FROM THE LOWER EAST SIDE
TO HOLLYWOOD

FROM THE LOWER EAST SIDE TO HOLLYWOOD

Jews in American Popular Culture

♦

PAUL BUHLE

VERSO

London • New York

First published by Verso 2004
© Paul Buhle 2004
All rights reserved

1 3 5 7 9 10 8 6 4 2

Verso
UK: 6 Meard Street, London W1F 0EG
USA: 180 Varick Street, New York, NY 10014–4606
www.versobooks.com

Verso is the imprint of New Left Books

ISBN 1–85984–598–3

British Library Cataloguing in Publication Data
Buhle, Paul, 1944–
    From the Lower East Side to Hollywood : Jews in American popular
    culture
    1. Jews – United States – Public opinion 2. Jews in motion pictures
    3. Jews in art 4. Jews in literature 5. Popular culture – United States
    6. United States – Public opinion
    I. Title
    305.8'924073

    ISBN 1859845983

Library of Congress Cataloging-in-Publication Data
A catalog record for this book is available from the Library of Congress

Typeset in Bembo and Gill Sans by YHT Ltd, London
Printed and bound in the USA by R. R. Donnelley & Sons

CONTENTS

ACKNOWLEDGEMENTS

Many of my personal mentors are described in this book, ranging from those whom I hardly knew, notably my boyhood hero Harvey Kurtzman of *Mad Comics*, to those who became real pals, like master filmmaker and critic Abraham Polonsky. Editor of what may turn out to be the last distinguished journal in the language, *Yiddishe Kultur*, Itche Goldberg comes up now and then in the following pages as the wise, ancient voice of history. I made an appointment to see him in 1977, in his small and cluttered office in mid-Manhattan, and he adopted me immediately, sent me on a decisive Miami Beach interviewing trip (even funding a bargain plane flight and a room in a threadbare, sandy-floored, little hotel for a few days) where I could find his devotees and meet dozens of octogenarians from all factions. If I stopped making regular trips to New York after most of this generation passed, Itche has always remained to me a model of what a cultured and committed figure would be and do. As of this writing, he is still at his desk writing and editing crisp Yiddish prose, at age 100.

My fellow editors and friends on *Cultural Correspondence* (1975–83), particularly newspaperman Dave Wagner (just about the only fellow Gentile among them), historian/musicologist George Lipsitz and media scholars Daniel Czitrom and David Marc, helped me greatly to make the transition from the 1960s to 1980s. Their cultural critique, with doses of Jewish content ranging from T.W. Adorno to Phil Silvers, kept me going in fruitful directions. In recent years Edward Portnoy, a young Yiddish scholar, has meant a lot to my continuing the work. So, too, Harvey Pekar and Joyce Brabner, celebrated for the biopic *American Splendor*; Art Spiegelman; R. Crumb and his underground comix nemesis, Trina Robbins; my new friend and collaborator on comics, Nicole Schulman, along with several of her collaborators on *World War 3 Illustrated*, including Seth

Tobocman, Eric Drooker, and Peter Kuper; Abbott and Costello screen-writer and Hollywood blacklistee Robert Lees; and Aaron Lansky, a casual pal in the years he was just becoming the maven of the National Yiddish Book Center; and master cartoonist Bill Griffith, like myself an adaptee to Jewishness.

Next, I would name my continuing flow of progressive-minded Jewish and part Jewish students at Brown, including a fortunate inner core who attended Camp Kinderland and kept the faith; not a single worthy social movement locally, on campus or off, is untouched by them. This expanded minyan continues to grow and is my joy as well as my inspiration, semester after semester. Then there are cultural mavens on the (often Jewish) avant-garde, especially gallery impresario Sara Agniel and comic book editor/artist Nicole Schulman; younger scholar-friends like Portnoy and Ari Kelman, now doing the badly needed study of Yiddish culture; and Henry Sapoznik, whose *klezmer* revival and recent Yiddish Radio Project performances (I'm proud to say that I was an advisor early on in this project) have reached live audiences and National Public Radio listeners in the tens and hundreds of thousands with hearty doses of *Yiddishkayt*. And the handful of email correspondents, old friends, and the new or renewed ones who responded to my essay on comics and scholarship in *The Chronicle of Higher Education* (16 May 2003) with enthusiastic interest, adding energy to the last weeks of my rewrites. And to Tony Kushner, a new friend who as much as anyone, anywhere, is the conscience and recreator of Jewish ethical traditions through entertainment.

So, too, I'm eager to acknowledge dozens of now vanished figures. They moved in and out of my life all too quickly, nevertheless leaving large impressions. These include Meyer Shticker, the last of the *Inzl* (island) aesthete Yiddish poets of the 1920s (amidst cigar smoke, he related proudly to me that he had translated Hemingway's *The Old Man and the Sea* into Yiddish); David Mattis, film reviewer for the Jewish *Forverts* and author of a Yiddish biography of Charlie Chaplin; Herbert Gutman, burgeoning from a teenage councilor at Camp Kinderland into a foremost social historian, encouraging a generation of emerging scholars to take cultural questions seriously; Irving Howe, with whom I had considerable disagreements both political and aesthetic, but to whom I could nevertheless pose important questions that needed to be asked; and many more less-remembered figures, rank-and-filers in the maintenance of *Yiddishkayt* and progressive political traditions, from Brighton Beach and Co-op City to Miami Beach and West Los Angeles. Finally, I wish to acknowledge my wonderful editor at Verso,

Amy Scholder, who has given this book both love and attention beyond the call of any possible duty. It is her book, too.

Speaking of most of the old-timers: I wish they were alive to read this book. I deeply regret not finishing in time for them. But perhaps I can manage to "make it new" for the latest generation of Jewish-American idealists, offering not models but examples that they can make their own.

INTRODUCTION:
ARTISTS AND CRITIC

Looking at the strength of Jewish actors, Jewish entertainers and Jewish executives, and knowing that my bloodline is part of that, gives me a kind of strength. Think about their positive contributions in this culture: Unionizing? Jews. Leftism? Jews. So to be part of that – the Norma Rae of it – gives me confidence.
                                                                          – Courtney Love

The trouble with Tobey McGuire's Spidey [in the film *Spider-Man*] ... is that he isn't Jewish enough.   – *The* (Jewish) *Forward*

Jewish? Entertaining? The introduction to the catalog of a premier Jewish Museum exhibition of 2003, *Entertaining America: Jews, Money and Broadcasting*, astutely points out that the very topic of American Jews and the entertainment industry is "charged and sprawling," and definitely threatening to become more so on both counts. Private conversations about the probable, but undisclosed, Jewishness of some celebrity or other have in recent times become not only public but audaciously intrusive. In the process, a subject once forbidden because weighted with threats of anti-Semitism has reemerged as the object of media scrutiny.[1] Without looking very hard, one is confronted with the inevitable question that underlies the entire discussion: What explains the impact of Jews on popular culture? And, more to the point, what's "Jewish" anyway?

No two writers – at least not those outside certain orthodoxies – are likely to have the same response to these intimately connected questions. My argument will be made below in analytical terms and then more extensively through examples. But let me first put the matter as succinctly as possible. In the first place, the Yiddish language was a natural territory for the emerging artistic vernacular, centuries in preparation, so to speak, for the moment when a mass, commercial, popular culture could be created. Secondly, the outsideness, the propensity to rebel, not only against the Gentile world but also against institutions and power figures of Jewish authority, forged the keen edge of innovation seen most vividly in districts of marginal capitalist enterprise.

In a twist that the nineteenth-century captains of industry could not have imagined, the all-powerful commercial engine of entertainment, including celebrity culture itself, really began here, in the most humble and seemingly improbable locations. Jews happened to be in the right place at the right time, and kept on being there, whether they personally identified with Jewishness or not. In addition, there was a section of self-identified Jewish artists and of Jewish audiences that scorned a bland mainstream and themselves created something more challenging and meaningful.[2]

I have organized my chapters around the topics of European background and the early Jewish rise to media influence, including music, theater and film, and graphic arts; the Americanizing generations; the avant-garde; and the putative postmodern that turned out to be a close cousin of the Jewish premodern. These categories are not strictly chronological, but their drift toward the present allows me to develop the large picture through many small ones. I hasten to add here that other books, an increasing number of good ones, offer insights into Jews and films. Dozens if not hundreds of book-length studies also have more to say about particular Jews and their music than I do here. Comics scholarship is by comparison only slight and recent. What I've sought to do in these pages is to move from genre to genre, over time, emphasizing certain themes central to my perceptions and my argument. I am not shy about my own personal connections, slight or sustained, with many of the artists discussed. As an oral historian, I learned long ago that the best preparation for interviewing is a mixture of scholarly preparation and life itself; as a writer of books and articles, an editor and even occasionally the publisher of cultural and political magazines, I have spent what seems like a lifetime looking for interesting material and meeting the people who are responsible for it.

One more additional, whopping complication should be noted at the outset, that of the infamous category of "identity," once a word under the virtual monopoly of Jewish writers, but in recent decades opening to a wide field of avid (and, as in more Jewish days, sometimes altogether tiresome) debaters. Had W.E.B. DuBois not proposed for African-Americans a "two-ness" of black and American identity in his memorable *Souls of Black Folk* (1903), the categorization might – especially when written – have been as suitable for Jews, but with an almost reverse series of spins. The starkly different yet vitally connected experiences of African-Americans and Jews indeed make up much of the ground of American popular culture, especially but not only in music, and will be treated repeatedly here, necessarily from a Jewish angle. The mysteries of "alliance," mutual disillusionment and wary rapprochement between the two groups are not going to be answered here, but it is safe to say that the attentive reader will have plenty of information and some insight to consider.

Not that I have all that much to say about exploitation and minstrelsy (its all-time perfect vehicle), for instance. Most participants at any point in the creation of popular culture, Jewish, black, or otherwise, simply went (as they continue to go) along resistless with individual opportunities, following whatever prospect has led to the most personal success. Feckless self-seeking is natural in a society that exalted the "main chance" long before Eastern Europeans passed through Ellis Island, and, until recently, largely denied African-Americans access to the same chance. But many Jews of the first, second, third, and fourth generation had, and have, an impulse to swim upstream, looking for allies along the way. To mix metaphors, that's where genius is most often born.

THE CRITIC ENTERS (STAGE LEFT)

What I have called reflexiveness marks an especially convenient point of entry for this critic, because most critics and other intellectuals have had a hard time accepting the implications of audience cravings for themes and objects that they can recognize as their own.[3] Bertolt Brecht, shortly before Hitler ended all antifascist experiments in German theater and film, theorized that through experiencing a conceptual distancing (not quite alienation) from the familiar existing form, the masses of viewers would learn to demystify what was offered them. His was a drastic conceptual error, although a provocative one attempted by Jewish avant-garde artists more often, certainly in the US, than by anyone else. For better or worse, audiences connect with a coherent narrative rather than cognitive dissociation, arguably because it is natural, even hardwired, for them to do so. As master noirist and the Hollywood Left's premier theorist (also notably a Yiddishist) Abraham Polonsky often observed, the various genres go back to primordial campfire stories and are not about to be dislodged. Learning must come in a different way.

There have long been suggestions of the reflexive within the texts themselves created by relying sympathetically upon audiences' own familiarities and their willingness to think about forms while enjoying the narrative. Way back in 1910, pioneering Jewish artist Harry Hershfield evidently had something quite remarkable in mind when he began drawing "three-minute movies" for the daily comics. He was able to embrace reflexivity by way of satirizing the clichés of silent films for readers who obviously went to the movies and loved them. Forty years later, as another new medium reached millions, Sid Caesar and Imogene Coca (with the inspiration of writers like Carl Reiner and Mel Brooks) burlesqued advertising and current television shows. *Mad Comics'* founder Harvey Kurtzman told me that bright New York kids like himself had grown up making similar gags about war films, melodramas, and comedies, and that he had known instinctively, in the same moment as Caesar and Coca's triumph, what path to follow with a new literary genre. *Mad Magazine*, tinkering with the model set by Kurtzman before his departure, subsequently made print media history again and again, in creating popular art styles and in circulation – a history that *Saturday Night Live* brought to the highest level of video sophistication, arguably until *The Simpsons*. Meanwhile, decades before the turn of the new century, High Modernism itself had more or less officially given way to a sort of internal dialogue within and about mass culture.

Individual Jews played fairly central roles in this reflexiveness all the way along, and a cynic would no doubt argue that their strategic location made it good business to do so: they recognized *any* incipient trend and got there before the other marketers. As we'll see, the once familiar story about the Gypsy bands actually made up of Jews, like the conflation of Indian tribes with the tribe of Moses in tasteless comedy sketches from vaudeville to television, gives us an early view of the nimbleness with which the ever adaptive Jewish entertainer would embrace alternative identities.[4] More than a little of the megasuccess that we will see from Tin Pan Alley origins to the film and comic book studios, and to the Brill building of rock n' roll fame, is indeed owed to a mixture of ruthlessness and bottom line savvy, with a built-in retro feature (the saleable qualities of near instant nostalgia) as one of its crucial components.

But to take the cynical view of (many, not all) Jewish entertainers and executives would be to see only the discolored tip of an iceberg. Jewish versions of modern culture have often been inherently reflexive in ways that move back and forth between the avant-garde and the mass. Again and again across generations, Jewish artists and entrepreneurs have probed deeply the form itself, seeking something that eludes the ordinary viewer or listener, and even the hard-working but unreflective musician, painter, or art critic. Sometimes they have looked down deep enough into the well to see something like a reflection of their own faces, not merely as Jews but as human beings with the fears and desires that prompted the original fireside story.

More than a few times, we find the same combination of deep Jewish traditions with the latest artistic experiments. Thus avant-gardists Marc Chagall and El Lissitsky undertook a survey of folk art in Russia's old synagogues in the 1910s with a fascination that will return again and again in the pages below. They delved folk forms in what would be called an almost scholarly undertaking, except that it was, and continues to be, conducted with a large degree of intuition, and with more contemporary artistic desire to transform and adapt materials than to understand them intellectually.[5]

If pressed to pick a single experiment that best illustrates the continuing impulse to recuperate and remix, I would point to a commercially doomed and largely forgotten project, the seven issues of *Arcade: The Comics Revue* (1975–77). *Arcade* was the premier effort of self-consciously vernacular artists not only to explore the kinds of connections of higher and lower forms of art and popular culture so vividly on display during the early 1950s in *Mad Comics'* treatments of superheroes and abstract expressionism alike. But *Arcade* sought to move the project one step further, adopting an explanatory purpose about the inner history of popular culture, framed with a necessary sense of irony about the whole project. It was the last as well as the highest form of the late 1960s-based "underground" culture closest to my own temperament. A creative moment had really passed and it was time for something else. Not entirely by accident, the year *Arcade* folded, I took a Yiddish class and set off on a small tour of Jewish retirement colonies, interviewing political old-timers and cultural activists who more or less adopted me.

That, in a microcosm, is the heart of the story that follows. We can see vastly better in the shadow of the postmodern than we could only a few decades earlier, but not because (as it so often seems) postmodernism flattens the landscape by making all things look alike. On the contrary, the kaleidoscopic flow of styles, genres, and traditions raises the possibility always close to the Jewish artist, the ability to get beyond himself or herself without losing the sense of self, the chance to try on the clothes of others, and then to look in the mirror and see the results better than the casual wearer of such clothes.

There is something else to be said for being so late in the day. The Cold War passions have cooled with the fall of the Soviet Union. The entertainment blacklist has mainly for this reason become a distasteful part of history, to be seen rather more clearly as a central episode in American life, impacting heavily upon culture, especially Jewish culture. The world of the blacklistees has been for years my chosen world as a sympathetic scholar. I taped as many of them as I could find, concentrating, but not entirely, on filmwriters as the most articulate of the crew, in their last years, watched their films, looked at their scripts and correspondence and struggled to understand their Jewishness. It has been one of the greatest experiences of my life.

Caribbean literature meanwhile provided me with insights that I could not have not obtained otherwise because, at least to me, it has always seemed so close to Yiddish literature in both its practical marginality and its communitarian assumptions. The Guyanese novelist Wilson Harris, a self-trained avant-gardist, known widely, if inaccurately, as the "James Joyce of the Caribbean," observes that any narrow self-consciousness "incorporates into itself a deafness to what it does not wish to hear," a defect all too typical of our time, even with such a myriad of cultural possibilities around us. But, he goes on, if "the burden of Memory alerts us to lapses from life-enhancing diversity into stereotypical purities," an alert that "would be unbearable if it rested on a singular or linear narrative of history," the potential of collective memory also allows us to "acquire a degree of density that steeps us in diverse personae ... which help us to see ourselves differently." That perception includes, most crucially, the "many players within ourselves and within strange cultures."[6]

It is a most difficult thought but a vital one for Jews within every realm of popular culture. Like the writings of Yiddish literary giant Y.L. Peretz urging the recuperation of Jewish folkishness into advanced forms, Harris's notion urges that the past "needs us" to recuperate apparently vanished memories and to find our own links to that past. This vital task, part of the project to escape the doom apparently written upon modern social relations along with the planet Earth, resonates vividly for me. The legacies of the generations shaped by *Yiddishkayt* and by its English-language descendents offer real antidotes to what ails us all. We do not reach out in vain.

Experiences described along the way implicate me all too much in ways that transcend scholarship, and their mention may be excused for a writer passing onward from middle age. It's time to take stock, and when I consider that various Jewish creators of popular culture have given shape to my imaginative impulses since age five or six if not before, it becomes clear that I am thereby joined to the largest question of Jewishness as well, however presumptuous that may seem. Every page of this book speaks obliquely to the vital issues involved in the question of Jewish identity, as frighteningly close to relevance as the Bush White House's favorite hawk intellectuals and as endearingly close to possible redemption as the peacenik/environmentalist countervisions heard (when at all) in music, comics, films, and the Internet rather than in the pages of big newspapers and other corporate news media. The version offered in this book, as will quickly become clear, is rooted both in centuries of European history and a century of popular culture, the latter imbibed at an exceptionally close range. I am thereby adding my own two cents to a secular Jewishness shaped by historical reality and touched by spiritualism, stubbornly convinced that it remains the most productive and appealing Jewishness imaginable.[7] It is my contribution to the unending puzzle of continuity, now more than ever bound up with the survival of civilization and of the planet itself.

SOME PERSONAE

Now, reader, let's visit some of the artists and examine what their work reveals, as a kind of overview of what is to come. First, a pleasant shock within a world of looming horrors: the Dramatic Grand Jury Prize of the 2003 Sundance Film Festival was won by the makers of *American Splendor*, a barely fictionalized biopic of the daily lives of Harvey Pekar and his wife, Joyce Brabner, the comic stripped soul of the nation so to speak, tucked away deep in Cleveland Heights, Ohio. The minute that I read the news, I got on the phone with Harvey, who had predicted it without the least bit of egotism or even cheerfulness, some months ago.

It had been a pretty bad period for Pekar until quite recently. Now, suddenly, his work can be found in *Entertainment Weekly* and even the *New York Times*, not to mention his voice (and Joyce's) on NPR's *Fresh Air*. He has struggled for almost thirty years, writing the comic book series *American Splendor*. Self-published since the middle 1970s, it was excerpted into book form by small publishers, with a couple of well-reviewed but low-selling volumes. A deep glimpse of Harvey's Cleveland, it was, and is, a real splendor in many ways. But it never paid the bills, let alone made a profit.

Pekar had an apparent breakthrough or two along the way. Praised to the skies by writers in the *Village Voice*, Harvey was invited onto the *Late Show with David Letterman* during the early 1990s and continued to appear occasionally for a few years, making waves (and getting laughs) with his gruff anticommercialism. His steady attacks upon the military-industrial connections of General Electric – the owners of the network – apparently grew unacceptable to management, or perhaps to David Letterman. Harvey thereafter disappeared back into Cleveland, where he grew up in the hybrid world of popular culture, *Yiddishkayt*, and the Popular Front. He has never gotten away for long, and never really wanted to.

When the film production crew for *American Splendor* settled in, as Joyce later explained to me, the pressure just got to be too much after all these years of waiting. Still recovering from cancer, Harvey took an early retirement, with a miniscule pension, followed by months of physical difficulty. The thrill of the award, redoubled by another at Cannes, seems lately to have snapped him out of it. He's had his artistic vindication, even if *American Splendor* (the comic, that is) happens to be selling as badly as ever. And the story *is* Harvey Pekar: a human frame, so to speak, for one kind of American Jewishness no longer so familiar in real life but all the more important to keep in memory.

Ben Katchor, with past awards, grants, and his own plays in almost steady production, is a world away from Pekar – as far away as New York's Upper West Side is from Cleveland Heights. But going to see the artist at his place in an early twentieth-century block of the Manhattan's west low eighties is not an adventure in luxury living. Katchor's building is modest, and the few people I pass by in the hallway are old; they've lived here since German accents marked the last Eurocentric, middle-class "cultured" immigrant Jews. It also would have been an almost perfect place for a Woody Allen set because you could walk to all sorts of places with heavy cosmopolitan Jewish associations (like the New Yorker Theater) that exist so vividly in Allen's early films and have now been wiped out of reality by the developers.

Ben hadn't exactly been a stranger to me even when I first met him years earlier. The not-yet-so-famous cartoonist Art Spiegelman had kindly brought Katchor's work to my attention in the 1980s because of my unusual interests in Jewish comic strip artists. I couldn't help being struck immediately, as Spiegelman had predicted, by the eerily Yiddish ambience of his strips' imagined neighborhoods. Hebrew lettering was scarce, but there was something about these oddly named streets (like real-life Brooklyn, where "Seagull Avenue" eventually became "Siegel Avenue") with the place and the characters, not so much the way they look or talk as the way they think, almost indefinably but still absolutely Jewish.

Our conversations on these subjects seemed drifty, because, as I came to understand, Katchor had grown intuitively outward from his father's Yiddish Marxism and away from the 1960s–70s underground comix, two beginning points of my own narrative framework. Artistically, he needed more distance. He was, at the same time, living proof that another generation of Jewish vernacular artists steeped in the past had begun in earnest.

By the time I came to see him in Manhattan, Katchor had been named a MacArthur Fellow – a first for a cartoonist, although a small number of Pulitzers had been doled out to such giants like Bill Mauldin, Jules Feiffer and, after the appearance of *Maus*, Spiegelman himself. Katchor was taking it in his stride. As he was quick to point out, the charisma lent by a "genius award" was not even close to that of the comic strip artists of old. On the other hand, Katchor represents the growing recognition of comic strip artists as real artists, a designation that not even Hershfield, whose *Abie the Agent* was the first popular Jewish strip in the English-language press, enjoyed, and something that the *New York Times* has only gradually begun to accord a select few, perhaps following foreign cultural critics, or perhaps capitulating to the academic vogue of popular culture subjects.[8]

In 1993, when *The New Yorker* ran an amiable profile by the keen-eyed Lawrence Wechsler, Katchor's reputation, apart from a few appearances in those august (but now more trendy) pages and Spiegelman's *Raw* magazine, rested mainly on a syndicated strip in about a dozen local-based alternative papers.[9] A few years later, two of Katchor's strips were dramatized by Jerry Stiller on NPR, a hilarious rendition with Katchor himself as the narrator and Stiller as the uncertain protagonist wandering through a time warp in a world that the actor must have been recreating in part from his own Brooklyn childhood. Katchor's still-underground reputation might best be reinterpreted, by this time, as referring to certain subway stops that everyone seems to have forgotten, leading to urban settings somehow untouched since, say, the early 1950s. Here, in the places where an imagined Katchor perennially walks, we find a world reinvented.

Looking at Katchor's world and then back at the underground comix art that signaled to me a vivid and vernacular canvas for the generation of the 1960s–70s, other hidden connections emerge. Somewhere behind the transgressive sex and dope themes could be found some of the best artists' referencing of a fragmented and disappearing urbanism. The genetically Gentile, but cryptically Jewish, R. Crumb's artistic rambles begin in the Cleveland of the early 1960s with the past etched in tenement skylines and oddball characters, alongside the anonymous art of outdated storefront signs and advertising logos. Likewise, arguably, Bill Griffith, of *Zippy*, never really leaves the Long Island of 1950s–60s, where he was raised within the garishness created by suburban devastation – not even now, while living in picturesque rural Connecticut. Not born with Jewishness, he was assimilated into it (no doubt with some help from his wife, Diane Newman, as

Crumb has had help from his two Jewish wives). For half-Jewish Justin Green, it's the Near North Side of Chicago, in more or less the same era, that taught him accents and angles. Pekar, of course, has gone on capturing in the urban memories of a wounded Cleveland the vanished Jewish generation, legendarily short and furiously gregarious, the lower-middle class, Jewish guys in particular who spoke for hours with self-created authority on any given topic, from politics to baseball.

There's another, still deeper and more curious connection between several artists whose work has meant the most to me. Katchor's immigrant father was on the fund-raising board of the daily *Morgn Frayhayt,* and a certain Mrs. Pekar in Cleveland was one of its loyal readers. The father of Trina Robbins, the most prominent woman among the early underground cartoonists, and chief founder of *It Ain't Me Babe,* one of the field's most memorable, just happened to be a *Frayhayt* writer. Thus three parents; all of them proud Jewish secularists, all staunch critics of both class society and of a bland assimilationism. The *Frayhayt* was a definitely left-wing – during its early decades, a Communist – newspaper, but it was also noted for having the finest Yiddish prose in the American Jewish press.

The humor that came to the *Yiddishe Gassen* (Jewish streets) of New York in the 1910s found homes in the theater and early cinema as well as left-wing Yiddish political meetings, where the biting phrase roared at the audience offered some of the sharpest shafts against the capitalist system and its ghetto lackeys. But it also came in the vastly popular satirical weekly *Groysser Kundes* (the big stick), whose intimate knowledge of ghetto life focused on personalities like *Forverts* editor Abe Cahan, whom it ceaselessly satirized, while reveling in the zest of ghetto life. In the same generation, near anonymous Yiddish poets probably delivered a larger quantity of published lyrics about New York's "cityness" than all their counterparts in any language for the rest of the century.[10] It was a humor thing, but even more, a street thing: the American counterpart to the Parisian flaneur's observations, or closer to home, the literary-vernacular counterpart to the Ash Can school of city painters.

Now, eighty years and more afterward, Katchor recalls particulars of that all but vanished world, freely inventing as he goes along. *Cheap Novelties: The Pleasures of Urban Decay* (1991) introduced his lasting protagonist Julius Knipl (whose surname is the untranslatable Yiddish *knipl,* meaning the handful of change or small bills required to get by or just get home from some unforeseeable misadventure), a real estate photographer and hence participant-observer of the scene. Then came the sequel *Julius Knipl, Real Estate Photographer: Stories* (1996) and *The Jew of New York* (1998), the latter an imagined historical epic in which a Jewish past in the American theater is traced to the early decades of the nineteenth century, with the retailing of seltzer water among other developments. *The Beauty Supply District* (2000) returns to where Katchor has spent most of his time in weekly strips, even if they sometimes take place on a vacation island where a kind of retro Miami Beach setting intensifies the urban *Yiddishkayt*, or in other odd spots of extended Jewishness in the countryside.

The spirit of anonymous invention highlights each strip, a subtle reminder of how the vast details of popular culture appear and disappear constantly, leaving behind tantalizingly ambiguous built environments. The original signage of apartment houses, oddly chosen names of dead presidents or favored daughters or even vacation spots, mostly painted over but half-visible, likewise the faded commercial messages not altogether effaced from old buildings of all kinds offer abundant clues for today's walker in the city.

A special note on the title page of *The Beauty Supply District*, tiny lettering acknowledging the store front techies who did the book's fine photographic work, indirectly reminds the reader about Katchor's quasi-artisanal phase in job shops that epitomize the print world of popular culture anonymity. Katchor and his fellow artisans had been, for a few years, marginally successful as cockroach capitalists, printing and typesetting everything from take-out menus to pamphlets of crank philosophy by self-publishing authors. The continuing experiment prompted him toward an art or philosophy of urban detritus. Meanwhile, *Raw*, the visually brilliant and financially disastrous venture put out by Art Spiegelman and future *New Yorker* art editor Françoise Mouly during the 1980s, was one of Katchor's best breaks because it introduced him to an international audience (that naturally appreciated *Raw* quite a bit more than its mostly baffled American readers) and encouraged him to syndicate Knipl.

Katchor, who speaks with such reserve that radio interviewers seem at loose ends to get something definite out of him, has a somewhat different explanation on issues of content and form. He's joking a bit when he says that his work is a cross between Nicolas Poussin and Harry Hershfield, but there's something to it. The revival of representational techniques back in the 1960s by artists as varied as Philip Perlstein, Alice Neel, and Alfred Leslie parallels, he insists, the efforts by Crumb and the keenest of the comix crowd to recuperate earlier twentieth-century vernacular images and comic techniques. The painters of the 1960s were going back a lot further, to seventeenth-century painters like Poussin, who looked in turn back to the models offered by antiquity, the Greeks, and Romans. Crumb might answer back that the real roots of his comics can be found in certain medieval caricature styles, specifically that of Hieronymus Bosch, himself a mysterious figure said to have been heavily influenced by a Jewish savant.[11] He wouldn't be wrong.

Katchor's technical breakthrough is to use the halftone printing that most comic artists carefully avoid. Through line drawings, by way of a gray wash, he achieves what he calls "watercolor in tones of gray." Instead of the cartoonlike street characters or line-drawing tenements that we might find in Crumb's urban landscapes, here we find rather more abstract images, impressions of something thicker and more atmospheric. There's nothing inherently Jewish about the technique, in my way of looking, yet the consequences are unmistakable.

Katchor gives off occasional deep, familiar signs to the wary reader. At moments of his most literal borrowing, the crank theories of old men in his strips about sexual hygiene offer direct analogies to the Marxist theories espoused by the autodidact Jews of his father's generation. In their own minds, they've got it all worked out, a near cryptic science of something or other, and now, if only the world would listen. Other Katchor conversations are more or less identifiably Jewish in the peculiarity of their pastness; no one else lived or talked about themselves and the world in quite this way. Very possibly, if you believe some of their descendents, no one else would want to. They certainly live in *kvetchland*, and although by definition nothing is ever really good enough, their problems seem a universe removed from the bored and sex-crazed Manhattan middle class of Woody Allen's films. Still, they also have many small satisfactions in the discoveries of detail that Walter Benjamin would surely have enjoyed.

Katchor offers not so much an in-joke or satire of these generations and their ideas as an oblique poetic comment on their world in dialogue and drawing, a sort of displacement that nevertheless sums (or summons) up the original. Yiddish pedagogue and critic Itche Goldberg once analyzed the paradoxical Jewish nostalgia for roots in the era of rebellious break from older traditions, resulting in what Katchor himself calls "remembering remembering." The recurrent impulse triggered by a semiconscious questioning of self-identity or self-location outside the bounds of either religion or nationalism thus finds its latest Dante in Julius Knipl. If Jewish conservatives disdain *klezmer* and Tony Kushner alike, it's because something vernacular, such as *Seinfeld* (and many *Simpsons*) reruns, is more accessible and is able to tap into feelings of Jewishness more easily than either the synagogue or the contemplation of Israel. You certainly don't even have to be Jewish for this vernacular kind of yearning, although it helps.

Dwellers in today's nineteenth-century-built cities, Katchor avows, can still drink in the ambience of the vanished Automats, where the coffee called for an iron stomach and the conversation lasted forever, just as they can relive visits to small shops whose very merchandise was a mystery. If this is a dream world, then more and more apparently want to join it. And if it offers an emerging public art, then perhaps in some alternative universe, everything is Katchoresque. It's a nice thought, hopeful in the way that André Breton used to promise his followers that someday surrealism would abolish the barriers between sleeping and being awake. This imaginative leap demanded something beyond the dreamed cooperative common-wealth of old, but Katchor's world bears a rather stronger resemblance to the old romantic phrase too rarely heard these days, "When you're in love, the whole world is Jewish." The phrase was common in an era when Jews were in vastly more danger than now; but then, *Yiddishkayt* was also more lively.

Seeing Katchor in these terms is apparently in contrast with the self-conscious avant-gardism of Spiegelman. By the 1990s, Spiegelman was the senior underground cartoonist of note (along with Crumb, Griffith, Robbins, and a few others), then a *New Yorker* illustrator of both political controversy and artistic acclaim. As for many other Holocaust survivors' children, the darkness of the soul is Spiegelman's best element, expressed as well in his satirical *New Yorker* commentaries on police brutality as his post-9/11 cover etching. A former bubble gum card illustrator with a life-long fascination with popular culture artifacts, he grants the vernacular no claims on him. "I guess I'm interested in mass culture insofar as I can appropriate it and make it part of my culture," he frankly admitted to an interviewer.[12]

Spiegelman follows, among others, Aaron Copland, who was nurtured on the avant-garde but grew into popular themes with the Popular Front and by the 1930s and 40s could selectively choose from the possibilities and create works with all sorts of idiosyncratic connections to the vernacular.[13] As he might have added, a certain kind of new Jewish artist (novelist Michael Chabon, who wrote the introduction to one of Katchor's early books, is perhaps today's most lauded example; detective genre favorite Sara Paretsky, with her left-wing real-life relatives and her imagined, tough and feminist protagonist V.I. Warshawsky, is likewise on the job in Chicago) draws from the common reservoir of what he or she wants, reordering parts by way of making serious art.[14] Fair enough but not far enough. We need to push this insight to its logical conclusion, as the opposite end of an axis of creative tension from the lives of mostly lower-class Jews in an earlier twentieth-century America. When we get there, we may find precursors not so different.

NOTES

¹ J. Hoberman and Jeffrey Shandler, "Entertaining 'Entertaining America,'" in Hoberman and Shandler, eds., *Entertaining America: Jews, Movies and Broadcasting* (New York: The Jewish Museum; Princeton: Princeton University Press, 2003): 11.

² Hoberman and Shandler·end *Entertaining America* with an editors' dialogue, noting the Jewish influence, yet warning against essentialism. But they also go on to restore the emphasis by suggesting that without the Jewish input, movies (to take their case in point) would never have had the particular quality of appeal to the immigrant (and other) masses. "The Last Word: a Conversation," in ibid., 274–79.

³ I have borrowed the term from David Marc, whose final chapter of his masterwork *Demographic Vistas: Television in American Culture* (Philadelphia: University of Pennsylvania Press, 1984) is titled "Self-Reflexive at Last," and offers a fuller description than I can provide here.

⁴ Mark Winokur, *American Laughter: Immigrants, Ethnicity and 1930s Film Comedy* (New York: St Martin's, 1996), 153–54. There are no known examples of Indians playing Jews.

⁵ Aaron Kampf, *Jewish Experience in the Art of the Twentieth Century* (W. Hadley, Mass: Bergin & Garvey, 1984), 36–41.

⁶ Wilson Harris, "Profiles of Myth and the New World," in Andrew Bundy, ed., *The Unfinished Genesis of the Imagination: Selected Essays of Wilson Harris* (London: Faber and Faber, 1999), 208.

⁷ Closest to my own sensibility is Irene Klepfisz, *Dreams of An Insomniac: Jewish Feminist Essays, Speeches and Diatribes* (Portland: Eighth Mountain Press, 1990), 195–96. Klepfisz, a Jewish-Polish immigrant who lost most of her family in the Holocaust, is a lesbian feminist and was a leading light in New Jewish Agenda, an organization for which I could perhaps best describe myself as shabbas-goy.

⁸ See Dave Eggers, "After Wham! Pow! Shazam! Comic Books Move Beyond Superheroes to the World of Literature," *New York Times Review of Books*, 26 November 2000. The others reviewed with him happened to be gentiles: Lynda Barry, Daniel Clowes, and Chris Ware. See also Grace Glueck, "Views of a Yiddish Past Spring Comically to Life," *New York Times*, 14 November 2001, on the traveling exhibition of Katchor's work.

⁹ Lawrence Wechsler, "A Wanderer in the Perfect City," *New Yorker*, 9 August 1993, 58–66.

¹⁰ Many of these are published in the oversized volume edited by Nakhman Maisel, *Amerika in Yiddishe Vort* (New York: YKUF, 1956).

¹¹ See, e.g., Carl Linfert, *Bosch* (New York: Henry Abrams, Inc., 1972). Linfert suggests that the insular Bosch and the Brotherhood of Our Lady, for which he

did most of his painting, were influenced by a certain charismatic Jew who took up Christianity and later returned to Judaism. If the influences can be said to have come through the connection between Jewish mysticism and the sense of medieval social crisis, i.e., the need to reinterpret some Biblical or pre-Biblical theme, then we can connect Bosch with the philosopher Jakob Boehme. The two sui generis figures painted and wrote centuries ahead of their time.

[12] Gary Groth, "Art Spiegelman Interview," *Comics Journal*, no. 80 (September 1995): 102.

[13] See Cal Levin and Judith Tick, *Aaron Copland's America* (New York: Watson-Gupthill Publications, 2000) for a wonderful range of examples and suggestions of influences on Copland.

[14] Many thanks to Paretsky for an email in October 2002, noting that her parents were staunch liberals in a conservative Kansas university town, her paternal grandparents met on a picketline, and one of her great uncles was a leading official of the Industrial Workers of the World, adding "I guess these things come together in how I imagine someone like V.I. Warshawski trying to fight for social justice, and the feelings of impotence that I and therefore she experience in working for change."

ONE

WHERE DID IT COME FROM? THE JEWISH CAULDRON OF POPULAR CULTURE

We no longer live in the era of unabashed mainstream (or elite) anti-Semitism where ethnic vaudeville humor refers to neighborhood shylocks collecting insurance by setting fire to their small businesses, or where Catholic film censors and congressional conservatives point darkly to "Hebrew influences" among the entertainment industry's leaders and employees. But the charge of "Jewish influence" has never really disappeared. Notwithstanding complaints from minority filmmakers, the too-familiar attack on movies for corrupting youngsters' morals, the intermittent threat of censorship has forever remained at base a Yahoo-WASP rage against supposed Jewish media liberalism and libertinism.

The same kinds of complaints have long been made toward Jews in the music industry. Until recent decades, the charges were mainly directed at Jewish musicians, nightclub owners, and record executives, those Jews purportedly directing a conspiracy to impose "jungle music" on white Christian youngsters. Since the shock of rock 'n' roll and the rise of a black business class, more complaints have also been heard from African-American musicians against the corporate-style behavior of Jewish businessmen at all levels of one of the nation's most influential businesses.

And yet it's never a surprise to learn, for instance, of contemporary hip hop fan publications that divide "authentic" from "inauthentic" based on race and related cultural criteria, publications with conspicuously Jewish editors (or self-publishers). Or to see the emergence of new stars, like hot Nuyorican Def Poetry performance artist Vanessa Hidary, the "Hebrew Mamita" restyled "Culture Bandit" (the name of her acclaimed one-woman show).[1] Anti-Semitic myth is thus recycled by a more benign reality of multicultural enthusiasts. Or perhaps those Jewish semi-Communists who did so much to create the audience for folk music and jazz during the

1930s–50s really *were* consciously and semiconsciously seeking to subvert an America that wouldn't let them in – as their successors, who are scarcely political, are still trying to pry open doors for something lurking outside. In short and despite appearances, some essentials may not have changed all that much.

No one has bothered to make similar charges about Broadway theater, doubtless because the sophisticated audience (for drama most especially) has historically been heavily Jewish. The historic Jewish subtext of musicals having now been replaced by a gay subtext hasn't changed matters much in that regard either because in the theatrical world, "Jewish" and "gay" so often flow into each other. Comic strips and comic books, more recently turned into the wildly expanding animation industry, have rarely been recognized as a Jewish domain. And yet many particulars, genre and artist, have an awfully familiar ring, as familiar as Mel Blanc's voices for urban-hip Bugs Bunny or the intonations of Krusty the clown or Hollywoodnik on *The Simpsons*. Perhaps only in organized sports have Jews been represented as sparsely as their population numbers would suggest, and even that assessment might disguise sportswriters, agents, and others whose out-of-the-spotlight moves help shape the professional and amateur fields.

Where did it all come from, and what does it mean? Only a true conspiracy theorist would arrive at a simple answer. The questions involved would also be far more straightforward, and to the same degree less interesting, if "Jewish" were synonymous with "Judaic." Nothing, indeed, could be much further from the truth, unless we consider all cultural creation to be religion with a backspin. Notwithstanding (almost vice president) Senator Joseph Lieberman and his conspicuous religious devotions, polls confirm what most close-range observers have suspected for several generations: a hearty majority of Jewish Americans understand "religion" not as theology (belief in the deity and certain ritual practices) but rather as historic identity – just as they scorn, more than any other group, the possible censorship of their cultural choices. "Non-Christian" has been offered to polltakers as their accepted alternative self-description, but this response only deflects the real issue. The Jewishness at the tangled roots of American popular culture must be located elsewhere.

It is a symbolic fact of great importance, if no literal fact at all, that this Jewish essence could be found in the famed Lower East Side of Manhattan. By the time the US entered the First World War, when the massive Jewish immigration was about to be cut off substantially, not even a quarter of Greater New York's Jewry actually lived in the Lower East Side. They never outnumbered Italians there, and a large portion were already on their way outward toward the Bronx, Brooklyn, and beyond, for a generation occasionally to neighborhoods *more* homogenously Jewish than the old neighborhood of yore. Twenty or thirty years later, the Sheepshead Bay of Woody Allen's *Radio Days* or the nearby setting of Neil Simon's *Brighton Beach Memoirs* offered Americanized versions just as Jewish, lacking in either case the massive tenements or troops of Hasids, but never lacking in Jewish ambience.

Nevertheless, the Lower East Side became to an increasing degree the symbolic home of Jewishness, for at least two generations. The very presence of the crowded streets, small peddlers in their stalls, factories, penny candy stores, and familiar landmarks (often, as cartoonist Ben Katchor would observe, the only surviving signs of vanished presences), connoted Lower East Sideness, like the street scenes and organ-grinder music of "The Sidewalks of New York" at the start of bottom-budget Bowery Boys films of the 1940s, scenes reimagined by the emerging Jewish artists of Hollywood, therefore almost as real as if they had taken place.[2]

This symbolic presence was urgently needed because the Jewish-American identity was otherwise lacking its own geographic home, and because no other neighborhood in the world was ever likely to seem so universal to Jews themselves – not even a neighborhood in contested Jerusalem. Other locations, like Vilnus (Vilna, Lithuania, once known as the "Jerusalem of Europe") or Warsaw before the Holocaust, made greater actual contributions to historic Jewish culture, and saw more historic tragedy. But neither was so likely to appear in cultural artifacts traveling around the world outside the Holocaust museums, especially among those many Jews who neither possessed nor sought an absolute Jewish identity. During my own brief stay in the Lower East Side in the summer of 1966 – just that year partly renamed East Village but still in some ways very much like the old, ungentrified neighborhood – I was fortunate enough to have happened across a Lenny Bruce Memorial meeting in the Judson Chapel at New York University, worked at a radical newspaper a few blocks from Tompkins Square Park, and heard Allen Ginsberg read his poetry at St. Marks Church On-the-Bowery. I could feel that I was somehow in a sacred space. The same summer, a fading cinema palace on Second Avenue, still earlier a Yiddish theater, was about to become Fillmore East: new generations, but somehow scarcely less of a Jewish-American culture.

How all this happened is a bit more than historical because it's history without the backdating that we normally expect. It's not that the past fails to fade, but it does not stay faded, never entirely. Long before the Holocaust (and associated Holocaust kitsch) dominated the identification of a collective past, the musical stage had proceeded to rework familiar stories again and again, an apotheosis of entertainment history with an apotheosis of Jewish history obscurely inscribed. We need to follow the bouncing ball.

YIDDISH ROOTS

The ultimate source will be found in the immigrant Jews' Yiddish language and within *Yiddishkayt*, the quality of Yiddishness. It marked the vernacular legacy of European Jewry's seven centuries and a then recent rebellion against the hegemony of rabbi and merchant. Yiddish was also, by no coincidence, the language within which Jewish Socialism and modern Jewish literature took shape simultaneously with the overrepresentation of Jews in and around the rapidly advancing media.

It would not be too much of a leap to call Yiddish a *lingua franca* of emerging popular culture, spoken by so many who created it – even if the immigrants mostly abandoned the language itself (or put it in second place, for intimate rather than public expression) as they advanced into a broader American mass culture. This end had been foreseen from the beginning, for Yiddish's very adaptability from one linguistic climate to another had conditioned the native speakers to "translate" their culture into new forms, according to the possibilities at hand. Whenever it has seemed to vanish, personal traces can be discovered, as in the life of magnum television producer Larry Gelbart, creator of the most popular (and antiwar) sitcom of all time, *M*A*S*H*, who reveals that until four, he spoke only Yiddish.[3] Not likely a coincidence, at least not entirely.

We follow the course of *Yiddishkayt* into popular culture most fruitfully through examining the immigrant generations' response to the complex possibilities of life in their adopted homeland, especially in the booming entertainment industries of mass society. A good beginning, but this is still not quite good enough. To look backward and to look forward, to see odd continuities among those who apparently identify themselves least as "Jewish," helps us grasp at the role of rebellion, the departure and return which encompass so often the subtle dialectic of adaptation, even assimilation, and self-identification.

The *apikoyres*, the self-avowed heretic, can nevertheless be the authentic believer in ways that no Talmudic portion could have predicted – not in existing religion, but in cultural equivalents of religious yearning and spiritual insight. This substitution relates intimately to the value of popular culture in an age of vanished meanings: truths or myths of everyday life, the snatch of melody or visual images, apprehended in distraction but called back to mind repeatedly, sometimes making accessible the highest (and least exclusionary) ideals of universal religious purpose.

There are more materialist answers too, of course. The limited range of entrepreneurial opportunities in the early immigrant generations, fortunate geographical location in the centers of cultural production, the striving for individual perfection in available fields, the intimate connections (and the accompanying contradictions) with African-American life – all these make good sense. But not convincingly, at least not by themselves. We return again and again to the subjective, the artist's self-description in the pages below, because motivation needs to be taken at its own value, as much for a song composer as a president or a general.

Popular culture is many things, but it invariably contains the particulars (of the creators) cast as the universal (of the audience): the special talent of Jews working in commercial entertainment. Because they worked the entertainment system but also because they often had the special capacity to see themselves in the Other, they responded more frequently, often more creatively than anyone else would or could to the inchoate yearnings (for meanings or for pleasure, often both) expressed in the only ways available to the masses of ordinary Americans, i.e., as culture consumers.

Tantalizing hints abound in the story of the Yiddish language, in Yiddish culture, and notably in the rise of Yiddish usage in the emergent form of mass communication of the nineteenth century, the press. Five million Jews in the Russian Empire, the overwhelming majority of them Yiddish speakers in their daily lives, had no proper newspapers of their own until the early twentieth century. The Czarist regime considered their very presence, especially when linked to the prospect of a collective expression in a daily Yiddish press, to be inherently dangerous to security. The small Jewish intellectual class agreed, for reasons of their own security within the power structures of their community. Placing their hopes in Hebrew (historically reserved for religious/ritual usage, and taught for many centuries in schools designated exclusively for males), traditionalists sought to hold on to a slipping leadership while newer elites planned to lead the orderly assimilation into western society, through the linguistic adoption of Russian or German.

Thus it fell ironically to American Jews, still few in number during the 1870s–80s, to publish the first range of semisuccessful Yiddish daily papers, harbingers in their small way of the modernization of Jewish life. What were these papers like? They might easily be described as the antithesis of the emerging popular press in the way they met the eye. By the Civil War, the successful English language dailies had already begun to use photo engravings and woodcuts, a bit later half-tone photographs, making the press more and more a prototelevision of visual entertainment. Judaism, the ultimate text-bound culture, as much as forbade illustration ("You shall create no graven images"), and the secular rabbis who launched the radical working class-oriented presses of the 1880s–90s so privileged the word over the picture that they were in that sense continuators of tradition. By the mid-1890s when Jews by the hundreds of thousands had reached American shores and had found no golden land – but instead found real-life victims of notorious suffering in depressed neighborhoods and sweatshops – the creative (to conservatives, heretical) process logically first took pictorial form in satire sheets.

In a formal sense, these early efforts were mere imitations of mainstream humor publications like *Puck* (one of them was entitled *der Yidisher Pok*).[4] But a clear line runs between drawings and gags about foolish fellow Jewish immigrants to the "I was raised on chicken fat" denizens of *Mad Comics* and to the Upper West Side crowd that an early Woody Allen ceaselessly lampooned. Humor, including a continually close assessment of popular genres through ridicule of the details, opens up a view on a world that need not be taken at official valuation.

How else are we to encompass, let alone comprehend, the myriad and almost limitless contradictions? *Rivington Street*, a booklet-length poem by one of the admired word-artists of the ghetto, Moshe Nadir (Itzakh Reiss's pen name, literally the actors' cheeky insult thrown at the audience, "Take This, Mister!"), decades later tried to capture them through retrospect. In an imagined meeting with an old man in a doorway on Rivington Street, the "old yellow-grey Jew with a peddler's pack ... a misty-man in a misty shadow of an era's end" explains street life of the 1890s in this way:

I remember Rivington Street
When the young girls wore bonnets
And blue worsted bloomers
And rode off on bicycles
Or together on tandems
Both singing away:
"A bicycle built for two."
On Shabbos there would be
A real assembly
Out for a walk
To great distances, West Farms.

I remember the time
When Union Officers wore ribbons
And rode horses
The bakers' delegates
Blazed the trail
And were slaughtered like calves.
I remember too
The first "Picture Shows"
On Columbia Street
Where movies were shown
Upstairs and Downstairs
And the "heroes" would fall off the canvas
To the floor below ...

Sha, the thoughts I have!
"Yes, We Have no Bananas
We have no Bananas! Today!"

And think of this!
I remember Rivington Street from the
Time when men were unashamed to have beards!
And women unashamed to have breasts.

I remember the stables
On Water Street
On Front Street
Famous horse-trainers
And gangsters
Little Augie
Dopey Benny
Ishka Nigger
Johnny Spanish
And other race-heroes
Of the East Side.

The fire escapes
And the air
The only summer resort
For Rivington Streeters
And sweat-shop workers.

And no sweeter word
Than "Europe" could be heard
Among the Rivington Street Jews.
Ah, Europe, Europe ...
Fools. They didn't have the money to return.[5]

Here was the deeper reality. Jewish immigrants from Eastern Europe in the last twenty years of the nineteenth century and first decades of the new century had left behind communities already in turmoil and crisis, and not only from the blows of persecution. The rebellion, conscious or unconscious, from an older collective enterprise toward newer forms of individual self-expression linked itself always, in one way or another, to the search for a larger unity.

Emigration from the world of the Pale to America was disproportionately one of artisans, skilled workers, and their families. As a group they had neither been dominant, nor at the very bottom. Since the origins of Eastern European Jewish life, petty merchants and some not so petty had flourished in places, and the religious class was a fixture. These two groups together ruled village life, often quite oppressively. Other categories could be readily found, including the unskilled worker, the agricultural laborer, the legendary *goneff* (thief), and in later centuries, musicians. But the craftsman and artisan, including a substantial number of skilled women employed from photographic to butcher shops, had come to set the newer tone as industrialization and urbanization dawned. All things being equal, they might have created a new Jewry around themselves.

These very modernizing elements faced, however, the combined effects of a declining Russian economy and special legal or extralegal constraints upon Jewish opportunity, including multiple exclusion from residence and business ownership – even from the manufacture of liquor within the ghetto. Under these conditions, further mechanization came slowly. Jews could not compete as workers or manufacturers with the prices of outside manufactured goods, placing them in economic oblivion.

The centuries-old solidity of the Jewish community, held firm despite internal tensions by Gentile persecution and threats, suddenly gave way. The temporal powers of the community seemed increasingly hateful, and for solid reasons. Existing Jewish elites decided who should be sent into the Russian army – often a death sentence, or, at best, a sentence so long that any prospect of social advancement would be entirely lost. Communal authorities naturally chose the defenseless poor, since rabbinical students as well as children from the better-off classes were exempted from service.

Discontent increasingly showed itself in breakaway synagogues, likewise in cultural and religious societies founded independently in a measured defiance of the regular civic and spiritual authorities. The cultural associations sometimes operated as embryo labor unions, bringing common Jews together against the protocapitalist (Jewish) masters determinedly expanding their enterprises and in the process making would-be journeymen into proletarians. Independent religious institutions, almost invariably more democratic than the ones that they abandoned, formulated their own codes of religious dress and behavior. All these breakaways were already taking steps toward a popular culture.

Class and cultural tensions assumed forms strikingly different, however, from those in surrounding Gentile communities. First, as Czarist decrees permitted more Jews to enter higher education and the professions, secularization spread as rapidly, perhaps, as anywhere on earth. Young Jews alienated from ritual and from religious centers of community power drank in the writings of literary rebels like Nekrasov and Pisarev along with the great Russian novelists whose furiously active pens offered a model of a new way for an educated man to live. They also turned to uplift Yiddish, the reviled "jargon" or "women's tongue," as a vernacular voice of and for the people, and to the world it encompassed. This was *Yiddishkayt,* literally Yiddishness, and to all but the empowered Hebraists, Jewishness as well, for to speak Yiddish meant to speak Jewish.

This last development received an extremely unexpected if vital reinforcement from the most intensely unsecular Jews in the rural villages of Galicia and other parts of Eastern Europe least touched by modernization. An established class of educated Jews, especially German Jews, had for a generation or more pressed the *Haskalah,* social-scientific Enlightenment ideas, as the proper way to save Jews from their own ignorance and to win them to German (or Russian or even Czech) *Kultur* and *Bildung* (self-improvement). The success of *Haskalah* was uneven at best, and not only because the lives of so many Jews were too insular or too difficult for the relearning of language and culture.

Neither German nor Russian, nor for a generation or so (if ever) even English offered the range for sensibilities expressible only in a folkish mother-tongue. The hard-core Eastern European Jews simply could not be assimilated into a "higher" culture. But many of them could be transformed when apparently new images and sounds offered something of an escape with a comfortably familiar feel. Many an erstwhile faithful boyish Hasid became a faithful Socialist (or at least a good union man), still waiting for the end of days – and that was not even the main story.

Yiddish almost overnight became, for large sections of the Pale and nearby cities, the literary medium for expressing the assorted contradictions. From its humble origins as a predominantly Middle-High German tongue spoken in the ghettos of twelfth-century "Loter" (a region between modern Germany and France), it migrated eastward under pressure of persecution with its speakers, and acquired larger doses of Slavic languages. As the keenest of literary scholars tell us, the first widely popular writers, styling themselves Mendele Mokhor-Sforim (Mendele the bookseller) and Sholom Aleichem ("Good Day!" or "Peace Unto You"), chose the vernacular as the only route to awakening the ordinary Jew. They thereby created an uplift with a difference, enlightenment by satire, that would become a standard in Jewish life.

No doubt they were also quite often entertainers by trade, a point made by recent critics who consider the growth of secularism to be suspect.[6] Historians now suggest that Jewish minstrels were at the very root of German folk music, as early as the fifteenth century.[7] By the later nineteenth century, they readily invented for their own purposes folk characters and folk songs that had never existed, made public appearances in outlandish outfits and displaced Talmud with nature-lore and modern romance. In doing so, they borrowed freely from the models and the familiar stories of surrounding peoples. The *klezmer* bands that grew up rapidly through large stretches of Eastern Europe in the later decades of the century required a repertoire large enough to entertain paying audiences of all kinds.

In fact, this form of collaboration went back centuries, with the richest musical interaction between those twin persecuted minorities, Jews and Gypsies. Not at all surprisingly, the "Gypsy orchestras" of the nineteenth century were often Jews, the composers also Jewish, like Mordechele Rosenthal, whose music was in turn snatched up by Franz Liszt for the much-admired "Hungarian Rhapsodies." The *Yidl Mitn Fidl* (Little Jew with Violin, subject and title of a later famous Yiddish stage musical) working alone on stage was already a cultural synthesizer, to say nothing of the clarinetist, trombonist, and *tsimbler* (hammered dulcimer player), all of whom invented and transposed as freely as the most eclectic early black jazz musician using instruments left behind in the South by the occupying Union troops (possibly including my own great-grandfather, a farmer-abolitionist who marched with Sherman through Georgia) of the Civil War.

From medieval times, rabbis had been known to curse the amateur musicians, storytellers, jokesters, and others for borrowing from the Gentiles, and not mainly because the Gentile audience could turn suddenly and dangerously hostile. Fusion and artistic reinterpretation posed a threat later to be realized in centuries in secularism, offering an indefinable something that could and did easily come to substitute for religion and the constituted structures of authority. In the tales of Sholom Aleichem that sustained Yiddish audiences for three generations (and found their reanimation in *Fiddler on the Roof*), father and mother are unquestioningly religious even when they express themselves most articulately in irony ("Thanks to God, we go on starving" or, in fear of the approaching final days, "God protect us from the Messiah!"). But the fulcrum of the narrative is rather more like an early version of *All in the Family* as adapted by Norman Lear from a more hard-edged British television version: young people's angst and eagerness for change goes up against the backwardness of parents. Tevye, the milkman, is a thousand times more sympathetic than Archie, the racist Irish-American dockworker. But he, also, advances through puzzlements and frustrations to loving descendents who depart from past ways once assumed to be eternal.

The same issues apply to theater, naturally. For countless generations, play-acting was possible only in the *purim-shpiel*, an annual reenactment of Jewish fate and rededication to its purposes. By the middle of the nineteenth century, even this religious pageant had become considerably more comic, with amateur performers beginning to borrow material and gestures from Gentile actors. Wandering groups of medieval-style acrobats and singers by that time created a sort of *shtetl* vaudeville, out of which the first Yiddish plays apocryphally appeared in 1870s Romania. By the early 1880s, the Yiddish theater took shape in New York parallel to developments in Europe, and in a short time became the sensation of the ghetto, from Warsaw and Vilnus, Kiev and Odessa, to the Lower East Side.

By the 1890s, a Yiddish art theater, launched to promote learning as well as entertainment and run by determined Socialists, offered a different version of eclecticism and not only because of the vision of proletarian universalism. *A Doll's House* would be played in New York nearly twenty years earlier in Yiddish than English, and all the while between the mid-1890s and 1910s, theatrical discussions of "free love" censored on Broadway continued to be rather freely heard on Yiddish Broadway, Second Avenue. These denizens – actors, playwrights, audiences – were the downtown bohemians before Greenwich Village gained its notoriety and radical flavor. In the new century, realists and romanticists had divided into separate theatrical worlds and their followers as well, helping set the genre-forms for films. This division fueled the atmosphere of evening entertainment that ended in the street with vigorous discussions, disputations, and occasional fistfights about the merits of a particular play, actor, or director.

The conditions and sentiments of immigrant ghetto life naturally played heavily in these developments. The "pull" of jobs far more than the "push" of persecution brought Jews to the new land. But after the crash of 1893 and before the recovery at the century's turn, jobs were relatively few and terribly uncertain. The needles trade industry was deeply regressive, in the modern factory sense, returning the bulk of work into the home where whole families worked together in the most miserable conditions to finish garments. Junk jewelry, cigar making, and nearly all the assorted light industries offered versions of same. Wholesale jobbers, many of them former impoverished immigrants (one of the very first Yiddish political cartoons jibed the moral indifference of these exploiters, and it was a lasting sentiment), ruthlessly underpaid the home workers. Naturally, the nascent capitalists got little respect even when they commanded fear. It was akin to the fragmentation back home, only more so because traditions of deference had frayed almost to invisibility.

Perhaps the Jewish writers and artists decades later would have reached the same high attainments if the Jewish ghetto of the 1890s-1910s had not been so rabid with radicalism. Perhaps. But the driving dynamic of radical humanism, bigger than any Marxist (or other) attempt to give it a singular shape, was to play a key role so often and so verifiably that the history of the little world of *Yiddishkayt* (not so little until the 1930s-40s, and even then boasting some of the best theater, with the best-paid actors and actresses, in the New World) must be given account.[8]

Sholem Aleichem thus began one of his best short stories with the phrase, "It seems to me that there is no better thing in the world than a strike," likening it to the pleasure of his walking out on an especially nasty and abusive Hebrew *kheder* (school) teacher.[9] Rebellion was in the life's blood of creative purpose. Jews were famous for their massive parades and rallies in which great orators, poets as persuasive as Pindar of antiquity, would beseech the workers to continue their sacrifices down to starvation rather than accept the indignity of crawling back on their empty bellies. At some of the same rallies, more so after the turn of the century, vaudevillian-style comics would warm up the audience for the serious oratory, and a chorus would finish off the program with stirring but also entertaining music. (One recalled to me a Lower East Side incident in 1915. The warm-up jokester, asked about Socialism, ad libbed, "Ask the baker [the speaker to follow], I am only the clerk." The remark reappeared in the next day's *Jewish Daily Forward* as the "vitz" of a "gruener," a new immigrant.[10]) Similarly, in the pages of the pre-1900 Yiddish radical press, melodramatic poems often ran on the front page, precursor to the dramatic illustration but also to the role of the popular song (and singer) in prolabor rallies and in similar film or television moments of the future.

Living conditions heightened the need for mental escape as well as hope for some future revolution. Dumbbell-shaped tenements with only airshafts separating them, dark and miserable rooms, bitterly cold from inadequate heating or insufferably hot as well as overcrowded, offered laboratories for tuberculosis and other easily transmitable diseases. The contrast to the countryside left behind was almost too much to bear, almost as much because of the industrial-urban pace as the congestion. Taking "de gez," or death by asphyxiation, a distinctly modern form of suicide, mirrored in real life the artistic expressions of despair. In the one-column short story, adopted as the basic popular literature of the Yiddish daily press in the very last years of the passing century, authors wondered aloud at how the beautiful flower (i.e., the lovely and characterful young woman) could bloom in the filth and rot of the tenements. If not the original "Rose in Spanish Harlem" several neighborhoods removed, a model that perhaps belonged to some earlier Manhattan Irish or even Dutch slum teen, it was nevertheless a memorable literary case in point.

Such "instant literature" sprang from the pens of Leon Kobrin ("the Jewish Zola") and other, mostly Russian-trained intellectuals who taught themselves Yiddish in order to make a living with the pen. They commented frequently on the comings and goings of Jewish mistresses to the rich, on the unfulfilled yearnings of the young (or the hopeless disorientation of the old), and on the bitter generational conflicts – usually religious orthodoxy versus radicalism – that drove parents and their children to alienation and worse. Among the range of other common subjects, these writers touchingly described the domestic scenes of conflict in the cramped tenements where modesty was an almost unattainable goal (especially with "roomers," nonrelatives renting rooms) and nonmarital sex as temptingly close as it was morally unthinkable to the senior generation. This was *Sex in the City* for Yiddish readers, a preview of attempted moral escapes that mainly brought no escape but instead reinforced the terrible sense of confinement.

Attempts at geographical escape were frequent but in some sense always chimerical. To the north (beyond the Bronx), to the west, even to the south, daily life could be easier for a Jew and many thousands made that choice – but not usually without looking back somewhat nostalgically. Never would Jewish life in Cleveland, Chicago, or the (until 1920 or so) almost unthinkably distant California be as fully Jewish as in Greater New York. Not even in Palestine, for those relative few who could afford the journey to visit or make the personal sacrifice to settle, because the central evolving Jewishness after 1890 did not belong as much in Vilnus or Warsaw as it did to the promise of the new world city, i.e., Greater New York. Nowhere else had the same critical mass with modern means at hand, nothing else was as city-like and rich with potential, notwithstanding multiple temptations to assimilate and leave Jewishness behind.

The old and now renewed sense of division (or permanently bruised feelings) within the community made things still worse for modern Jewishness in some ways, in others mainly more confusing. Jewish patrons of art and culture, like Jewish relief agencies, sprang up on all sides, and were by a considerable degree greater in resources and outreach than in any other ethnic community. But these agencies, with few exceptions up to at least the 1920s, had one class of patron and one boss: the wealthy German Jews, male or female, indubitably philanthropic-minded but simultaneously repelled by the language, the manners, and, it often seemed, by the very physical presence of the Eastern European immigrant. Thus "kike" and "kikey," not WASP taunts but German-Jewish sneers directed at "greenhorn" looks and Eastern European lower-class behavior such as hand-waving during conversation.

These upper-class Jews (derisively called "Yehudim") and the Eastern Europeans who managed to join them in the class of wealthy merchants could make mighty claims of institutional accomplishment. German Jews in particular rushed into civic orchestras during the last years of the century. One of the most prominent of the families launched Julliard; Adolph Ochs meanwhile bought the nearly defunct *New York Times* in 1898 and rendered it "cultural" – destined to become, in time, the ultimate high-class tastemaker; and Walter Domrosch took over the New York Symphony. But with some keen-minded and strategically important exceptions, they shunned the kind of culture, religious or otherwise, closest to *Yiddishe Hertzen* (Jewish but really Yiddish hearts), which in their eyes was definitely *not* the culture that could lift ordinary Jews out of folkish tastes and into something better.

Anarcho-Zionist Baruch Rivkin, the most insightful of the Yiddish literary critics, wrote later that the first Eastern European immigrant generation slipped unconsciously into American life, removing its heritage like an old overcoat suited to the bitter East European winters. This drastic oversimplification contained a kernel of truth.[11] Empowered German Jews and their successors sought to replicate the elite forms of European culture on American shores. But for them, too, as the emerging middle class and upper middle class, the "culture of consumption" was taking center stage. Words like "discipline," "character," and "sacrifice" had begun to be displaced in their own circles by "personality," "celebrity," and "leisure," as the existing Gentile ideals to be attained. Jewish Socialists and anarchists called these energetic upper-class consumers the "shoddy aristocracy" or "moneybags," and borderline anti-Semites like Henry James nailed them as mere *arrivistes*.

Immigrants of a lower sort had a long, long trip to make from the *shtetl*'s age-old familial longings to the comical American Jewish vaudeville lyric version, "Oy Oy, Gib Mir a Boy!" and the hope that the generation to come might at least be able to get rich and respectable if not supply a future president to the nation. Immigrants themselves, in large numbers, naturally made the trip in their own fantasy lives, not in reality. At least for most of them, such cravings did not cancel out the personal value of collective memories. Abraham Cahan, a bridge between Jewish lower and middle classes, thus remained a firm assimilationist to the end of his life (which is to say, the end of his editorial career on the *Jewish Daily Forward*, in the middle of the twentieth century), adamantly against the teaching of Yiddish as a second language in New York schools on the grounds that it would slow Jewish upward mobility. The same milieu also increasingly celebrated consumer capitalism. Yet the *Forward* carried on its masthead long after Cahan's passing, until the mid-1980s, the old Marxist phrase, "the emancipation of the working class is the task of the working class itself," an idea potentially more incendiary than "workers of the world, unite!" The paper offered daily reinforcement of Yiddish and *Yiddishkayt*, and served until its end (it went weekly in 1989 and on that basis still continues) as the largest publisher, by way of serialization, for Yiddish literature.

For the Socialists who defined so much of the working class spirit of the 1890s, universalism offered a vocabulary or school of different meanings. The German immigrant Socialists, whose newspapers, unions, sickness, and death benefit societies and cultural associations set the model for the Jewish immigrants (and extended a hand, often automatically, because leading German Socialist intellectual activists were themselves Jewish), lived in a transported mental world of radical German romanticism and *Bildung*. Commercialism and its associated mentality had in this view utterly misdirected civilization, but workers of hand and mind would one day redirect it toward what might be called an aesthetics of daily life. If another model offered itself, English poet laureate (and leading Socialist intellectual)

William Morris epitomized the quest to turn back industrial society's ugliness and to realize the artistic possibilities of human endeavor. His death in 1896 brought an apotheosis from the young Yiddish press that the passing of Frederick Engels hardly equaled.[12]

Jewish editors quickly took up the call, albeit with a crucial difference in what critics now like to call "cultural production." The socialistic German-American newspapers' weekly supplements essentially reprinted literature and criticism from the Old Country, adding a few interesting immigrant authors, for the most part newspaper editors fresh from the homeland who continued their familiar stylings. By contrast, Yiddish writers and Yiddish editors had to invent form even more than content, both because an Old World Yiddish press hardly existed (the first Yiddish workers' paper had been published in London in the 1880s by Morris Winchevsky, an intimate of William Morris and later a leading Jewish-American poet/critic) but also because the situation obviously demanded something dynamically new. Jewish socialistic readers accepted the notion of uplift, but they also demanded – far more than the fairly insular German immigrants – real entertainment.

No 1890s ghetto dweller put the philosophy of art and culture into action so well as the father of the Jewish-American theater, Jakob Gordin. Stressing the promise of ancient cultures and the demoralizing effect of Christianity, Gordin sought to unify the realism of material existence (especially working-class existence) with the poetry of romantic renewal.[13] For a time, he and Cahan worked in harness, Gordin writing the kind of realistic, uplifting plays that Cahan considered a proper model, their success a warning against *shund*, mere trashy romanticism. But Gordin's realism was never absolute, any more than that of the writers and readers who treasured Morris's fanciful visions of nature and a different human future. In the end, Cahan used his pages and his polemical skills to try and destroy the reputation of Gordin while the theatrical giant was dying of cancer (Winchevsky for his part delivered one of his most ambitious Yiddish texts, a book-length memoir of imagined time together, "A Day With Jakob Gordin," i.e., the final day of the dramaturge's life in 1909).

But Gordin, as theatrical impresario and senior philosopher, had already been a ghost within the theatrical world for years. When the Socialist movement of the 1890s failed, life and culture moved on. In the rushed pace of American culture, many important changes had already taken place as the famous generation of "1905ers" (named for their arrival time) set down their own roots. Two apparently opposite tendencies in Jewish immigrant life actually reinforced each other and set the stage for our main subject.

YIDDISH STREET LIFE AND ITS CARTOGRAPHERS

Reader, try to imagine yourself as a young intellectual in New York in 1910, recently immigrated to America, or as the child of Jewish immigrants growing up with the old culture and language close at hand. Our so-called Jewish life, the life of the *Yiddishe gassen,* or Jewish streets of the city, is by now one of the most intensively Jewish ever, certainly ever lived in America. But there is no contradiction to say that it was nevertheless full of other and very contradictory elements. We Jewish intellectuals-to-be not only ride the subway with the *goyim* every day, but we also go to dance halls – no matter what our parents say – and even flirt with the *goyishe* opposite (or even same) sex. We go to the movies at least as often as other urban young people in America. We go to Coney Island. And although we mostly hate it, we go to work. In nearly all these circumstances, fresh data flows in. We live with our own multiple identities.

These identities have to do with being Jewish in new ways, and simultaneously recuperating selective traditions. One speaks of the rebellious young people as the first large generation of secularized Jews, prototype for future smart alecks that will become respectable parents (decades later the type of parents likely to answer back, at every wild claim of the next adolescent generation, "Hoo-hah!"). But budding artists quickly used the advantages of education and leisure, however limited, to reach back into obvious sources in Jewish folk traditions, the musical, visual, and, in modified form, religious.[14] For aesthetes in particular, this is a new form of rebellion, an unstable if exciting mixture. Brought together with the situation of the current day, from the Triangle Fire to the Paterson textile strike pageant to the war, the terrible suffering of European Jews, and the Russian revolutions, these influences produce a Jewish nervousness, a state of heightened attention to detail and nuance, as veteran critic-observer Jakob Milkh pronounced in 1919.[15]

Beneath every gesture to reach the artistic self, the artistic-minded could discover a kind of Jewish transcendentalism waiting to be brought back to consciousness. At the ultimate vernacular level of cheering hoi polloi, Fanny Brice, one of the most popular vaudeville performers for 1910s-20s Jewish audiences, noticed (with some coaching from Irving Berlin) that she could win applause and tears by slipping into Yiddish, a fact all the more remarkable (but by no means unusual for performers) because she had no background whatever in the language. The comic gestures that gained her fame were likewise alien to her, discovered at the same time by accident – altogether the veritable picture of the immigrant pathos, expressed with typically Jewish humor. Yiddish was for Brice, as for future art film director Jules Dassin taking part in the Yiddish ARTEF theater as a youngster twenty years later, at once an American and a Jewish thing to learn.

At the other end of the artistic spectrum, the post-Impressionism of the Russian scene so influencing young Jews from Moscow and Budapest to Berlin, to Paris and New York had led roundabout to rediscovering folk symbols of a Jewish art. Demanding more than a realist treatment, this impulse commanded an appropriate modernism with flowing lines, surface play, shading, and the intersection of planes through a curious two dimensionality realized most clearly in Chagall's work, but common in the Jewish world from book illustrations to painting. It was the artists' counterpart to Fanny Brice's appeal to the masses demanding to be entertained.

In sum, as the Yiddish language and *Yiddishkayt* had drawn from the cultures around the Jews for centuries, the new country offered the opportunity to do so at great cultural advantage. The Jewish *shtetl* dweller even one or two steps removed understood the weight of oppression that rested upon the new immigrant from everywhere, and the search at leisured moments for something that promised escape and more. In the commonplace of the emerging cultural critics, the Jew who shunned both the synagogue and whorehouse found a solution in the theater. It satisfied the diverse urges that, psychologically speaking, were not so diverse after all. (It also had a vast appeal to women, a notion that the original aphorism completely failed to recognize.) The same cultural critic was slower to recognize similar solutions in the movies, considered more whorehouse than theater, and still more appealing to young Jewish women.

To view the larger process with greater depth, we need to step back a bit and begin from a seemingly unlikely direction: urban life of the progressive era, especially urban immigrant life, self-reflected in the new technology thanks to the concentration of potential audience. It is here, in the early decades of the century, that we first find our subjects, the lower-middle-class, first- or second-generation immigrant Jews who will overwhelmingly make up the cast of future blacklisted artists.

In an admirable study of art and the city, Rebecca Zurier points to the role of the 1910s Ash Can school of painters and to their subjects, the Lower East Side inhabitants (especially Jews), as offering the educated middle class a first glimpse at the new, urban life redefining popular culture. These artists, most of them Gentiles, invented what Zurier calls a "thematics of sight that both participated in and commented upon the urban visual culture of their day." John Sloan, George Bellows, and Robert Henri artistically realized what a larger group of urban illustrators had been working on since the 1890s.

The "urban visuality" of the evolving public culture, an astonishing leap of interest and information access, included consumer goods, public spectacles such as labor or political rallies, and "cheap amusements" like films and amusement parks.[16] In some crucial ways, this urban visuality has been the undying inspiration for the century, fading and reappearing in dozens of guises, culture high to low but most obviously where high and low meet, the artistic pages of the *Masses* magazine to *West Side Story* and hip hop versions of today's once again drastically changing, somehow flourishing multicultural reality.

A city life that Henry James had pronounced "unspeakable" thus began to "speak." The most skilled artists, in every medium, can be said to have composed their work similarly to the early filmmaker, utilizing costume and other informational clues, subtle or unsubtle, to indicate to the audience the meaning intended. The artist is not detached, nor is the subject: they collaborate, much as the live audience and actors collaborate. The Ash Can sobriquet, at first intended as insult and then adopted proudly by the artists themselves, stood as a challenge to previous aesthetics of affirmative or uplift culture, "sweetness and light." Not surprisingly, the People's Art Guild announced to the public – in Yiddish and English – its formation. Dropping all specific Jewish identification, the Guild nevertheless continued to aim its search for subjects and plan its exhibitions within the East Side. Indeed, its prime organizer, John Wechsel, taught at the Hebrew Technical Institute (he also devised the first systematic design for the future Jewish Museum) and he appropriately held the Guild's most ambitious show at none other than the offices of the *Jewish Daily Forward*. Projects were also on display at Alfred Steiglitz's gallery, and Weichsel himself published in the gallery's journal, *Camera Work*.[17]

This sort of operation was definitely something new, at least to Americans. It adamantly opposed the exploitation of artists by commercial art dealers in the name of an avant-garde. To issue a challenge in the name of high art was not, of course, the same as an immanent critique from out of the heart (or bowels) of mass culture, and its advocates might actually scorn the masses. But these early beginnings nevertheless offered an important step along the way to a self-conscious popular art.

In the midst of this process, immigrant and specifically New York area Jews passed from cultural object to cultural subject, part of the throbbing city that through the eras of booming suburbs and exurbs – with Jewish Americans among the most suburban – has seemed the locus of real life and interest, a resonant source material for naturalism and superrealism, comedy, and tragedy of every kind. The sources of this crucial transition need to be traced carefully, and much of the evidence will be seen along the way through the individuals whose lives and work make up this book. A broad background will suffice for the moment.

If it's clear that every emerging genre of popular culture demanded a synthetic approach, it remains little understood just why some of the particulars appealed so readily and came so easily to the children of *these* immigrants. Music offers an apt microcosm, or perhaps not microcosm so much as macrocosm of modern Whitmans seeking with great success to cry out, "I hear America singing – *my* songs!"

First there was Tin Pan Alley. From the mid-1880s, music publishers based in New York had a booming business in sheet music. Meanwhile, middling and working-class German-American Jews who felt themselves part of a cultural Germania (where anti-Semitism was the privilege of ardent Christians but anathema to many immigrant free-thinkers) were among the prime customers and most often the performers in the musical culture of family-oriented taverns that dotted German-American neighborhoods with names like "Over the Rhine." The Americanized version of this culture, carefully described in popular novels, brought together a love of music, beer, and good times that contrasted vividly with Yankee Protestantism and therefore instinctively appealed to urban and irreligious "new immigrants," Jews in particular. Gus Kahn, arriving in Chicago in 1892, ended up being one of Al Jolson's chief suppliers, including vaudeville standards like "Yes, Sir, That's My Baby," "Toot, Toot, Tootsie Goodbye," "Carolina in the Morning," and the score for Eddie Cantor's show *Whoopee*.

Bright Jewish boys born abroad or shortly after their parents' immigration also devised the synthetic sentimentalism that made a vaudeville tune, "By the Banks of the Wabash Far Away," the perfect state song of Indiana – although inspired by a Chicago Jewish gaze at Lake Michigan. Another German-American Jewish stylist wrote "Take Me Out to the Ball Game" twenty years before he actually went out to one. "By the Old Mill Stream" or "School Days" would do as well for a wider audience, and for strangely similar reasons. As the older rural society slipped away, its evocation became steadily more precious, scarcely less to those who happily plunged into modern materialism than to small-town Americans with a minimum of change around them. Jews L. Wolfe Gilbert with "Waitin' for the Robert E. Lee," and Harry Von Tilzer with "Down Where the Swanee River Flows" could obviously deliver the goods. Asked what made a hit tune, Gus Kahn answered frankly and cheerfully, "'Mother,' 'Sweetheart,' 'Home,' and 'Longing for You,'" essentially pleasures of the past with hopes of renewal in the future.[18]

The German-Jewish Witmark family, whose company grew to one of the largest in Tin Pan Alley by century's turn, had actually been in America since before the Civil War (one of them fought for the Confederacy!), distributed liquor, and among the younger generation envisioned a prosperous future in the rising music business. Isidore Witmark thus composed a wedding march to commemorate and profit from the impending marriage of President Grover Cleveland; he also turned out show tunes, hypersentimental "mother's songs," and even African-American genre tunes for the cakewalk, as the public tired of the sentimental Germanic waltz. How far did his race tunes diverge from the minstrel melodies written earlier by the dozens? In one sense, a lot, because the first modern black commercial composers worked with and for the Witmarks. "Dat Old Wagon," published in 1896, written by Ben Harney (albeit passing for white), was arguably the first authentically African-American popular sheet music. On the other hand, the Witmarks had a big success in the same years with "All Coons Look Alike to Me," which caused African-American lyricist Ernest Hogan and the company itself deep embarrassment due to black audience protest – also marking the first consumer complaints launched by African-Americans against any entertainment corporation, and specifically a Jewish one.

The further range that made the Witmarks both the sponsors of an early black musical written by Paul Lawrence Dunbar and the sponsors of the first black members of ASCAP also prompted them to devote a whole division of the company to minstrelsy (and publish a *First Minstrel Encyclopedia*). Likewise, the middlebrow pop melodies of Victor Herbert – a big part of Eubie Blake's early inspiration, according to Blake himself – helpfully further complicate the picture. Isidore Witmark's autobiography, a bit defensive on racial points, described American music as encompassing "white, black, American Negro, Jewish, Yankee" culminating in jazz, whose heritage he traced to "the old minstrel shows." Unlike the Domrosch legacy or even Julliard, both of which championed the continuity of Old World music in the New World, this was Jewish American, commercial opportunism but with more than a touch of the familiar Jewish idealism. Instinctive pacifists, the Witmarks let loose a last burst of antiwar music as President Woodrow Wilson prepared for war and for his administration's comprehensive suppression of peaceniks, Socialists, and Wobblies.

The dance craze that caught on in the last years of the nineteenth century had meanwhile also prompted hasty entrepreneurialism in many related forms – but most important for us, Jewish young people's pursuit of pleasure and self-realization. Nearly all New York's numerous dance halls stood adjacent to saloons. The sale of liquor hastened the process of ungenteel and unchaperoned behavior (in this first case, Americanization) through a precocious teen culture of dancing and necking. The steadily changing argot of the dance floor, parks, and surrounding streets in turn spurred up-to-the-minute lyrics by young Jewish song pluggers. Few of the events were racially integrated among the dancers; but among the musicians, theater owners and booking agents, the mixture of black artists and Jewish entrepreneurs was by the early 1910s reaching the big time.

The print world of 1910, meanwhile, was suffused with observation and light verse that so far owed little to Jewish immigrants save as big city readers, but which they were soon to make their own. The famed "Conning Tower" of the *Herald Tribune*, the sports commentaries of Ring Lardner, Sr., contemporary political and cultural writings of all kinds promised amateurs with an ear for rhyme a quick way forward. Why did Jewish boys like the future music giants the Gershwin brothers and their companion E.Y. ("Yip" for "Yipsel," Yiddish for "squirrel") Harburg leap so readily into the fray? Here the evidence is exceptionally good because they lived long enough for detailed memories. Harburg attended the Yiddish theater often with his father, meanwhile reading light matter, and was drawn to Gilbert and Sullivan's published lyrics even before his childhood friend Ira Gershwin played an operetta on the gramophone, ending Yip's hope that music had not already been written for these clever phrases.[19]

Brother George Gershwin naturally disappointed his parents by leaving formal education behind for Tin Pan Alley – almost literally as scripted in part by Clifford Odets for a film audience in *Rhapsody in Blue* (1945). Ira went on to CCNY where, with Harburg, he invented the humor column "Gargoyle's Gargles" in the school daily, titled after the stone mascot outside the entrance and full of ingenious, irreverent verse. By no coincidence, a near generation later, in 1930–31, CCNY undergraduate Abraham Lincoln Polonsky took over the column. The Gershwins and Harburg were by this time world famous; Polonsky, son of a Bronx druggist, was a few years away from writing *The Goldbergs* for Gertrude Berg, one of the biggest hits on the radio of the 1930s–40s.[20]

It would be a mistake to separate such developments from further ones taking place in the seemingly secluded world of Yiddish. In truth, Yiddish music, drama, and the art world of Yiddish speakers intermixed freely with the English-language world, adding to it a global network of innovations and a treasure house of available legacies. Nor did the influences pass only one way. Any look at the Yiddish cinema (Yiddish titles before 1930), as much in Eastern Europe as the US, would show rebellious jazz babies rejecting the backwardness of their parents for the dream of stylishness and individuation.

The timing and content of the last great burst of immigration proved crucial for these developments. The 1905ers who had personally lived through (or heard plenty about) the Russian pogroms amid the national humiliation and political uprisings of the Russo-Japanese war, had also lived through an intensification of Yiddish culture unthinkable a decade earlier. Jews who came after the turn of the century were more urban and urbane, more in touch with working-class life, Gentile or Jewish, than their predecessors, more politicized and in many subtle ways also more self-consciously Jewish. Not only did they provide the main audience for large competing dailies in New York — easily the most circulated of any Jewish publications in the world — but also for a booming Second Avenue theatrical district and soon a world of *klezmer* music with its own popular "ethnic" labels.

Yiddish song pluggers could be just as topical (as "Kapitan Dreyfuss," about the Dreyfuss Case, showed early on) as their English-language counterparts and found their way to the new United Hebrew Record Company or lesser competitors, until overtaken by the Gentile but shrewd executives of Victor, Columbia, and Edison records with their own "ethnic" lists of titles. "Sell your foreigners!" urged the in-house organ of the Victor Corporation to its sales force, as distribution from Eastern Europe was cut off in wartime and America boomed. The boom continued through the 1920s, lifting stars like Yiddish vaudevillian Molly Picon into fame and fortune equivalent, in its own narrower way, to anything in the Gentile world. Fanny Brice, with her risqué "oy oy oy," and her transgressive phrasing of "hammm" (jolting listeners to turn over the record) demonstrated that violations of old-fashioned religious morality were exciting, part of becoming American. She was also the sweetheart and later wife of famous gambler Nicky Arnstein, thus on the edge of the mob and Arnstein's pal Arnold Rothstein whose own protégé was Meyer Lansky, Jewish founder-leader of Murder, Incorporated.[21] A transgressive Jewishness, indeed.

Did these Americanist themes diminish the energy of the workers' choruses (so popular from Zionist to Socialist, later Communist Yiddish groups) or the amateur "mandolin orchestras" which often entertained political gatherings? No more than the magnum recording hit, "A brivel der Maman" (a letter to mama) by one Solomon Smulewitz extinguished the perceived need for political movements to rescue Mama's extended family, still in Europe, from the anti-Semites. Aging Socialists might brag in the 1910s that *their* movement's youngsters didn't bother with ragtime and other such foolishness, but anyone younger knew better.

"Yiddish vaudeville," never big outside New York, thus rehearsed the old quarrels (regional Galitzianer vs Litvak, Galacian against Lithuanian) with comic effect but in the long run, mainly trained new talent. Some of the emerging talent is painful to remember, like the "hebe" humor of "Cohen" records, with vaudevillian Monroe Silver offering ethnic stereotypes from deprecatory stinginess (not that far from Jack Benny) to the minor criminality of storekeepers setting insurance fires. Some told a different story about New World life. "Yente Telebende," originally a short story by B. Kovner in the *Forverts* about an aggressive matron on vacation, driving crazy all those around her with her monologues, coined the noun "Yente," for the annoying chatterbox. Later on stage and on record, *Yente* was performed by actress Clara Gold as the self-possessed woman who knew America every bit as well as the men in her circle.[22]

All this could be said to come together within the details of George Gershwin's supreme rise − details of the story left out of the Hollywood biopic but very much present in the history of his compositions. Yip had literally been on the street with the two brothers when workmen delivered the famous piano to the Gershwin household and Georgie sat down immediately to play (he had been secretly practicing at a friend's). Working as a song plugger, George was noticed by Yiddish impresario Boris Thomashevsky as a potential theatrical composer. The plan to match Gershwin with another young composer (and unlike Gershwin, an authentic Yiddishist) Simon Secunda failed because the latter had Julliard training while the "American" Gershwin wrote by ear! Most of his compositions owed virtually nothing whatsoever to Jewish music and precious little to black music. And yet one wonders. Perhaps it was Gershwin's very adaptiveness that allowed him to incorporate elements of Jewish melodies into other compositions that is the true connection.

Yiddish film, altogether lacking a soundtrack until its fading final decade, offered another fascinating venue for experimentation. Not only did Jews pioneer and continue to exert a large influence in mainstream films but for a crucial generation or so generated a unique transition from stage to cinema in technological culture. Responding to the immigrant New York audience, Gentile director D.W. Griffith himself scripted and directed *Romance of a Jewess*, one of his biggest box-office hits. Fox's *Bar Kochba, Hero of a Nation* first romanticized the Hebrew uprising against the Romans, in six expensively produced reels. Utterly fanciful, it was far from the apolitical escapism common in mainstream cinema. Old country persecution closer to the present inspired a cycle of Yiddish films about pogroms, escapes, intermarriages, and arriving in America. Silent film hits like *Heart of a Jewess* and *Bleeding Hearts* (both starring Gentile Irene Wallace) simultaneously imported the Yiddish story into English-language (i.e., major studio release) film for Americans and also demonstrated that (Jewish) movie entrepreneurs could expect success in a Yiddish-speaking audience.

Yiddish filmmakers successfully sliced off a section of this audience for themselves. Practically every Yiddish film, as J. Hoberman points out, is riveted to the themes of separation (generations, immigrants and stay-at-homes, man and woman, religious and secular) but each also speaks to "the urge for totality, the desire for a complete and self-contained Jewish world."[23] One could say that the major impact of *Yiddishland* upon American film lay in the era ahead, when the Method acting of Group Theater along with other bodies and techniques framed in left-of-center politics and Jewish backgrounds impacted heavily upon cinematic realism. But it would be as true to say that Yiddish film, not only as produced in the US but in Europe, too, previewed the spin on heroic resistance to authority, the angst of the immigrant and the *haymishness* of actors whose next emanation would be Paul Muni (in this case, literally stage actor Muni Weisenfreund) and John (aka Julie, for Julius) Garfield (né Garfunkel).

SEARCH FOR A METHOD

Before that leap into the materials of the rest of the book, let's stop and ask: Where have we come so far? The reader seeking a causal (which is to say, definitive) status for the Jewish role in American popular culture will not find it in these narrative strokes. Or perhaps the reader will find his or her own version of it, for the question is both too large and too intimate for a one-size-fits-all answer. But let's try out some theories, as epochal and improbable as the imagination of the theorist reaches. These can be highly useful as we proceed, so long as no claim is made to finality.

Hannah Arendt once suggested that for Walter Benjamin, "the smaller the object, the more likely it seemed that it could contain in the most concentrated form everything else," rendering the familiar relationship of superstructure and substructure, art and its material basis, altogether meta-phorical.[24] To adopt the more favored word of the surrealists whom Benjamin so much admired: analogical. This book, as should be obvious by now, works mainly through analogy.

To offer one example, doubly removed by intent yet, thanks to analogy, still very useful to us: Yiddish. Literary theorists Deleuze and Guattari have insisted that a "minor language" (they refer to Prague German, in a discussion of that favorite Jewish writer, Franz Kafka) inherently holds a universe or universality unto itself; and that it binds the writer to the fate of the speakers as a more global and imperial language (English, French, German, Chinese, etc.) does not.[25] The proper language for this theory is of course Yiddish, because of its *veltlikhe* ("worldly" in the sense of material) status – set apart starkly from ritual Hebrew, and regarded as a mere jargon – and its artists' burning aspirations for emancipation of the masses and of themselves as artists. It's a thought, and not the last time that Franz Kafka comes under our gaze to think it further along.

There is another, more intimate case: identity. Any searcher in today's computer equivalent to a library card catalogue who pursues this subject far enough, book by book and presumably article by article, will still find an overwhelming preponderance of Jewish authors, whether the object of study happens to be Jewish or not. It can't be an accident. Hopis, Armenians, and all manner of smallish language groups have ancient and often continuous traditions of a collective self. None have had so much access as Jews have to print. But other possible answers lurk, and I beg the reader's indulgence for a trial leap into theology as it touches upon the crucial issues of popular culture.

Back at the mythical beginning we inevitably find the creative word, the naming power which contained all other powers. Moses asks God to name Himself and YHWH answers, "I am what I am."[26] In this cosmology, Man takes up godly powers when (on command) he begins to name the animals – and right there, something begins to be lost. As Adorno would have appreciated if he had attributed Reason to the Hebrews rather than the Greeks, the departure from Egypt confirmed the abandonment of mythos for logos. I believe that this narrowed scope may be the key to the otherwise puzzling phrases of the seventeenth-century cobbler-philosopher Jakob Boehme – the "theosophicus teutonicus" (in Hegel's phrase) and reinventor of the dialectic from the ancients, setting loose Romanticism (especially the German variety) and ultimately Marxism, when he insists that Moses, "that dear man," somehow got the ideas backward.

In the Boehmist way of thinking, drawn from Jewish mysticism (by way of the Radical Reformation and the violently suppressed utopian uprisings in Boehme's Silesian home district), a cosmic dialectic rendered inevitable the Fall of Eden; but the long-hidden hand of the deity would be felt again in the revival of demigoddess Sophia. Her long-degraded womanliness at the dawn of existence was – this is strictly my interpretation – a first signification of the vernacular, with the capture of the vitality from the designated holy. What has been degraded as unholy, mundane, and hence vernacular will *become* holy, not by the doings of existing religious (or secular) potentates, nor by the single-minded conquest of Reason, in the liberal version of progress that radicals have shared all too willingly (and that Communism or pseudo-Communism drove to a self-destructive conclusion). Some other long-hidden means, some other cosmic vision must ultimately prevail. Then, and not before, the fruits of the tree of life will be freely available. Jakob Boehme and his cosmological anticipation of Romanticism (including dialectical idealism) thereby opened the way for a simultaneously modernist and primitivist view of culture, free from existing religious controls but all the more open to a renewed spirituality. As intellectuals, artists, and outsiders, perhaps also as village (urban) dwellers, Jews were the natural explorers of this possibility.[27]

Now consider the proposition from another angle, the angle of American life's peculiarities as seen through the "great American novel" of the type that generations of Jewish novelists have so wished that they could write, in reality, Herman Melville's *Moby Dick*. Although the early European colonists often described themselves as bent on a (then) modern-day exile, their explicitly Mosaic mission demanded the conquest of Nature, including the Indians, and the unprecedented transoceanic importation of slaves to serve the real gods, those of economic expansion. True to this tradition, the whaling ship Pequod's officers, bound to follow the maddened logic of conquest even unto collective self-destruction, continually whip the multiracial crew of mariners and castaways into submission. Melville's protagonist-intellectual and the only possible leader of a counterforce, Ishmael, is inveigled by the authoritarian power of Captain Ahab, the perfect twentieth-century totalitarian, at once dictator and global market force harnessing the emotion and intellect to the exploitation and devastation of nature's prodigies.

Meanwhile, crewman Queequeg, a Polynesian with his own highly developed cosmology, remains wholly outside this Mosaic construction. Ishmael is certainly drawn to him, as they sleep in each other's arms and perhaps do a good deal more. If – skipping a few generations – Ishmael happened to have been a Jewish intellectual of a certain type, interracial political organizer or jazz impresario, he might have seen matters more clearly. He might be more than a bit like Group Theatre actor Elia Kazan's character in the Warner Brothers' *Blues In the Night* (1941) who abandons pursuits of professionalism, despite his mother's pleas, in favor of a materially insecure life of playing black music. Why? Because he would see himself not as the distaff Yankee Ishmael, but half-insider (half-white) at best, outside far enough to see in Queequeg the other half of a potential alliance against Ahab and against the thoroughly coopted or whipped ship's officers. The crew, promising to rise to collective self-consciousness with the help of the alliance, can rely only upon itself to abandon the quest for the whale and bring the ship safely home. At least it's a tempting interpretation of America's literary classic, in this case put forward by a Caribbean intellectual (my own savant) who for nearly a decade helped lead a small, almost entirely Jewish syndicalist-minded radical movement.[28]

The sheer heterogeneity of the American workforce, the layers of race privilege that outdid but also dramatized the ethnic prejudice faced by several generations of Jews, made working-class prospects for an egalitarian society unlikely for some time. But egalitarianism might evolve in a different way. By being submersed in and working within a world of objects alienated from them as their work is alienated from them, the ordinary folk might familiarize themselves, educate themselves, learn to denaturalize the objects, demystify them, and make new sense of them. At least that would be the theory of popular or mass culture as portending self-healing and total democratization rather than exhaustion of resources and an endless individual isolation.

Romanticism and modernism offer theories for why it didn't happen, what substituted for the sublime reconciliation, and how we all seem to have been left rudderless today. Wouldn't mass culture be the last place to look? "Yes, but with an explanation," as one of Woody Allen's protagonists answers when asked if he's Jewish.

The late nineteenth- and early twentieth-century middle classes, observed the critic Harold Rosenberg, had invented "the modern" in order to free themselves from all remaining encumbrances. Modernness would finish the job of replacing the "standing friezes" that once demonstrated historical continuity with the only surviving reality, i.e., motion itself. The agency of total transformation (for young Rosenberg, writing in 1949 under the influence of Rosa Luxemburg's essays), the working class, could then best be defined through the negative, as "the modern itself experienced as misery,"[29] the misery of an apparently incomplete destiny.

Rosenberg evidently didn't know well his real-life contemporary American proletariat of bowling leagues, tract houses, and oncoming generational mobility symbolized in the GI Bill. Or the memories, both positive and negative, that it dragged along from the vanishing working-class neighborhoods of Manhattan or the Bronx to Queens, Jersey, and beyond. But in a despairing, roundabout way, Rosenberg was better equipped to deal with the next stages of rambunctious Jewish lower-middle-class behavior than his more determinedly genteel colleagues around the *Partisan Review* like Lionel Trilling or celebrity-driven ones like Leslie Fiedler. Turn Rosenberg's despair neatly on its head, turn Adorno's despairing repose on its head,[30] and you might arrive at ideas something like the following, inspired by Hegel rather than Luxemburg. If mass culture can be described with necessary difficulty as a "total response by Capital to the historical possibilities of the specifically modern mass which it first creates and which now continues to create itself," then the culture of the masses, acting both as the subjectivity of capital *and* as the demand for collective self-recognition, must hold a hidden key. Ordinary folks thus struggle to move toward a universal subjectivity in their own ways. Not that they necessarily succeed. But if society manages to last long enough without destroying the ecological basis of life, then its members should be learning to live in new and more self-conscious ways, shedding the forms of an inherently alienated consumerism for something better. This would be the realization of popular culture as well as a truly egalitarian society, with Jews thoroughly implicated in the process. It remains my own fantasy, a readout from the data absorbed during a childhood of seeking a kind of cosmology within the pages of *Mad Comics*.[31]

But is it Jewish? To quote an unpublished line from the author of these Germanic quoted phrases, another mixed Yankee- and German-American like myself, "nicht Yiddish aber noch Yiddish," not literally Yiddish (or Jewish) but still *somehow* Yiddish or Jewish. What follows is a rumination on the process as the unconscious (but also occasionally conscious) dream of certain kinds of Jews involved in the creation of popular culture, all too well aware of themselves as hired hands in the factories of mass culture, but also hoping and sometimes intuiting in the responses of the audience an ending different from the one demanded by media (and other) CEOs and by our politicians. No one but the Jewish intellectual-artist has probed the question so often and struggled so hard for a happy, democratic, truly egalitarian ending.

This is never likely to be a respectable view among intellectuals of any political coloration, I'm afraid, even at a historic moment when (some) comic strips begin to be praised as art, albeit always a little apologetically about the subject matter, in the book review section of the *New York Times* and in the august pages of the *New York Review of Books*. But it comes closest to how we all feel when we identify with a film, a song, even a television show as bearing the contradictions of the age. That the favorite film, the song, and the show have almost certainly passed through Jewish hands or been shaped by earlier such productions should be no mystery.

When Irving Howe (in the best-selling *World of Our Fathers*: the one widely read volume of a notable literary and political career perpetually frustrated west of the Hudson) explains that Jewish success in popular culture is due to location and ambition, he only seized a corner of the connection.[32] Certainly, Jews were in New York at the crucial moment, most of them lacking the necessary connections and ethnic identification to join the gentility or even progress to respect and public admiration along other lines, let alone fame and riches. But if there had been nothing more than hunger and talent (along with a keenly strategic business sense), then the peculiar, reflective quality of the Jewish contribution could not possibly matter so much.

The most popular of all Yiddish writers, Sholom Aleichem, it is sometimes forgotten, did not die in his imaginary *shtetl*, Kaserilevke, of the Pale, or in Moscow or even the East End of London, but in the Bronx. I could still feel a deep connection in 1981 as I recorded the recollections of his volunteer day nurse, by this time in her nineties, a retired Yiddish pedagogue and widow of a sculptor, living in a basement apartment in the Sholom Aleichem Houses of the same Bronx. But for a few hours, the greatest of Jewish fiction writers would have died in her arms. We held hands during the conversation, she and I, and occasionally we kissed. Perhaps she saw in me, if only a little, her only child, a small son who had run into traffic in the Lower East Side during the 1930s and been instantly killed. Or she perceived me less mystically as a young man who suddenly appeared and asked her about her old friends, all of them now dead. She herself died a few months afterward (as Itche Goldberg wrote in the pages of *Yiddishe Kultur*: "So a generation passes"), and I never saw her again.

I felt a different kind of connection while talking on the phone with National Public Radio staffer Rebecca Perl about her late father, a black-listed radio writer who first staged *The World of Sholom Aleichem*, a 1950s set piece performed mostly in Jewish cultural centers, then with adaptations on Broadway and a 1959 educational television special presentation. After several emanations, another but definitely related version of the writer's stories reemerged as *Fiddler on the Roof*. Arnold Perl, the original dramaturge, a radio and television writer of grippingly realistic scripts, also left behind a version of the film script for *Malcolm X* that Spike Lee rewrote for the epic film of modern African-American life.[33] A coincidence? I don't think so. At any rate, the connection has the quality that shines like a beckoning North Star as we continue our journey.

NOTES

[1] David Thorpe, "A Mamita for the Hebrews, and Everyone Else," *Forward*, 30 May 2003. Vanessa Hidary, a Sephardic Jew raised by secular parents, fell in with black and Latino schoolmates. Her show has been optioned for a film.

[2] In particular Carl Foreman, the former carnival barker, much-admired screenwriter of *High Noon* among other features, and blacklistee: his first two films in Hollywood were Bowery Boys subfeatures.

[3] Dan Miron, *A Traveler Disguised: The Rise of Modern Yiddish Fiction in the Nineteenth Century* (New York: Schocken Books, 1973). A recent study has added rich musical emphasis to this interpretation: Henry Sapoznik, *Klezmer! Jewish Music from Old World to Our World* (New York: Schirmer Books, 1999). Larry Gelbart, *Laughing Matters: on Writing M*A*S*H, Tootsie, Oh, God!, and a Few Other Funny Things* (New York: Random House, 1998): 9.

[4] Thanks go to Edward Portnoy for my being allowed to see an unpublished essay on the origin of the Jewish humor magazine in the US.

[5] Moshe Nadir, *Rivington Stritt* (New York: Morgn Frayhayt, 1931), unpaged. My translation.

[6] A point held with particular polemical interest and a certain lack of sympathy in David G. Roskies, *A Bridge of Longing: The Lost Art of Yiddish Storytelling* (Cambridge: Harvard University Press, 1995).

[7] Yale Strom, scholar-musician, notes that the first German songbook with vocal polyphony, published in 1440, was composed by Woelffle von Locham. Strom, *The Book of Klezmer* (Chicago: A Capella/Chicago Review Press, 2002): 23, a fascinating tidbit borrowed from earlier Jewish musical scholarship.

[8] Also, socialistically organized musicians like "di Rusishe Progressiv Muzikal Yunyuon No.1 Fun Amerike," the earliest discovered *klezmer* union, evidently launched in the late 1880s, playing weddings, balls, and parades, especially for workers' organizations. The vernacular description of a musician as "professor" may have begun here.

[9] Sholom Aleichem, "We Strike," translated by the editor, in Henry Goodman, ed. *The New Country* (New York: YKUF, 1961): 85.

[10] In 1978, when I interviewed the elderly "Uncle Sam" Liptzin, known as "Feter Shepsel," in the Allerton Avenue Coops of the Bronx, he had published more than thirty volumes of "vitzen," reprints of his columns from the left-wing daily *Frayhayt*, and in the early 1920s, published his own occasional humor magazine, *Der Humorist*. He gave me his bound volumes of *Der Groysser Kundes*.

[11] No one was more aware than Rivkin of the oversimplification. One of the subtlest thinkers in a world of subtle thinkers and the greatest of Yiddish anarchist critics, he explored Yiddish-Jewish consciousness as no other. See the tri-

bute volume selected (if not apparently edited) by his widow Minna Rivkin, *B. Rivkin, Lebn un Shofn* (Chicago: L.M. Shtein, 1953).

[12] Miguel Abensour, "William Morris: The Politics of Romance," in Max Blechman, ed., *Revolutionary Romanticism* (San Francisco: City Lights Books, 1999), 125–62, best restates the Morrisian themes in terms that the old Yiddishists would have relished.

[13] See Jakob Gordin, "Realism and Romanticism," in Steven Cassedy, ed. and trans., *Building the Future: Jewish Immigrant Intellectuals and the Making of Tsukunft* (New York: Holmes & Meier, 1998), 81–86, an essay that rather overstates Gordin's own implicit romanticism and understates his socialistic politics.

[14] A noted ghetto aesthete, I. Entin, thus complained in 1909 that dour Yiddish literature desperately needed the gusts of romanticism introduced into other cultures by folklore and fantasy. I. Entin, "A Yidisher Romanticism," in I. Adler and I. Slanik, eds., *Treumer un Verklikhkayt* (New York: Shriftn, 1909): 14–24.

[15] Jakob Milkh, "Reaksionare Shtremungen," in *Shriftn* (New York: Shriftn, 1919): 3–35. *Shriftn* was the primary organ of the Yunge, the young rebel aesthetes.

[16] Rebecca Zurier and Robert W. Snyder, "Introduction," to *Metropolitan Lives: Ashcan Artists and Their New York* (New York: W.W. Norton and Museum of New York, 1995): 14–15.

[17] Avram Kampf, *Jewish Experience in the Art of the Twentieth Century* (S. Hadley, Mass.: Bergin and Harvey, 1984): 63–64.

[18] Michael Alexander, *Jazz Age Jews* (Princeton: Princeton University Press, 2001): 156.

[19] Much thanks to the Harburg Foundation, especially Ernie Harburg, for giving me a taped interview with E.Y. Harburg. My personal memory of Yip is limited to a 1978 conversation at a reception for Alger Hiss in Harburg's Central Park West apartment. Yip had a habit of exclaiming, in cheerful moments, "I see a rainbow!"

[20] See this book's Postscript on Abraham Polonsky; he lived long enough for me to know him well.

[21] That Lansky's persona should be revived in a recent film vehicle, of the same name, for Richard Dreyfuss offers some poetic justice; regrettably, the script is not up to the potential.

[22] Henry Sapoznik, "That's Jewish: You Don't Look Funny," *Shmate*, no. 13 (Summer, 1983): 13.

[23] J. Hoberman, *Bridge of Light: Yiddish Film Between Two Worlds* (New York: Museum of Modern Art and Schocken Books, 1991): 11.

[24] Hannah Arendt, "Introduction," to Arendt, ed., *Illuminations*, by Walter Benjamin, translated by Harry Zohn (New York: Schocken, 1969 edition): 22–23.

[25] Gilles Deleuze and Felix Guattari, *Kafka: Toward a Minor Literature* (Minneapolis: University of Minnesota Press, 1986), translated by Dana Polan: 16–18.

[26] It is barely a digression to note that some thousands of years later Elisar Segar, under heavy Jewish influence if not Jewish himself, has his protagonist amend the phrase for the American vernacular of the protean proletarian: "I Yam What I Yam/That's All That I Yam/I'm Popeye the Sailor Man" – Toot toot. Marx could not have phrased better the contemporary Jewish belief that the working class, the universal class whose triumph would abolish class society to establish Socialism, was "the answer to the riddle of history that knows itself to be the answer."

[27] One of R. Crumb's chief inspirations, Hieronymus Bosch, Jewish-influenced as earlier noted, created a series of works depicting an Edenic innocence, fantastic creatures commingling with humans (including sinless blacks) in a spectacle of communal pleasure with little pain, and then the fall from grace into disgrace. Bosch lacked the optimism to see any redemption. But with the reverse messianism of the faithful – suddenly aware that priests along with warriors were corrupting everything they touched – he got the most important part right.

[28] The Three Stooges, progressive entertainers who put themselves on the line in public support of the Seaman's Rights Bill (directed against the long-accepted tyrannical power of ship officers) may even have had something like this in mind, or maybe only Moe, the intellectual, who toured campuses late in life, denouncing Richard Nixon. Much scholarly attention has been given in the last decade or so to the multiracial proletariat of the Atlantic Sea Trade, first described by C.L.R. James, *Mariners, Renegades and Castaways* (London: Allison & Busby, 1986 edition), as the original factory workers. His own parent organization was the Workers Party, of Trotskyist derivation, peaking in the mid-1940s and composed of lower-middle-class Jews, remarkably fixed on a near-time proletarian uprising. Among their ranks could be found prominent intellectuals who, disappointed, turned sharply to the Right. Irving Howe and Harvey Swados remained the most progressive. But a handful of future neoconservatives, most prominently including Irving Kristol and Gertrude Himmelfarb, anticipated neoconservatism and played leading roles in its creation, with the considerable help of intelligence agencies and right-wing foundations. My story of James's life and the milieu is told in the authorized biography, *The Artist as Revolutionary: C.L.R. James* (London: Verso, 1989). My account of the Pequod also owes something to an unpublished essay by L. Goldner on the Mosaic in Melville's writings and specifically in *Moby Dick*.

[29] Harold Rosenberg, "The Pathos of the Proletariat," *Kenyon Review*, XI (Autumn, 1949): 604, 609.

[30] "That there is no longer a folk does not mean ... as the Romantics have propagated, that the masses are worse. Rather, it is precisely in the new, radically alienated form of society that the untruth of the old is first being revealed." Theodor Adorno, *Minima Moralia: Reflections from a Damaged Life* , translated by E.F.N. Jephcott (London: Verso, 1978): 204.

[31] Dave Wagner, "Philosophical Steps," *Cultural Correspondence*, I (August 1975), quoted in Paul Buhle, "Introduction," to Buhle, ed., *Popular Culture in America* (Minneapolis: University of Minnesota, 1987): xxi. This is the founding manifesto, so to speak, of a doomed journal (1975-83) edited by Paul Buhle, Dave Wagner, George Lipsitz, and Danny Czitrom: doomed because the recuperation of popular culture was as unpopular an idea on the Left (at least during the 1970s) as on the Right. See the introduction to the anthology and the contents, drawing some of the best contents of the journal several years after its demise. In its last phase, it was attached to New York artists around the Nuclear Freeze movement of the early 1980s, the "Radical Humor Festival" of 1982, and the multiple legacies of C.L.R. James as well as of Adorno's dialectics.

[32] In conversations, Howe seemed to sense that there was something missing in the volume as well; the Yiddish sources had been translated for him and in the *Vitze* or little in-joke of the season, "Buhle's Yiddish is better than Howe's." If true, it was only because he had neglected his first language and restricted himself to "improving" Yiddish translations by collaborators. We clashed a bit over my critique of *World*, during a 1979 academic convention; my main complaint was not about the politics (he had actually softened slightly toward the determinedly Yiddish left-wingers of an earlier generation), but his disdain for the premodernist Yiddish poetry of the 1890s. Still, Yiddish gave us something in common and allowed me to see the pain in his harmful and unfair attacks on the campus peaceniks and the Women's Movement; he had missed his moment, again, and predictably, he blamed cultural tastes quite as much as politics.

[33] Perl worked from a first draft written by James Baldwin. See Paul Buhle and Dave Wagner, *Hide in Plain Sight: The Hollywood Blacklistees in American Film and Television, 1950–2002* (New York: St. Martins Press, 2003), 255–58, for a fuller explanation.

TWO

FROM JEWISH STAGE TO SCREEN: HOW SHOW BUSINESS JEWS REORGANIZE THE WORLD AND FIND THEMSELVES IN THE PROCESS

The secret of the Jewish role in Hollywood, the undisputed center of world filmmaking, was never really a secret except perhaps from semi-literate or rural audiences unaware of the ethnic identity of key moguls, producers, directors, actors, and, above all, screenwriters. But nevertheless, from the early sound films until the 1950s, a remarkable pretence or convention remained formally intact. The altered names of so many Hollywood Jews in writing and production affirmed their self-constructed collective identity as merely one group within the great human melting pot of the burgeoning film industry. Likewise, Jews or Jewish-seeming characters with "American" or generic immigrant identities filled the screen, from drama to comedy.

Many later factors, notably public guilt about the Holocaust, the passing of the old studio giants and the studio system, eased this virtual ban and accelerated the process of assimilation into a Jewish-American status on screen and off. By the later decades of the century, Jewish themes and unabashed Jewish personalities flourished in Hollywood despite an uneasiness whenever so-called "Jewish influence" became the object of discussion. Steven Spielberg's *Schindler's List* (1993) was more than totemic: for many younger generation Jews, at least, it redefined Jewish identity as no political campaign, no documentary project, no religious or Israel-based publicity effort had managed to do in the several decades since "continuity" had become doubtful. It thereby continued Jewish identity among an increasingly assimilating and intermarrying people, reflecting a major concern in Jewish institutional life.[1] And yet the old difficulties of Jews in Hollywood, two in particular, failed to go away.

The first problem springs from the proportions of Jewish participation in Hollywood. Not only African-Americans but assorted ethnic and racial groups far more numerous than Jewish-Americans have a point when they complain that they are not particularly well represented in film, at least not compared to Jews. The complaints usually fail to confront the fact that the human content or personalities of the film business, like television or theater, has its own inner logic. Every American, perhaps everyone in the Western world and many millions far beyond, has shared the fantasy of being a movie star. But for at least four generations, American Jews in considerable numbers have grown up with the expectation that they could become successful in some area of entertainment. Whether they have the contacts (and talent) or not, they have often had this crucial element of self-confidence and the insight that working behind the scenes is a more probable route to worldly success. Therefore, when scriptwriters, composers, and directors – to say nothing of actors – draw upon themselves, upon their own experience, they draw disproportionately upon Jewish experience.

Since films must also represent in some ways the lives of those watching, the difference between the watched and the watchers cannot be abolished. Considerable numbers of American Jews, including some of our greatest artists, will go on acting as "others" – writing, directing and in all manners seeking to present and represent the lives and feelings of non-Jews. As commercial entertainers, as artists or both, they have no choice. For this reason among others, the nonidentified "Jewish type" or Jewish-image-within-the-generic-American protagonist has remained a fixture of film, and will inevitably remain a source of friendly or bruising speculation. So will the presumably straightforward treatment of Gentile lives and dilemmas by the Jewish artist.

The second problem appears at first glance more historically specific but remains, decades after the key traumatic episode, central to Hollywood history and its Jewish saga. In 1947, Representative John Rankin of the House Committee on UnAmerican Activities warned Congress about the true identities of various actors, including Danny Kaye, Eddie Cantor, Edward G. Robinson, and Melvyn Douglas. Like others using stage names, they were essentially parading under Gentile labels, a practice that Rankin considered prima facie evidence of their "UnAmerican" intentions.

Over the next few years, Congressional hearings convened ostensibly to examine the dangers of Communist influence in Hollywood, and again and again hammered at the Jewish role in front or behind the camera in certain kinds of films. Not long before, the Committee Chair had opened the hearings to notorious anti-Semites on the premise that Jewish control of Hollywood demanded redress. By the later 1940s, internal FBI memos complained that the Jewish press failed to take up its patriotic duty of supporting the blacklist. That support would come, soon enough, from the Anti-Defamation League's Los Angeles office, from *Commentary* magazine of the American Jewish Committee, and from other sources, but it never managed to persuade the Jewish community itself that the persecution lacked some larger purpose beyond the defense of supposed national security.

After all, no one bothered to accuse screenwriters (the main culprits), directors, and actors of subversive activities like the stealing of secrets, passing on "Moscow gold" to spies, or any such sin. Hearings conducted to prove that their moves had a pro-Russian taint managed to tag no more than a half-dozen films, wartime features that had been lauded on their appearance by most critics and sometimes welcomed by the White House.

The transparent intent of these hearings was to create a far-flung blacklist against left-wing political or labor activists and their sympathizers to drastically narrow the themes and to reshape the treatment of subjects in the then leading medium. The tactic has been tried out frequently in Congress since – in recent years, most notably by Senators Larry Pressler and Joseph Lieberman – but never with such devastating results. Movies such as *Gentleman's Agreement* scoring anti-Semitism, those like *Pinky*, appealing for racial egalitarianism, others upholding the dignity of the poor, casting aspersions on the rich or appearing to call for a redistributive social justice all indicated suspicious deviations from the acceptable standards of the Cold War political mainstream – just as FBI field reports claimed. After hesitating, Hollywood's power brokers fell in line with the blacklist, conducting it themselves with the help of notorious anti-Semites and of some noted Jewish institutions alike.

Government and private witch-hunters consistently exaggerated their case, making wild claims for the subversive content of films with comfortably liberal or merely patriotic messages. But they nevertheless had their crude conceptual hooks into something real. Back in the later 1930s, isolationists like Congressman Gerald P. Nye had quite accurately charged "Hollywood" (meaning Jews as much as liberals) with making films urging US participation in the coming war. Within a decade, the film industry had changed so drastically that Jewish left-wing sympathizers *could* write hundreds of pictures, albeit mostly in the "B" genres best noted for predictable plots and low production values. Like Gentiles concerned with the tragic fate of Jews and those fascinated with the active role of Jews in contemporary society, such writers found ways to carve out and multiply Jewish cinematic roles recognizable to anyone looking at them carefully.

Such roles had existed from the first moment of film, and intermittently provided thematics for box office hits from the early 1920s onward. But not until the 1940s had what might be called the "crypto-Jewish film" been made in the numbers or variety approaching the potential of the available Jewish talent, and rarely with such subtle underscoring of Jewish experiences and insights as dozens of films now offered. Like films in general, whose production fell sharply after 1946, the implicitly Jewish roles of certain kinds – from political moralists to soldier-vaudevillians and just plain working stiffs – would never actually rise to this scale of output again.

For exactly these reasons, the ghost of John Garfield, protean proletarian and martyr to the blacklist, has never left the set and is not likely to do so. Archetypes of other remembered types likewise persist: Sam Levene the battered Jew but otherwise the cerebral proletarian; Howard Da Silva, the petty criminal (or morally corrupt official); Groucho Marx or Phil Silvers, the fast-talking con man; Sheldon Leonard the mobster with the heart of gold; master of excess Zero Mostel; not to mention character-actresses like Gertrude Berg who helped create the ethnic relative at her unneurotic loveable best, or the Jewish writers, directors, and technicians who made possible in so many ways the laughter and tears that the people in front of the camera successfully evoked. Lovably annoying cameos of aging Jewish types in Woody Allen films, perhaps the most convenient sample of Jewishness in film in recent decades, are properly a last look at, and homage to, what went before. Like their Yiddish-American accents and neighborhood slang, they represent an absence in anticipation: soon, no one will remember the life of the *Yiddishe Gassen*, the Jewish urban streets, as they once existed. Not even the proletarian neighborhoods of Israel can recreate their counterparts, and not only because the historic moment is gone. "Nothing like it since Valentino," observers pronounced at the 1951 mass mourning of Garfield (dead at thirty-nine) in a Jewish working-class New York destined to be Jewish no more.

In the decades to come, as cinematic Jewish became matter-of-fact Jewish, less and less as a semidisguised persona within the framework of a social problem, it advanced into a more evident part of daily life. Jews had uneasy adolescences, unhappy or happy marriages, silly and occasionally compelling adventures, and so on. Measured in those terms alone, the several hundred American films made in the second half of the twentieth century with Jewish themes certainly marked a considerable step forward. As in the professions and formerly exclusive clubs of real life, they had been "normalized."

And yet there was something unmistakably ambivalent about this coming

out. Since early Hollywood days, Jewish filmmakers, from actors to technicians, had wanted something more for themselves than a confining or
comforting shell of an identity that seemed destined, in one way or another,
to limit artistic choices. With relatively few exceptions, they did not choose
to be "only Jews", whether they shunned ghetto characteristics as embar-
rassing or, as leftwingers, felt little warmth in a Jewishness dominated by an
increasingly wealthy and rightward-drifting Jewish establishment. Not
infrequently, the available Jewishness tended to become a template for the
immanent critique of the morals and manners that artists abhorred. Nobody
did the 1960s rebellion fit quite as well as the young man breaking away
from the suffocating materialism and the smothering sex-repressed
motherhood of home. Dustin Hoffman, Richard Dreyfuss, and dozens of
lesser artistic figures were, at their best moments, the new Paul Munis and
John Garfields, with all the contradictions implied in the shifts from aspiring
homeboy to rootless rebel.

Another Jewishness, distanced just enough to dispel maudlin treatment,
has had far greater warmth. That "Other" is imaginary as well as historical,
closer to the film world's 1940s "hidden Jew" than to the real-life Jewish
identity a half-century later. Just as the generic ethnics and idealistic
intellectuals or workers of earlier films are often not only more interesting
or admirable as characters but also more real as Jews than the real Jews set in
films close to the present, so the Jews-as-Other in the recent era often
continue to carry the torch of artistic integrity or political morals. Seemingly outdated figures in the New World Order that determinedly pro-
tected the lowly against the rich and reclaimed spiritual homelands bear a
relation to a past that strengthens and haunts us simultaneously. If the
present, with no more futuristic radical promise or terrible fears for Jews
than for anyone else, seems to have less to offer Jewish self-identity, and if
even the highly sophisticated Jewishness of David Mamet or Barry
Levinson, to take two examples, often dwells within or upon the diasporic
past, the 1930s and 40s become all the more emblematic. This is, like
Hollywood's golden age, an experience that remains alive for Jews and
Gentiles alike when so much else slips by.

In our first chapter we surveyed the ghetto background of popular
culture. Here, we take up the media in the making: the popular stage, radio,
and film. Jewish immigrants were in and (even more importantly) behind
the triumphs of Broadway and their creative reformulations of themes and
methods, as an integral part of the newness required for films at a series of
crucial points, both political and aesthetic. The special demands of film
animation, that little-appreciated art form beloved to moviegoers, seemed

to bring out the essence of the vernacular, with a handful of talented Jews eager to make a mark.

MUSIC AND THE STAGE

The history of Jews and film logically begins back at theater, from the moments of ubiquitous Jewish prominence to the appearance of serious film in Hollywood. Broadway, as we have seen, already owed much to German Jews, from melodies to booking agents. Unlike vaudeville, where Jews entered a developed field, Broadway offered Florenz Ziegfeld an arena for debut as a producer in 1896 that already suggested a kingmaker role. The musical theater of the all-male minstrel genre was passing, and the new entrepreneur offered the girly show, with higher admission prices paying for sumptuous sets and outfits as vaudeville moved up into a heterosexual extravaganza. The naughty queen of the *Folies-Bergères* appeared in *A Parlor Match,* and the Ziegfeld Follies was, in effect, born.

The prosperity following the worst depression in national history – not to mention the imperial conquest of the Caribbean and Pacific, through a one-sided Spanish-American war – prompted many outbursts of patriotic cultural "Americanization." The rich merely dragged trinkets from Europe, outfitting mansions from Manhattan to Chicago and beyond with evidence of Continental tastes (and no real understanding of them). Opening his own version of the *Folies* in 1907, Ziegfeld outdid Paris in ornateness of costumes and spectacular performances. It still wasn't Paris, but it was impressive.

Whatever Busby Berkeley would later do in films, Ziegfeld had already accomplished in 1908 when the "Taxicab Girl" number showed dozens of dames marching around wearing little more than tin flags, headlights, and signs reading "For Hire" as the lead sang "Take Me Around in a Taxicab." Two years later at the Follies, Bert Williams became the very first African-American (actually, Afro-Caribbean) to share the spotlight in a major Broadway revue (featuring his own composition, "Nobody"). Europe had nothing like it. Nor did they have Eddie Cantor, the synthetic comedy and singing talent featured by Ziegfeld for a decade after 1917. Erstwhile street performer, Coney Island singing waiter, and burlesque theater comic, Cantor had built a signature number in "Waiting for the Robert E. Lee," wearing a shoddy gentleman's outfit and intoning gag lines in a faux-Dixie, half-Yiddish accent.[2]

Back in 1900, Sam Lee and J. J. Shubert, German Jews of Syracuse, New

York, leased the Herald Square Theater and regularized the system of strict contracts intended to monopolize actors and performing space. A decade later, the full force of the song pluggers kicked in, with results seen and heard in shows shaped around so many composers like Irving Berlin and the very young George Gershwin, and singers like Al Jolson (from an early standpoint, just another Jewish "coon shouter"). This was, of course, only the beginning.

The producer, rarely acknowledged as an artist, was always crucial: he was the moneyman, in Yiddish *hondler*, the guy who got things done. He produced, not only a show but a pseudoreality. "I left Russia to make my fortune, whatever my confused aspirations," magnum promoter S. Hurok later remembered, and (with no little boasting here) "I carried the singing of Russia with me."[3] Son of a successful businessman and commercial farmer in the Ukraine, young Hurok headed for the big city (Kharkov) ostensibly to learn hardware. The 1905 Revolution had changed the face of Russian politics and he recollected that he might have stayed behind as a political organizer, but he headed onward to America. He resettled in the materially poor but spirited Brownsville and worked furiously for the election of local Socialist candidates, his own talent best expressed in getting musical accompaniment together for street rallies. He dreamed of becoming a manager-promoter and actually got then famed violinist Efram Zimbalist to perform in the neighborhood to benefit the Socialist Party. It was a beginning.[4]

Out of it came *S. Hurok Presents*, a calling card for a half-century of entertainment. By the mid-1910s he had created what he called *Music for the Masses*, an effort at popular uplift that failed, and a series at the Hippodrome wildly successful because of his prodigious promotions in every imaginable immigrant language and venue. The "Hurok Audience," as it came to be called, was born. In the years to come, he sponsored Chaliapin, Anna Pavlova (who claimed her father was Jewish, and longed to return to Russia but was blocked by her husband), Isadora Duncan, German avant-gardist dancer Mary Wigman (until she leaned toward Hitler), Marian Anderson, and countless others, defending performers against charges of Bolshevism and lewdness alike. He brought the Russian Opera Company, Arthur Rubenstein, Isaac Stern, and even the Lippanzer Stallions to the same mixture of culture seekers. In 1965, Holocaust survivor and future magnum rock promoter Bill Graham put a sign on his first producer's desk simply reading "S. Hurok": a homage and perhaps an expectation as well.

Broadway reached its apex as a source of high-class national entertainment during the 1920s, in terms of box office receipts and as an influence on the coming sound film. But it is just as true to say, as another producer, Max Gordon, later recalled, that the 1920s found burlesque adapted to the legitimate theater and thereby the surest audience for musicals in what Gordon acidly called "the sex-hungry and the thrill seekers."[5] The Shuberts themselves offered more bare female breasts in *Artists and Models* than had ever been seen on the American stage (or perhaps outside a bordello). The boom market in revues afforded a place for the sophisticated comedy relying upon satire and sophistication rather than grand sets and costumes. These were the cerebrally sexy hits, father and mother to the film screwball comedy. At this crucial moment in modern entertainment, the structured musical and the serious drama took form with almost the same degree of Jewish connections.

The historic role of Jewish summer theater from the Catskills to the Adironacks in this process is often neglected as a mere sidebar to the Borscht Belt-style entertainment. In such a tiny and off-center venue as Camp Copake, of the Adirondacks, future film lyricist Edward Eliscu served as social director, dancing with lonely girls but also writing, directing, and acting in the plays put on for residents. His camp assistant, Mortimer Offner, later on a writer for several Katharine Hepburn films, helped him put on Oscar Wilde, Noel Coward, and so on, along with some original dramas, one of them by a certain refugee from Minnesota, Sidney Buchman. From Camp Copake, Eliscu graduated quickly (at Ira Gershwin's suggestion) to the Song Writers Protective Association, an early syndicate that placed him in the same circle (often the same elevator, en route to or returning from a pitch session with the same producer) as the Gershwins and Jerome Kern. When Oscar Hammerstein overbooked shows simultaneously and left a gap, Eliscu and his friends filled in.

Since 1914, Jerome Kern had been creating book musicals in the tiny Princess Theater, while the operetta style continued to dominate musical Broadway. Richard Rogers met Larry Hart just as the theatrical world was about to change drastically. Hart and Rogers brought the Garrick Follies to Broadway in 1924, and the Gershwin brothers had their first show. Songs from the young composers became national hits, but something more important happened to Broadway with *Showboat*. Its successful debut in 1927 demonstrated that music, lyrics, and plot could be fitted together into a virtually seamless story. The lesson did not strike home immediately, but it was there to take.

The challenge to the lyricist was perhaps suited perfectly for the new crop of writers. Ira Gershwin had been actively collaborating with brother George since *Lady, Be Good!* in 1924, the show that arguably established a syncopation or sophisticated urban, jazzy tone to the hit musical. He passed on the skill to his close friend E.Y. "Yip" Harburg, who took informal lessons separately from Russian-born Jay Gorney (the two were to collaborate on the Depression epic "Brother, Can You Spare a Dime?"). Gorney wrote for Eddie Cantor and scored with the big 1927 hit *Merry-Go-Round*. What Ira Gershwin and Gorney taught Yip, he reflected later, was that the feeling of the "authentic" now measured the difference between success and failure. Songs had to be written for plots, actors, and actresses, no matter if others would sing them in films and popular recordings. Harold Arlen, a Buffalo rabbi's son, had gotten there already. Yip learned fast. By 1932, he had collaborated with no less than twenty-five composers, including Gorney, Arlen, Johnny Green (with whom he had his first smash hit: "I'm Yours," in 1931), Sammy Fain, and Oscar Levant. By that time, he had also written the lyrics for three Broadway productions. The nimble Harburg invented the serio-comic lyric, as distant from *The Mikado* as Depression New York was from Gilbert and Sullivan's Edwardian London and "Brother, Can You Spare a Dime?" was from *The Mikado*'s "I am the Captain of the Pinafore."

Meanwhile, other Jewish writers and lyricists moved to revolutionize the musical and, arguably, Broadway as a whole. The Great White Way peaked, in the same year as *Showboat*, with some 264 openings. Second Avenue Broadway, the Yiddish stage, counted over a hundred thousand in attendance that year. Drama influenced by the Russian playwright Vsevolod Meyerhold (who practically organized the Soviet stage following the Revolution but within a decade, ardently denounced its offerings as mere agitprop) quite as much as Leftist politics brought a new brand of realism into theater. Race and class themes, along with new forms of presentation, were in the process of taking hold.

Thus Vincent Youmans, another Jewish Tin Pan Alley musical maven, would stage repeated interracial musicals and dramas in a few years, just as future screenwriter John Wexley, nephew of the famed Yiddish actor-producer Maurice Schwartz, scored a huge hit with *They Shall Not Die*, about and for the Scottsboro defendants (nine African-American youths falsely accused of raping a white woman in a Southern freight car). Kern, *Showboat*'s composer and lyricist, had reached his peak by adapting novelist Edna Ferber's lightweight fiction into a plea for black folkishness, which became all the more real when Paul Robeson sang the show's signature "Old Man River" in London and made it his own signature piece. At least on the stage, Blackness had become something more than background, if something rather less than counterpart to white character development.[6]

Whether this innovation and all that followed along the same or similar lines was a Jewish way of becoming American (as some scholars have empathetically insisted), or a way to make a good living from a highly exploitable American culture, surely depended upon the writer, the source, and the historical moment. Arguably, *Showboat* itself was all of these. Gershwin's *Porgy and Bess* marks a further advance, in any case: as the earlier theatrical hit set the musical drama in place, the latter instated the black musical drama, however picaresque and to some degree exploitative.

Critics would later complain that all the clichés of the black folk opera of sharecroppers shouting for "de Lawd" had been born here, along with another phenomenal and still more stylized stage hit, *Green Pastures*. But so had a precedent for those breakthrough performance films of the 1940s, *Stormy Weather, Cabin In the Sky*, and the unjustly forgotten *New Orleans*, all of them heavily salted by the work of future Jewish blacklistees or their intimates, even Oscar Hammerstein's *Oklahoma!* Jewish-Americans were redefining American identity in its purest entertainment-based form.

The same critics would better have complained about the eliding of layers of complexity, impossible without the background of African-American culture but ambiguously situated in relation to it. The Jazz Age musical circles and their descendents on stage and in film generally buried such uncertainties, as in *Rhapsody in Blue*, a film that dwelt heavily upon the theme of "American Music" and Jewish adaptation, but did so in ways woefully ignorant of or indifferent to the larger racial implications. As the tale of a life made famous by commercial success in bringing "the blues" to a wider public, it glamorized Gershwin's first hit "Alexander's Ragtime Band," a total swipe from the idea of black music, the more so because it owed so little musically to ragtime, adding insult to injury when bandleader Paul Whiteman (playing himself) promised to bring jazz out the slums and "make her a lady" at Aeolian Hall in 1924 – with Gershwin's tunes.

Like the sex musical that opened space for the sophisticated musical, the black-as-told-by-Jew musical on stage or screen nevertheless opened the doors to something better – even if the better did not, for a long time afterward, include black songwriters, directors, or business interests. Some Jewish performers went further. Sophie Tucker and the early Fanny Brice, comediennes but also soul singers, pitched black accent songs with a depth that Al Jolson never approached, no doubt because of the gendered emotional energy: with them, suffering deep personal longings as well as desires, soulfulness was no act.[7]

Other factors meanwhile lent musical theater an unanticipated Jewish ambiance that it has never entirely lost. The standard minor-key melody, for instance, was properly an Eastern European musical inflection of a wider kind, but on Broadway it could only be Jewish, redolent with the mixture of tears and laughter, nostalgia and daydreaming. Enough of the composers' fathers, uncles, or grandfathers were cantors to more than suggest a liturgical link. The cleverness of internal gags, the sophisticated phraseology, and references to Manhattan landmarks and exotic vacation-spots abroad (or as close as Miami Beach) could have been connected by any educated New Yorker in the audience – but that New Yorker was usually Jewish. So was the possibility of the sharp political satire as viable entertainment. Even George Gershwin, the less political of the two brothers, wrote satires of politicians and privilege-based American economics. The outbreak of Depression brought waves of commentary by and for Jews who felt badly let down by America. Ira's partner, Yip Harburg's *Hooray for What!* (1937) savaged pseudo-patriotism and its partner, the American style of militarism then taking shape once again.[8]

The influence of the stage on the wider culture also spoke strongly to the survival of cultural geocentrism of a certain kind within a sprawling nation. The center of prestige American show business before Hollywood, Broadway remained amazingly so during Hollywood's golden years, if steadily less so after the Second World War. Scholar Stephen Whitfield suggests that the Broadway musical *was* New York, as much as the waltz had been Vienna, and it was also more consistently Jewish than Hollywood. (Generations later, Edward Koch pronounced Joseph Papp – not only a magnum producer of Shakespeare for the masses but a HUAC victim from a Yiddish-speaking household – to be Manhattan personified.) The audience, too: late estimates have the paying crowd at least half-Jewish, proof that the genteel middle classes of the old theater audience had always been somewhat Jewish (especially German Jewish) and the newer middle classes, especially with the fading of Yiddish theater, even more so.[9]

But there is also something more subtle and internal to the rise and changing forms of commercial entertainment. As scholars have observed most keenly in recent years, the very essence of the musical inclines toward the retrospective, its most single recurrent theme the backstage story. That its other favorite theme has been the American pageant only reinforces the point. Whatever the formal subject, the search for roots perpetually renders musicals the "mass art which aspires to the condition of a folk art," as Jane Feuer puts it, with props that don't appear as props, choreography and precision dancing that must be made amateur-looking, and stars intended to look like writ-large members of the audience.[10] The transfer to film was therefore almost seamless, a reinvention that was only an expanded and technically improved form (albeit heavily censored version in many ways, from politics to sex and ethnicity) of the original.

What Broadway musical comedy did for film in one way, drama did for film in another. Not only Broadway drama, however. The emerging melodrama of 1920s Broadway (and even before) was largely of the domestic kind. When Jews wrote for it (and not many did, at the upper-most levels of pay and prestige), they wrote faithfully within the English stage style, adapted for Americans but not adapted so much that its roots would be obscured. In a typical plot, an unhappy marriage feeds the neurosis of a young woman still full of life and hope. On sophisticated Broadway, she may reach the point of desperation (or plain boredom) with her husband's adulterous behavior and make a liaison or her own. Less seriously and more sit-comishly, romantic mix-ups and gentle social satires, rural/city tales destined to be replayed for domestic and backstage plots in endless variations continued much as before but shaded with more sophisticated sexual innuendoes. Hollywood recensored the dialogue and, by the mid-1930s, sought to censor the very inferences that audiences could draw. But the White Telephone films of luxurious life in the Depression could not have been made without the example that the stage provided; prestige comedy sound film, with marked exceptions, drew less from the Keystone Kops than from Noel Coward and the "funniest man in America," playwright-gone-Hollywood Donald Ogden Stewart (a notably left-wing Gentile surrounded by Jewish comrades).

It's well to look in another direction for the sources of Hollywood's subsequent breakthroughs. A glance at the Yiddish stage and particular segments of the Yiddish stage reveals the kinds of dramatic seriousness only glimpsed in contemporary Broadway productions of work by Irwin Shaw, Maxwell Anderson, or Eugene O'Neill. Productions on Second Avenue (and the adjoining East Broadway café scene) could be just as silly as Broadway, but they began losing their audiences by the Crash, thanks to the cutoff of new immigration and resulting assimilation. But Second Avenue and other ethnic venues offered a discerning minority crowd something different and more important to future English-language entertainment, from stage to film and television. The touring European theatrical company had the kind of impact upon American Yiddish audiences and productions that European neorealism might have had on the 1940s–50s Hollywood art movie without the impact of the Blacklist. Some of the finest actors, directors, and set designers who trained in Moscow and Berlin made their way to New York, and some stayed on. Impresario Maurice Schwartz's

Yiddish Art Theater meanwhile boasted impressive productions of Gorky (a special favorite), Chekhov, and immigrant talents like left-wing poet-playwright H. Leivick.

ARTEF, more serious by a large degree, was an openly radical troupe whose productions always left the company at the verge of bankruptcy (it survived only thanks to "benefits" and bloc ticket-selling), but whose successes foreshadowed in some ways almost every serious Hollywood Jewish drama to come. Director Benno Schneider, who had been trained intensively in Habima, the Soviet Jewish folk troupe steeped in Yiddish, would end his days miserably, as an assistant to a Hollywood producer. Yet from an artistic standpoint, ARTEF had imported contemporary Russian and German drama, combined realism, impressionism, naturalism, and agitprop, with a heavy emphasis upon the ensemble of actors rather than the star. The emphasis upon speech and expressive movement, thought to be particular strengths of the Jewish actor, had its political result in dramas like *Strike!* (preceding and preparing the way for Clifford Odets's *Waiting for Lefty*, almost a decade later – even offering Odets' play its famous crowd-rousing tag line, "Strike! Strike!" cued to be picked up by an aroused audience), which had been conceived by amateurs in 1927 at the apex of real-life strikes by cloakmakers and furriers.

For a decade from the late 1920s, Carnegie Hall, and sometimes Madison Square, intermittently rocked with productions that could be described as something encompassing both theater and political demonstration. Sometimes its dramatic achievements were so great that even the non-left Yiddish press, which made a habit of ignoring the ARTEF on principle, took notice. As a proper troupe, ARTEF was at once too successfully boycotted and too caught up in the internecine controversies of the Communist orbit to hold on to the success that it had achieved. ARTEF was destined to yield to the English-language theatrical and cinematic radicalism of the younger generation, in any case, much as the left-wing and Jewish-heavy Group Theater of the early and mid-1930s was to yield its talent to Federal Theater and to Hollywood. But as late as the mid-1930s, these final developments were still not fully in sight.

The successes of Sidney Kingsley best showed the transition. A sophisticated New Yorker suited to merge the documentary spirit of contemporary artists (including many left-wingers, but also nonpolitical folklorists) with winning theatrical plots, Kingsley saw sudden and overwhelming success with *Men in White* (1934), produced by Group. Formed by an overwhelmingly Jewish and left-wing circle of young artists heavily influenced by the Russian example of Constantin Stanislavsky and his

American disciple, Lee Strasberg, Group transmitted Method acting to the American stage and film. They sent out the decisive message that actors needed to understand, and live, their parts rather than just being directors' automatons with golden voices and interesting bodies.

In *Men In White*, arguably for the first time on the English-language stage in America, a workplace was painstakingly reproduced, demonstrating (apart from its soapy but necessary romance features) in detail operating room procedures, with a set by Mordecai Gorelick and direction by Strasberg. It won Kingsley a Pulitzer. It also notably inspired, after the 1934 film version, something just as Jewish and as timely: the Three Stooges' only Oscar-winning short, *Men in Black*, illustrating perfectly the high-minded doctors ("For duty, and humanity!" the Stooges chant at every absurd act of theirs) and the tyranny of the hospital loudspeaker (Moe guns it down in the final moments, eliciting the mechanical version of the gangster/cowboy lament, "Ya got me!"). Never again for very long would American media lack an idealistic but emotionally torn doctor and his faithful nurse. Sometimes, at least – Adam Arkin and Mandy Patinkin on television's 1990s *Chicago Hope* – the doctor would be recognizably Jewish. Rarely would the form be satirized as effectively as the Stooges had managed.

Dead End (1935) by Kingsley was similarly location-set. The slum saga was made into a 1939 film by playwright-become-screenwriter Lillian Hellman, director William Wyler, and a troupe of actors that included both Humphrey Bogart and the core of the future Bowery Boys (archetypal Lower East Siders somehow both Irish and Jewish). This time the action took place below the skyscrapers overlooking the Hudson suites and the tenement dwellers at the bottom. The crippled architect (in Hollywood inevitably Gentilized and played by Joel McCrea) aspires to rebuild the city New Deal-style. He is counterposed to the mobster (played by Bogart) who returns to the scene of his youth to find his mother unforgiving and his old sweetheart a streetwalker with syphilis (in the film, she gives an unconvincing tubercular cough).

Group Theater could be more consistently serious. Odets's oeuvre after *Waiting for Lefty* (the first of his Depression classics actually put on by Group), *Awake and Sing!*, *Paradise Lost*, *Golden Boy* (the Group's most successful drama in its short history), and *Rocket to the Moon*, would by themselves constitute a map of Jewish angst and aspiration in interwar America as well as a condemnation of class society in the name of Jewishness. But they were hardly alone. Beyond Group, politically minded theatrical and heavily Jewish groups sprang up across the early to middle

1930s. Most are forgotten, but dozens if not hundreds of their members went on to Hollywood or a lifetime in some end of the entertainment business.

THE MOVIES MOVE (AND RADIO IS HEARD)

That the Hollywood of the golden age grew up thanks to the grand entrepreneurial talents of mostly Jewish entrepreneurs is no revelation. That it established sound film and consolidated film art through Jewish products of Broadway and Off Broadway is a story less known. That a distinctly related, emphatically internal struggle among Hollywood Jews went on almost every step of the way – essentially a struggle for a different Holly-wood with creative control by those who wrote, directed, shot, and acted in films – is a tale still largely unknown.[11]

Former scrap dealers, jewelry merchandisers, dancehall bosses, bicycle shop owners, and movie house operators moved in swiftly on a promising line of business, outmaneuvering the wily Thomas Edison, who sought to monopolize the field, and shifting the weight of moviemaking to southern California. There they lived like kings, not the beloved "good fathers" to the screen folk that they had their flunkeys of various kinds purvey, but more like tyrants passing out slots to relatives and quietly arranging for purges of those who displeased them. The movie moguls, not so different in some respects from the mostly Jewish Communist Party leaders who struggled with limited success to keep their Hollywood faithful in line, were cultural philistines. In the Hollywood version of life, endangered women in every imaginable dangerous situation from shipwreck to battlefield some-how managed to have their hair perfectly coiffed, just as good children who obeyed their parents (or guardians) managed to overcome all possible obstacles to get a solid family tie of sorts by the end of the last reel, and as criminals born to be caught or killed met their final and deserved end. Tragedy could sometimes be found, but melodrama triumphed, along with lighter entertainments.

In their capacity as captains of industry in a one-industry town, the moguls thus presented models of assimilation and conservatism upset only – but what a big only – by the Depression and the struggle against Fascism. As manufacturers of a sort not so far from garment center operators, they also developed a close relation with organized crime, especially with the pro-prietors ("elected" officers) of the International Alliance of Theatrical Stage Employees (IATSE) union, led by an erstwhile Chicago Jewish gangster

Willie Bioff, who kept their own members and most of the other potential studio unionists safely in check. It was a normal way to do business, American-style.

And they kept intimate company with bottom-feeders in multiple other ways. Walter Winchell, the newspaper gossip columnist and radio broadcaster whose style lowered a generation of journalists, could intimidate Hollywoodites with his revelations of their peccadilloes, sexual ones especially. He could also go after Hitler (notably, as a secret homosexual) early and often, unlike his sometime employer William Randolph Hearst, who stopped apologizing for reliably anticommunist German and Italian dictators only on the brink of world war. He could even favor unions, under certain circumstances. But this son of Russian-Lithuanian Jewish immigrants was, more than anything else, a child of his own craving for power and celebrity. As the FBI, deeply racist and quietly anti-Semitic, infiltrated Hollywood circles with paid and unpaid informers, Winchell struck up a working relationship with J. Edgar Hoover that would be exceptionally fruitful for both in the witch-hunting days ahead. Unlike more kindly smaller-fry like Leonard Lyons (the son of Roumanian immigrants and a columnist first in the *Forverts*, where, ironically, he already ceased to be Leonard Soucher), Winchell personified Burt Lancaster's portrayal of the driven, greedy columnist-beast in Clifford Odets's *Sweet Smell of Success*.

By the 1920s, when filmmaking blossomed with a large, enthusiastic and international audience, one- or two-reel length films dealing with Jewish life proliferated, albeit mostly in the comic vein and often hurtfully so, with endless gags about bearded storekeepers torching their own shops. The Jewish moguls destined to dominate large parts of Hollywood through the golden age also consolidated their strength during this time, men like Carl Laemmle, Louis Mayer, Harry Cohn, Irving Thalberg, and the Warner brothers, with decidedly mixed effects on the possibilities of Jewish themes and Jewish writers, producers, and directors. On the one hand, family connections and sympathies opened the flourishing Hollywood commerce to thousands of transplanted New Yorkers, in turn offering possible career escape routes to Jewish filmmakers in Europe. On the other hand, the moguls themselves firmly believed in, and personally practiced, the wealthy Americans' version of the benevolent melting pot, usually exaggerating its virtues on the screen.

Looking to its immigrant audience, the Hollywood of silent days nevertheless turned out a string of successful films modeled on *Humoresque*, itself adapted from a short story about a proletarian violinist and his doomed wealthy melancholic patroness, by assimilated Jewish writer Fannie Hurst in *Cosmopolitan*. Some of the most commercially successful of these films starred Yiddish stage actress Vera Gordon. By the end of silent days and early talkies, more Jewish stars had emerged in front of the camera – if never as many as behind it. Once again, they were most often comics like Eddie Cantor, prone to display the very traits condemned by the Anti-Defamation League seeking to purge films of stereotypical Jewish images. Bad table manners, Jack Benny-like cheapness, suspiciously lecherous behavior toward blondes (the ultimate Gentiles), and hilarious broken English mark the genre.

Only now and then, as in the 1927 spectacular *Ben Hur*, does a heroic and muscular Jew save the day, or (as in the later *Disraeli*) shape the history of a great nation. Surprisingly, if by no means pleasantly so, the first sound-synchronized epic of the talkies, *The Jazz Singer*, gave us stage headliner Al Jolson as the ethnic who succeeds grandly in the world of commercial entertainment through adopting the minstrel pose, sublimating (or eradicating, depending on the interpretation) his own *Yiddishkayt* through the simultaneous adoption and mocking of African-American stage traits. Even the huge success of *The Jazz Singer*, written by the premier Jewish screenwriter Samuel Raphaelson, did not, however, prompt a rush of films about Jews. On the contrary.

Even as MGM became known among jokesters as "Mayer's Ganze Mishpokhe" (Louis B. Mayer's entire family) and Daryl Zanuck's Twentieth Century Fox was regarded as the virtual Gentile holdout among the big studios, the Jewish contents of films actually receded with the sound process (after, that is, *The Jazz Singer)*. Harry Cohn was reputed to have barked at a director who wanted to cast a Jewish actor, "around this studio the only Jews we put into pictures play Indians." It wasn't even remotely true.

The Red- and Jew-baiting congressmen who ran HUAC investigations were not fooled by the stage names of Melvyn Douglas or Paul Muni, among a large handful of leading players and many extras engaging in the then common name changes for Hollywood, not to mention the dozens of others who changed their names but made no special effort to hide their identities. But it was true, especially for the 1930s, that Jews or Gentiles rarely played Jews. As Hitler closed in on Europe and Jewish intellectuals played roles in an American presidential administration previously considered inconceivable – not to mention the contemporary Jewish role in labor and social movements – the screen remained very largely a zone of all but invisible ethnicity. The embrace of Gentile values extended even to shaping them: Mayer was famous, or infamous, on the set of the Andy Hardy series issuing pronouncements on "how the Gentiles behave."

Those of all ranks who came to Hollywood with artistic ambitions usually found disappointment waiting. From the viewpoint of ordinary workers including most writers, the studio system was more than a little like a plantation in the southern California sun. Entrepreneurs and executives, Jew and Gentile, naturally saw things differently. Before the stock market crash, a few years afterward, and some even during the worst of the period, they raked in enormous profits, paid most of the help very badly, and made it clear that Jewish issues were not going to surface all that much in films made for the *goyishe* masses. These power brokers did not at first understand the young Jewish radicals, or comprehend what an impact they could potentially exert upon the system.

That it produced some magnum management figures, as creative as they were vulgar and grasping, is a tribute not perhaps so much to them as to the possibilities of cinema. Harry Cohn, ruthless executive of Columbia (reputedly uncertain how to spell his studio's name), had been a mere song plugger and vaudevillian, secretary to Universal's founder Carl Laemmle, and then founder of Columbia in 1924. From a minor studio, it blossomed by the 1940s into one of the most profitable, if not biggest studios, thanks in no small part to Cohn's eye for talent and audience possibilities.

Thus Frank Capra, the Sicilian-born son of a Los Angeles blue collar family, came to fame. He was an artist who by no coincidence broke into silent movies thanks to his brief marriage to a Jewish actress whose brother owned a tiny studio. Capra hit the formula of the "little guy" film before he joined Columbia in 1929. But Cohn gave him extraordinary freedom and the permission to work with liberal-to-radical Jewish writers like Sidney Buchman and Robert Riskin on classics like *It Happened One Night* (1934), *Mr. Deeds Goes to Town* (1936), *Mr. Smith Goes to Washington* (1938), *Meet John Doe* (1941), and *It's a Wonderful Life* (1946). That Capra never understood how much he owed either to radicalism or to a certain Jew-ishness was clear in his later failures. Cohn, who understood better what the loss of relative political and artistic freedom in Hollywood meant, was still trying to stage secret shootings of films with now-forbidden Communist writers like Albert Maltz – only a few years earlier one of Hollywood's favorites – when the blacklist came down tight.

More influential than all these in what might be called Hollywood political aesthetics was Jack Warner. Youngest of twelve children of a Polish Jewish couple, actually born en route from London to America, he grew up mostly in Youngstown, sharing the work of the family bicycle shop business. His folks then bought a nickelodean operation in Newcastle, Pennsylvania, and young Jack sang during intermission. Four growing brothers attempted repeatedly, over the next decade, to get into film distribution. By 1917 they had set up shop in Hollywood with Jack as a twenty-five-year-old production chief. Acquiring several production companies and many theaters, they were set for the sound era and *The Jazz Singer*.

It was Warner Brothers and above all Jack Warner's response to the social crisis of the Depression that made them, and especially him, unique among the moguls. A Republican like his counterparts, although not as vociferously reactionary as Louis B. Mayer (who cochaired the California Republican Party), he saw the light in 1932 – or perhaps caught a glimpse of the changing box office. In September, weeks before the fall election, he staged a Busby Berkeley-style motion picture electrical parade and sports pageant for Roosevelt in Los Angeles' Olympic Stadium, guaranteeing huge waves of added publicity. Having won with FDR, Warners released the New Dealish *42nd Street* to coincide with the inauguration, and with tardily opportunist MGM, provided the starlets and even Tom Mix for the inaugural counterpart parade (practically, in severely depressed but movie-crazed America, an anticlimax) in Washington.

The moguls at large responded with genius in another way, facing the nation's worst ever depression. Only radio prospered among the major media in the early Depression, with falling prices of radios destined to bring down the huge inventory overstock and with continuing profits for the major networks. Most of the major studios, by contrast, lost money hand over fist during the early Depression years. RKO, Paramount, and Fox all went into bankruptcy by 1933, a trend that accelerated consolidation and control of Wall Street that was already underway from investment in equipment for the new sound films.[12] Moviemaking, however, soon resumed with a newly burnished corporate-style bureaucracy firmly in place, turning Hollywood from a society of semimavericks into a complex and carefully structured system designed to turn out and (just as important) to market a more regularized product.

The Warners, to take a case in point, produced a decade of social films treating the massive disillusionment with the system and economic struggle of a type that had been seen only at the margins earlier. It was a shrewd marketing strategy, paired with low budgets and a furious production schedule with no special favors for the directors and writers. They managed to turn out respected and profitable films about sympathetic gangsters and slum-dwelling kids, uncaring businessmen and hard-working heart-of-gold chorus girls. Whether Jack Warner was sincere or insincere (he later turned to anticommunist themes as readily as he had turned to reform and wartime antifascist themes) was never the crucial question; as a businessman who also craved the prestige of attachment to the New Deal and war effort, he accommodated the radical Jewish creative upsurge that the era allowed.

Below the moguls, and substituting in small ways for them, were the producers, sometimes extraordinarily creative, more often just carrying out orders. Rather less often Jewish hacks (compared at least to Hollywood's Gentile hacks), the best were far more often Jewish geniuses, like David Selznick, Irving Thalberg, and Joseph Pasternak. Thalberg, who claimed to have been a teenaged Socialist soapboxer in New York before the war, was supervising the shoot of *The Good Earth* when he collapsed fatally at age thirty-seven. Posthumously, he or his spirit could take credit for *The Story of Louis Pasteur* and *The Great Ziegfeld*. For sympathetic critics these were the models for the biopic exploring rather than exploiting personalities.

The "Thalberg system" signified integrated production at every level, from bankers' financing to filming, making MGM the masters of the new sound medium. No one else came up to this level. Warners depended upon Hal B. Wallis and others for production, using the Depression outbreak and rebound as an opportunity to transform production facilities and expand market shares. "Junior" Laemmle, acting as a surrogate for his father, became by force of circumstance a producer for underfinanced Universal, to reemerge later as the maker of outstanding weird and horror films with heavy German Impressionist (often immigrant Jewish) influences.

David O. Selznick was the most sincerely aspiring artist of the bunch. Son of mogul Lewis Selznick, sometime near-leading executive and attempted rebel (his bid for an independent production unit was crushed by multistudio agreements in the early 1930s), he took over badly wounded RKO that made some of the first Katharine Hepburn films, and then rejoined MGM with a fair degree of autonomy. There he had his success, foreshadowing the efforts of stars, producers, and writers to break off from the suffocating contracts and begin anew.

But the young Selznick was, perhaps, more successful as a model of the artistic filmmaker than in reality. Literary masterpieces became his beat, defying the Hollywood wisdom that they could not be done seriously, with *Little Women, David Copperfield, Anna Karinina,* and *A Tale of Two Cities,* all before he moved on to his own company, Selznick International in 1936. The box-office success – if not the unacknowledged moral-historical disgrace – of *Gone With the Wind* helped him launch Hitchcock (with *Rebecca*) as an American director. His producing of *Spellbound*, *Since You Went Away*, *Portrait of Jennie*, and *The Third Man* remain tributes to his efforts. But name and influence did not spare him major disappointments. Like a less influential writer and director, he saw favorite projects unproduced and forgotten, his lasting impression on movies slight.

Walter Wanger was another executive genius, at some points better realized because more instinctively cinematic than Selznick. Born Walter Feuchtwanger, the son of a German Jewish salesman and garment producer and nephew of the surrealist painter Florine Stettheimer, he managed to make himself rather more independent and frequently more artistic. He also took more chances. The antifascist *The President Vanishes* (1935) and *Blockade* (1938), the "little guy" *Stagecoach* (1939), the feminine alcoholic treatment *Smash-Up* (1947), the heavily stylized *Joan of Arc* (1948), not to mention his role as a leading Hollywood liberal, drew the enthusiasm of leading intellectuals like Norman Cousins and Carl Sandburg as well as of Hollywood's talented and influential Communists.

Joseph Pasternak was a third and more distinctively European-Jewish variety. A Transylvanian-born producer who returned to Europe and cinematic success and then fled Germany in 1935 for Hollywood, he is credited with the lavish kitsch of the Popular Front. Creator of the Deanne Durbin musicals (saving Universal from collapse), he also guided Marlene Dietrich after her preliminary stumble, and made other sui generis films that included *Destry Rides Again*, an all-American Western like one never seen before, with a distinct Viennese comic twist. Among the left-leaning crowd, Joseph Pasternak had the gravity to make films that emphasized the Russian–American alliance, like *Song of Russia*, joined to themes of common men and women taking their own place in society. Only occasionally were they obviously Jewish, but then sometimes in small but vital ways. Credited for good or ill with popularizing sweetened versions of classical music through film, and for musical extravaganzas like *Anchors Aweigh*, *The Great Caruso*, and *The Merry Widow*, Pasternak's Popular Front kitsch may even (as some critics have charged) have foreshadowed Holocaust kitsch – one Jewish stylization replaces another.

Next, there were directors, perhaps the least Jewish of the Hollywood professions (apart from starlets) but among those best placed to see their own auteurist creations through final hurdles. None was more commercially successful than the gay Jewish Hungarian George Cukor, none more political in their art than the Russian-born Lewis Milestone, and none more vernacular than bargain basement auteur, Viennese Edgar G. Ulmer.

Cukor, actually born and raised in New York City, was already a stage manager barely out of his teens, a distinguished theatrical director in his twenties, debuting in Hollywood with *Tarnished Lady* (1930), one of the several kinds of women's films for which he had a great sensitivity. Cukor followed his friend David Selznick to RKO and MGM, leaving in his wake such extraordinary Hollywood products as *Bill of Divorcement, Dinner at Eight, Camille, Little Women*, and *Holiday*. Breaking with Selznick on the set of *Gone With the Wind*, he went on to direct, among others, *The Philadelphia Story, A Woman's Face, Adam's Rib, Born Yesterday, Pat and Mike*, and so on up to *My Fair Lady* and beyond. Among the most theatrical of mainstream directors, he had the appreciation of actresses like Hepburn and the rapport that realized the promise of the women's film already strong in the theatrical plots of so many early 1930s films written by Sidney Buchman among others.

Out of that rapport came a kind of sex or gender comedy not quite like any other. Cukor was not just sympathetic to women. He grasped the distortions and hidden weaknesses of male culture as perhaps only a gay artist of the time could. His Cary Grant of *Holiday*, Grant and James Stewart of *The Philadelphia Story*, Spencer Tracy of repeated Hepburn–Tracy matchups, did not simply adore Hepburn, as men do with women they place upon a pedestal away from the grime and action of life. They came to see something in her character and not just potential uplift that was otherwise lacking within themselves and their world. That unbuxomy Hepburn shone brighter than the Hollywood types around her was in itself a revelation that could hardly be described as Jewish but had much in common with the old Jewish theatrical avant-garde's attachment to the themes of Ibsen.

Milestone was more the showman, but an altogether serious one. Scion of a wealthy Russian Jewish clothing manufacturer, Lev Milestone literally ran away from his family's professional aspirations in order to immigrate at age eighteen in 1913, taking ordinary factory jobs until he managed to become a photographer's assistant. Enlisting in the Army for war service, he was assigned to the Signal Corps' photographic unit, learning there much about technical shooting, including the possibilities of filming under war conditions. In Hollywood, the very first Oscar ceremonies saw him winning with a comedy direction, *Two Arabian Knights*, the story of soldiers who escape from a German prisoner of war camp, in Palestine.

This antiwar hit with definite Jewish undertones led him toward the most expensive and (aside from Chaplin films) most radically pacifist film in cinematic history to that point, *All Quiet On the Western Front*. Never before had anyone expressed the overwhelming Jewish repulsion at armed conflict so perfectly, or captured the public disillusionment with war that swept across America and Europe by the late 1920s. It is often said that he never returned to this level of accomplishment, but that view fails to recognize the difficulty of what he repeatedly attempted. *The General Died at Dawn*, Clifford Odets's first Hollywood film, *Of Mice and Men*, the second Steinbeck adaptation, *Edge of Darkness* (in which the mass of a Norwegian town rises up heroically against the German occupation, anticipating the crushing response), *Purple Heart* (one of the John Garfield war films ruminating on anti-Semitism), *North Star* (a pro-Soviet musical with a score by Aaron Copland), *A Walk in the Sun* (the most realistic war film made to that date), and the fabled noir *The Strange Love of Martha Ivers*, among other – actually, too many others – lesser efforts to follow.

Then there were the screenwriters, Jewish by a considerable dis-proportion except at the very top levels, where some, but by no means most, of the true aristocrats of the trade were Jewish as well. The coin-cidence of the Depression and the need for real screenwriters (not mere "titlists" as before) with the advent of sound film brought a veritable tidal wave of New Yorkers to Hollywood. A decade or so later, success on Broadway and the boom of wartime cinema prompted newer Jewish playwrights, by the dozens, to make the trip. As in other sections of the entertainment world, supply and demand meant that some prospered while many faced long stretches of unemployment. Until the achievement of a real contract in 1942, supply and demand were unregulated by the Screen Writers Guild. This meant that even those working with some regularity often merely scraped by, wondering if they'd chosen the wrong line of work.

Success usually came by following well-worn formulas, rearranging parts of melodrama, romance, comedy, and so on to match the image of the stars chosen. Rarely did it mean writing a script that would be used in anything like the version that left the typewriter, and only occasionally did the writer even appear on the set for production, let alone rewrite for the final take. Those Jewish writers who cared about the craft found it perpetually heartbreaking, as they found Los Angeles a pale counterpart to Manhattan. And yet it was a living, especially with the union in place, sometimes even a chance to do something lasting.

Could the studio powerhouses and mere screenwriters have done more to introduce the Jewish character and for that matter the Jewish actor, whose talent could be seen everywhere across contemporary theater, to touring WPA troupes? It's an intriguing question. The inner logic of the much-touted "genius" system of the majors was especially obvious in

Hollywood renditions of theater, where the Jewish role could hardly be denied and the cutting edge (as Clifford Odets's explosive mid-1930s hits) sometimes pinpointed a contemporary Jewishness, or reflected on showbiz history full of Jewish ghosts. John Howard Lawson's *Success* (renamed *Success at Any Price*) was especially painful for the playwright, because the very contradiction that bore upon the conclusion was the tragic self-denial of the left-leaning Jew who wanted the Bitch Goddess of success so badly that it ruined him. *The Life of Emile Zola* starred Paul Muni, Hollywood's biggest former Yiddish stage actor, *Golden Boy* had William Holden playing a Jewish boxer whose Jewishness is just barely suggested, and *Having Wonderful Time*, notably Gentilized from the stage drama, retained its Bronx factory-girl heroine craving culture and her Catskills boyfriend envisioning a social system where folks would only work two days a week – but Ginger Rogers was the filmic dame and Douglas Fairbanks, Jr., the beau. (Even the Catskills comic was Red Skelton).

Not that Jews as Jews disappeared in celluloid, but they usually played a version of themselves in minor or narrowly defined support roles only. *Street Scene* (1931), at the dawn of sound film, actually had a Jewish father preaching socialism to the other inhabitants of the neighborhood. In a foreign (he reads a Yiddish newspaper) manner, actor Max Montor thus managed against every expectation to cast this role in a positive light usually reserved for upfront (but English-speaking) Jewish progressives in war films, like militantly antifascist midshipman Sam Levene explaining Americanism to a would-be duty shirker in *Action In the North Atlantic*. Back in 1934, the Oscar-nominated *The House of Rothschild* more typically cast its heroic Jewish character as a financial manipulator hiding his fortune from tax collectors. Arguably, the handsome proletarian-type John Garfield was Jewish for Jewish viewers, Gentile for the Gentiles. Meanwhile, operating mostly under the radar, low-budget B films had more Jewish lawyers, bankers, junk collectors, treasurers of boys' own societies, as well as long-suffering mothers. Perhaps they were made to appeal to urban neighbor-hood audiences, or perhaps just made to fill out a second bill on the cheap. At any rate, the muscular Jewish hero, the real Jewish intellectual, and the seductive Red Jewess of anti-Semitic lore were all late-blooming, from 1940s to the Cold War era.

Radio was another story, although not entirely. To say that Jews were on the ground floor of the industry would be a less dramatic statement than the Jewish role in films, because the corporate control and military uses of radio had been more firmly established before newer entrepreneurs could make a beginning. David Sarnoff, a boy genius of radio and the boy genius of television – the very inventor of the National Broadcasting Company – exemplified the character of the power exerted by individuals from the top down. This left scant room for the less controllable expressions of talent.

Thus a *New Republic* essayist who complained in 1924 that entertainment entrepreneurs were "admirably fitted to assemble orchestra, pianists and singers; but when it comes to lectures and addresses they are about as competent as Florenz Ziegfeld is to run Columbia University" had engaged a double irony.[13] The complainant's magazine had itself a predominantly German-Jewish bent, its savants, like Walter Lippmann, determined to avoid the embarrassment of association with Eastern European immigrants' vulgarity. But radio was never seriously intended to educate. Whether propagandizing or selling more normal commercial products, it had the malleable consumer in mind.

Radio Jews like Eddie Cantor offered a distinctly more benign ethnic humor than, say, *Amos 'n' Andy* (at least, Cantor and other Jews got to play the stereotyped Jews) because the Jewish characters were more "normal" than ghetto blacks: they had regular families with sympathetic members, more varied social types and so on. A good example was *The Goldbergs*, which starred, was produced, and purportedly (if by no means entirely) written by Gertrude Berg, with a longevity rarely exceeded in radio. Housewife Molly and her garment district husband Jakey, their kids, and neighbors might almost have been any American family, except that they talked "funny," hung their washing on lines strung between tenements, and exhibited among the usual traits of good will a certain New Dealish affect.

Jack Benny, a veteran vaudevillian, had no such progressive bent, but used a solid formula of tight-fisted Jack, and a marvelous cast of characters including Mel Blanc, the most inventive voice in the early decades of animated features, playing the other stereotypic Jew, Mr. Kitzel.[14] Benny also invented, with George Burns, the *arriviste* Los Angeles Jewish comedian who plays something very much like himself on television week after week, obviously wealthy and famous, but nevertheless beset with life's little problems (very often, the sitcomic confusions of social relations). Other comedians making the successful shift from vaudeville to radio and television had no reason to appear Jewish any more than band leaders like Harry James or Benny Goodman had cause to appear Jewish in any discernable sense. To be successful within the great melting pot was quite enough for them.

These carefully cultivated images disguised the other central Jewish role in radio: the writers. The Radio Writers Guild, a few hundred of almost homogeneously Jewish practitioners, many of them originally from New

York, by the middle 1940s effectively represented the creative minds in the entertainment end of radio (the news end, with more intellectual prestige, was ironically less Jewish, and considerably less likely to be left leaning). Usually denied writing credits but paid decently, they ground out scripts week after week, using familiar formulae but occasionally striking out in dramatic directions.[15]

The approach of wartime gave the radio writers social issues to treat and a patriotic responsibility to take up problems like the traumas and the later readjustment of GIs to life on the homefront. Despite earlier experiments, like the *Columbia Workshop* (in which Orson Welles played a large role), and the continuing rendition of serious dramatic films into radio versions, as well as a handful of regular drama shows, artistic projects never gained real traction on the radio networks. Mostly it was gags and melodrama, adult fare, family, and strictly kids' shows, worked out along models of pathos, humor, and heroism that any screenwriter would recognize as American mainstream entertainment. It was, with some notable exceptions, an educational and artistic opportunity squandered.[16]

JEWISH AT THE MARGINS

At the media margins of respectability, where Jews so often found and also discovered themselves, animation had first caught public attention when Windsor McCay's short-lived "Gertie the Dinosaur" became a hit. In an expanded vaudeville act, the famed cartoonist actually appeared on the stage, and pretended to throw a ball to his on-screen creature. Full animation followed quickly, but for the first era of film, no one did it like Max and Dave Fleischer, two sons of an Austrian-Jewish immigrant tailor. Dave was already a film editor at Pathé, and with the inspiration of McCay's work, tinkered with live scenes (Dave dressed as a clown while brother Max worked the camera), then developed film outlined in ink. Thus Koko the Clown was born. The boys dubbed their process "rotoscope" and persuaded Pathé to invest in a cartoon, but army hitches put the two out of business until the armistice.

Out of the Inkwell, the brothers' first series, might be accurately described as the vernacular *Nude Descending a Staircase* and in its way just as formalist in its modernism. Koko refuses to obey his creator's commands. Sometimes he is drawn, sometimes he does the drawing of himself or his supposed creator. Intellectualized observers might conclude that he was a product of the unconscious, never far from the dream state, and indeed Koko appears and disappears with the artist's supposed sleep. It was brilliant, but like all animation in the presound era, slowed down by being dependent on dialogue balloons and expensive to produce for the seven-minute between-features niche. The Fleischers were doomed even before the crash – but they didn't know it.

Walt Disney and his invention of Mickey Mouse brought cartoons roaring back in the sound era. The Fleischers, their work now distributed by Paramount, countered with their version of sound (including their own version of Mickey Mouse, the clown Bimbo, jumping out of an inkwell) and eventually Betty Boop. Betty, destined to be one of the most copied camp sexy items in novelties history, her return in the 1960s and 70s, a sort of postmodernism in itself, was made with a kind of Group Theater method (though no one would have called it that). Actors invented lines and pre-sumably the necessary meaning after the film footage was shot. In stunning moments with a real Cab Calloway, Betty offered a total contrast to the shy but red-blooded Mickey, himself modeled after the *goyishe* and anti-Semite aviator sensation Charles Lindbergh. Then again, she was probably destined to have that "it" quality, after all, as the only female cartoon "star" of the 1930s.[17]

Boop, a dame with a low-cut dress, had a teasing manner that more than hinted her sexuality as evildoers visibly stroked her thighs and breasts. No one east of the Hudson, at least, would describe her as a Gentile: at times her parents have Yiddish accents, and Jewish in-jokes can often be heard (like the Samoan islanders who greet her with a roaring "Sholem Alei-chem!"), Hebrew lettering and all. Sometimes she even sounds like Fanny Brice. Most of all, she radiates musical syncopation, the gravitational force of constantly "animated" creatures and often equally animated inanimate objects, all of them apparently moved by the liberation of the urban space, while also being threatened by its spooky downside. Like *Mad Comics* decades later, she also places herself within a field of sight gags that threaten, along with the music-inspired waves, to overwhelm any possible narrative – altogether a good thing because the story-line, a weak point with the Fleischers, is paper thin.[18]

In the first half of the 1930s, Betty becomes more and more an impersonator, taking on Joan Crawford and Mae West ("She Wronged Him Right") in particular. These turned out to be animated Betty's last moments of glory. With the Film Code, Betty lost her cleavage and double entendres, became a college girl and then faded away. A bit character in one of her films, Popeye the Sailor Man, replaced her in the Fleischer lineup.

Popeye and Olive Oyl (featuring the incomparable, aural Mae Questal, former Betty Boop voice, vocalizing "Pop Oyy!"), sans Betty's double entendre, sans the eerie constant animation, sans jazz, sans almost everything but the occasional wild stroke of animated supernaturalism, were a giant hit. But in 1937, amid the fever of the sit-downs and the formation of mass industrial unions, the badly paid Fleischer studio employees went on strike, a precursor to the set-to at Disney's four years later. Max went all out to bust the existing union and failed. The subsequent efforts to rebuild the studio with full-length features fell flat. Now a part of Paramount, the Fleischer studios' Capraesque *Mr. Bug Goes to Town* (1941) had an insect community fighting the bulldozers of the monopolists, a cartoon version of *Mr. Deeds Goes to Town*. It was promising but it came too late. After Pearl Harbor, Paramount decided not to promote the film, and fired the two brothers who had not already quit.[19]

When the relaxed censorship of World War II allowed Tex Avery and MGM to produce explosive animation like the feline Red Hot (the protagonist who evoked howling wolves whenever she sang), and even Bugs Bunny was made erotically agitated under the collar at the sight of dancing dames, the Fleischers were no longer around to benefit from the loosening of censorship. Further down the road, one might argue that the repeated rebirth of animation actually brought back from Fleischers's styles the pared-down animation and the jivey musical thematic that eventually pushed animation beyond the straightforward (if often marvelous) storytelling of Bug Bunny and the rest of the 1930s to 50s mainstream.[20]

Another Jewish immigrant had overseen that mainstream. Leon Schlesinger, former publisher of silent film dialogue cards, made himself a fairly independent producer of cartoons for Warners in the early 1930s by investing his cash in the seemingly risky *Jazz Singer*. Under his tutelage, two former animators, Hugh Harman and Rudolph Ising, now created the blackface Bosko for early sound, sharing comic race traits with his girlfriend Honey, and even their dog, Bruno. Not that beak-nosed Jews (also oily-looking Mexicans and so on) were absent from the Schlesinger studio cartoons for Warners, but Bosko was a bigger star. When Harman and Ising walked out on Warners in 1933, Schlesinger found a new crew of writers and artists, future animation legends that included Tex Avery, Chuck Jones, and Bob Clampett. Of these, only Mel Blanc, already famed for his voices, was noticeably Jewish. Schlesinger was also notoriously cheap (the animators gave Daffy Duck his voice: a little creative revenge), so much so that his animators worked on a fraction of the budget that Disney allowed per cartoon, and took home next to nothing. Schlesinger was, in short, a typical sweatshop operator.

In any case, a notable middle term could be found within this semi-

Jewish animation history: *Fantasia* (1940), the last of the great Disney animated features before the strike drove many of its best hands out of the studio and, some years later, onto the blacklist. A Jewish abstract painter working at the studio, Jules Engel, was hired by the studio to guide dance choreography and design so as to reconcile animation and classical music. Arguably, *Fantasia* simplified background drawing (perhaps to save cash in an exorbitantly expensive production) into something like contemporary abstract art. Engel went on to UPA, as the left-leaning United Productions of America was popularly known. For someone like him it was the meeting point of a democratic political agenda and a space for the most creative animationists to experiment.[21]

Some things never changed, at least not until computer animation. The notorious marginality of the animated trade garnered no respect; a Warners executive bragged in the 1950s that he didn't know where on the lot the cartoons were created, but he knew that the studio had a winner in Mickey Mouse (in reality, of course, never a Warners product). Marginality was after all a Jewish specialty, familiar to that majority of Jewish actors and actresses who never successfully became filmic Gentiles or hit the payroll big time, but managed to hold on. The Three Stooges, Marx Brothers on the cheap, offer a good example.

Sam (invariably known as Shemp), Curley, and Moe Horowitz, growing up in Brooklyn, sons of a garment cutter and a housewife who dabbled in real estate, were grade school mischief makers fascinated by silent movies. Moe wormed his way into Vitagraph by doing errands for stars and successfully snagged a few parts. Always the aggressive brother, he formed a friendship with a Scotch-Irish lad from business classes, later to be known as Ted Healey. By the early 1920s, Moe, Shemp, and Healey had an act with Larry Fineberg, appearing as Ted Healey and his Three Southern Gentlemen. Healey passed out the slaps but it was already Stoogery in the making. They made their film debut with sound, in 1930, where they were joined by bald brother Curley and then abandoned by Healey in short order. By 1934, they had signed with Columbia to make two-reelers and there they stayed for just under a quarter-century, never paid more than a small fraction of their box office value. Writers and directors working with them came and went, even genius brother Curley went (a heavy drinker, he died in 1942), but the Stooges continued, a thwarted (at least in Moe's estimation) Abbott and Costello. They made up for some of the difference through endless personal appearances. But they could be headliners every summer in Atlantic City for years and still unappreciated near nobodies in Hollywood.[22]

The Stooges's counterpart at the bottom of the Bs was doubtless Edgar G. Ulmer (1904–72). At the distant opposite end of production values from Joseph Pasternak, who could not imagine a cast of less than hundreds and a budget less than hundreds of thousands – the equivalent of today's blockbuster multimillions – Ulmer's reputed 150 features were mostly shot in under a week with a bare minimum of retakes. That he guided one of the mightiest horror films (and antiwar allegories) ever made, a top Yiddish box-office attraction, early race films, one of the classic noirs (and later, a classic noir western), as well as several remarkable antinuke SciFi features surely makes him also the most diverse Jewish filmmaker. More than that, by choosing a most peculiarly vernacular art over the usual Hollywood commerce, Ulmer was in some ways the ultimate popular culture artist and legatee of *Yiddishkayt* that he knew only by second remove.

Born in Bohemia, son of a socialistic wine merchant, he grew up mostly in Vienna, where he eventually studied architecture at the distinguished Academy of Arts and Sciences. Homeless and impoverished by war, he was as much as adopted by the family of later famed actor Joseph Schildkraut. Ulmer began in the film industry as a set builder, and late in life insisted that his true introduction to the industry had been working on *The Golem* (1920). He came to Hollywood in 1923 with Max Reinhardt, and dividing his time between California and Berlin, worked with many greats such as F.W. Murnau, Erich Von Stroheim, Emil Jannings, Ernst Lubitch, and others.

Most memorably, he codirected *Mennschen Am Sonntag* (1929) with young Robert Siodmak, written in part by Billy Wilder and Fred Zinnemann, an experimental quasi-documentary look at a typical Sunday in the lives of ordinary Berliners. By the early 1930s a refugee, Ulmer directed minor westerns and the first solid documentary about the danger of venereal disease. He most urgently wanted to make an antiwar film, the kind of project made possible by the great success of *All Quiet On the Western Front*. But Ulmer, with his background in Expressionism, had a very different notion of how it could be done.

The Black Cat (1934) had virtually nothing in common with Edgar Allen Poe's original story of the same name. Instead, it was an extraordinary revisiting of a battle scene, years after the war stopped. Rather than analyzing the lives of protagonists as Lewis Milestone and his scriptwriters did in *All Quiet*, Ulmer created an elaborate metaphor of mechanized horror. A Bauhaus stylization framed a castle and its subterranean bowels, erstwhile allies become enemies, Bela Lugosi and Boris Karloff squaring off, with the dead wife and the daughter of one as trophies of the other and stark horror as the consequence.

Ulmer may have killed his career by stealing away the wife of the head of Universal, but more likely he had resolved to go it alone anyway. Actually introduced to Yiddish while attending so-called Second Avenue Broadway, he found his new métier in film adaptations of the Yiddish stage dramas, comedies, and musicals. Uncertain in the folkish tongue, he employed Yiddish stage directors while he oversaw the process.

It was a propitious moment, as well as the last extended major moment, for Yiddish film. Actress Molly Picon, who had turned to Broadway in the early 1930s without success, had led the Polish cast in *Yidl Mitn Fidl* (Little Jew with Violin), shot in 1936 in Warsaw and in a small Jewish town on the Vistula River. A bittersweet, nostalgic trip through Jewish life with Picon as a daughter, disguised as a boy and featuring real *klezmer* music, *Yidl Mitn Fidl* offered the actress the rare opportunity to display a full repertoire of her vaudeville talents. It even closes with a stage triumph in New York, as befits a proper Hollywood ending. Highlighted by a wedding scene using real-life poor Jews as guests – convinced that they were attending a real wedding – *Yidl* cost $50,000 and was not only the top moneymaker among Polish films that year but also the first Yiddish talkie to play in a major American theater chain.

Ulmer may have been encouraged by this success, but he clearly made his own plans. Raising money from needle trades unions, from former Yiddish actor Paul Muni, and from the Household Finance Corporation on the collateral of his own mortgaged home, he filmed *Gruene Felder* (Green Fields) in New Jersey in 1937. It is rightly considered the most artistic Yiddish language film ever made and was also the most commercially successful. During the next three years, Ulmer also completed *Yankl der Shmid* (retitled in English, The Singing Blacksmith), *Di Klyatsche* (The Light Ahead), and *Amerikaner Shadhken* (The Marriage Broker), none as successful as *Gruene Felder* by either standard but sturdy examples of the last wave of Yiddish cinema before the combination of the Holocaust, American assimilationism, and the Israeli demotion of Yiddish had condemned *Yiddishkayt* to generational memory and the ultraorthodox Hasidic communities.

In these four Yiddish films, Ulmer, the writers, technicians, and above all, the actors themselves succeeded in creating something literally out of time, a fantasy version of Jewish life of the Pale unseen in Hollywood until *Fiddler On the Roof.* As in all good fantasy, they project a mixture of folklore, unfulfilled aspirations, and keen sensibility of personal fate's merging with that of the collective. Unlike real-life Zionism and rather more like the projections of anarcho-Zionists such as literary savant B. Rivkin,[23] Ulmer's Yiddish films do not need to exclude or expropriate anyone in order to suggest the possibilities of autonomous development; love and music create the bridge between the everyday and the possible.

Gruene Felder in particular, unsparing in its uncinematic starkness and not only because of the razor-thin budget, is correspondingly excessive in its romanticism for the Yeshiva *bokher* (student) who travels to the *shtetl* of unlettered Jews and falls in love with the land as he falls hard for a local girl. Shot on the barest sets in New Jersey, it drew upon the success and the name of the famous play by Peretz Hirschbein. Jacob Ben-Ami, who had starred in a theatrical version fifteen years earlier, cast and supervised the script readings, in effect the dramaturge, adaptor, and acting coach, while Ulmer himself oversaw the camera work and general direction.

The process was not so different, in Ulmer's mind, from silent film days in which two directors had performed parallel tasks. But he sought to produce something beyond the existing Yiddish film. He called his intent "the same decision that Sholem Asch made, which Chagall made," i.e., to create real art from a mixture of folk culture and vaudeville.[24] In critic-scholar J. Hoberman's phrase, the "dreamy pantheism" of *mise en scene* with alternating sunlit and dark scenes and flavored by Vladimir Heifetz's soul-rending score resembles Jean Renoir and avant-gardist Jean Vigo more than the work of any other director.[25]

Ulmer even had to bargain to get the negative printed, and offered a new theater near Times Square a guaranteed ten-week run, in exchange for eighty percent of the gate (not counting members of the ILGWU, whose chief had bought a block of seats in the Jewish institution-supported theatrical tradition). The first weekend, the manager had to beg filmgoers to leave the theater so that the patrons for the next show could be admitted. Failing that, he called out the police. *Gruene Felder* broke all film box-office records in Jewish neighborhoods, then more characteristically ran (as a somewhat shortened B feature with subtitles) on the Keith's circuit theaters at the bottom of a double bill. There had been nothing like it, and, sadly enough, there would be nothing like it again.

The evocation of nature's store as the essence of wholeness and of honest labor was the key to achievable paradise that has rarely been equaled, except perhaps in the virtual repeat moments of the otherwise improbable *Jive Junction* (1943), where patriotic jivers reconcile themselves to classical musicians, Ulmer honoring apple picking (i.e., agricultural production for antifascist unity, to the sound of the "Bell Song"). Ulmer's musical comedy/melodrama *Yankl der Shmid*, based on a David Pinsky play and starring Yiddish stage tyro Moishe Oysher, boasts a plot still more bare, if that is possible: a village smithy who makes the girls swoon.

A psychological drama in the original, *Yankl der Shmid* became a vehicle for matinee idol Oysher to learn the necessity, and joys, of faithfulness to a good woman. Ulmer shot *Yankl* through his own prism of psychology, odd camera angles that suggest *The Black Cat* and Ulmer's noirs ahead. Reviews were overwhelmingly positive, nowhere more so than in the Left press, where *Yankl*'s labor anthem and the progressive/socialistic commentary of his bride-to-be seemed a real, even Soviet, example of appropriate cinema.[26]

Di Klyatsche (1939), shot as Polish Jewry was falling under German and Russian occupation, was an adaptation of two stories from the nineteenth-century literary father of Yiddish short stories who called himself Mendele Mokher Sforim (i.e., Mendele the Bookseller). Gently (sometimes not so gently) mocking Jewish backwardness and the costs of class-divided *shtetl* society, rabbinical school dropout Mendele fashioned an allegory of the Jewish people who had been reduced from noble steeds to old workhorses, and Ulmer joined it to a more famous novel, *Fishke der Krumer* (Fishke the Lame), about the fate of Jewish beggars. Left-winger Chaver-Paver (the nom de plume of Gershon Einbeinder, taken from the game of reconciliation Jewish children play after a fight) had adapted *Fishke* but the ARTEF troupe had been unable to stage it in 1936 due to a more heavily funded rival production by impresario Joseph Buloff. Ulmer bought the rights to the Chaver-Paver version in 1939 and set about production, again in New Jersey. It starred David Opatoshu, nephew of a famed Yiddish short story writer Joseph Opatoshu, and late in life (1970) scriptwriter and supporting actor of *Romance of a Horse Thief*.[27]

The *Klyatsche*, in this respect the most literal rendition of its original, is also the least sentimental American Yiddish film about the age-old *shtetl*. Here, the narrowness of life mirrors the power and privilege of the merchants. A generational drama without any glimpse of American optimism, it features, as Hoberman says, not only the most erotic couple in Yiddish cinema, Opatoshu and Helen Beverly, but also the most didactic dialogue, as the wise elder pronounces the dangers facing Jewry. It was also weirdly Expressionistic, which is to say true vintage Ulmer, as if his Expressionism had overcome his folkishness in this moment of extreme political crisis. It opened in Detroit rather than Manhattan, suffered bad reviews from the non-Left Jewish press, and despite some good notices in the mainstream English-language press could not reach the heights of his musicals or his cinematic sentimental journeys home.

The last of Ulmer's Yiddish films was yet another musical. *Amerikaner Shadkhn*, shot on the slimmest of budgets even for Ulmer, with precious few exteriors, is a comedy about the *schlemiel* and the marriage brokerage, with the struggle for a Jewish-American identity that sometimes looks surprisingly like Woody Allen with one crucial difference. This Woody is ultimately redeemed by a good woman. With the story credit to Ulmer's cousin, a Viennese operetta librettist of the 1930s, and the script itself by Ulmer (with his wife, Shirley), it bore many signs of the director's later work: haste, visual flatness, and unexpected turns or moments. The film died in the theaters, and Ulmer's Yiddish phase was over.

Consider that in between these Yiddish films, Ulmer had shot *Moon Over Harlem* (1939), a low-budget melodrama with no white actors, showing the victory of a Popular Front-style reformist minister over gangster elements; *Cossacks in Exile* (1939), a musical romance about Ukrainians fleeing into Turkey and then returning to their homeland; and *Clouds in the Sky* (1940), a documentary in English and Spanish about the dangers and treatment of tuberculosis. Over the next few years, he made educational material for the armed forces, and antifascist morale-building melodramas and comedies of other, mostly oddball, varieties featuring generational and gender tensions. He was scant few years from making the classic noir *Detour* (1945) and several equally dark films (usually with the participation of his left-wing friends), en route to an obscurity and fantasy-horror series so strange and low budgeted that he might properly be considered an artistic version of Ed Wood, Jr. – except that even when confined within extremely sharp limits of dreadful scripts and hopelessly small budgets, Ulmer's talent and his redemptive vision never entirely flagged.

Other notably Jewish margins of popular culture meanwhile continued to percolate. The emergence of sound films had of course been prompted by media competition, the power of radio to detract from the film audience to be exact. Some Jews, though markedly fewer than in films, were at the base of corporate radio development. But nowhere could vernacular Jewishness be as complete as at the utter margins, in other words, Yiddish radio. It was never seriously intended to compete with its English-language counterpart, but had far more listeners than any other "foreign" language American radio, and a highly concentrated potential advertising base in and around New York City.

The first "foreign" license for Yiddish radio was issued by the I.C.C. only in 1923, and the station never reached the air, an abortive move by the editor of the Yiddish *Forverts*, recognizing that the *Forverts* had begun to lose readers to assimilation and was destined to increasing future hemorrhages. By writing to RCA Chairman David Sarnoff, *Forverts* official and East Side giant B. Charney Vladek was in effect appealing from Jewish margin to

Jewish mainstream. The appeal was unsuccessful (so was an effort of Vladek to get future Folkways record executive Moses Asch – son of the most famous of all Yiddish novelists, Sholem Asch – a job at RCA) and Yiddish crept into regular stations one program at a time. Only in 1927 did WEVD open its doors, thanks to the Debs Memorial Radio Fund honoring the martyred Socialist leader and its promise of a "militant voice of the American labor movement." Shortly, it became more entertainment than social cause, but with enough socialistic politics to make WEVD a unique presence within American popular culture, even apart from its *Yiddishkayt*.[28]

One of the ironies of the approach of global war and, then, Pearl Harbor followed by American entry, was that Jews would be accused of manipulating American popular culture in two different ways simultaneously. On the one hand, they were said to be guilty of demoralizing American youth, sapping manliness through a corrupt Hollywood (and stage-dramatic, and musical) product. On the other hand, they were even more guilty of urging war upon a nation that obviously didn't want it. That a vibrant Yiddish neighborhood culture locked into the most American of consumer interests – live radio broadcasts from fruit markets bustling with customers, or amusement parks with joy seekers – could be seen as anti-American would be ludicrous if the accompanying prejudice were not so widespread.

And yet it might also be said that the anti-Semitism alive in American life, together with the status of blue collar and lower-middle-class city dwellers, continued to give Jewish contributions to popular culture an edge that they might otherwise have lacked. Even when strictly apolitical, they favored a more European notion of organic society, the crowd as a living creature, and culture as a possible means for crossing the divide between the life of art and the muck of daily life.

NOTES

[1] And yet in Peter Novick's widely acclaimed and exhaustively researched *The Holocaust in American Life* (New York: Mariner Books, 2000), *Schindler's List* appears only marginally: one more sign that popular culture doesn't signify to the critics.

[2] See the charming classic overview, David Ewen, *The Life and Death of Tin Pan Alley: The Golden Age of American Popular Music* (New York: Funk and Wagnalls, 1964): 89–104.

[3] S. Hurok, in collaboration with Ruth Goode, *Impresario: a Memoir* (New York: Random House, 1946): 13.

[4] Ibid., 23–25.

[5] Max Gordon and Lewis Funke, *Max Gordon Presents* (New York: Bernard Geis Associates, 1963): 124.

[6] Stephen J. Whitfield, *In Search of Jewish Culture* (Hanover, NH: Brandeis University Press; New England Universities Press, 1999): 73–78.

[7] See, e.g., "Sophie Tucker" and "Fanny Brice," in Linda Martin and Kerry Seagrave, *Women in Comedy* (Secaucus: Citadel Press, 1986): 76–77, 110.

[8] A few years later, "Over the Rainbow," in the *Wizard of Oz*, won an Oscar for Harburg. A poll of 365 recordings by the Recording Industry Association of American and National Endowment for the Arts in 2001 put "Rainbow" at the very top in a measurement intended to serve as a framework for a music education program in US schools. From 1950 onwards, Harburg himself had been blacklisted from the Hollywood his early plays bitterly attacked. Only decades later was he rehabilitated, and then never in the eyes of liberal Cold War critics like Pauline Kael and Andrew Sarris. Thanks to the Harburg Foundation for this information.

[9] Whitfield, *In Search of Jewish Culture*, 60–61.

[10] Jane Feuer, *The Hollywood Musical* (Bloomington: University of Indiana, 1982): 3. See also Richard Barrios, *A Song in the Dark: The Birth of the Musical Film* (New York: Oxford, 1995).

[11] See Paul Buhle and Dave Wagner, *Radical Hollywood* (New York: New Press, 2002), for a general political overview.

[12] Maurice Rapf, *Back Lot: Growing Up with the Movies* (Lanham: Scarecrow Press, 1999), 47–49, is particularly good from the standpoint of a mogul's son looking at the practical effects of the Wall Street takeover process.

[13] Quoted in Susan Douglas, *Inventing American Broadcasting, 1899-1922* (Baltimore: Johns Hopkins, 1987): 313.

[14] Benny thought that ethnic stereotype humor was predominantly a form of melting pot Americanism, valuable until the Second World War if considered tasteless after that. He received some of his heaviest mail when fictional Benny asked the fictional chauffer Rochester to punch him – and Rochester knocked him over. See Jack Benny and Joan Benny, *Sunday Nights at Seven: The Jack Benny Story* (New York: Time Warner Books, 1990): 108–110. George Burns wrote the foreword to this volume, or is described as writing the foreword. At any rate, he, too, always had writers.

[15] Typical of the hard-won space for real drama was an adapted radio version of *Our Town*, produced 1940–41 by future blacklistee Leonardo Bercovici, made possible by his earlier success in producing two highly successful afternoon family programs; or a children's series dealing with the need for psychological counseling, written and produced by William Alland, later a horror producer of note and a friendly witness. Neither show would have survived as long as it did without an indulgent sponsor (in the latter case, stations of the Canadian Broadcasting

"Paayper Reggs," by Harvey Pekar and Robert Crumb, from
American Splendor (1987). Courtesy of author/artist.

"The Cheap Novelty District," by Ben Katchor, from *Cheap Novelties: The Pleasure of Urban Decay* (1991). Courtesy of the artist.

"Meine Rue Platz," by Sharon Kahn Rudahl, from *Wimmen's Comics* (1978). Courtesy of the artist.

Marx, the Wonder-Worker, leads the children of Israel through perils to Paradise.

"Marx the Wonder Worker," reprinted from *Der Groysser Kundes* (c.1915).

Moshe Nadir caricatures by
Zuni Maud and Yosel Kotler, from
A Bukh Moshe Nadir (1926).

שאַרזש פֿון ז. מאָוד

Still from *Gruene Felder*. Reprinted from J. Hoberman,
Bridge of Light (1991).

מיר זעהן אלעקסאנדער גראנאך מיט ווערא, "מענטש", דעזשורנע, אלעקסאנדער ע און א׳ נוסינאוו, סמאמבול

ARTEF scene, c.1927, from *Tseyn Yor Artef* (1937).

"Fascism," by Maurice Kish, from *Images of American Radicalism* (1999).

"With apologies to Rube Goldberg," by Art Spiegelman, from SHIMATE (1983). Courtesy of the artist.

"Zog nit keyb mol," by Trina Robbins and Sharon Kahn Rudahl, from *Wimmen's Comics* (1958). Courtesy of the artist.

"Good Girl" comic cover, 1947.

Lionel Stander, the "original Hollywood Red," dressed for "Pal Joey,"
c.1950. Courtesy of Bella Stander.

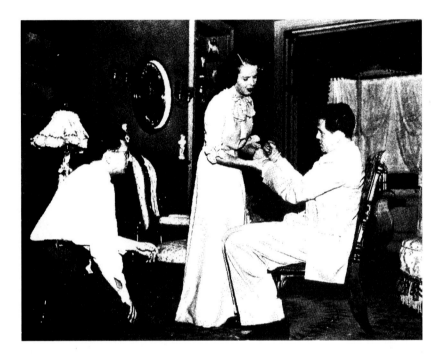

Abraham Polonsky directs John Garfield and Beatrice Pearson.
Courtesy Hank Polonsky.

Service eager for shows professional and educational). Thanks to the late Bercovici and Alland for interviews.

[16] See chapter four for a most important exception: Norman Corwin.

[17] See Amelia S. Holberg, "Bubbie Boop," in L.Hoberman and Jeffrey Shandler, eds., *Entertaining America*, 164.

[18] Norman M. Klein, *Seven Minutes: The Life and Death of the American Animated Cartoon* (London: Verso, 1993): 81–90.

[19] Ibid., 84–88.

[20] See below, chapter six.

[21] Klein, *Seven Minutes*, 232–33.

[22] Moe Howard, *Moe Howard and the Three Stooges* (Seacaucus: Citadel Press, 1977), especially pages 10–32, 53.

[23] Rivkin spent a lifetime interpreting Yiddish writers, but one of his least famous essays, "Pesach" (Passover), best captures this spirit, reprinted in Minna Rivkin, ed., *B. Rivkin: Yidishe-Tovim* (New York: Morris S. Sklarsky, 1950): 101–43. In Rivkin's interpretation, religious holidays for the *shtetl* are "out of time," in a zone of timeless utopia. I would like to acknowledge a meeting with Rivkin's daughter, herself once a semianarchist "Junior Wobbly," for her insights and for giving me this volume.

[24] J. Hoberman, *Bridge of Light: Yiddish Film Between Two Worlds* (New York: Schocken Books and the Museum of Modern Art, 1991): 248.

[25] Hoberman, *Bridge of Light*, 253. As Hoberman says, Ulmer claimed that French critics awarded the film best foreign feature of the year, in a year when the Popular Front cinema peaked in Paris; the claim remains unconfirmed.

[26] Ibid., 268, quotes one of the most intelligent reviewers, Ber Grin of the *Morgn Frayhayt*; by the time I met Grin (or Green) at the *Frayhayt* office, he was so crippled by arthritis that he could hardly type and walk, but kept up his poetry-writing to the end. Film reviews were an extension of his poetic sense.

[27] See the afterword on Polonsky and *Romance of a Horsethief.*

[28] Ari Kelman, "'All Right, Dear God, I Give Youth Aleph-Baiz and You Make up a Sketch for the Radio': The Culture of Ydidsh Radio 1923–1928," unpublished dissertation chapter. TheYiddish Radio Project, headed by Henry Sapoznik, has in recent times made public presentations of the ambience of Yiddish radio, and I am in debt to this project along with Kelman for material and orientation.

THREE

THE PRINTED WORD AND THE PLAYFUL IMAGINATION: HOW PULP ENTERTAINMENT TRANSFORMED LIFE AND EVEN ART

Jewish comic art, even more than other forms of popular entertainment with Jewish creators, was born postmodern. It turns back in upon itself so often and so adeptly that, as film writer, director, and theorist Abraham Polonsky once sagely observed of Jewish culture, the things thrown out in the production process are remade and revalued – after generations of disrespect – by the successors of those who threw them aside in the first place. That thought nicely sums up the whole world of Jewish caricature, and its late elevation into art.

Cartoonist Ben Katchor has in recent years delivered to various audiences a comic lecture about the issue of portrayal as violation of an ancient Jewish taboo. If the result of the "mat," a rubber insert for the most mundane continuing advertising in the Yiddish newspaper of past decades, looked ghostlike and fraying after repeated reuse, it is due not only to wear and tear, but because (in Katchor's richly symbolic imagined universe) the publishers did not want to redouble their guilt by ordering an early replacement. This is an absurd but fruitful premise. Real-life Jewish caricature began very late and is thoroughly imitative, but like Yiddish literature, quickly acquires its own character out of the fragments at hand. It looks rougher than a clear, genteel print should. It is also somehow more intriguing, because it acquires something unanticipated in the process.[1]

Jewish comic strip artists were as rare in the first several decades of the art form (and the century) as Jews were becoming common among the fine arts. But cartoonists had several key contributions to make during the first half of the century. They saw the city, specifically New York City and environs, as vividly and uniquely as their fellow short story writers and poets. They were early experimenters among the modernists, influenced by and influencing the plastic arts, but tainted by popular culture. Later on, both "Metropolis" and "Gotham City" became theirs. By the time the Second World War arrived, they had introduced cinematic action into comics, a move of enormous value to a hitherto stolid form. The same latter generation, by a high proportion of numbers and key figures, made the comic books a premier juvenile art form never destined for real respect in the US but that nevertheless received great admiration from millions of ordinary readers and enormous popularity. When, over further time, the form began to mature, *Mad Comics* to Art Spiegelman and Katchor, it revealed an introspection that had been, consciously and unconsciously, on hand all along.

But that introspection had, for most of the time, hardly been either self-conscious, or, for the most part, rewarded either commercially or critically. There were exceptions: Gilbert Seldes proclaimed comics an authentic American art in *The Seven Lively Arts* (1926), and *Krazy Kat* was already an opera in the 1920s. The 1930s and 40s saw film comedies with *Joe Palooka*, *Blondie*, and others, almost entirely in the B category. A rare strip might be flattered by liberal commentators: Al Capp and his *Li'l Abner* were favorites, the matriarchal hillbilly society hailed as a metaphorically accurate picture of Middle America. But a relatively small number of artists, and only a few of them Jewish, enjoyed the benefits of a popular readership built through newspaper syndication. If movies – at least until television – were derided by genteel critics as no art form at all, what chance did comics have for respect?

Thus the inner history of comic books in particular includes at its economic base just the curious sort of marginality that a range of Jewish entrepreneurs (and others, most likely extending institutionalized pulp publishing empires) found inviting. Looking for talent in the 1910s, newspaper syndicates had hundreds of local artists around the country to choose from, most of the successful ones destined to move to San Francisco, Chicago, or New York in order to enter the big time. A similar talent search for comic book artists hardly extended west of the Hudson and took in practically anyone, including teenagers (practically all male) willing to work in spurts of long hours for very low wages, with no union, and with artistic prospects that rarely extended beyond well-paid but definitely philistine advertising work.

It was a crazed crowd, often hardly more mature than its childish audience that included, by the Second World War, not only youngsters and semiliterate adults but also hundreds of thousands of GIs who regarded comics as basic literature. Its artists, and many executives who were former artists, operated like sign painters in a boomtown, borrowing freely from each other, suddenly opening up new shops and just as suddenly shutting them down, shifting art and content with any new and apparently salable trend. Their pulp writer counterparts – often getting checks from the same parent publishing corporations – had some chance to reach the middle (or lower-middle) levels of mass literature by turning story writing talents into writing novels. Occasionally, these same writers even got to Hollywood. Comic book artists lacked such openings. They had only talent and, in the best cases, an inner compulsion to discover the possibilities at hand for one of the nation's most avidly consumed cultural items.

This chapter traces the story from the earliest Jewish comic artists into the works of the genre's golden age, and slightly beyond. More than vaudeville, more than the movies, it may be the ultimate story in the unrespected art form that made its artists beloved without ever (with the rarest exceptions) making them respectable as art creators. For that reason alone, it would be the perfect expression of vernacular Jewishness, of Yiddish-gone-mainstream.

COMIC ORIGINS

The first Yiddish, that is to say, Jewish, satire magazines date to the 1890s, the same time as the Yiddish (and usually Socialist as well as secular) press began to run humor columns in the US and parts of Europe. The small-scale literary parody was the creation of the *zeyde*, the grandfather of the secular and Socialist Yiddish press, Morris Winchevsky, and his 1880s *Meshugina Filosof* signature column in the *Arbeter Fraynt* (Workers' Friend) of London, shortly before he brought himself and his humor to the US. The *Fraynt* was the first widely circulated Yiddish labor paper, beloved of garment workers, small shopkeepers, and starvelings of London's East End.

Winchevsky, grandson of a noted Polish rabbi martyred during a past Russian invasion, had adopted the Russian realist critics adopted the contemporary Russian litterateurs as models, gone to work as a clerk in Koenigsberg, written for the Hebrew as well as the early Yiddish press, and shifted to London. He was a fighter, but also an ironist, for this mad philosopher knew that the world was crazy, unwilling at the moment and perhaps ever to accept the vision of a cooperative order. His pen strokes were intended to rouse readers through appealing to their courage and idealism – and Jewishness – but also their sense of irony, between the possible and the current miserable reality. His other humor columns included comic strip inspired repartee, acidly anticapitalist: "How much does a policeman make in America, Michael?" "As much as he can steal, Schmeikl."

The Yiddish satirical magazine, more barbed by a thousand degrees than television's *Politically Incorrect* a century later, was decidedly commercial by intent but inflected, for its audience's tastes, with roughly socialistic values. Modeled after the German *Simplissimus* (itself socialistic in its satires of bourgeois society and values) and the British *Punch*, a succession of failed experiments led to the *Groysser Kundes* (1907–26), the most distinctive publication of the Lower East Side after the daily *Forverts*.

Founded and guided by erstwhile melancholy poet Jakob Marinov who settled upon commercialism (and avid exploitation of his writers) without losing his Jewish nationalism or his political populism, the *Kundes* flourished by holding up a mirror to ghetto life and personalities. Every major editor, every lecturer, every Jewish writer went under its political/satirical microscope and was simultaneously lampooned and recognized. As a comic weekly, the *Kundes* had its share of fat lady jokes, also what the American comic magazines like *Puck* and *Life* called "he-she" humor (in an early version of the modern sex war), and so on. But unlike *Punch* or the contemporary *Life* (not yet a photo magazine), strikes, especially Jewish strikes, would be hailed in the *Kundes*, May Day and Socialist electoral victories would be celebrated, war would be attacked, idealists exalted as the real geniuses of Jewish art, of Jewish disappointments, and of Jewish hopes. Indeed, ghetto giants like Winchevsky or the neighborhood's "teardrop millionaires" (successful writers of tragedy-bound short stories about immigrant life) could be understood here as the realistic guides to the heartbreaks in store for so many Jews in modern urban America.

Perhaps most interestingly for future generations of Jewish humorists of all kinds was, however, the *Kundes*' stance of uncompromising iconoclasm. Abraham Cahan, by any standards the most formidable literary figure of the ghetto with the power to puncture local reputations and shut down stage productions, was treated unsentimentally, with special contempt for trading on or selling out his Socialist faith. Cartoonists of the *Kundes* depicted him as a ringmaster at the office, whipping his own nonunion staff into line, or as the emperor of the vast commercial enterprise that ultimately catered only to the bottom line. Like Lenny Bruce going after the Jewish establishment in future generations, the *Kundes* relished these kinds of contrasts between socialistic (in later generations, liberal) ideals and reality.

More than politics or unionism was at stake. If Cahan refused on principle to publish the emerging writers of *di Yunge*, blue collar aesthetes of the 1910s experimenting with literary form, the *Kundes* recruited them to make a little money with jokes and commentary – otherwise, outside of their own small-circulation anthologies, the *Yunge*'s work appeared only in the anarchist *Freie Arbeter Shtimme*.[2] The *Kundes* could, at stressful moments, be militantly Zionist in appealing for a Jewish army to create a state in Palestine. Yet it remained, in its editor and artists' eyes, antibourgeois on grounds both aesthetic and political, its caricatures the definitive signature of the printed page jokester.[3]

Jewish progress in the comic pages of the mainstream English-language press, quickly becoming the most popular section of the metropolitan dailies, was slow by contrast, although markedly interesting in its spare personnel. Richard Outcault's *Yellow Kid*, a single box first appearing in the *New York World* in 1896, could easily be described as an Ash Can vernacular study of urban chaos, and might have been Jewish in its depiction of what could have been the Lower East Side, but what was actually an inhabitant of *Hogan's Alley*, an Asian boy among Irish-Americans. The first comic strip pages, a precursor to television in reaching the home with pictures, acquired a filmlike narrative sequence and daily appearance (rather than only in the Sunday supplement) a few years later. The first Jewish artist who crossed over the genres from cartoon to strip was Harry Hershfield.

For forty years a real American celebrity, from his comic strip spiritual home to the editorial and theatrical review pages of prestige dailies and from radio shows to a host of best-selling books, Hershfield was a productive force of nature. Born far from swarming immigrant neighborhoods, in Cedar Rapids, Iowa, of business-class, Russian, Jewish parents, he placed his first strip in the *Chicago Daily News* before his fifteenth birthday. The young man proceeded to move from one big paper to another, Chicago, then San Francisco, and back over the next years, until heading for the big time at Hearst's *New York Journal* in 1910. *Abie the Agent*, not a spy drama but a running commentary on the life of a Jewish salesman, ran from 1914 to 1940. Meanwhile, in the manner of the day, he had multiple other strips running concurrently.

Hershfield established his reflexive self, so to speak, with two genre satires, *Desperate Desmond* and *Dauntless Durham of the USA*. At once commentaries on the nature of the standard melodrama (villain chases innocent dame until halted by hero) and of the primitive character of silent screen, they commanded readers to disassociate melodrama from serious presentation and to ponder the absurd conventions. "Thirty Second Movies," a strip-within-a-strip of *Dauntless Durham*, perfected the form of effortlessly switching readers from one logic to another and simultaneously one media to another. Already, thanks to Hershfield's visual suggestions, casual readers were thinking about watching movies while looking at the comics. Presumably some also thought of his comic strips while watching filmic melodramas.

Hershfield's rise interestingly parallels the appearance of Jewish censors; the Anti-Defamation League (most significantly, first known as the "Anti-Caricatural Committees") was organized in 1913 by German-American Jews to police and reduce the stereotypes of Jews seen or heard across American commercial culture. Best known in later decades for business class political-economic views and its quiet collaboration with investigative agencies like the FBI against radical unionists and left-wing civil rights activists of the 1930s and after, the ADL also pressured Hollywood and the comics syndicates early and often. In 1916, the Jewish creator of the *Samuel and Sylenz* daily strip surrendered his salary rather than continue the offending strip. The ADL was offended by many stereotypes, but most of all, caricatures of the ADL's own version of respectability, such as Jewish capitalists with large noses, a very favorite butt of the *Groysser Kundes* drawings for Jewish-only readers. The guilty cartoonist, Samuel Zagat, also happened to be the artist of *Gimpl Benish*, the most successful of the Yiddish comic strips (it ran in the *Forverts'* rival, the daily *Warheit*), which related the frantic pursuit of single men by a professional matchmaker on behalf of unwed ladies. Beginning a few years later and for forty plus years to follow, Zagat supervised the art work in the *Forverts*. On the sly, he drew for more left-wing Yiddish magazines and the *New Masses* under the pseudonym of G. Molan. Zagat was thus a most typical Jewish popular art creator, the quiet subversive.[4]

Most of Hershfield's strips meanwhile employed characters straight out of white-bread America, although often in such metropolitan settings as Coney Island. But *Abie the Agent* ("Abe Kabibble," one of a long line of Yiddish-sounding nonsense words, like Jack Benny's "Schnook") was renowned from its first appearance for its language: vaudeville Yiddishized English, phonetically transcribed on the page to play up the comedy of malapropisms and misunderstandings. A little guy with a big head, arms and legs perpetually in motion, Abe's specialty is "autermobile" sales – but cars are, finally, just a commodity with no intrinsic fascination even for the salesman. He really wants success, and with it the culture symbolized in his fiancée, later, bride, Rheba Mine Gold, a sophisticated tootsie both noticeably taller and vastly better dressed than Abie. Rheba, it was widely known, happened to be a somewhat idealized version of the artist's wife, a comic artist who abandoned her career for marriage but sometimes contributed a strip or two.

In the artwork of an anti-Semite, Abie would have been a cruel caricature Jew, grossly materialistic and ugly to boot, the oily type who craves
beautiful American-looking women. In Hershfield's hands he is a harmless
alrightnik lacking conscience when it comes to sales and commissions, but
bearing his own definite sincerity in strictly personal matters. For the sake of
family, he will even play "Sental Claus" for Christmas. As artist, Hershfield
told a Chicago women's club in 1916 that Abie was intended to be "a
clean-cut, well-dressed specimen of Jewish humor," a sharp contrast to "the
big-nosed banker so often seen in films and sometimes other comic strips,
too."[5] Obviously the artist was being a little defensive. By the last decade of
the strip, during the 1930s, Abie lost his Yiddishisms altogether.

One can appreciate Hershfield better from a different angle by
contrasting his work to that of a contemporary who made his own
breakthrough in the same decade and with a similar eye to transforming the
possibilities in front of him. Max Weber, the artist (not the sociologist), was
born in Bialystock, Russia, in 1881, immigrating with his family ten years
later to Williamsburg, Brooklyn. Weber graduated from the Pratt Institute,
where many of the best in the following generations of comic book artists
would learn their basics, and he taught drawing in the deepest parts of
Middle America, Missouri to Minnesota, before heading for Paris in 1905.
At the moment when Hershfield would have been absorbing the skills of
fellow comic artists, Weber was taking up Cézanne, Matisse, Picasso, and
especially the work of his friend (a later favorite of the underground cartoonists, as we've already seen), the bizarre Henri Rousseau. Weber
returned to New York in 1909 with another pal acquired in Paris, fellow
immigrant and soon-to-be famed modernist, Abraham Walkowitz.

Within months of his return, Weber visited Coney Island and began a
series on vaudeville. He also painted a series based on Isadora Duncan's
dancing. He became a vital part of vernacular culture and the Village scene.
It's no surprise that he was soon living on East fourteenth Street and
spending time with Alfred Steiglitz, the assimilated Jewish genius of the
salon crowd drawn to the physical mystique of the city and the use of the
photo as an art form. Two decades later, Weber would be dubbed the
"dean of the moderns." In this era, still a young revolutionary, he sought to
render art a spiritual truth that merged mathematical geometry, the interior
life of the artist, and the burning hope for a different kind of society. His
Cubism, which he rendered in poetry and essays but mainly in his paintings,
had everything to do with the city, its masses, the discovery of movement,
the "look" of music, and the possibilities for plastic arts raised by the
achievement of films. One cannot call Weber a popular artist, because his

following was always limited to an avant-garde. But he is one of the first who found his subjects squarely within popular life and culture.

Hershfield had become steadily less Jewish with growing success, but Weber declared his Jewish focus in the 1940s, obviously moved by the crisis of Jewry. He had been in his deepest sensibilities a Socialist with an intuition for the romantic-revolutionary view destined to become surrealism. But a look at his early Cubist paintings (especially the famed *Women in Tents*) again and again reveals the Jewish image or the daily scenes in his Manhattan, then as now, the capital of the Jewish world. His vision was very much what *di Yunge* saw and wrote about in the most experimental publications ever produced in Yiddish, and like them, intimately related to the artistic conceptions arriving with Dada, surrealism, and the cinema, not at all excluding the comic strip.

Rube Goldberg, a vernacular and undeclared surrealist, born in 1893, grew up in almost the same generation as Hershfield and Weber. But the West Coast businessman's son followed stern parental commands to stay in college (where he drew for the new student humor magazine at Berkeley) and began work as a civil engineer in San Francisco. Within a few years, he quit to join the press as an artist. Soon, he began to evolve the characteristic style of his masterstroke, syndicated across the major dailies.

His first success was with *Foolish Questions* (as in the old saw: ask a silly question, you get a silly answer) in which questions were resolved visually, with enormously inventive sarcasm heaped upon the questioner. For a few years, he also appeared on vaudeville stages in a lecture and movie combination, showing the animated cartoons for which he had supplied the completed cell-by-cell drawings. Only his perfectionism prevented him from further film animation work that might easily have revolutionized the young field; it was physically impossible for anyone to do that much work unaided, and he was not one to launch an animation company.

By 1914, Goldberg had begun the *Inventions* series that brought him permanent fame and his name a niche in the *Oxford English Dictionary* as the very definition ("A Rube Goldberg") of an absurdly complicated device to carry out a simple task. His imaginary machines, which he invented and described by the thousands in loving visual detail, gently satirized the American obsession with modernism and mechanized optimism. These machines actually made work *more* difficult, encompassing animals, furniture, and pain, while their obvious ingenuity outwitted the straightforward logic embodied in the do-it-yourself projects of garage tinkerers armed with back issues of *Popular Mechanics*. At the end of the process, a pencil was sharpened or something more useless accomplished. His drawings can be seen best, perhaps, as the counterlogic of the machine age, a different way of viewing the claims of progress that suffused American life.[6]

A phenomenally hard worker, Goldberg produced no less than sixty distinct comic strips, including that model of humane ethnic détente, "*Mike and Ike*," subtitled "They Look Alike." Any contemporary would know by the names that these two apparent twins are Irishman and Jew, sharing the inanities of urban life. *Boob McNutt, Bobo Baxter, Lala Palooza*, and *I'm the Guy* – or "I'm the Guy that put the Con in Congress": a delightfully cynical slogan adopted, with the accompanying illustration, for campaign-season buttons and signs – among others had the same qualities, simultaneous visual and dialogue playfulness in the extreme, examining culture from what critics would later call the surreal angle.[7] Indeed, the curators of the first Dada show in America, the veritable stalking horses of surrealism in 1917, actually hung a *McNutt* frame among the works of Marcel Duchamp and others. Goldberg claimed not to understand what the Dadaists were all about, but the canny artist was likely being modest: praise in Paris meant little to him when he had millions of readers at home.

Pseudorealist trends in the comic pages drove him out in 1938, though he continued as a popular comic and fiction writer, illustrating his own stories, in the *Saturday Evening Post* and elsewhere, and a public personality with pals like Charlie Chaplin and Jimmy Durante. He returned to editorial cartoons in wartime, best remembered now for his antifascist sentiments, commentary on poverty at home, and his plea for the public to wake up to the dangers of atomic warfare. He won a Pulitzer for a 1949 cartoon warning that the world was now teetering towards annihilation.

Harry Hershfield's and Rube Goldberg's only true counterpart in Jewish comic strip status and antic humor was Milt Gross, the artist, dialect humorist, and creator of *He Done Her Wrong* (1930), the first graphic novel published in the US and one of the first anywhere. Born in 1895, raised in the Bronx, Gross joined the *New York World* as an office boy, skipped higher education, and began commercial art straightaway in one of the very first animation studios, meanwhile turning out random strips and panels. The *World* handed him a full Sunday comics page in 1918 and he gained overnight celebrity status. Another fanatical worker, Gross managed to draw or script up to a dozen comic strips simultaneously during the 1920s, producing an astonishing array of sight-and-sound gags. *Count Screwloose of Toulouse, Dave's Delicatessen*, and *Banana Oil* (whose title quickly became the punchline of the day, the permitted equivalent of "Bullshit!") each had an abundance of crazy characters and fantastic elements, a wild scrap with the logic of contemporary urban life. But the strip that he made into a comic literary volume, offering an infinite series of language gags, lifted him up to another level of celebrity. Through *Nize Baby,* a collection of his *World* pieces, he truly found his poetic métier.

Gross had his characters abandon gentle ribbing, within the usual comic fashion, for sheer comic pathos. The sharp phonetic jokes that Yiddish speakers could read in the *Groysser Kundes* of the 1910s, like the poet who upon drifting into pure slapstick sentimentalism becomes "a reglar Sharlie Shaplin," in *Nize Baby* is rendered the all-important Baby Isidor, "a Cholly Chepman." Around him, the Three Stooges theater of comic cruelty ruled:

> "So, Isidor!!! Benenas you swipe from de pushcart; ha? (SMACK). A Cholly Chepman you'll grow opp, maybe, ha? (SMACK!) I'll give you (SMACK!). Do I (SMACK!) swipe? Does de momma (SMACK!) swipe? From who you loin dis (SMACK!)?"

Isidor never learns (or loins).

Nize Baby was a self-illustrated best-seller in the era just before sound movies found the Three Stooges. The similarity is not altogether accidental, but Gross was more incisive. After all, Gross had creative control of his material. Yet *He Done Her Wrong* retitled *Hearts of Gold: The Great American Novel,* surely would have been better done a decade earlier when sound pictures were nowhere in immediate prospect. A tale of the Yukon with a wronged beauty, an exceptionally stupid-looking muscular hero, and a brilliant cad of the Oil Can Harry variety who convinces her that her true love is dead and lures her into the city, the saga has her saved after seemingly endless misadventures and near-miss reconciliations with her soul mate. (Perhaps the best part is the ending for the villain: the polygamist is forcibly turned over to six betrayed wives, all of them awaiting his return with a rolling pin in hand.) In any case, *Hearts of Gold* marked the beginning of a downward trend for Gross. Increasingly deprived of his newspaper readers and lacking Hershfield's and Goldberg's other outlets, he drew his own strange comic books without much success.

The initial descent of these giants as the great figures of the funny pages coincided with the famed 1929 stock market nosedive. Their continuing strips offered a glimpse of the persistent wildness in early comic strip styles confined and almost obliterated by the advancing stylization. Changing tastes that can be attributed to the craving for a middle-class (but also more realistic, cinematic) "look" demanded another kind of Jewish artist.

The ranks of the famed funny pages artists of the 1930s and 40s, including

Chester Gould, Hal Foster, and Milt Caniff, contained few Jews and embodied a decidedly conservative style and emphasis in tune with the WASP suspicions of Franklin Roosevelt and social change generally. Ham Fisher, who drew *Joe Palooka*, and Fisher's sometime assistant Al Capp, were exceptions in some respects but by no means entirely. Fisher placed himself right at the center of the mainstream in the sustained narration, day-by-day story development (however achingly slow) highlighted by the Sunday strip. Capp, a Brooklyn-born lad raised in New Haven with the stigma of a wooden leg, made an imaginative leap into the supposed Appalachian culture of Dogpatch and its inhabitants. Although the folkish art of the New Deal era honored the very culture that he disparaged, Capp considered himself a New Dealer until after the war when, like a certain type of liberal, he began a trek toward the distant Right. A handful of his lesser characters, from General Bullmoose (styled after the antiunion General Motors Chairman of the Board, "General" Bulwar) to the hapless Schmoo (whose edible body promised a cornucopia bordering on socialism – if only humankind could use resources intelligently), arguably the last glimpses of his left-of-center jabs, meanwhile became staples in the popular imagination. His other greatest contribution may have been a Hershfield-like lampoon of the action-adventure drama, through the misadventures of a Dick Tracey type. Most of the time, it was hackwork, sampler for a commercial.[8]

Capp also displayed a meanness absent from the first generation of Jewish comic artists, his visuals and dialogue not only ridiculing familiar gendered elements of rural (i.e., American) culture, but above all the mom image. Hell on wheels, more powerful than either lazy pop and immature son, Capp's Mammy Yokum may well have inspired the stereotypes soon etched in acid by another not so different Jewish intellectual, Philip Wylie, in *Generation of Vipers* (1943), a phenomenal misogynist best-seller. Capp may be seen as a trendsetter in another important way: he was never much interested in the art element. Practically from his earliest successes he turned over most of the daily work to uncredited assistants, interesting himself more in the packaging of his images for a variety of consumer items. No doubt growing up yearning for the status of Yalies and the coeds that they wooed, Capp had never had much else on his mind but becoming a success. By the 1950s, he could count notable Cold War liberals (such as Arthur Schlesinger, Jr., who wrote the introduction to one of his collections) as his biggest fans. A decade later, he had become a frightened and vicious old man, lashing out at peaceniks (Joan Baez became Joanie Phony, and all young protesters were drawn dirty – an echo of the "dirty Jew" canard he heard as a child?) while taking advantage of naive Republican coeds.

Eventually he was arrested for rape and sodomy, ending his personal crusade for campus values.

The issues of style and politics were larger than personalities, of course. Hershfield, Goldberg, and Gross were not simply the victims of a diminished public imagination for the printed sight and word gag. What the comic strip gained in technical expertise during the 1930s and 40s, it lost in imaginative content. A rare conservative comics scholar who praises the triumph in artistic day-to-day story continuity and identifies with the distinctly middle-class, idealized version of realism, nevertheless observes that the change signaled a visual and thematic blandness within the funny pages.[9]

What *Buck Rogers* (or *Flash Gordon*), *Blondie*, and *Little Orphan Annie* lacked, among other things, was the residual humanist flavor of *Yiddishkayt* or anything resembling the reflexive self-consciousness of many earlier (and some later) Jewish strips. Standard adventurers *Captain Easy*, *Smilin' Jack*, and Terry of *Terry and the Pirates* like so many others, heroically commandeered the underdeveloped zones of the world that included lots of funny-looking people and a few exotic femme fatales, along with a sampling of good natives eager to serve their racial superiors. It was also, notably, a *Judenrein* (Jewless) world.

In comics like these, gender set the rules more absolutely than for Abie the Agent and his Golden Reba, who subtly ruled: the sex war here persists, but white American tomboys grow up to become exquisitely feminine, hopelessly in love with two-fisted male heroes. (The occasional female protagonist like Winnie Winkle, at the center of their own strips' heavily gendered attention, remained amazingly feminine even under the most extreme circumstances.) If there were amazing exceptions to this large rule within the funny papers mainstream – *Krazy Kat* or *Popeye*, not to mention the frankly surrealistic *Smokey Stover* and by the 1950s, even *Pogo* – the exceptions were not Jewish, and creative artistic energy was almost certainly elsewhere.

THE BLOODY PULPS, THE DEPRESSION, AND THE JEWISH INTELLECTUAL

It's amusing as well as informative to observe how much of American popular culture outside Manhattan and Hollywood, even the rebellious elements of popular culture from the nineteenth century to around 1930, was demonstrably Gentile precisely because the regiments of rebels would never again be lacking in plentiful Jews and Jewishness. Pulp literature offers a first example, as the earliest case of the suspect lower-class culture given literary form. From the 1850s onward, penny story papers, the earliest of fictional tabloids, practically flooded the market with melodrama, often the preliminary version of soft-core, and hard-core, pornography with innocents all but ravished by villains and saved by heroes. Yellow Backs, early cheap novel editions bearing the same kind of stories but also joined by thousands of the original Westerns with tough-talking cowboys literally riding rough shod over the otherwise unconquered range, had huge contemporary readerships from the 1850s onward.

Rebellious hints were ever-present, from the Ricardian Socialist novels of George Lippard in the 1840s savaging the rich for their immorality, to the minor genres of labor romances during the tumultuous 1880s.[10] But race and sex lines held firm, despite the occasional female pirate or noble Indian. In the Protestant and middle-class version of American life, the detective (a type invented in part by Edgar Allan Poe, but first sweepingly popular during the 1880s) Cap Collier tracks down Jewish-looking subversives – led by the seductive Jewess – threatening to plant bombs and to disrupt the good relations between well-meaning bosses and their all-too-credulous workers. In the adventure story, perfected by Jack London during the early years of the next century, likewise in the sentimental seduction novel reworked to explain the evils of prostitution as products of capitalist corruption and in the social muckraking literature like Upton Sinclair's *The Jungle,* denunciations of existing conditions at last found legitimacy and large audiences. Immigrant Jews by the thousands eagerly read such works in Yiddish translation or in the original.

Until the 1930s, however, the deeply Jewish best-sellers were most often enjoyed in the newspaper pages of the Yiddish press. It is difficult now to grasp the significance of the one-column story for the 150,000 readers of the *Forverts* and the reverence in which the writers were held (except, of course, by a cash-stingy management). Leon Kobin, B. Gorin, the little capmaker Z. Libin, and at least a dozen others wrenched tragedy and humor out of the East Side suffering, unrequited longing (for nature, for sex, for normal family life), rage at the system which persecuted them and at the fellow Jews who profited from it. As time went on and the writers along with the readers became more sophisticated, naturalism acquired more depth, and many of the stories gained a lighter touch. The calamity of the First World War and the suffering of European relatives set a keen edge of irony upon the advance of consumerist pleasures, even cheap ones like a day at the beach or the cooled air of a movie theater. Materialism, a fact of life now based on a modest prosperity, was all the more suspect, subjected to

Socialist critiques and to ancient visions of the golden day, as well as the living memories of the egalitarian sharing in a vanishing (and partly mythical) *shtetl* community.

In the aftermath of sharp disillusionment with the First World War, increasingly felt not only by immigrant Jews but by the American public at large, popular literature began to take a shape more suitable to the fusion of iconoclasm and popular art.[11] Of the "bloody pulps" deplored by the gentility as bringing down the readers' cultural aspirations, the sensationalistic *Black Mask* practically invented noir, a genre about the darkness of modern life. It made former Pinkerton detective Dashiell Hammett, forever linked with his largely Jewish circle in anti-capitalist sentiment, into a major creative force in American fiction and soon film. It thereby extended the limits of bottom-rung literature to include veritable cities of evildoers destined to die in literary bloodbaths, deaths as pointless in their way as the Great War, which had come to seem repulsive and meaningless to most of the nation by 1922 or so. In short, it turned the "invader" or "dangerous stranger" narrative inside out; now the stranger was the victim of the community which did not want or deserve to be redeemed through heroics or any other action. It would provide a perfect frame for Jewish artists suffering a second or third disillusionment, this one from the collapse of egalitarian hopes for America with the outbreak of cold war.

Meanwhile, toward the end of the 1920s, the first of the science fiction pulp magazines was born, and by the early 1930s, along with the Hollywood fan magazines and detective or crime magazines, filled out a large zone of the booming newsstands. The science fiction magazines had a buoyant side and juvenile qualities, the bug-eyed monsters that predictably (especially on the covers of the magazine) threatened scantily dressed earth women. But science fiction and its sister fantasy pulps, notably *Weird Tales*, had another side. Younger writers, hit hard by the Depression, had often been escapists in the first place, never much in sympathy with the society that had crashed. Thus Frederik Pohl, a Gentile among mostly Jewish peers, recalls the Futurians of the later 1930s as exemplars of the moods among budding pulp writers of the time. A dozen or so bright lads including Isaac Asimov gathered to publish their own ephemeral mimeo texts, share experiences at getting their stories published (or not published) at penny-per-word rates, and speculating on the more "scientific" future awaiting in a postcapitalist world.[12]

The adolescent milieu only lasted a few years, but it created much of the infrastructure of the emerging SciFi world of editors, their publishers, and a generous share of the stock of writers who would dominate the field well into the 1950s. In large part this literary ghetto continued to be a field of BEMs, stories badly written and often just as badly edited, produced on the model of any mass literary output, by formula wrung thin with constant use, and sadly, in large part, as conservative as comic strip characters swashbuckling through Asia and Africa. Adventurers straight out of the old western pulps now advanced into space where they encountered creatures who might be made of any imaginable molecular structure but needed conquering, just as the dames on the cover of the magazines needed rescuing, in endless repetition. The moon shot of 1970 finally wore down the SciFi press, along with the nagging weight of television competition, until only a few of the most hardy pulps survived.

But SciFi was always, to some extent, also a world of naysayers and lyrical fantasists, and here the spark of Jewish otherness could most often be found. Not until the 1970s would writers stake an avowed claim to Jewishness. The liberal idea that science had a happy ending different from corporate marketing continued to mark the vision of Isaac Asimov, the most prolific and best-read writer of the field. But even Asimov glimpsed what others saw more clearly, the darker notion that the misuse of science for profits and power might plunge all humanity, along with the earth's flora and fauna, into destruction. The themes of supercorporations taking over the public classrooms, of guiding a futuristic interplanetary system with the same old business values, the suggestion that current standards (or double standards) of love and marriage might make no sense in some other worlds, were all voiced or written in ways that reached the adolescent, innocent, and apolitical reader like myself.[13]

In a career sense, pulp writing never ceased to be a lousy way to make a living, demanding a massive outpouring of words. For the lucky and the exceptionally skilled, a ticket to better things like films (usually low-budget films) and television beckoned. For the unlucky or less talented, it was at the least a world of increasingly organized interest amid the fans of fandom who published a growing number of mimeoed magazines, and mounted conventions that honored otherwise unrecognized figures of the field. Fandom was never a particularly Jewish thing, but there was something strangely familiar about the campy and theatrical costuming of crowds gathered around the celebration of the fantastic.

Out of the pulps as much as the comic strips had come the comic book. This story goes back to the early 1930s and the inventive bundling of Sunday strips into book-reprint form, and to one extremely curious figure: Max Gaines. A politically liberal German immigrant with a Jewish wife – and a son, William, who would launch *Mad*, certainly the most Jewish and easily among the most influential comics ever – Max worked as a struggling salesman living in the Bronx. He chanced upon the idea of selling booklets of reprints to assorted companies like Wheatena or Canada Dry, which would give away the booklets as promotions. As a trial balloon, he adventurously put a few hundred copies of *Famous Funnies* (1934) on newsstands with a dime price. Soon, he took the idea to another company, using some spare presses at *McClure's* and adding one original strip by a Jewish seventeen-year-old named Sheldon Mayer. By 1937, just as Gaines was looking at the prospects of a small, independent company that had been the first to produce an entire book of original material, Mayer spotted a unique strip by a couple of Cleveland Jewish teenagers. It was *Superman.*

Here the narrative turns to Cleveland's deeply ethnic East Side, a few years earlier. Adolescents Jerry Siegel and Joe Shuster were honing their talents on the high school paper, along with equally hungry for success classmates who would in the future write scripts for *Howdy Doody*, pen *Auntie Mame, How To Succeed in Business Without Really Trying*, and *Inherit the Wind*, and edit *Seventeen* (another became a manager of Liberace).[14] They had their eyes on prizes. But it was by no means unusual in 1932, at the depths of the Depression, for such Jewish youngsters also to be socialistic, if less likely in Cleveland than, say, Washington Heights, Manhattan. Everyone was looking for a superpower of some kind to save society, and Siegel first penned a fictional "The Reign of Superman" on the aftermath of the elections. Possibly he had Socialist candidate Norman Thomas in mind; Thomas, a great Jewish favorite, got almost a million votes, more than any Socialist since 1912, albeit far less than expected by his followers. Jewish idealists in the next few years turned, almost unanimously, to Franklin Roosevelt.

Meanwhile, the Clark Kent-like Siegel, a bit shy socially and considerably less than muscle-bound, literally dreamed up the two-sided character from a distant planet, armed with superpowers and even X-ray vision.[15] Given the poverty of the family, his collaborator, Shuster, was said to have made the first Superman drawings on leftover wrapping paper and the reverse side of wallpaper samples. On no budget, Siegel somehow managed to put out a mimeographed SciFi magazine titled *Cosmic Stories.* That was their first step in publishing. [16]

In 1936, they sent off their *Dr. Occult* to *New Fun Comics*, then renamed the character Dr. Mystic for *The Comics Magazine*. The same Sheldon Mayer, doing the pasteup of Gaines's repackaged *Popular Comics*, was spending his time arduously stripping newspaper material and then placing it in comic book format but also acting like a future executive on the lookout for talent. In Shuster and Siegel, he found it. Gaines, looking to make a deal with another publisher of comics, proposed the superhero with the red cape. Gaines's new partner was dubious, but then the kid buyers went wild, demanding more comics with "that superman hero." As news dealers begged for more, one of popular culture's leading icons had been set into place.

In return for that first feature, the art and story team signed over all the rights along with thirteen pages of *Superman*. They were paid $130. Eventually, they made several hundred thousand dollars at a cost of being fired and losing all control of their creation, which made and continues to make vast fortunes in merchandise of all kinds. Siegel, the more determined of the pair, later scripted an exceptionally dark comic strip: *The Spectre*, a dead cop in the suspiciously familiar-sounding city of Cliffland, who talked with the deity, got crime clues from departed souls, and personally laid waste to criminals. It was no success and one in a long series of disappointments after the boyish creation of the great superhero.[17]

Superman outgrew his creators overnight. Pulp publishing had suddenly entered a new era and the businessmen moved in. Comic books had been coming along, gradually and in small way, in any case. With the Depression easing, millions of kids had the dime necessary, and something would be needed to fill the pages. Though up to 1937, nearly all of it remained either reprints or imitations of newspaper strips. *Superman* imitators spun off literally hundreds of male and a couple dozen female characters during the genre's own golden age, which ended by the early 1950s with the spread of television. *Superman*'s success also introduced the comic book sweatshop of badly paid artists and scripters in Greater Manhattan, most of them Jewish and young.

One Jack S. Liebowitz, like a garment manufacturer of an earlier generation discovering a new territory, had no small role in the coming consolidation and attendant exploitation. Born in the Ukraine in 1900, growing up in the Lower East Side, he went into the magazine distribution business almost by instinct. Soon, he teamed up with Harry Donenfeld, a successful publisher of the most lurid pulp magazines of the time. Through the insiders' route of first publishing similarly glossy covers on comic books – with sex and violence stylized and domesticated – the partners struck a gold mine. They established Detective Comics and thereby invented the future company logo, DC. Here, *Batman* first appeared. Donenfeld launched *Action Comics*, and for that purpose personally bought *Superman* from Siegel and Shuster. He was also a partner in All-American Comics, those purveyors of *The Flash*, *Green Lantern*, and most notably, *Wonder Woman*.

But it was former accountant Liebowitz, who was shrewd enough to turn his acquired property from others' brainpower into films and television swiftly, after the golden age of comics had crested.

What kind of businessman was Liebowitz? Like a garment manufacturer without a union contesting him, the comics giant fought Siegel and Shuster across decades of litigation, refusing to yield an inch or dollar. When a settlement was finally reached he was ordered to pay twenty thousand dollars per year (later thirty thousand dollars) to the aged creators who had made him so many millions. In the meantime, he also led DC through its legal action against *Superman* rival *Captain Marvel*, finally succeeding in the suppression of the rather more comical figure (or rather the living duality, Marvel and his human teenage alter ego, Billy Batson, who had to utter the acronym SHAZAM to make the change). Simultaneously a noted figure in the Jewish philanthropical community, Liebowitz remained an active board member at Warner Communications (later Time Warner) until he retired at ninety. In short, Liebowitz was truly a man of his generation. Others had seen comics as a fad or a low-yield enterprise: he saw them as potential big business.[18]

Surely no worse than art business moguls, ruthless figures like Liebowitz definitely set a limit on the status of the comic book artist and probably on the work as well. Art Spiegelman was to observe, decades after the golden age, that if *Krazy Kat* and *Little Nemo* had been finally accepted into the pantheon of modernism and given real respect (he might have added his own work to this list), the lowly comic book seemed destined never to get that kind of respect.[19] The business bounced back repeatedly, but never achieved anything like dignity for its artists, and usually remained a factory production line for those who did the work. As an old-timer once told Spiegelman, mental breakdowns, alcoholism, and such symptoms were common here, by-products of long hours, stress, and repetitive tasks. To last fifteen years in the trade was a long time, even if the combination of factors wiping out most of the business had not decimated comics by the mid-1950s. Many artists hoped for careers in advertising that they never achieved. More than one made a meager living in later years freelancing for *Playboy*, and more than one chose suicide, by faster or (more usually) slower routes.[20]

A decisive contrast to the Liebowitz type could be found in the combination of creator and promoters. Sheldon Mayer, now little remembered outside the fan press, was still a teenager when he began drawing the very first of the superman satires *Scribbly*, a hero more often in trouble with the cops – or his mother – than rescuing the endangered. At a tender age, he took the editorial chair in All-American Comics. Mayer is credited with being the first to package different superheroes as a team, the Justice Society of America. In the same years, his supersatire *Red Tornado* proved to be even better. "Ma" Hunkel, who ran the neighborhood grocery store, also put on a pair of red long johns, a cape, and a saucepan and became the scourge of neighborhood crime. Mayer went on to draw the much-beloved *Sugar and Spike*, a kids' comic about the 1950s that responded to the success of *Dennis the Menace* with a view of the world as seen by kids themselves. A pioneer in this region of popular art, Mayer ended as a kindly figure with what might be called the Carl Barks touch (the much-admired work done in the adventures of Donald and his three nephews, that is), exploring the widening sensibilities of young readers without condescension.

No doubt the war had a major impact in the craving for the *Blue Beetle*, the *Green Mask*, the *Flash*, *Hawkman*, the *Human Torch*, the *Sub-Mariner* (similar to my personal favorite as a kid: *Aquaman*), a sort of Johnny Appleseed of the ocean, who got the sea creatures on his side in return for defending them), the *Green Arrow*, the *Green Mask*, and the rest. If violence needed a new sanction, the daily reports of military action provided plenty. But before the war, from the very first appearance of *Superman*, it was already apparent that children, boys in particular, craved a visual fantasy of the power that they lacked in the world around them. There were destined to be no super-Jews, but perhaps some readers really could intuit "Jewish" from the Cleveland adolescents' wild projections. An essayist later observed that the character of Superman would, despite his renown and super-strength, always remain Jewish because he "will always be of Krypton, subject to laws … foreign to his countrymen" and no matter how apparently assimilated he is as Clark Kent, "haunted by a past [that] he relives over and over" as he fights for Truth, Justice, and the American Way.[21] Perhaps some Jewish boys took the subliminal hints, but it seems highly doubtful that Gentile readers ever saw the Supe that way.

Meanwhile, down in the real-life comics sweatshops, early hopes for unions and improvement of conditions were brushed away, pressures for more intensive hack work multiplied. Among several hundred now for-gotten artists, another Bronx genius emerged: Bob Kane, who, at the tender age of eighteen, created *Batman*, in 1939, in collaboration with writer Bill Finger. Later generations were inclined to see Kane's art as Expressionist, but probably the first readers, if they lacked the vocabulary, already found it brilliantly dark in motif and implications. In *Batman* as in film noir – but earlier and more like the weirdest of Weimar film of the 1920s – inanimate objects loom strangely huge in size while human figures shrink, living their adventures in the shadows.

An exceptionally thoughtful figure, Kane later recalled the sting of the Depression and the wasted talents of the vast majority of his colleagues in a field that no one took seriously, especially when it came to dialogue, plots, and narrative structure. Kane had, he dolefully recalled, "crossed off content" as hopeless and put his energy into form. It was an uncharacteristically candid observation, from an artist who had been frustrated or self-frustrated for nearly all his creative life. But thoughtful Jewish writers of all kinds of popular materials, from potboiler novels to superficial musicals to movies, could say more or less the same. Those who made the transition from artist to businessman (emphatically including master artist-entrepreneur Will Eisner) enforced the code that an adventure comic allowed only a certain style and sequence for the expected market.[22] One of the most talented, Kane found himself in what he considered a backwater for the artist who couldn't escape into advertising, or didn't want to, and didn't find some other way out. He practiced, then, the Expressionism of the innocent, the angularity of the constant pursuit, the somber hues of Gotham City and visual weirdness of villains like the Penguin and the Joker.

If we ask whether *Batman* is somehow the Jewish creation of an artist with memories still in the Bronx, we might better ask why he is so endlessly iconic. An ordinary physical being with no apparent superpowers, Batman lacked Superman's alien origins but also the good cheer that the defender of the American way occasionally managed to express along with righteous determination. It's not that Batman's characters are, in themselves, even particularly interesting (scripter Bill Finger was clearly the weak side of the team), although the Congressional hearings into comics accused the dynamic duo of a hinted homosexual relationship, but that the atmosphere of gloom surrounding the "weird figure of the dark" (as the first installment of Batman in 1938 put it) simply could not be dispelled by any sort of happy ending.

Kane was also simply one part of a production team. He had the good luck, after an early phase with Fleischer animation studios, to move over to the Eisner-Iger shop. The less-remembered partner, Samuel "Jerry" Iger, born at the turn of the century, had done assorted work before setting up the S.J. Iger firm in 1939, as a master of administration. The more famous partner was Will Eisner, who was to introduce a cinematic reach into comics and thereby transform the field, during the 1940s, in ways analogous to the Gershwins' introduction of the integrated music and book on Broadway. Leaping technologically ahead in his microcosm, Eisner integrated filmic views and the comic form. No artist offers a more dramatic contrast to Kane's innocence and art-centeredness.

Eisner, another Bronx boy but notably the son of a small garment manufacturer, apparently always considered himself in equal parts entrepreneur and artist. He located, trained, and underpaid talent, ranging from a somewhat experienced Kane in the early 1940s to a completely inexperienced Jules Feiffer a half-decade later. As Eisner rewrote his own story, in effect, through a series of graphic novels published during the 1970s and 80s, his was a lower-middle-class world struggling for recovery from the Crash, with its good and innocent folk dogged by bad characters, criminals, and their political counterparts, Red union organizers. (He later characterized the differences among his studio's artists as "Socialism and anti-Socialism."[23]) But this was mostly hindsight. Until the Cold War, real-life Eisner was surrounded by sentiments around him of unionism, social solidarity, and the Jewish Left; his own work was serialized in *PM*, the radical spirit among New York's major dailies.

Eisner found his own inspired creation with *The Spirit*, in an eight-page weekly comic book distributed through newspapers beginning in 1940. It was a brilliant marketing stroke and an instant success. Thought dead but actually living in a cemetery, this masked hero was beloved by police and feared by outlaws. In addition to assorted villains and a very Irish police captain, the Spirit is surrounded by "characters," from campily caricatured femme fatales to a diminutive African-American assistant (inevitably named Ebony) straight out of minstrelsy. With a dash of humor and wartime patriotism, it might have been an attractive mixture in any case. But Eisner looked at the comic strip in a new way, as if from the eye of the movie camera; his angles shifted wildly from panel to panel, and the texture, thanks to a compulsive "feathering," made for a subtlety tenderly mocking the pseudo-realism of the usual newspaper comics.[24]

The downside of the hard-headed entrepreneur's perspective was never absent. *The Spirit* frankly appealed to prejudices as raw as the white sentiment towards nonwhites, of the ridicule of funny fatties, effeminate men, and masculine-looking women, ugly foreigners, and after 1945, Russians of all possible types. They looked worse under Eisner's pen than in the mocking caricatures of other strips because of their comic strip variety realism, with neat human proportions or disproportions. Crime in his perception had no social causes, nor could any kind of opposition to the "American way." When comics began to fade, Eisner set up a military contracting enterprise and stayed with it until an early retirement. A subsequent revival of comics brought his own memorable return, both his own expanded (and reprinted earlier) work and his substantial documentation of American comic art. By that time, his appreciation for the accomplishments of underground comix artists – notwithstanding his vehement rejection of all the political and social values they held – demonstrated his own catholicity and his eagerness to play Dutch uncle to the makers of a new phase of graphic art. The Eisner awards came to play the role of film Oscars in a field where the remunerative benefits had never improved very much.

Indeed, one has only to read the recollections of assorted comic book artists barely younger than him to realize what Eisner the artist and Eisner the editor and publisher did for the field in its early decades. Comic books in Eisner's entrepreneurial days were still decades away from artistic maturity, and Eisner had no role in the more oddball and educational end that marked other promising avenues for Jewish artists' expression. But within his limited sphere, he successfully nudged the industry along from the prewar into the postwar era when ninety percent of American children between the ages of eight and fifteen were said to read comic books regularly.

Eisner and Iger had actually begun as a packaging shop, creating photo-ready copy to order for various comic titles that publishers put out under their own imprints. Eisner allowed his partner to buy him out in 1939, so as to gain more creative control and publish the cash cow newspaper supplement of *The Spirit*. Iger, handling the hack work, notably churned out new lady stars straight out of what was expected to be the interplanetary era of the 1970s, heroines and heroes traveling around scenes that looked like a ruined Miami Beach or Hollywood, in a world apparently wrecked by Fascism, and wearing mighty skimpy clothes to protect what was left of it.[25]

This was a propitious moment, with Eisner by no means the only creative force. In 1940, the largest number of enduring heroes, ever, first saw the light. That year readers gobbled down newly minted characters Flashman, Hawkman, Captain Marvel, the Skyman, the Face, and the Cloak and dozens more, down to the Purple Zombie, Black Owl, the Green Lama, and the miniscule Doll Man, a sort of human Mighty Mouse in an otherwise full-sized world.[26] Unlike Hollywood, where more and more films suggested the existential reality of Jews in the US and Europe, these comics remained virtually absent of ethnicity – at least American ethnicity, as its heroes battled funny-looking foreigners along with the usual bad guys. And unlike the movies, it was exceptionally hard here to separate the military antifascist theme from personal contempt for German, Italian, and Japanese leaders and followers (with the caricatures of Japanese people especially racist, almost to the point of eliciting violence). Comic book patriotism was rarely dialectical.

Behind the patriotic bluster, some subtle minds and pens could be detected. Richard Briefer (aka Dick Floyd), born in 1915, began work at the Iger studio and is remembered for his contributions to *Crime Does Not Pay*, a million sales per month series that is regarded as the most noirish of nonfiction crime accounts.[27] Briefer considered Mary Shelley his foremost influence, and turned at the first opportunity from conventional work to his own pet Frankenstein satire in 1940. Like the Abbott and Costello send-ups of horror films just a few years later, it used the knowledge (in this case also the intuitive sympathy of the audience for the creature) as a source of humor. Briefer's Frankenstein (he even used "Frank N. Stein" as his nom de plume) was a bumbling fellow, a giant with a small head, surrounded by educated would-be savants who are closer to nincompoops. As "Dick Floyd," Briefer simultaneously drew *Pinky Rankin* for the *Daily Worker*, another comical but more human character who needed to teach the lessons of Socialism through social solidarity, again and again, to fellow workers and others. In tune with the McCarthy Era, Briefer later drifted to horror comics during the 1950s, and hardly outlasted the worst of the Red scare.[28]

Behind Briefer in the comic line stood a veritable army of "funny animal" artists, those who helped comics grow out of the humor strip newspaper reprints of 1930s and the sterile heroes of the war years, and would carry them far beyond during the bad years of the 1950s. In a sense, the funny animal lines had been the most thoroughly monopolized from the appearance of *Mickey Mouse Magazine*, because Walt Disney's animated film triumphs and his eye for packaging (as well as notorious underpayment of his own artists) put the Disney empire way in front. *Mickey Mouse Magazine* was more an anthology-style kids' magazine than a comic, but the appearance of the Mouse and Donald Duck in the daily and Sunday funnies as well as much related merchandise gave them more visibility than any other comic book character was likely to gain.

Walt Disney's Comics and Stories (the only comic named after a CEO, an unwarranted namesake: he didn't draw the comics or write the stories inside[29]) appeared in 1940, many of its covers drawn by the young Walt Kelly. Among other funny comic lines, Sheldon Mayer personally edited All-American's animal books and did a fair amount of the drawing (including a recycled *Mutt and Jeff*, bringing back the oldest major pair of the daily newspaper strips). Milt Gross, at the end of his long career, had his own *Milt Gross Funnies*, and Stan Kaye (collaborating with later-famed SciFi novelist Alfred Bester) invented a *Gyro Gearloose*-like *Genius Jones* as haywire Henry Ford. By the end of the war, teenager comics (several of them conceived by yet another Jewish youngster barely out of his own teens, Dan Gordon) leaped into production. These comics, with the exception of Milt

Gross's under appreciated efforts, weren't actually very funny. And not all that many of the artists of the funny animals were Jewish, an odd detail to say the least. But as Kurtzman recalled, the new generation was training itself through close observation of popular culture, from newspapers and films to comics, at once analyzing and satirizing the details of commercialism. Their day was coming.[30]

Until then, it was mostly a matter of technique and especially boldness with color schemes that made artists themselves admire the especially talented among them. Lou Fine, considered one of the finest draftsmen, was a blue-collar New Yorker who trained at Grand Central Art School where he picked up that rare (for comics artists) skill of feathering with a Japanese brush, giving more to *The Ray* in *Smash Comics* than most of his readers likely noticed. His Flame, another favorite character, could materialize out of smoke and fire, and worked with an equally ethereal Flame Girl. Fine's high point arrived when Eisner went into the army and Fine (kept out of service by a crippled leg) took over the strip, adding still more garishness to it.[31]

The young artist abandoned comics for work at an advertising agency shortly after the war, transforming his style in the process and all but abandoning its most original touches. Perhaps, his friends suggested, he had actually wanted to be an illustrator in the bygone age of the great illustrators. Returning to daily comic strips in the 1960s, he retrained himself to draw as if he were just one more of the realists who cranked out *The Heart of Juliet Jones*, scripted by Al Capp's businessman brother, Elliott Caplan.[32] In the high times of the 1940s especially, Fine's talent prompted scant admiration beyond his own circle because skill was at no particular premium: sales were huge and critics few. In 1943, twenty-five million comics were printed monthly. Two years later, sales reached 102 percent, signifying the purchase of damaged copies, i.e., anything that looked like a fresh book. DC itself was selling something like twenty-five million comic books in each fiscal quarter.[33]

ODD ART

What remained, then, of artistic interest in the work of the 1940s was mainly the strange, odd, misshapen, and otherwise semiconsciously reflective. A wonderful example is so-called Good Girl Art that offered up semi-naked heroines obviously attractive to preadolescent boys and evidently to some girls as well. Take the *Blonde Phantom* as drawn by Syd Shores: a conservatively dressed secretary by day who then let down her hair, donned a low-cut dress, traded her glasses for a black domino mask, and solved crimes that baffled the authorities. Or the "headlight" comics of jungle goddesses armed only with knives and clothed only in bikinis, fending off wild animals and protecting evidently helpless males. Eisner and Iger's first joint product had in fact been none other than the *Jumbo Comics* that introduced Sheena, the semiclad jungle girl, to eager boyish (no doubt including GI) readers.

Some of the most fascinating examples looked like an extended version of SciFi pulp covers: *Planet Comics* thus offered women of the future, simply stunning in their metal bras, shorts, and gun belts, as the first comic ever devoted solely to SciFi. It was also the chief purveyor of Good Girl Art, until *Planet's* 1953 demise. The post-Eisner Iger shop continued to produce some of the most garish ones, like *Rulah, Jungle Goddess*. Iger artist Alex Schomberg also drew a space-pirate lady or two who looked suspiciously like Sheena gone interplanetary. Perhaps the most notable trait of a few of these feminine futurists was not the shapely girl rocketeers but the ruined America of the 1970s.[34]

Some comics, never more than a handful, aimed higher. The elder Gaines sought to make *Stories from the Bible* his métier. In 1941 *Classic Comics* was launched by former salesman and small-time manufacturer, Albert Kanter. The comic was inspired by a wave of public rage at the supposed ill effects of action comics upon the juvenile mind, and coinciding with an early series of HUAC hearings, aimed at pinpointing subversive Jewish influences in Hollywood. *Classic* was obviously intended to do well by doing good. Some critics suggested that success might be due at least in part to the discovery that book reports for school could be based upon skimming *Classics* (a sort of visual CliffsNotes). And they were badly drawn for the first several years, by especially underpaid artists. Then Iger took over production for a decade, the finest of the run, including the title change in 1947 to *Classics Illustrated* by which they are best remembered for dozens of titles and hundreds of millions of copies. It's where I read *William Tell* and imbibed the idealism of the historic struggle against aristocratic privilege.

Classics were, in style, fairly close to the Catholic magazine *Treasure Chest's* comic section, which was drawn rather realistically even if frequently treating martyrs with grisly fates like boiling in oil. *Classics* never showed this taste for violence, and the painstaking re-creation of literary plots no doubt took a toll upon the artistic imagination. Yet they were, for readers, an easy road into the originals and more than that, they were educational for children who would never delve into those sources. Close in this sense to the illustrated Young Readers editions of the same classics, they genuinely treated children like grownups-to-be. According to anecdotal evidence, some of them, especially the tales of rebellion, from *Robin Hood* to *William Tell*, were sometimes scripted by blacklist victims seeking work.[35]

Unlike other comics, the *Classics* titles also had the advantage of being essentially ageless (they were kept in print and reprinted as the market offered promise). And their competition in self-described educational comics was weak: *True Comics*, edited by Elliott Caplin, were stodgy and unexciting. Similar experiments like *Real Heroes* and *Real Fact Comics* also fell flat.[36]

Most comic books were not nearly that serious or inventive. The champion survivor, as the congressional investigations demonized publishers and as television swallowed up much of the audience, turned out to be the artist-entrepreneur with more staying power than Eisner. Jack Kirby, born Jacob Kirtzberg, the son of Jewish immigrants, could be described as the reinventor of comics after their first death. Kirby late in life observed to an interviewer that "Jewish artists and writers were those people who lived by the stories told them by their relatives," and that Jewish storytellers were naturally the founders of comic books.[37] The deeper meaning of a more obviously commercial story was clear from the beginning.

Kirby practically began with Eisner and Iger in 1937, after a spell doing animation in the abysmal factorylike conditions of the Fleischer studios. Self-taught, "with no role models except the people I met" and no serious aspiration except success, the young artist took rapidly to the professionalism of the new field.[38] A former street brawler, from the beginning Kirby embraced a sort of lyric mayhem, what he called the "beauty in violence" and in competition with the filmic version of violence and action, by portraying people (almost invariably men) posed against each other in the most extreme physical situations. It was, as Eisner recalled, something new in comic book formula; previously, everything including the violence had come out of the storyline, however limited that might be. Kirby was "competing with the movie camera," not as films developed narratives but rather as they leaped out of the stories and directly into the imaginations of the audience.[39] Ironically, the outcry against comic book violence by critics of the field had helped suppress everything *but* the violence of the re-emerging superheroes.

Leading comics scholar Ron Goulart sympathetically calls these qualities of Kirby's a "freshness and energy in his work," the "excitement of heroes who were less like Batman or Superman than like super-stuntmen, wild with action."[40] By the time he was drafted into the infantry of World War

II, Kirby and his collaborator Joe Simon had already invented *Captain America*, a superhero who did the usual things but always against the nation's enemies, in a red, white, and blue costume. Some issues of *Captain America* sold nearly a million copies. After the war, his erstwhile partner Simon became a publicist for Nelson Rockefeller while Kirby went back to comics, emerging as the key figure in Marvel.[41]

In the comics industry revival that he, more than anyone else, sparked, and especially through the extension of the audience to college agers, Kirby proved himself more and more the Liebowitz type, the shrewd printed-page capitalist who foresaw marketing in toys and films. Still, he was a comics man. In middle age, Kirby invented *The Hulk*, that Frankenstein-like creature tortured by humanity's misunderstanding of him. In old age, he continued to experiment with Star Wars-like dramas, in which Captain Victory fights the extraterrestrials who don't want to be conquered by the likes of us – but obviously need to be bested, for the earthlings' own good. His staff artist Stan Lee, aka Brooklyn-born Stanley Martin Lieber, himself a brilliant entrepreneur mainly interested in art for the sake of merchandizing, claimed to have created *Spider-Man*, a giant hit in comic books and then comic strips. Its film rendition, the surprise smash of the 2002 spring season, was cut from the same endurable cloth: even with superpowers and married to the world's hottest babe, Peter Parker is still uncertain of himself and his identity.[42]

Still another set of ironies hurtled the field forward one more time. The pop art postmodernism that gave the most banal comic strips previously unthinkable prestige (at least when retraced onto canvas) and the tastes of post-baby boomers prompted a cinema of comic superheroes. *Superman and the Mole Men* (1951) was peacenik propaganda in disguise, an appeal for tolerance and peaceful coexistence in an America facing home-grown legions of what the Supe called "Nazi storm troopers" as he took away their guns.[43] *Superman* (1978), shot at the high point of Vietnam disillusionment, was practically a showcase of Hollywood progressives (albeit few of them Jewish), its remakes climaxing in *Superman IV* (1987), an antinuke overkill directed by Sidney J. Furie. The various Batman films, *Batman Returns* (1992) being the most interesting (conservative Jewish critics thought they saw anti-Semitism in the visage of the Penguin, an abandoned freak baby with a caricatured Jewishness who seeks revenge upon the civilization that tortured him), were also pointlessly violent enough to realize a certain impulse in Kirby's Marvel comic characters.[44] Soon, the comics of the 1930s–50s became source materials for films mostly no better (the Superman films and the Hulk television series aside) than their sources, and often worse.[45] It was just another phase of self-exploitation. But the legacy of Jewish comic art was already taking new life elsewhere in American popular culture.

Michael Chabon's *The Amazing Adventures of Kavalier & Clay* (2000), hailed by admiring critics as the most important Jewish-American novel of the post-post-Holocaust generation (i.e., born after 1970), and cursed by others (the neoconservatives) as a wrong-headed celebration of undeserving, thoroughly un-Zionist mass culture types, has brought the issues of the comic book artists to an audience scarcely suspecting the Jewish role.[46] The conjunction of comic book collecting and the rise of fannish scholarship around the industry, the surge of films based on comic characters and plots, and the transformation of the root story into literature, is no coincidence.

Chabon's protagonists, two cousins (one of them gay) and a wife whose love and everything else but sexual intimacy they share, at different times, are themselves the pulp creators. One cousin is Brooklyn-born, with the not unusual aspirations of a New York Jewish teen in the late 1930s for making it big in the comics trade; the other is a Czech refugee who has left his family behind and dreams constantly of saving them, especially his little brother, from the rapidly impending doom. The two come to know each other and discover that immigrant Joe has the European art training and background in stage magic to visualize a new character, while homeboy Sammy is ideal as scripter. Rosa (named for Rosa Luxemburg), the girl close to both of them, is the daughter of urbane, middle-class, and left-leaning New York Jews, the German cultured type once so frequently seen around the Ethical Culture Society. She, too, has some artistic talent, but treats it as a hobby useful for her straight job in the slick magazine world until she takes up comics later and somewhat reluctantly.

Their collective genius comic creation (and naturally Chabon's as well, even if we never see a single drawing of it) is the Escapist. This superhero is first of all unique, in the years just before Pearl Harbor, as openly antifascist, slugging it out with thinly disguised members of the Axis. By dint of occupation alone, he is arguably more Jewish than other superheroes. More to the point, he becomes the object of Expressionist artistry, vastly more surrealist in drawing styles and coloring than, say, real life Will Eisner's Spirit. At the Escapist's artistic apex, Joe's brother is known to have died when a ship ferrying orphans is sunk by a Nazi sub. Following his instincts, he has chosen an invisibility akin to suicide.

Chabon bypassed opportunities to make points about the comic industry in its postwar evolution, including the role of EC's stunning achievements, the rise of Harvey Kurtzman's *Mad Comics*, and so on. But there's some-

thing he does not miss: the corporate law suits faced by all supposed imitators of *Superman* (*Captain Marvel* was more clever by far), even the congressional hearings that so eerily paralleled the Hollywood hearings and the
Blacklist. Indeed, cousin Sammy is actually called to the docket, and is
accused of the crime for which he is guilty and for which most of the fired
government officials of the early 1950s were also guilty: not of being a
Communist, but of being a homosexual. Worse yet in this case as in perhaps
hundreds of others (since the New Deal had been a natural career path for
Jews), he was a Jewish homosexual.

Kavalier & Clay is weakest in its description of a Jewish lower-middle-
class life in which old collectivities, reinforced and legitimated by the New
Deal, retained for a while longer the moral as well as a political conviction
that old-fashioned piratical capitalism was undermining itself and could not
finally survive. Chabon, a great devotee of Jack Kirby, has written a mostly
Kirbyesque reconstruction of comic industry history, with the creators of
action figures displacing the generally more oddball artists of the others,
from diverse funny animals to *Psychoanalysis Comics*.

The ending of the novel is rounded off for the sake of literary style and, if
not historic, then at least for metaphoric accuracy. *The Golem*, source of
endless Yiddish folklore – its very title one of the most important Jewish
plays and, later, silent films – has been on Joe's mind since his European
childhood. As he reasoned it out, nothing less than a supernatural creature
could save the Jews from their enemies. Contemporary Jewish Socialists and
Communists reflecting on their own religious background might admit that
they hoped irrationally for a supernatural event: the overthrow of capitalism
and Fascism in one fell swoop.

It seems very likely that the pair of Cleveland boys who created the man
of steel drew upon the same Golem mythology, consciously or unconsciously. Chabon's Escapist, despite a high degree of irony, suffers from the
same absence of psychological depth as those in Kirby's commercial
empire, neurotic gods like the Fantastic Four, the Hulk, the X-Men, and
the Eternals. It's an irony that Chabon does not explore, perhaps because
the real tragedy, decades after the golden age of comics, continues to
consist of the stunted or purely cynical work of the artists in a field that
long promised (and still does promise) the possibility of something far
better.

Perhaps the generation born in the middle 1940s, reading comics during
the swiftly passing golden age (which to say, my generation) would be the
last one steeped in the mass-manufactured lore of the practically anonymous. From the flatly superheroic to the contrasting funny animal, from the

EC science fiction or war series likewise contrasting to the mainstream bug-eyed monsters (or heroic GIs unsullied by battlefield fear and gore), all of them leading to the scrutiny of the hyperconscious *Mad Comics*. That was the great dialectical negation, never quite undone by the subsequent taming of *Mad*.

R. Crumb once remarked, in response to a written query from me for a symposium I was to publish, that he had spent his artist's life trying to reach that holy of holies, the apex that Harvey Kurtzman gained back in Crumb's childhood.[47] His abnegation was unnecessary and comparisons of this kind, across the eras of comic art, are about as relevant as comparisons of center fielders in the 1920s and 1990s. But Crumb properly suggested the awe that we felt for the art and social commentary offered us, plain American kids of the McCarthy era, within such a modest setting. And he was right, too, in a way: after those savage critiques upon assorted hypocrisies from advertising to the depiction of military glory, nothing could ever really surprise us again. We had been truly educated.

NOTES

[1]   This rings a very particular bell. In the summer of 1966 (when a section of the Lower East Side officially became the East Village), living on East Tenth Street between First and Second Avenues, I worked as the seasonal substitute at the *National Guardian* ad department, where mats for regulars like the one that began "DANCE WITH MURRY SHERMAN IN KERHONKSON" were normal fare, usually adding "KOSHER MEALS" and "OPEN FOR THE HOLIDAYS." It was all new to me. Our other fare, indirect sales at discount prices to subscribers, featured Vitamin E supplements and Paul Robeson records.

[2]   A point pressed on me by Arne Thorne, final editor of the anarchist *Freie Arbeter Shtimme*, which folded in 1976. Several of my elderly interviewees, notably the long-reigning editor the Yiddish press, Pesach Novick of the *Morgn Frayhayt*, had in their youth been occasional contributors to – in Novick's case, a short-term staffer of – the *Kundes*.

[3]   It may be also useful to note, for later generations, that as popular culture items within the Yiddish world, labor Zionist and Communist dailies were not so far apart that they did not share considerable readerships: the Poale Tsionist daily *Tsayt*, with a good list of literary contributors, folded around the time that the *Morgn Frayhayt* was launched, with an even better list. My gratitude to the late Pincus Caruso, the managing editor of the *Tsayt*, a young ninety-two when I interviewed him in Miami Beach, for these insights.

[4] John J. Appel, "Abie the Agent, Gimple the Matchmaker, Berl Schlemazel, et. al.," *Midstream*, no. 28 (January 1988): 13–14.

[5] Peter C. Marzio, "Would You Buy a New Car from this Man? How Comic Strips Went Into Business with Abie Kabibble," in *Abie the Agent: A Complete Compilation, 1914–1915* (Westport: Hyperion, 1977): viii. This volume and *Dauntless Durham* (Westport: Hyperion, 1977) offer extremely useful samples of Hershfield's work.

[6] The best rendition of Rube Goldberg's genius can be found in Maynard Frank Wolfe, *Rube Goldberg: Inventions* (New York: Simon & Schuster, 2000).

[7] The Chicago surrealist circle that entered literary production with the various projects of Franklin Rosemont from the mid-1960s forward, praised Goldberg repeatedly in assorted surrealist publications as genius and precursor. I'm happy to have been publisher of some of these effusions, which include the anthologies "Surrealism and Revolution" (special 1970 issue of *Radical America*) and "Surrealism and Its American Precursors" (special 1978 issue of *Cultural Correspondence*) along with *Free Spirits: Annals of the Insurgent Imagination* (San Francisco: City Lights, 1982). Art Spiegelman paid his own tribute to Goldberg in a Goldberg-like drawing reprinted into the "humor" issue of *Shmate*, no. 13 (Summer, 1982), which I edited.

[8] See Robert C. Harvey, *The Art of the Funnies: an Aesthetic History* (Jackson: The University Press of Mississippi, 1994): 71.

[9] Ibid., 116–24.

[10] When Lippard died in 1854, he was a youthful literary giant of the weekly story tabloids, but his most faithful audience, the one that turned out the mourners, was said to be the German-American societies of Philadelphia, likely to be led by German-American Jews.

[11] Not only the fiction itself, of course, but also the illustration. In recent years, the 1920s–40s pulps' illustrative art has become almost, but never quite, respectable. See the characteristically condescending review of a recent show of "Pulp Art" at the Brooklyn Museum – Roberta Smith, "An American Vision Far from Apple Pie," *New York Times*, 13 June 2003 – taken from the collection of a retired stockbroker, Robert Lesser. In my examination of earlier collections of this material, I turned up only a minority of Jewish artists – a marked contrast to the comic book trades, and due perhaps to the violence and semifascistic ambience of the field, or simply to which artists got the assignments from the executives in pulp magazine firms.

[12] Frederik Pohl, "The Futurians," in Mari Jo Buhle, Paul Buhle, Dan Georgakas, eds., *Encyclopedia of the American Left* (New York: Oxford University Press, 2nd edition, 1997): 251. The H.P. Lovecraft Collection at the Hay Library, Brown University, has much fascinating correspondence between the young Lovecraft and fellow fictional amateurs. Some of the closest of his letter-writing friends

were young Jews. He later spent an unhappy several years in Manhattan, married to a Jewish woman and closest to Jewish science fiction-writer Frank Belknap Long, who granted me an interview in 1976 (his wife was a set designer in the Yiddish theater). Nevertheless, a borderline anti-Semite, Lovecraft realized his error after the rise of Hitler, and spent his last years as a Socialist. Into old age, meanwhile, Fred Pohl was true to the ideals of his youth: *O Pioneer!* (New York: TOR, 1997) has a protagonist on a distant planet who realizes that his fellow earthlings are plotting to wipe out the alien races with which they have formally agreed to colonize the pioneering zone cooperatively. Responding as the Popular Front-era Pohl had himself responded to anti-Semitism, our hero defends those who look different and have a different form of logic against his own kind.

[13] Gratitude is extended here to the late Donald Wohlheim, a Futurion member who went on to decades of editorship and his own DAW imprint; he spoke with me at a SciFi convention in Providence in 1975.

[14] Dennis Dooley, "The Man of Tomorrow and the Boys of Yesterday," in *Superman at Fifty: The Persistence of a Legend* (New York: Colliers, 1988): 21.

[15] In what must be considered a happy ending, Siegel wooed and won his model for Lois Lane, Joanne Carter, from another Cleveland high school.

[16] Dooley, "The Man of the Future," in *Superman at Fifty*: 28.

[17] "The Spectre," in Ron Goulart, *The Comic Book Reader's Companion*: 151–52.

[18] Eric P. Nash, "Jack Liebowitz, Comics Publisher, Dies at 100," *New York Times*, 13 December 2000.

[19] Art Spiegelman, "Comix 101: Forms Stretched to their Limits," *The New Yorker*, 19 April 1999: 77–78.

[20] This is the story of one of Spiegelman's own favorites, Jack Cole, artist of the hilarious *Plastic Man*, later a sort of staff cartoonist for Playboy in the magazine's early years. Cole killed himself with a gunshot in 1958. He was just forty-four.

[21] Scott Raab, "Is Superman Jewish?" in *Superman at Fifty*: 167.

[22] Decades later, as teacher at the School for Visual Arts in Manhattan, he held to the same rules. He had, as young artist Bob Fingerman put it, a "rote way of teaching . . . this is the way to tell a story, and that's it." Interview of Bob Fingernan with Kent Worcester, *Comics Journal*, no. 207 (September 1998). We'll meet Fingerman again in the final chapter.

[23] Eisner interview with Gill Fox, in *Will Eisner's Shop Talk* (Milwaukee, Oreg.: Dark Horse, 2001): 159.

[24] See the evocative interpretation of Eisner's significance in Robert C. Harvey, *The Art of the Comic Book: an Aesthetic History* (Jackson: The University Press of Mississippi, 1996): 66–99. The downside of Eisner's contribution is, however, lost on the critic-historian.

[25] "Planet Comics," in Ron Goulert, *The Comic Book Reader's Companion*: 129–30.

[26] Mike Benton, *The Comic Book in America: an Illustrated History* (Dallas: Taylor Publishing, 1989): 25–32.

[27] See Ron Goulart, "Comic Book Noir," in Lee Server, Ed Gorman, and Martha H. Greenberg, eds., *The Big Book of Noir* (New York: Caroll & Graf, 1998): 341.

[28] Alex Malloy with Brian Kelly and Kevin Ohlandt, *Comic Book Artists* (Radnor, Pa.: Attick Books, Ltd, 1993): 74–75. (His colleague at the *Daily Worker*, Louis Furstadt, drew the more memorable "Little Lefty," a kids' strip with humor and political punch outside the Party line; Furstadt's work in the mainstream was strictly standard hero-stuff, but his unpaid studio assistant was the young Harvey Kurtzman, destined to be the cerebral genius of *Mad Comics*.)

[29] Comics genius Carl Barks described himself as a "sharecropper on the Disney plantation" for a quarter-century.

[30] Buhle, "Interview with Harvey Kurtzman," *Shmate*, no. 13 (Summer, 1983): 24.

[31] Over at a competitor's shop, the departure of Jack Kirby, Stan Lee, and others from Timely Comics prompted the company's bosses to drop the pulps and pick up new talent, including Otto Binder, Alex Schomburg, and Syd Shores. New comic titles included *Tessie the Typist, Funny Tunes, Super Rabbit, Gay Comics*, and *Miss America Comics*, later *Miss America Magazine*, followed by girls' comics that turned from superheroines to teens interested in fashions and boys, like Millie the Model and Nellie the Nurse.

[32] Eisner interview with Gill Fox, *Shop Talk*: 168–78.

[33] Matthew Pustz, *Comic Book Culture: Fanboys and True Believers* (Jackson, Miss.: University Press of Mississippi, 1999): 27.

[34] Ron Goulart, *Comic Book Culture: an Illustrated History* (Portland: Collector's Press, 2000): 192–95; Goulart, "Planet Comics," in *The Comic Book Reader's Companion*: 129–30.

[35] This anecdote from Annette Rubinstein, a PhD who could not, as a woman, be hired as a professor during the 1930s, and served as a teacher and the principal of a private secondary school (and leading Upper West Side organizer for radical congressman Vito Marcantonio) until the blacklist drove her out. She re-emerged as a prominent Marxist literary critic, global lecturer, and mentor for many young people, including myself, in a small way. Other blacklisted former teachers wrote science popularizations for young readers, scoring great successes in a parallel field.

[36] "Classics Illustrated," in Ron Goulart, *The Comic Book Reader's Companion*, 32–33, "True Comics," ibid., 172–73. Special thanks once more to Annette Rubinstein.

[37] Thanks to Fabio P. Barbieri, in a 16 December 1996 letter to the author; the interview was published in an obscure British fanzine, Kirby interviewed by noted anarchist cartoonist Chris Harper. Barbieri is publisher of the *Jack Kirby Quarterly*.

[38] Kirby interview, *Will Eisner's Shop Talk*: 200. Kirby has lately, in the light of the cinematic *Spider-Man*'s vast success, delivered a memoir, *Excelsior!* (New York: Fireside, 2000), relating his childhood fascination with strange figures and superheroes of the radio, his workmanlike, i.e., nonartistic approach to scripting comics, and his eventual successes.

[39] *Will Eisner's Shop Talk*, 210–11.

[40] Goulart, *Comic Book Culture*: 125.

[41] Actually, Simon bounced back as pulp publisher (including *Sick* magazine, a slightly bohemian takeoff on *Mad*), comic editor, and even worked at DC for another stretch until he left comics for good to go into advertising in 1973. "Joe Simon," in Alex Malloy, *Guide to Comic Book Artists*: 289.

[42] *Will Eisner's Shop Talk*: 222–23.

[43] Supporting actor Jeff Corey was about to be blacklisted at the time. Director Lee Sholem became a director on the first Superman television series.

[44] The counterposition of Batman/Michael Keaton and Catwoman/Michelle Pfeiffer successfully explicated a sexual tension repressed in the comic books, and the mise en scene of a dark Gotham was the closest the films have ever gotten to the original. It is easily the best film of the often thoughtless director Tim Burton, who squandered the opportunity to remake *Planet Of the Apes*, scripted in the original as a brilliant satire of McCarthyism.

[45] Indeed, *The Incredible Hulk* (1979–82) was in line with a long history of progressive-leaning family-oriented television shows, featuring a tortured Bill Bixby who when not transformed into the raging Hulk (Lou Ferrigno) is an innocent victim on the run, assisting common folks against such villains as corporate swindlers and purveyors of harmful pesticides. In short, it was a show that the blacklistees could easily have written from their humane, Jewish sensibilities. Only *Beauty and the Beast* (1987–90) with sometime avantgardist Ron Perlman as the pursued creature of New York's literal underground, assisting fellow undergrounders (and beloved of the empathetically wrinkle-browed *shiksa* assistant district attorney, played by Linda Hamilton) thumped the familiar themes of poverty versus wealth more effectively in the family TV zone.

[46] Michael Chabon, *The Amazing Adventures of Kavalier & Clay* (New York: Random House, 2000).

[47] Crumb interviewed by Paul Buhle in *Cultural Correspondence*, no. 5 (1976), reprinted in Buhle, ed., *Popular Culture in America* (Minneapolis: University of Minnesota Press, 1987): 132–34.

FOUR

ASSIMILATION: STYLES OF AMERICANIZATION, 1941–65, AND THE HIDDEN COSTS

The war changed so many things about Jewish-American life in the long and the short run that merely to recount its effects would be impossible. By 1950, so much unforeseen in 1945 had become finalized that formerly large dimensions of Jewish-American life had been rendered all but invisible. Suddenly, Jewishness became virtually synonymous with Judaism, defying the fundamentally secular character of Jewish immigrant communal leadership within unions, also eclipsing the left-leaning political or fraternal movements and cooperative housing that largely dominated the thought of the previous immigrant generations – or at least their most articulate sections. The institutions' material base, the light industry districts of Manhattan, were about to shrink dramatically, along with the Jewish working class at large. Along with secularism as the true faith, went millennialism of the old kind, the expectation that a post-New Deal America would become at least a social democratic America on the European model, controlling wealth for public welfare. The postwar welfare state, with corporations unleashed and (some) Jewish businessmen along with intellectuals rising to the top, was something very different, its culture drastically altered.

Millenialism of the new kind was based metaphorically around the state of Israel, realization of a vision not several hundred years old (as European-based Socialism and its communal precursors) but several thousand years old, in Jewish national triumph. Meanwhile, in more than a few ways, the crabgrass frontier resembled the moshav, conquests of land previously held by non-Jews and now fiercely claimed as secure escape from discomfort and/or danger posed by nonwhites. Most noticeably, the old sense of shared oppression, making of alliances against the powerful, now turned toward a feeling of special oppression or at least potential persecution at the hands of others stigmatized by poverty or racial discrimination. Soon enough, the wartime analogies widely drawn between Nazism and American racism were quietly dropped. Key Jewish intellectuals would soon be saying that the problem of black poverty was mainly psychological. Jewish institutional leaders added thoughtfully that, anyway, it was not *their* problem. Jews themselves already had enough to worry about.[1]

But it would be a great error to condense or exaggerate the process. If you ever forget that you're Jewish, as the old saying goes, the Gentiles will remind you. Accumulating wealth, pursuing power and influence previously accorded to WASP counterparts, Jews still experienced those exclusions for several generations, formal and informal, that kept them out of locker rooms of exclusive clubs and the boardrooms of most giant corporations, therefore logically in the offices of marginal enterprises capable of sudden expansion or equally sudden collapse. Here, creative energy thrived, and a certain vital Jewish liberalism repeatedly established itself, filling a vacuum that otherwise might not have been recognized, let alone realized, in the bastions of entertainment powerbrokers. It was only one of many Jewish contributions in the postwar period, but along with the daring of the perpetual Jewish avant-garde, unquestionably the most distinguished.

Aaron Copland offers one splendid example of roads to popular culture patriotism that led from the avant-garde and the Left, through the Popular Front, to the forefront of American cultural acclaim. This major figure in American music began life in Brooklyn, in 1900, the child of Jewish Russian immigrants who were far from proletarian. His father owned a Brooklyn department store, and two of his sisters played musical instruments.[2] Like the acclaimed public intellectual Lewis Mumford, the illegitimate son of a Jewish businessman (and a German immigrant maid), Copland quickly discovered a world in the public resources – not, like Mumford, the New York Public Library and Natural History Museum, but the Brooklyn Public Library and Brooklyn Museum. Copland was already attending avant-garde musical recitals as a teenager, and was a reader of *The Seven Arts*, and in a few years, the *Dial*. Modernism was his credo, and modernist Waldo Frank (another future prominent Jewish artist cutting across modernism and radical politics) his savant, proclaiming the need for American music to discover its true roots in black and Indian life.

Copland had to go to Paris, where he studied with Nadia Boulanger, to interact with the leading lights of the global avant-garde, like Marcel Duchamp and the surrealists, who he admired at a distance, and with future American avant-gardists like his Paris roommate, Harold Clurman. Back from Paris in 1924 and starting up a long-term relationship with German Jewish critic Paul Rosenfeld, Copland moved through the cosmopolitan world of Mumford, Frank, Hart Crane, e.e. cummings, and Edmund Wilson, sometimes providing a musical interlude for their gatherings on Irving Place.[3] His compositions of the time included "Music for the Theater," inspired by jazz and by the erotic expressions of burlesque comedy babe Fanny Brice. Years later, as the Depression opened, he was still seeking to connect his musical projects with international avant-garde figures like his friend, Spanish surrealist painter Joan Miró.[4]

An interest in folk materials – Mexican, Jewish, and Middle American – prompted Copland toward more didactic social themes. This was also the path of friends like Ben Shahn, with Copland an admirer of Walker Evans's documentary photographic style, and with Shahn also close to documentary filmmaker Paul Strand. Shahn and Copland had together protested the execution of Sacco and Vanzetti (Copland's friend Marc Blitzstein began but did not finish an opera about the victims), a most Jewish cause for the saving of two Italian-Americans legally murdered through characteristic Yankee injustice.[5]

It has probably grown more difficult for Copland lovers of all kinds to comprehend why a young composer who wrote "In the Streets, May First!" for the Communist milieu collaborated two years later on a score of "The Second Hurricane," directed by Orson Welles, about American Revolution-era themes. Revived in Copland's centenary year, 2000, the score's original libretto describes six children boarding an airplane to rescue flood victims, thus beginning a voyage of discovery and self-discovery constituting "an idea of what life could be like with everybody pulling together." It is believed to have inspired Earl Robinson's "Ballad for Americans" (Copland was Robinson's teacher) and also the work of Leonard Bernstein, who oversaw the Boston premiere of "Ballad" in 1942, reviving it for television in 1960.[6] The latest version, not surprisingly, was framed as an affirmation of multicultural democracy: exactly what had been intended in the original.

The semifictional character of Billy the Kid was, like the heavily romanticized Jesse James, perhaps the most popular of the "good/bad" cowboys rebelling against an unjust social order, and Copland leaped at the chance to take a commission to create something for the Ballet Caravan on this theme. His adaptation of cowboy songs informed his approach, and "Billy the Kid" (1937) dramatized the era's niche for making folk themes middle-brow. In much the same spirit, Copland's film score for *The City*, two years later, accompanied the footage of Ralph Steiner and Willard Van Dyke and featured Morris Carnovsky as narrator, intoning the commentary written by Lewis Mumford. The masses had their own history, and in the shadow of the New Deal, that history could become the national saga. In1942, he collaborated with Agnes DeMille in creating "Rodeo" (in tune with DeMille's work on *Oklahoma!*) and climaxed in his "Fanfare for the Common Man" (1943), and the Popular Frontish "Appalachian Spring" (1944).

Years earlier, Copland had composed the score for *Of Mice and Men* (1939), his work receiving Oscar nominations for both the Best Score and Best Original Score. He also wrote the scores for Milestone's *The North Star*, *The Red Pony*, *Our Town*, and *The Heiress* (which won him another Oscar). As he observed about writing in Hollywood, "Composing music for film is not in itself 'easier' than writing concert music except that the form, length and general tone are set in advance, so the composer does not have to make those initial decisions."[7] In other words, he was happy enough to give himself over to the necessary techniques and mechanisms of popular culture, when the opportunity arose. Those opportunities ended suddenly with the Red Scare and the Hollywood Blacklist, even if he personally escaped formal blacklisting. Under pressure from the Right in the 1950s to display greater patriotism, he composed "The Tender Land," drawing upon *Let Us Now Praise Famous Men*. Late in life, he returned to the avant-garde, penning "Inaugural Fanfare" (1969) for a fellow late-surviving member of the painterly old Left, Alexander Calder. In Copland, as so often happened in American life, the Jewish Left had found a way to go mainstream.[8]

Or was it only that an acceptable remnant of the Jewish New Deal Left had somehow remained behind to collect plaudits? The saga of Norman Corwin as radio savant has no such happy ending. Raised in tenement East Boston by Jewish Hungarian and Russian parents, a printer and a frequently ill mother, Norman experienced the uplift of a family move to quasi-suburban Winthrop by his early adolescence. He went to work as a cub journalist at seventeen, in a small town of the Berkshires. In a few years, he moved up to the *Springfield Reporter*, where he wrote his first radio column, meanwhile editing an anthology of contemporary quotations, many of them from the pen of his mother's hero, the radical journalist Heywood Broun.[9] He also launched a small radio station devoted to poetry, a most unlikely idea in the commercially tyrannized medium. Pretty soon, he was working for the famed Cincinnati station WLW, with a half-million watts. But the job lasted two weeks, because he tried – against the edict of management – to report one of the spectacular strikes of 1935. It was a vivid radio lesson for the twenty-five-year-old whiz.

Corwin came to New York, thanks to a boost from his brother, working in the publicity department of Twentieth Century Fox. He also did a poetry program for WQXR, the Long Island-based high-toned "station for people who hate radio." Amazingly, but also a tribute to the times, CBS invited him to direct the *Columbia Radio Workshop*, its most serious and experimental dramatic show. The founder and first director happened to be Irving Reis, a prominent Hollywood progressive in years to come and a major source of encouragement.

Corwin, who had visited Nazi Germany in 1935, quickly put across a series of stunning original shows about the Fascist takeover of Spain and invasion of Ethiopia, programs that literally made him a national figure. Rarely adverting to his own Jewish status, he rendered a serious, universal, and even reflective persona.[10] It was Corwin who suggested rearranging "Ballad for Americans," which became a giant hit (it was adopted by the Republican Party convention of 1940) and a giant source of embarrassment for Paul Robeson haters in later decades. He shifted bases to Hollywood in 1940, and was primed for liberal antifascism. "We Hold These Truths," broadcast by several networks simultaneously on the 150th anniversary of the Bill of Rights – felicitously just eight days after the bombing of Pearl Harbor – captured the nation's imagination and was said to have boosted enlistment hugely. *This is War!*, carried over the largest national hook-up for a radio series ever (700 out of some 925 stations), was no mere entertainment; it engaged the issues with total seriousness and frankness. Through the remainder of the armed conflict, Corwin seemed at or near the center of American radio's public voice. He may be said to have carved out the role of Walter Cronkite, Bill Moyers, and so many others who were to follow in radio and television afterward.

How quickly things changed. In his highly influential, book-length political essay of 1949, *The Vital Center*, Arthur Schlesinger, Jr., attacked the "vogue ... for the incredible radio plays of Norman Corwin" that "only results in betrayal of taste." These were the marks of "the adaptation of slick advertising methods to politics," sufficiently degrading in themselves but also certain signs of the "Communist penetration" of American life that required isolation and eradication.[11]

By the time Schlesinger's polemical classic went to press, Corwin had reemerged from the war not much of a political figure at all, but rather a leading supporter of opera and poetry within network radio. He had joined United Nations Radio and had received the prestigious Wendell Wilkie "One World" award, named after the former Republican liberal candidate for president. But in 1947 he had also personally produced a spirited radio defense of Hollywood against the Red Scare, with a handful of the biggest stars in the business on hand for a national radio show to denounce the

House Committee on UnAmerican Activities and all efforts to blacklist certain writers, actors, or others in films. That was very likely Corwin's real crime in the eyes of Schlesinger, Jr. Corwin had never been a Communist (although some of his friends were) and eventually he would be cleared. But he refused to bend, and as he observed, he considered himself honored to be in such named company as Leonard Bernstein, Aaron Copland, John Garfield, Judy Holliday, Burgess Meredith, Zero Mostel, Howard K. Smith, and his old *Columbia Workshop* producer, William N. Robson.

By the time Corwin's career reemerged from McCarthyism's grip, network radio was dying. He wrote a bit for films and television (and even for radio again, creating in 1955 a ten-year anniversary celebration of the UN) but his creative time had passed and in some ways, more than passed: CBS executives had decided to send all the recorded *Columbia Workshop* shows to the dump. (Corwin himself personally intervened at the last moment in 1955 and salvaged, for historians and others, many of the medium's best dramatic moments.) Not even as his career closed did he make an issue of his Jewishness. His generational circumstance had meant, in effect, that by becoming a distinguished radio journalist, creative writer, and producer, he had put his own quietly but undeniably Jewish self on display.

The forgotten sideman Max Kaminsky, another Bostonian, offers a more average entertainment world example of the Jewish lower-middle class going mainstream thanks to the war, and of the costs eventually extracted. A Dorchester prole, trumpet prodigy, and born hipster, educated on "race" records and playing at the local YMHA, Kaminsky made his way up through jazz circles, still avidly reading books (a not unheard of, but most unusual, trait for a professional musician). Listening to Louis Armstrong live convinced him that jazz was an art. An adolescent in the late 1930s, during the heart of the swing era, he was already playing in Artie Shaw's band.

Kaminsky later claimed that he helped originate the arrangement for "Begin the Beguine," Shaw's signature number, but the connection had a greater significance. The most intellectually sophisticated of contemporary jazz band leaders, self-taught Abraham Isaac Arshawsky had brilliantly adapted his clarinet playing to the styles of the period and achieved his big breakthrough with Billie Holiday's vocal accompaniment. Shaw's Gramercy Five continued to adapt, hot or sweet, according to the live audience and record sales, and the bandleader made himself the minor movie star that Louis Armstrong might have been in another time or perhaps another civilization.[12] The Jewish trumpeter saw the other side of Shaw's adaptability in the programmed music of the big band, its inherent merger into exploitation and *schlock*. Kaminsky rationalized it as well as possible through his presence in the inner circle, who knew better than they played. Similarly, he rationalized the fact that he was in a white band by the presence of Billie Holiday as its true voice.

Kaminsky split with Shaw, but reunited in the antifascist effort via the bandleader's famed navy band, playing across the Pacific and often in dangerous conditions. He suffered shell shock while actually loading guns on a liberty ship as they returned home. The war, as he recalled, was meanwhile "opening a path a mile wide for jazz ... troops all over the world were clamoring for jazz band, jazz records, and jazz broadcasts."[13] Arnold Stang quipped at the time, "I knew [Kaminsky] before he changed his name." That is to say, when he had remained identifiably Jewish. At the time, it wasn't a problem.

But in the years shortly after the war, what Kaminsky called an "incredible nonsense about Jazz" suddenly proliferated, with fan clubs, popularity polls, and the emergence of the record buyer or club goer with very specific and often very confused taste. Jazz was elevated, and made more black simultaneously. But for him, as a self-educated Jew sensitive to classical music, jazz was best when spontaneous and for that very reason a sort of minor art, like the Viennese operetta or the Italian grand opera. Kaminsky therefore rejoiced at the success of his generation fighting Victorian propriety but mourned the cool jazz to follow, and not only because it left him on the sidelines of innovation. The glory of the Fifty-Second Street clubs in New York so vivid during the 1930s and 40s passed quickly, although a lot of good music remained behind, some of it his own.[14]

Ghettoization could intensify the audience for a certain kind of Jewish performance, while rendering it steadily more accessible to young Jews. Famed musical joker Sammy Katz, who trained with Spike Jones in the early 1940s, and for a decade after the war happened to be the hands-down most popular upfront Jewish musician (at least of Jewish music) in record stores and on the radio, observed laconically that he had no real competition. Until the revival of *klezmer*, he did not even have secular successors.[15]

Something very different happened in other quarters, among them television, where a fresh medium offered talented Jews near-perfect opportunities to express a widening Americanism (that is, one no longer marginalizing them), along with the more benign side of the remaining tensions. Here, a limit would be reached with the encompassing blandness, the networks' and sponsors' counterpart to McCarthyism not far from the censorious intent of the original. Assimilationism tended to expose its own defects, but not necessarily in the short run, or ever, for the careerists who cared only about the bottom line. Sensitive souls and committed Jewish artists, acutely conscious of their Jewishness or not, learned to abandon illusions about a cheerfully homogeneous American culture. We follow their lives and work below, mapping the alternatives.

FILM'S LAST GOLDEN AGE

Wartime brought the largest American audiences and the most public acclaim that Hollywood was ever likely to get. Afterward, tax breaks, foreign (and television) sales, and the marketing of feature-related products would prove decisive. For decades into the future, executive giants like Lew Wasserman (the last of the moguls) would create strategies to repackage Hollywood products, finding niches the size of elephants (Wasserman personally turned MCA talent agency into a production company for film and television), planning film spectaculars and new marketing schemes until ushered out by '90s international corporate mergers.[16]

But for the final era when movies constituted the single central icon of popular culture, consider the fate of some key contemporary Hollywood films tackling in one fashion or another the Jewish question. Many of them could be described as either patronizing or mere showbiz history and inaccurate history at that. *Mrs. Skeffington* (1944), written and produced by twin brothers Julius and Phillip Epstein (best remembered for collaborating on *Casablanca*), has Gentile beauty Bette Davis marry aptly named Wall Streeter Job (played by Claude Rains), bear him a son (who is killed in the war), cheat on him repeatedly and then realize that he is her one true love. *Easter Parade* (1948) was almost a literal parade of tunes by Irving Berlin with a sketchy plot about a pair of dancers played by Judy Garland and Fred Astaire back in the 1910s and 20s.

Berlin personally got six hundred thousand dollars for the songs and the use of his name. It was an all-time good investment because *Easter Parade* proved to be the biggest moneymaker of MGM's year, garnering assorted awards for producer Arthur Freed, coscreenwriter Sidney Shelton, and composer/jazzman Johnny Green. In short, a vast Jewish triumph with no Jewish story and no evident Jews on screen except cinematic newcomer Jules Munshin as François, the French headwaiter. Bing Crosby quipped about Berlin, "He's the guy who holds the patent for Easter and Christmas." The aphorism was thought by some not to be quite on the mark because the composer had actually de-Christianized the holidays. But it was more authentic than that: the popular celebration of those holidays had, after all, been a merchandizing ploy in the first place.[17]

A representation of Florenz Ziegfeld, Jr., of the 1946 *Ziegfeld Follies* might have added a twang of real Jewish entertainment history, but that degree of realism was nowhere to be found. The hoofing of Fred Astaire, Lucille Ball, and a huge cast of cameos (including Fanny Brice) merely gave the entertainment king a chance to recall his star-studded triumphs from beyond the Pearly Gates. It was, in short, just a production-number version of *The Great Ziegfeld* (1936), itself scarcely more than an excuse for singing and dancing, with the same William Powell improbably playing Ziegfeld. In *Ziegfeld Girl* (1941), coscripted by leading female screenwriter Sonia Levien with lyrics by Gus Kahn among others, the producer's character never even makes it onto the screen.[18]

By contrast, *Rhapsody in Blue* (1945) stands, with *The Jazz Singer*, as the big film demonstrating the most Jewishness in Hollywood history to the time. Written by Howard Koch and Elliott Paul (but with Clifford Odets and Robert Rossen among others contributing dialogue), produced by Jack Warner and directed by Irving Rapper, it moves tunefully through the life of George Gershwin, as we've seen, inventing or ignoring various aspects of private life as suited the plot. And, although perhaps it should go almost without saying, starring a Gentile, Robert Alda, as Gershwin. The title song, said to be influenced by black melodies – but actually an attempt to "Europeanize" vernacular American music – expresses the inner tension of the film hardly seen as tension at the time.

More vigorous if still more absurd attempts at happy assimilationism were certainly attempted at the same moment. *Abie's Irish Rose* (1946), an update of a *schmaltzy* 1920s Broadway play and 1929 silent film of the same name, has VE Day just announced in London, and a Jewish soldier (played by Michael Chekov) in love with an Irish-American USO singer. They are married by an army chaplain but they keep the wedding secret as each comes home to waiting family. During the second and third (respectively Jewish and Catholic) weddings, one side or another is bitterly unhappy with the couple. Things change only with the arrival of a son, Patrick Joseph Levy, and a daughter, Rebecca. As everyone on camera seems to cry together, a kindly Irish cop standing by sings first Jewish, then Irish lullabies, and the families reconcile. The thoroughly Jewish *Variety* called it a "topical misfit" of screaming minorities that can't get along, and a radio show based on the film was cancelled after listener complaints. With Bing Crosby's imprimatur (his company produced it) and the film's OK by the equally conservative Catholic Legion of Decency and the Anti-Defamation League, *Abie's Irish Rose* made money without ever erasing the memory of studio embarrassment.[19]

And so it went. By 1958, Hollywood rendered Herman Wouk's *Marjorie Morningstar*, what might be called still Jewish, a melodrama of middle-class life after a brief sojourn in bohemian circles. The mere introduction of the Jewish gangster, after *King of the Roaring Twenties: The Story of Arnold Rothstein* (1961), and of the Jewish madam, in *A House is Not a Home* (1964), in a sense completed filmic assimilation to multicultural society, if it ever could be completed. Recovering Jews, Jewish mobsters, and whores could all be real Americans.

To the considerable surprise of Hollywood itself, a frontal attack on anti-Semitism had meanwhile suddenly proved to be a good business, even if it led HUAC to dramatic assaults on the writers and directors of the hits. *Crossfire* (1947), one of the most prestigious of the socially relevant postwar melodramas, produced and directed by two future Gentile members of the Hollywood Ten, offers a violent contrast. It has a prejudiced and distraught war veteran brilliantly played by Robert Ryan beat an amiable Jewish host (a civilian, played by Sam Levene, who meets several GIs in a bar and invites them back to his place for a drink) to death. Much of the action in the film comes with the pursuit of the killer by a humanistic detective, and without the Jewish theme would have remained a mere police drama. But *Crossfire*, released a few months before the more prestigious *Gentleman's Agreement*, had been prepared as a social shocker, prescreened to representatives of religious groups who had already been carefully polled prior to production about the subject matter.

Hollywood, eager to test its new subject matter before deciding upon heavy investments in promotion, had shrewdly gone for gold. Audiences would not have known that novelist Richard Brooks' work, *The Brick Foxhole*, was about a homosexual beaten to death by a veteran with pretty much the same intent and ferocity. In Hollywood, a shift of plot device ("motivation") was perfectly normal. And in this case lucrative: it cost less than six hundred thousand dollars to make and proved to be RKO's biggest film of the year, garnering millions.

Still, the theme of prejudice offered no guarantee of success. Most others seeking room to discuss anti-Semitism did not do nearly as well, and no small part of the problem remained studio sabotage. *The Vicious Circle* (1949) was an independent production intended to dramatize the historical background to the Holocaust. Its plot revolves around a Czech liberal lawyer in late nineteenth-century Budapest fighting for the rights of Jewish citizens. Just a year after the film's limited release, it was recut, retitled *The Woman in Brown*, and shorn of all references to Jews or even to Europe. Miraculously, in what must have been an interchangeable society of white folks in that century, these European-looking people were actually Americans living out an unstated and evidently unpolitical populist grievance. Historical dramas had generally done very badly at the box office, and as receipts fell throughout the industry, the theme of Jewish persecution was (at least for a decade or so) considered still worse.[20]

A raft of little films, a mere handful still in Yiddish, but most in English, tackled issues from which Hollywood continued to back away. Thus *Open Secret* (1948), a low-budget melodrama scripted by future blacklistee Henry Blankfort and future television dramatist-savant Max Wilk of early anthology series, has a murder plot against a crusading Jewish journalist, organized by a right-wing veteran determined to revive the nativist movement.[21] Perhaps such second-bill features might have had a chance, even in the Jewish neighborhoods amid the throes of highway construction and outward bound mobility – if their political connections were not suddenly so unpopular.

Jews, or rather the Jewish presence and image, usually did better on the sidebars of the story, like the sincere second lead who nevertheless moves the story along and helps the main character get the girl or the guy. Meanwhile the familiar pattern of the 1930s, where known Jewish stars like Paul Muni, Melvyn Douglas, or John Garfield signified Jewishness to in-the-know viewers, held on most amazingly.

But a (usually) lone Jewish face was also needed in many a GI adventure, like the stunningly realistic *A Walk In the Sun* (1946) where Jake Friedman, played by George Tyne, is the native Brooklynite among the embattled platoon, and who has some of the best lines. Sam Levene is likewise the proletarian hero in *Action in the North Atlantic* (1944). Evidently an auto-didact, he explains why democracy is worth fighting for. The same year, Jewish-labeled Levene also played the unofficial lawyer for himself and his fellow captured airmen in *The Purple Heart* (1944) abused in a frame-up trial and then himself executed by the Japanese. John Garfield, another supporting star in *Action* and also Jewish largely by virtue of a neighborhoodish identification, was the best cast in a half-dozen other 1940s films, including *Destination Tokyo* (1944, an ordinary seaman, behind Captain Cary Grant) and *Gentleman's Agreement* where, unlike faux-Jew Gregory Peck, he is the real thing who rejects condescension toward the "poor little Jew" and demands justice for all.[22]

Just as Jewish were some filmic expressions of American democracy winning out at home, hardly at the center of the plot but useful to make necessary points. *Till the End of Time* (1946, directed by Edward Dmytryk and produced by Dore Schary, the new liberal boy wonder on the scene) has GIs striving to get their lives back amid trauma, not only refusing to join a veterans' group openly prejudiced against Jews, but personally punching out the bigots. In fact, the resulting bar brawl restores the sense of vitality to one of the three GIs, and sends another to the hospital, from which he can reunite with his family. All in all, a unifying experience. Now a better America can move on.

This set of images was successor to what might be called the victim film, with its roots in the earliest antifascist movies that the studios, fearful of lost European profits, actually permitted to be produced. *So Ends Our Night* (1941), based on a popular novel by Erich Maria Remarque, has a German Jewish refugee, played by Fredric March, denied entry into Austria. The character, jailed for illegal entry, shares a prison cell with the unwanted of various countries, then continues a miserable adventure across Europe seeking personal safety. It was the first screen credit for a young Jewish production assistant headed for great things: Stanley Kramer. *Tomorrow The World!* (1944), adapted from a highly regarded Broadway drama, has a propagandized German orphan boy brought into an American home, learning to his horror that his father was Jewish and repelled at the Jews (and "Jew lovers") around him. After denial and violent rejection of America as well of his true self, he sees the light.[23]

That orphan may in fact represent the ultimate divided state of the 1940s filmic Jew. In Europe, dramatized best in the low-budget classic *The Search* (1948), directed by Fred Zinnemann, where the orphan is discovered to be Jewish, the escapee is not so much fleeing from prejudice but from extermination. Back in America by contrast, the main risk, apart from a return to 1930s Depression economic conditions, was undoubtedly neurosis. It could be uncharitably suggested that the Jewish types needed head shrinking by their kinsmen because they were so frequently the most visible screen neurotics. Oscar Levant was only the most famous, playing himself more or less in a handful of films, while actually one of the highest-paid concert pianists on the planet. *Humoresque* (1946), seemingly a prewar relic, gained new life as a vehicle for the emotionally torn figure of John Garfield as a crypto-Jewish violinist. This project was launched when Odets's script for *Rhapsody in Blue* got rejected, obviously leaving the neurosis narrative (and deeply, if implicitly, Jewish) possibilities for the taking. Hollywood was not the place for anxiety about the differences in the emotional lives between a fictionalized composer and a fictional fiddler.

Instead, the new *Humoresque*, updated to the Depression years, has a Lower East Sider burdened by his poor family while offered uplift by a heavy-drinking, heavily neurotic, and definitely *goyishe* socialite played with great tragic effect by Joan Crawford. In order to realize his art, he must at once struggle against the overwhelming guilt of abandoning his background, and against the temptations of obsessive love with an immoralist. In the end, and faced with the fact that she would certainly drag down her lover's career, the benefactress-mistress drowns herself, precipitating a solution to the artist's own uncertainties by reminding him that art is indeed for art's sake above all. It seems a strange lesson for 1946, but one that many a Jewish musician or devotee doubtless appreciated in a world gone mad.

After the Lower East Sider as soldier or artist, and apart from the continuation of the vaudevillish Jewish types on screen, the psychoanalyst or M.D. with a psychological specialty was probably the most identifiable screen Jew. Fictionalized Freud would not make a major appearance until 1962, when Montgomery Clift in *Freud* (at least Clift was psychologically troubled, if not actually Jewish) played the great analyst.[24] But Barry Sullivan, playing Dr. Alexander Brooks in *Lady In the Dark* (1944, based on a musical with book by Moss Hart, music by Kurt Weill, and lyrics by Ira Gershwin), one of the admired films of the time, had famously prescribed a return to femininity for the Manhattan career girl played by Ginger Rogers. Two battling shrinks played by José Ferrer (in his dark looks and cerebral talk almost definitely perceived as Jewish) and Richard Conte (doubtfully so) in *Whirlpool* (1949) contrast an unorthodox and orthodox therapist, a badly botched adaptation (by Ben Hecht) of a novel by Jewish Hollywood Marxist Guy Endore. And so on, from the darkest corners of noir angst to the constant mugging of slapstick, where the Viennese psychologist probably made the most frequent appearances of all.

At least one other Jewish role of importance remained for the postwar years to explore: the Bronx gamin, gum-chewing and slangy, but wise to the world's tricks. Only a blind person could fail to see the Jewishness of Judy Holliday (1921–65), a Bronx-born daughter of a piano teacher who had rushed to the hospital for delivery immediately after watching a Fanny Brice live performance. It was kismet, or something like that. A teenage receptionist at the Mercury Theater, one of the group of left-leaning improvisationists who made the Village Vanguard a hip spot in wartime, Judy had an unsuccessful tour as a bit actress in Hollywood, returned to New York, and won best supporting actress in a hit play that established her persona.

Holliday replaced an ill Jean Arthur in Broadway's *Born Yesterday*, and again in the 1951 hit film. With an IQ established at 172, she had managed to become America's favorite dimwit – but only to those who failed to look carefully. Adopting the same character in her testimony to HUAC, she confounded the "red baiters" (and quietly dropped her contacts with progressive organizations), although she was informally blacklisted in film and television for years. Coming back in *The Solid Gold Cadillac* (1956), this time she plays the stockholder who realizes that the corporate types are a bunch of crooks and organizes a campaign to outsmart them. Miraculously, she manages a combination of Katharine Hepburn's self-possession and Shirley MacLaine's playfulness. All in all, Holliday offered an example of what clever Jewish comediennes could have done for decades if given the chance, and others, but especially Barbra Streisand, would do so in the self-consciously Jewish era to come.[25]

Holliday's fate was not unfamiliar. Jews lost most heavily in the McCarthyism and Blacklist period to follow in Hollywood, not only because they constituted a majority of those writers, actors, editors, and musicians actually driven from the industry, but also because they were so often the studio executives, producers, and directors deprived of the needed talent. Harry Cohn desperately attempted to protect his writers, and Jerry Wald, up-and-coming producer of the 1940s, was to tell oral historians in 1959 that he spent a decade not being permitted to make the films that he wanted.[26] From another standpoint, the certainty of the FBI field office that industry and LA-area Jews were hostile to the Bureau suggested how the ascribed qualities of Jewishness still seemed threatening to J. Edgar Hoover, Walt Disney, and the downright anti-Semitic congressmen of HUAC alike.[27]

Hollywood, successfully cowed, now produced filmic Jews, shrunk down to their 1930s predecessors, either bland or stereotypic but most of all, generally absent. There was something Jewish about John Garfield, even if only New Yorkers seemed to know for sure; there was nothing apparently Jewish, in the era immediately to follow, about Tony Curtis, aka Bernie Schwartz, his ethnicity drained out of him along with the Method acting that he had imbibed before settling into silly roles (with the marked exception of his Method casting in *The Sweet Smell of Success*) amid the Hollywood mainstream. It was almost as true at the top: Louis B. Mayer was fired by MGM in 1951, two of the three Warners sold their shares in the studio, Harry Cohn died, while David O. Selznick and Samuel Goldwyn made their last films before 1960. The next generation of moguls would be proportionally almost as Jewish but definitely more corporate, often talent agency executives, and the broken accents were gone.

The most hilariously awful portrayals of Jews by Jews and others were certainly the biblical spectaculars created to outdo television offerings. *The Robe*, easily the best (and the one written by a Blacklist victim, albeit without credit, Albert Maltz), puts the Jews into the background as the rebels against Rome whose would-be savior convinces Roman consul

Richard Burton finally to martyr himself. *David and Bathsheba*, *The Ten Commandments*, and *Solomon and Sheba* among others placed Jews in supporting roles when they looked too Jewish, reserving the premiere status like Moses for Hollywood Gentiles with a universality that hardly seemed Jewish at all. Perhaps Elizabeth Taylor (a real-life convert) made the best Jewish appearance when as the Egyptian queen *Cleopatra* (1962) she pleaded to save the grand library of Alexandria from destruction by knowledge-hating barbarians. It was an all-time studio money loser.

The fire of passion and commitment still burned (or was allowed to burn) in comedy and showbiz nostalgia, along with a little corner of the melodramatic spotlight.[28] Danny Kaye's movies almost always looked something like *Me and the Colonel* (1958), with Kaye as the little guy who exhibits great courage when the chips are down, often enough by imitating a pompous Gentile, rather as Charlie Chaplin did before him in *The Great Dictator*.[29] *The Eddie Cantor Story* (1953) seems to do as little as possible with the singer-comic's background and the militant unionism, not to mention the burning antifascism that the background spurred – but something of the past remains unavoidable as his character.

Interracialism offered a marker for the real progress toward a transformed Americanism into which Jews might proudly assimilate. While the dark side of the rise of sound films up to the war years was stained in more than one way by *The Jazz Singer* and *Gone With the Wind*, cabaret had presented another side of Jewish/black cultural collaborations. *Café Society*, the Village venue opening in 1937, alone held a remarkable story. Part Weimar, part left-wing fundraiser and stand-up shtick, part jazz experimentation, it placed black performers in front of disproportionately Jewish and highly sophisticated audiences week after week. It defined, in its own small way, the New York sophistication of the Popular Front, and its spirit might have remade a corner of Hollywood, given the chance.

If Café Society and the larger milieu had done nothing more than to place lyricist Abel Meeropol's verse in front of the young Billie Holiday, the experiment would have been monumental in American culture. Appearing the same year as *Gone With the Wind*, "Strange Fruit" defied every expectation of the commercial lady singer of the Ella Fitzgerald type, outraged Southern politicians beyond measure, and put left-wing Meeropol onto the FBI's list. The Bronx High School English teacher, composing music in his off-hours, had just walked into Café Society with the lyric in hand and coaxed Holiday to sing it. Although the song's success owed much to Danny Mendelsohn's arrangement, she had captured what the lyricist could not have done himself; the *New Masses* called it, anomalously, but not entirely so, the "first successful attempt of white men [i.e., the lyricist and composer] to sing the blues."[30]

Abel Meeropol had just one more hit, with circumstances just as unusual. In 1945, by this time living and working in the film capital, he was asked to provide a song holding together a special human rights short vehicle for Frank Sinatra, then very much a supporter of antifascist idealism. Thinly scripted by Albert Maltz, *The House I Live In*, running less than fifteen minutes, played in theaters across the country and won a special Academy statuette. It was a spectacular Jewish intervention in redefining American-ism. Sinatra's character, himself as hit singer stepping out of a studio, came across a poor kid being bullied and threatened by other boys, and fended off the attackers by explaining what democracy was about: "all faiths/all reli-gions/that's America to me." He could not say, or sing, about Jews or African-Americans, let alone Japanese-Americans returning from camps with their worldly possessions purloined. The boy must have been an inexplicable Catholic in a Protestant neighborhood or vice versa. When Sinatra sang it again, as a staunch Reagan Republican late in his life, he didn't need to change a word or intoned phrase.[31]

And yet serious progress had seemed possible, perhaps just ahead, amid the public mobilization for the great war against Fascism. In 1943, *Cabin in the Sky* appeared on stage, a too-folksy fantasy musical about the soul of one seemingly lost African-American male, but containing several crucial songs written by Yip Harburg and sung by the likes of Ethel Waters and Lena Horne. The show, it is said, contained the first integrated theatrical road cast. In 1945, *Stormy Weather* saw the light, with book by future blacklistee Hy Kraft (whose previous work, mostly on Broadway, was most notable for the re-creation of pre-1920 Yiddish theatrical atmosphere of the coffee houses on Second Avenue), dancing by the Katherine Dunham troupe and show-stopping work by Horne and Fats Waller, in his best moments of a disappointing cinematic career.

Things went pretty much downhill thereafter. Films about musicians proliferated during wartime and after, but a Negro "problem" never sur-faced any more than any Jewish "problem" that musicians might continue to face within American society. In *Rhapsody in Blue*, the young composer's career takes off when he becomes a lyricist for Al Jolson. Near the end of his short life, the film's George Gershwin writes "Porgy and Bess," but he is cheated from life's real triumph when he dies before his classically oriented Concerto in F is performed (by his friend Oscar Levant, as in real life) on a live NBC radio broadcast.[32] Black music ultimately has a kind of domestic folkishness, which Gershwin, like his European counterpart Ravel, can render into real music, but which is definitely not at the classical level of real art. That Sidney Buchman contributed script to *The Al Jolson Story* (another contributor was Clifford Odets) and produced as well as wrote *Jolson Sings Again* only drove home the contradiction.

Nor were Jewish-written interracial dramas in the Hollywood big time more notably successful. A young Jewish screenwriter from Chicago, Carl Foreman, penned *Home of the Brave* (1949), in which a psychologically broken African-American soldier regains use of his body, with the help of a psychiatrist (naturally Jewish, played by Jeff Corey), by understanding that all soldiers are equal beneath the khakis and polished brass. At a historic moment when Jewish teenagers were seen on the cover of *Life* magazine idolizing Dizzy Gillespie, and romantic crossovers across race lines more often united Jews and blacks than anyone else, the Hollywood response was all so pathetically inadequate. The Cold War's repressive edge and the crash of box-office receipts ended hopes for nearly a decade, meantime squeezing Jewish innovation into hiding, like the humanist sentiment delivered by Jewish left-winger Ned Young working under a front for Oscar-winning *The Defiant Ones* (1958).

But the boldest television drama had already done interracial themes before *The Defiant Ones*, and in the larger sense, television success, television writers, directors, and actors would be required to reinject the topicality and verve back into Hollywood by the end of the 1950s. In the meantime, the filmic burden of Jewish humanism and experimentation with the forms of popular culture was more likely to go under the radar.[33]

A now forgotten producer, William Alland, offers a large case in point. He could easily be called the first king of the "creature feature," one of the chief cinematic innovations of the 1950s, when only drive-in receipts managed to buck up a severe decline in general attendance. Not that this kind of film was otherwise unknown to Jewish movers and shakers, far from it. Low-budget hucksters like Samuel Zarkoff would extend the process into dozens of pictures and mega-million box offices. But Alland had something rather different in mind.

Growing up in an abusive, working-class family two generations earlier and several neighborhoods over from Barry Levinson's middle-class Baltimore, Alland later recalled being enraged enough to murder his father, or run away with his mother. Instead, he just ran away to Manhattan in the midst of the Depression with only a few dollars and a cardboard suitcase. There he did some amateur stage work and was both seduced and practically adopted by an older woman (she also happened to be a Marxist theoretician). Through her, the young would-be actor became Orson

Welles's gofer, also a bit player for *War of the Worlds* and other Mercury Theater radio broadcasts. At twenty-three, he personally chauffered Welles from New York to Los Angeles, and played the narrative-relating reporter in *Citizen Kane* with his back to the camera (also providing the voice for the newsreels). That anonymous role was, if not Alland's finest moment, at least the high point of his aesthetics. But aesthetics aren't everything.

After service as a combat pilot, the still young man returned to Hollywood and minor film work but poured his talent into producing a Peabody Award-winning radio show, *The Golden Doorway*, the first network radio devoted to the psychological problems of children. It was not, however, a commercial success. By the early 1950s, Alland moved into film production at Universal. His career moment had almost arrived. Amidst work on low-budget westerns, he was called in by HUAC and presented the usual alternatives: testify and betray your friends, or disappear professionally. He chose the first, set on realizing a delayed Hollywood career.

Alland claimed afterward to bear no guilt and to have put his left-wing life behind him. But a look at his films offers the oddest combination of creatures who mean no harm but are to be captured for display, like commodities; aliens who discover the real monsters are human beings; aliens whose commitments to scientific society are unmistakably, if allegorically, Communist; and rebellions against domineering aliens that seem not at all like the familiar Americanism of standard monster-feature good guys but very much like Trotskyism or anarchism (the *revolutionary* alternatives to Stalinism). "The basic principle is all right," a scientist thus remarks in *This Island Earth* (1955), but the means had not been found to save the home planet without endangering humankind.[34]

Alland's *Creature from the Black Lagoon* (1954) and *Revenge of the Creature* (1955), although thin on plot, nevertheless perfectly recaptured the Frankenstein motif of film's classic monster era. These monsters were innocent; the guilty ones are the humans, either innocently scientific and seeking a gillman surviving in a South American swamp, or exploitatively kidnapping the creature for a Sea World-style amusement park in Florida, chained to the bottom of a pool and destined, like real-life dolphins, to a short and unhappy existence.[35]

That kind of liberalism, the furthest possible during the 1950s, was the marker for a generation of mostly younger men and women from lower-class or lower-middle-class backgrounds who had come of age during the war years and found a place for themselves in entertainment. Largely if by no means exclusively Jewish, they offered a way for Jewishness to equate with the ideals of an inclusive society and with their own aspirations.

THE TELEVISION ERA

Radio, apart from Gertrude Berg's *The Goldbergs*, was never much of a place for Jews to identify themselves as Jewish. Eddie Cantor drastically toned down his stage ethnicity and set the pattern for other Jews thereafter. One might almost say the most promising field was the perfectly imagined Gentile. Zeke Manners, the top so-called hillbilly on radio during the 1940s and ruler of "Mountain Music" in Manhattan, was born Leo Ezekiel Mannes. Young Mannes entered the medium through kids' shows, rising to his New York apex. Afterward, he became the nation's first cross-country disk jockey on the ABC radio network, playing assorted musical instruments, and later worked in Las Vegas with a bluegrass group. Finally and perhaps most appropriately, Manners appeared as a support actor in the film *Lost in America*. He remains most famous for writing the *Pennsylvania Polka* in 1942, for the virtual Jews as all-American girls imagined them, the Norwegian-Greek Andrew Sisters of "Beï Mir Bist Du Schoen."[36]

Television did not seem at first to promise more Jewishness or more artistry. Many of the same censorious advertising agencies at work in radio guided the new shows as well. The captains of the visual medium nevertheless had so much open space to fill that many kinds of experiments flourished – for a while. Not unlike film's early days, the east of the Hudson audience helped lay out basic interests with many peculiarly Jewish themes (and creators, at all levels). Unlike film, the post-Holocaust atmosphere served to legitimate Jewishness into something bold, sometimes garish, and occasionally poetic.

But the electronic projection of images had been excruciatingly slow in evolution. Russian-Jewish immigrant David Sarnoff played a crucial role almost from the beginning. Commercial manager of the American Marconi Company in 1915, he urged the mass production of radios, and by twenty-eight, he was general manager of the newly formed (and government-chartered) Radio Corporation of America, RCA. By 1926, as network radio raced ahead, television had become a technical possibility, and it grew up as a shadow form. A bit more than a decade later, at the World's Fair in 1939, Sarnoff brought television to the public officially. "A new art so important in its implications that it is bound to affect all of society . . . an art which shines like a torch of hope in a troubled world," he told the small viewing audience.[37]

RCA and Dumont sold sets for a bit under $400 each, and about 2,500 people in New York owned them by 1940. Because major film studios shunned the competition and kept their wares out, and the cost of sets restricted most viewing to bars, sports practically dominated the screens for a decade. But not entirely.

Once again, location counted heavily for the new participants. NBC live from Chicago, but especially from New York, immediately featured Jewish talent galore. A very young Imogene Cocoa, Judy Holliday, Leonard Bernstein (a mere pianist), and others were ready at the mark. Allen Dumont, another Jewish whiz (but from a comfortable upper-middle-class family), actually invented the first successful electronic receiver and beat RCA to the market. Meanwhile William Paley, a cigar maker's son who purchased an independent radio network in the middle 1920s, was an experienced radio executive and major owner of CBS by the time television began to show commercial possibilities. In 1937, Paley hired the able critic Gilbert Seldes, one of the first to write intelligently about popular arts, to head up a new television station in New York. Seldes in turn hired Worthington Miner, a journeyman theatrical director who got his start in the Works Progress Administration's Federal Theater, to help create an atmosphere of genuine experiment and creativity.

It was a genius stroke all around. Seldes practically invented the news format of cutting in with film and using maps and charts to break up the talking head. But the creative prospects for television were dimmed by the coming war and the disappearance of most of the personnel. With peace, programming began to expand rather rapidly, although the first serious nonsports projects had to wait until 1948. That year, thanks to major advertisers like Ford and Kraft, real theater, i.e., live theater, came to television. So did the variety show, vaudeville reborn one last time, and the radio sitcom, the least altered genre across the mediums. Within a few years, the nightly talk show emerged out of the kinds of revues familiar in sophisticated Manhattan.

Within the thriving west-of-the-Hudson local television scene, down-home Chicago, heavily Slavic and full of assorted Gentiles, veteran Federal Theater actor (and the very Jewish) Studs Terkel organized and presided over *Studs' Place*, an unscripted weekly show that closed out when the Red Scare reached television. It was a world in which hand puppets Kukla, Fran, and Ollie could perform (sometimes Studs took one of the parts). But it was a scene due to break up in any case when the big time opened up, by the middle 1950s, for local talent to go national.

The big time was ultimately New York, and, a few years later, Los Angeles. It would be a mistake to suggest that Jewish personalities, from cameramen to executives, dominated the new medium. But like no other identifiable group, more than in radio and almost as much as in Hollywood films, they were there, at the scenes of the creation. In aging viewers' memories, television's clowns, the fading Ed Wynn, and the rising Sid Caesar and Milton Berle (with their staff of some of the funniest Jewish writers ever born) stir the warmest memories.

Berle, with his campy vulgarity full of Yiddishisms, was at the top of the charts so long as television sets remained mostly in metropolitan and, especially, east of the Hudson living rooms. Caesar, another stage comedian, found his métier in the same era and with many of the same gestures as *Mad*: ridicule of television advertising, current films, high-culture effeteness and intellectualism. Phil Silvers, playing the irrepressible Sgt. Bilko (with a multicultural cast that replicated the Second World War film, this time with comedy effect, improved by interracialism), was the new medium's greatest fast-talking wise guy.[38] Jack Benny, George Burns, and game show host Groucho Marx along with an abundance of supporting actors offered other Jewish personae; one is tempted to say *the* Jewish persona because the roles were actually relatively few, and terribly familiar.

Behind the scenes, the Jewish role was of course greater. Carried over from the film industry (a simpler process when studios began to produce television and shot most of the shows from Los Angeles, at the end of the 1950s) or rising up in fresh careers of a new medium, Jewish writers, directors, executives, and others were ubiquitous. Without producer Nat Hiken, *You'll Never Get Rich* could never have surfaced. But Hiken had few other successes. His show *Car 54, Where Are You?* may possibly be the most Yiddish-inflected sitcom of all time and the one with the most Jewish character actors until *Barney Miller*, another deeply urban-*mentalite* comedy decades later.

Of the industry's power figures that were creating shows, the most influential, and in a way also the most characteristic, was Sheldon Leonard (1907–99). A Cornell graduate and film actor cast repeatedly in the sentimental gangster role, Leonard began writing for radio in the late 1940s, then turned to teleplays. After directing *The Danny Thomas Show* or three years, he became its producer in 1956 while occupying both spots on various other shows (including the pilot of *Lassie*, one of those shows in which blacklistees worked frequently under assumed names). With Danny Thomas, he formed T&L Productions in 1961, a company that (after another internal transformation) created *The Dick Van Dyke Show* and most of its spin-offs, and he also bears the highly commercial responsibility for the Andy Griffith comic persona. Occasionally seeking more serious ground (like an unsuccessful but prize-winning series based on James Thurber stories, or the *Damon Runyon Theater*, which must have been close to his own heart), Leonard is regarded as the father of the sentimental sitcom.

After the sitcom, the Jewish role was simultaneously heaviest and least apparent to the outsider in the crime drama. *Naked City* (1958–63) has captured more attention from scholars and from reminiscing actors of serious dramatic and comedy films from the 1960s to the '90s for one chief reason: location. In many ways a standard policier not so different from others of the time, it was in some respects the stepchild of contemporary live teledrama. It retained a Manhattan location shooting even after other shows left, and went them one better: each episode opened with the proud claim that the drama was shot in the naked city itself.

Naked City was, in many ways, really about the city and its outskirts all the way to Fire Island, its physical contours as much as its human inhabitants. In that sense it was very much the child of the 1948 film of the same name, directed by young left-winger Jules Dassin (and produced by the writer of the original story, Mark Hellinger), as one of what Abraham Polonsky had called the "fable of the streets" type, where the camera drew upon archetypes of collective personalities in their native location. For the final scene of the cinematic *Naked City*, as the perpetrators are about to be nabbed by police, Dassin had a camera hidden in the back of a van, and directed actors to weave through the thick crowds of the Lower East Side without revealing themselves.

This style of experimentation was badly damaged by the Blacklist, for the simple reason that its creative artists were plainly on the Left. The telltale police drama on the small screen, *Dragnet* – supposedly documenting police procedures and code phrases – scarcely bothered to treat its own city, Los Angeles, as a sociological subject, let alone a spectacle of everyday life. Nor did most of the other popular television cop series, from *Highway Patrol* (1955–59) to *The Untouchables* (1959–63), do so in any sustained way. But in a place like *Naked City*, as one contemporary critic observed, the cops both lacked the poise of their counterparts on the *Untouchables*, as well as their sense of revenge on wrongdoers. "Gentle creatures," these police were "almost disabled by pity" and an "infinite capacity for being pained" as social workers witnessing humanity's "folly and anguish." The crimes themselves were far from conspiratorial power plays by mob bosses who viewed themselves as businessmen. Rather, they were likely to be pointless acts of desperation by broken men and women in the dark city; in sinning, they mainly brought destruction upon themselves.[39]

Naked City also made dramatic history, and not only for television. To play those marginal characters and others casually involved, bystanders, victims, petty crooks, the show readily grabbed the talent at hand. A producer later recalled,

> *Naked City* was the big window on New York talent that people from the West Coast watched. I had people like Alan Alda and Marty Sheen in one-line parts. Marty Sheen came to me one day and said, "Can I play an extra?" I said, "I don't cast extras, and I have a script coming in with a lead part for you in a few weeks." And he said, "Yeah, but I've got to pay the rent now." So I said, "Okay, get in the background and don't let anybody see your face." Sure enough, in a couple weeks, he had a lead. Bobby Duvall was in a lot of the episodes, and one day he said, "Listen, my roommate has seven years in the theater and he's never done a film thing." So I said, "Bring him in." I had a part I had to cast that was opposite a big scene-stealer. I gave him a couple pages and said, "Go in the corner and read it, and come back and read it for me." And I said, "Fine, you've got the job." Anyhow, that was Dustin Hoffman.[40]

Hoffman and Duvall, Sheen, and Alda were joined by a galaxy of character actors that included Geraldine Brooks, Dennis Hopper, Caroll O'Connor, Gene Hackman, William Shatner, Ossie Davis, Martin Landau, Ed Asner, Cloris Leachman, and Geraldine Fitzgerald, and among the older Holly-wood actors Mary Astor, Lillian Gish, Sylvia Sidney, and Ann Harding, not to mention blacklistees John Randolph, Howard da Silva, and Jack Gilford – the first return to television or film work for these last three Method actors. The admired Sterling Silliphant wrote many of the early shows. He was replaced by a long list of writers including blacklistees Arnold Manoff and Ben Maddow, and joined by unblacklisted Marxist Al Brenner, among others.[41]

No television drama, however prestigious, could or perhaps ever would exceed this extended wealth of talent, week after week. *Naked City* was thus the logical connecting point in a career between early television for progressive Method actors such as Jack Klugman, from the lowest to the highest genre, *Captain Video* (at sixty-five dollars an episode) to *Studio One,* later *The Odd Couple* – and the social teledrama of Klugman's own crusading melodramatic vehicle, *Quincy, ME.*[42]

After *Naked City,* the most important liberal crime show by a long stretch was *The Defenders* (1958–65). *Naked City* made the city the real center of the drama rather than the crime, but in *The Defenders,* the law itself became the subject, and all the contemporary police and civil liberties issues, such as no knock police entrance into home and apartments, capital punishment, abortion, passport policies, and so on were brought home to the viewer.

The Defenders owed its existence to two Jewish television giants, David Susskind and Herbert Brodkin. Susskind, a talent agent turned Broadway producer, first became a liberal darling with the landmark series *Justice* (1954–56) that rehearsed many of *The Defenders'* themes. Here, dedicated public interest attorneys defend the rights of the indigent, seeking the spirit of the law in addition to the letter. Shortly following the cancellation of that show, television industry insider Brodkin produced a double episode of *Studio One* in 1957, called "The Defender," with Ralph Bellamy playing the fatherly role later memorably occupied by E. G. Marshall with William Shatner as the son, once again defending the poor and miserable against the power of the prosecution. Years went by and the memory of that two-hour piece eventually served as a kind of prepilot, when Brodkin brought it back as the civil liberties show par excellence, employing Silliphant to write many of the first season's episodes.

Looking for fresh blood after the first season, Brodkin added Al Ruben to the staff – a bit of a revolution, because practically all writing for dramatic series, including *Naked City* and *The Defenders*, had been done on a more or less freelance basis up to that time. Ruben was a former journalist, a story editor of *The Adventures of Robin Hood* series made in the UK by expatriate Hannah Weinstein and secretly written by a small handful of Hollywood blacklistees. Ruben returned to Los Angeles to work on a series of television shows, including especially liberal episodes of the artistically admired Richard Boone vehicle *Have Gun, Will Travel*.

Ruben got a guarantee of credit for either a teleplay or payment for a revision of some other writer's work, not quite creative control of the show but something close to it. That the most successful Jewish progressive writer on television would be guiding the most liberal show on television, and one of the most admired, marked a quiet return of a kind of dissent. Working with Ruben, the other most interesting writer for *The Defenders* was Ernest Kinoy. Brother to the famed left-wing civil liberties lawyer Arthur Kinoy, Ernest was a veteran radio writer in the last decade of that medium's network programming. He wrote widely for television's *Studio One* and *Playhouse 90*, and in future years he would specialize in telefilms, often about Jewish-American or Israeli themes. His most famous work after the 1960s was undoubtedly on the original *Roots* (1976), and the miniseries successor *Roots: The Next Generations* (1979–81), for which he served as principal scriptwriter. He had already earned two Emmys for *The Defenders*, including a memorable episode with James Earl Jones thrown into prison with a racist white man, and probably risked his career with "Blacklist" (1965), the very first television show to dramatize a victim of the Blacklist, a local Jewish actor (predictably played by Klugman) who lost his career to nefarious supposed investigators.

Only one show went further and that one could not last. *East Side/West Side* (1963–64) replaced the gun with the social worker lobbying agencies. It was also memorable for violating the network rules on how stars should look on camera. Produced by Susskind, it was a much tougher dramatic series than television was prepared to take before the 1980s, and it lasted only thirty-nine episodes. Yet *East Side/West Side* has remained memorable in the chronicles of media history. Set in a poor section of Manhattan, it centered upon the many problems of the contemporary poor. A single, remarkable episode could crowd racial discrimination, slum housing, joblessness, children's endangerment, gender issues, and the civil rights movement into the fifty-minute frame, with the good white liberals of the Community Welfare Service both validating the grievances and striving to mitigate the worst of them. Its writers and directors were skillful enough to strive for a kind of theatrical balance within the drama.

Thanks to location shooting – by this time still more rare than in the first days of *The Naked City* – it shared the earlier show's most important asset, some of the best younger stage actors and some of the most visible blacklistees just coming up for air, including Martin Sheen, Maureen Stapleton, Coleen Dewhurst, Ruby Dee, and blacklistees Howard da Silva and Lee Grant. The editor of the pilot was Ralph Rosenblum, future editor of many Woody Allen films. But its most distinct qualities may be traced to its sometime executive producer Arnold Perl (as we have seen, creator of "The World of Sholom Aleichem," and original screenwriter of *Malcolm X*) and its occasional writer, Millard Lampell.

Lampell (1919–98), whom we have seen earlier, had joined Pete Seeger and Woody Guthrie on the famed Almanac Singers, wrote the then-famous "Lonesome Train" cantata, and turning to films in his last years before the Blacklist, wrote *Saturday's Hero* (1951), perhaps the best movie about the gritty reality of college football ever made. Later in the decade, still without real work, Lampell staged his own drama, *The Wall*, about the 1943 Warsaw Jewish Ghetto uprising, gaining the attention of Susskind, who recruited him to *East Side/West Side*. One of Lampell's most controversial scripts for the series, "No Hiding Place," plunged into the world of unscrupulous realtors successfully prompting panic among white home owners as a black neighbor moves in. A savaging of liberalism as much as of bigotry, it thereby went further than any network executive would consider comfortable, for a very long time. The episode reminded viewers that no easy solutions were likely to be found in general expressions of kindness or abstract humanism. America's race troubles were, in short, not going to go away easily, if at all.

East Side/West Side was troubled from its beginning by internal divisions of authority and temperament, and by the refusal of many network affiliates (mostly in the South) to air a dramatic show with a black colead, Cicely Tyson. But the real problem was the perception of the show as too realistic, i.e., too depressing. Real-life liberal Jewish Republican Senator from New York Jacob Javits even praised it from the floor of Congress, to no avail.[43]

For television drama connoisseurs *East Side/West Side,* whatever its virtues, was almost a decade too late for the grand golden age. The era of conformity, of Eisenhowerisms and bomb shelters, had also been the age of the live action drama anthology.

It would be impossible to trace the Jewish credits and noncredits of *The Armstrong Theater, Playhouse 90, U.S. Steel Hour,* and dozens of other short-lived anthologies of the 1950s and early 1960s, *Top Plays of 1954* to *Theater '59* and *Star Theater.* But among dramatists and for the general public alike, one name is a mile ahead of all the rest: Paddy Chayevsky. The son of Russian-Jewish parents one step ahead of the Czarist police, he grew up with an amateur actor for a father, a needle trades worker and autodidact for a mother. Growing up in the Bronx, he worked in a print shop, mingled with other ethnic groups, went to City College and wrote satirical ditties attacking the local red hunters. In Europe during the war, he began writing shows for Army camp tours, met left-leaning cultural types from Garson Kanin (who "discovered" him) to Marc Blitzstein and Arthur Penn.

It was Chayevsky's intersection with the Method teaching and acting crowd that set his path decisively. A few serious theatrical efforts had already been made on television. Worthington Miner had overseen, beginning in 1948, a series of adaptations building off the radio's *Studio One.* The same year, the Actors Studio (spun-off from the Group, under the leadership of Elia Kazan and others) saw its own dramatic anthology awarded one of television's first Peabody Awards.

Television, it was quickly recognized, had huge benefits for the realist or melodramatic stylings of Method with the camera's training upon the individual, showing to every viewer what only a few theatregoers could see, and emphasizing the live action akin to a theater setting. Of course, it remained to be seen whether televised theater could be commercial. Writer Max Wilk, one of television's first memoirists, began work with the *Ford Television Theater* in 1948 and watched the progression of drama across most of the next decade. The audience was a small percentage, perhaps twenty percent, of what it would become by 1960; and the taste of that audience lent itself to drama.

Chayevsky wrote nine teleplays in the single season, perhaps a record for a high-profile theatrical anthology. Unlike the earlier Group drama, wartime film, or film noir, but very much in consonance with television's special features, the scale of human drama had been reduced from the social to the person or from the problem that demanded great solutions to one which called for more personal choices, personal solutions acceptable to the modulating ethos of individualist America.

Marty, a 1954 teledrama made into a film the next year, and overwhelmingly the most acclaimed drama of network television's first fifteen years or so, made that point in spades. Chayevsky had already moved his ethnic choices from Jewish to Irish (catching up with the "Paddy" he had adopted in place of his own "Sidney," during wartime) and placed his famous Bronx drama among the unhappily unmarrieds. The character in question, so lovingly played by Ernest Borgnine, was dramatically revolutionary by being homely yet a romantic hero. In another age, the hinted homosexuality or at least homosociality might have played a more central role in the protagonist's inner life; instead, it is the urgency of his quest to be normal, to marry, leave home at last, perhaps to move out of the Bronx to the suburbs, but in any case to establish himself within the parameters of what middle-class America has to offer.

Other Chayefsky characters of the time have similar problems: they are unsuccessful businessmen; their suburban life makes them feel claustrophobic; they don't know what to do with a mother (much like Chayefsky's own mother) who refused to move in with the kids and instead insists upon going back to work in the factory as a way to cope with the empty nest; or they have other generational problems. In any case, they are ordinary folks facing problems more ordinary than desperate unemployment (1930s) or battlefield action (1940s) for themselves or relatives. They are the old urban working class seen through the rearview mirror of suburbanites, suburbanites with memories and difficulties going back to their ethnic, urban upbringing. They suffer most from the consequences of transition.

Chayevsky later observed laconically that he wrote large sections of *Marty* as satire and was stunned to learn that viewers wept through scene after scene. This anecdote is suspect because Chayefsky was hardly a satirical scenarist. But the point is a good one, nonetheless. Viewers, emphatically Jewish viewers, could not only feel the pain, but felt it over worse troubles, like prospective atomic war, because they made the personal troubles their own. The penchant for introspection suited the era of psychoanalysis, even for that vast majority (practically everyone between New York and Los Angeles) who had never seen a psychoanalyst; they now looked inside themselves, hoping to find happiness.

And yet, its essentially humane quality could not be denied, nor could the status of the city, actually highlighted in some ways by its abandonment for the suburbs, because the city contains the irrationality of the crowd and the historic setting – in a country with precious little history and less memory – of buildings and scenes that resonate with mass experience. "New York" was becoming the exotic zone, at least for suburbanites, that the Lower East Side and Harlem had been for previous generations.

Like Chayevsky, who was said to have shuddered every time he received a letter under his birth name (fearing it was a HUAC subpoena), television's leading Jewish dramatists of a better, more inclusive America often lived under a cloud themselves. To take a spectacular example: at the apex of quality shows was undoubtedly *You Are There* (1953–57) with the most famous newscasters of the time, remembered, during the 1950s, for their stentorian coverage of the war, narrating historical events ranging from the fall of Rome and the trial of Gallileo to the surrender of Lee at Appamatox and the burning of the Hindenburg. Most of the top production staff were Jewish, along with the most talented director on the series, former Yiddish child actor Sidney Lumet. But the writers of the prestigious first series (1953–55), working under assumed names, were uniformly Jewish as well as radical: the blacklisted screenwriters Abraham Polonsky, Arnold Manoff, and Walter Bernstein. Their interrogation of society tended backward frequently to the man of conscience on trail, that is to say, to their own stories. They had found the way to challenge the threats to American democracy, even though at least in a career sense (a consideration for men who had lost their occupation) it could do them no good.

For much of the rest of Jewish acting, writing, and directing talent, of course, television was just one more way to reach the big time and big money.[44] Even so, somehow their vision of assimilation was often not the vision of propriety forced upon them. Take a seemingly most unlikely example: Soupy Sales.

Born Milton Supman in 1926 and raised to age seven in small-town North Carolina, son of dry-goods business owners who shifted from Baltimore in search of virgin territory, he and the family moved on to Huntington, W. Va., still the South, but in another world, in fact a world where a Soupy Sales Plaza ultimately came into existence. Sales later claimed that before leaving Franklinton he had witnessed a lynching and mutilation by the KKK (and the "gruesome spectacle left an indelible, lifelong impression on me . . . as vividly as if it all happened just last week").[45] It was a Jewish observation, if not only a Jewish observation; the young observer had evidently not only been terrorized by the sight, but by his own identification with the victim.

He started stand-up comedy in high school, did club dates before he enlisted in the Navy during the war, broke into radio, then local television in Cincinnati, Cleveland, and Detroit (his show is most kindly remembered for the appearance of jazz musicians like Duke Ellington), where he found his métier with a noon-time show, *Soupy's On*. Much of it was a soft version of vaudeville, and getting a pie in the face always seemed to climax Sales's antics. Then Soupy went national, even hosted *The Tonight Show* for a week, and proceeded to act in some films, many television shows, and made more public appearances of the Macy's Parade type.

In 1965, he pulled a gag (telling his young viewers to take money out of dad's wallet and mom's pocketbook and send it to him – he received nearly eighty thousand dollars) and got himself fired until a demonstration of college students and others outside the studio got him back inside. ("This . . . has been a recurring theme in my career," he complained, and rationalized, "I've often had trouble with management. It's not that I was working against the establishment, it's just that the establishment always branded me as undisciplined, which is pure bullshit . . . ".[46]) Known for his over-the-top jokes, he seemed to have his last outré moments in the 1960s appearing with Jimi Hendrix and Little Richard, before fading into showbiz nostalgia.

Those who rightly complained about the end of live television, the removal of production from fertile urban Manhattan to suburban, sterile Los Angeles, and the increasing imposition (in the later 1950s) of sponsor censorship of "neurotic" social themes, were not mistaken. The takeover of the airways by westerns by 1960 confirmed a dismal trend. But more was ahead.

Meanwhile, Jewish talents like director Martin Ritt, writer Walter Bernstein, and a host of younger writers, actors, and cameramen would find their way from television training into many of the best films of the 1970s, '80s, and '90s. Others, including Steven Spielberg, would later claim to be educated by the best of television, giving them the sense of loss and of yearning that the ordinary person felt, a sense that could belong to anyone but seemed to belong best, in drama at any rate, to postassimilation Jews.

And, for a long time, there were living remnants, not so much in television where youth increasingly ruled but in other avenues where the old task of lifting up the masses seemed to pass from social movement to the control of one staggeringly talented or massively energetic individual.

CULTURAL CONNECTIONS

The visionary assimilationism or unnamed multiculturalism of the New Deal enthusiast took decades to die away and may never have vanished altogether. For a while, audiences, performers, and promoters could easily convince themselves that the anticipated transformation of society still would or at least could happen. "Spirituals to Swing," the most important showcase for African-American musical talent heretofore, was Carnegie Hall's most vivid productions of 1938, cosponsored by the *New Masses* with indelibly Popular Front material, staged in 1939 by future Marxist (and exile) film director Joseph Losey. Meanwhile, the critical acclaim of Marc Blitzstein's *Cradle Will Rock* and Harold Rome's *Pins and Needles* in 1939 – both definitely radical, neither of them notable for African-American participation – led the Hollywood Theater Alliance to stage a "Negro Revue" which led to *Jump for Joy*, with music mostly written by Duke Ellington, produced by B film writer Henry Blankfort.

Opening in Los Angeles in 1941, *Jump* not only introduced Dorothy Dandridge and "I've Got It Bad (and That Ain't Good)," it capped off Langston Hughes's half-decade effort to showcase black talent with politics undisguised, built upon Hughes's own Harlem Suitcase Theater, Cotton Club acts, and protests to defend the Scottsboro Boys. Comic skits, dance numbers, ballads, including a musical history of African-American life by Ellington – and an audience very largely Jewish as well as left-wing. To illustrate how far the alliance extended, parts of *Jump for Joy* were broadcast on NBC radio during 1941 in a national "Salute to Labor" hosted by noted liberal (and Jewish) actor Melvyn Douglas. By 1943, amid the war effort, a "Black, Beige and Brown" revue premiered in Carnegie Hall, with the usual cast of blues, folk, and jazz entertainers and the usual Jewish audience. Like Aaron Copland, they were sketching a new world of peace, cooperation, and mutual prosperity that never happened.

There were many deeply Jewish successors to this effort, whose trajectories belong to another chapter. One of the best belongs, however, closer to Shakespeare than to *Jump for Joy*, but somehow close to both. Joe Papp, accused of "gutter mentality" by prestigious critics while making the bard available to the masses in New York City's parks, is a marvelous case in point.[47]

Growing up in Brownville poverty, Joseph Papirofsky (1921–91) was the child of Polish refugees, reputedly awed by *The Jazz Singer*, but far from being able to make an assimilationist dream possible. In Williamsburg, as a teenager in the Depression, Papirofsky left orthodoxy for Marxism (or left one orthodoxy for another), became president of his high school's Dramatic Society, [48] heard Paul Robeson and Pete Seeger at rallies, and after a short spell of attempted union organizing, joined the Navy in 1942. Like many other Jewish boys, he learned in the service that he could organize entertainment (his first show starred Bob Fosse). Upon leaving the Navy, he used his GI Bill money to enroll in Actors Lab in Los Angeles. He was close to his teachers, some of them like Morris Carnovsky, Lee J. Cobb, and John Garfield, classic actors who nevertheless took pride in their Hollywood movies. It was a lesson.

The denunciation by columnist Hedda Hopper of "race mixing" at a Hollywood Lab social event sent Papp into print, writing angry letters to the press about racism in film and theater. [49] To an FBI acutely conscious of Reds who pressed this issue exactly, it was an invitation to investigation and to the Blacklist, and not only for Papp. The Lab closed, and the young man who served as manager and janitor locked the door on its unsuccessful successor. Papp went to work in a sheet metal factory, then took a job as stage manager for a touring company doing *Death of a Salesman*. After a few more months, he got a job as a stage manager at CBS. Within a few years, helped by friends he made at CBS, he had created the Shakespeare Workshop in New York. True to his politics, the Workshop was determined to be multiracial and multicultural, and just as determined to make the bard understandable to American popular audiences.

Opening in the parks with Shakespeare in 1958 was a return to the vision of 1930s theatre, and brought with it the inevitable FBI investigation. He was still stage manager for *I've Got a Secret* when hauled onto the stand by investigators. Fired by the network, he got rehired after a court case, but quit. Although Robert Moses (among others) tried to dump Shakespeare out of the parks, Papp finally triumphed. In the next ten years, he made the careers of some of the more exciting younger generation of actors, like James Earl Jones, Colleen Dewhurst, and George C. Scott. He also plunged into the political controversies of the later 1960s, settling on *Hair*. By 1971, when CBS backed out of an agreement to broadcast David Rabe's terse drama about a traumatized Vietnam veteran, he launched a campaign against the network's censorship. He also joined demonstrators against the war in Washington, and returned to protest on assorted issues. Before his death, he could be found protesting a president, this final time against the arts censorship intended by the first Bush administration.[50]

Papp did not work in vain, nor did official efforts to memorialize him as yet another visionary of Manhattan self-promotion capture what he really had in mind. He belonged to another legion, a lost legion whose message would nevertheless endure because no substitute would salve the wounds of the society or even attempt to give generation after generation of immigrants (especially after the change in immigration law in 1965) a way to join the society not only in the family pursuit for jobs and homes but in spirit, as part of a moiling, constantly evolving, uniquely modern democratic project. Out of the frustration at this project, the Jewish avant-garde was born and reborn, time and time again.

NOTES

[1] Michael Staub, *Torn at the Roots: The Crisis of Jewish Liberalism in Postwar America* (New York: Columbia University Press, 2002): 108–09, 116–17. The shifts of Jewish opinion-makers were naturally resisted, but not successfully.

[2] Gail Levin and Judith Tick, *Aaron Copland's America: A Cultural Perspective*: 11.

[3] Ibid., 29–30.

[4] During the early 1940s Blue Note Record founder Max Margulis would take Copland and Willem and Elaine de Kooning around to jazz clubs. Ibid., 74.

[5] Ibid., 70–71.

[6] Leonard J. Lehrman, "Storming Into a New Century with Aaron Copland," *The Forward*, 17 November 2000. In Chicago, Bernstein's daughter Jamie Bernstein Thomas cocreated a new version for the Chicago Humanities Festival. The Houston Grand Opera also staged a concert version of "The Tender Land," commissioned for NBC and rejected during the Blacklist days. Later in the 1930s, Copland taught at the Henry Street Settlement's school; my mother was a settlement nurse-worker there at the time, and I like to think that they passed each other in the hallways.

[7] Ibid., 105.

[8] The centennial of Copland's birth brought museum exhibits and a new version of "Second Hurricane," his 1930s piece forecasting Marc Blitzstein's "Cradle Will Rock." Ibid.

[9] R. LeRoy Bannerman, *Norman Corwin and Radio: The Golden Years* (Birmingham: University of Alabama Press, 1986): 14–20.

[10] Thus in "Seems Radio Is Here To Stay," written at the behest of the network's quest to make radio seem meaningful, he closes some lines,

All this by way of prologue, listener

And prologues should not be prolonged.
Let our announcer do what he's engaged to do:
Announce
What this is all about.
And let there be, when he is done, some interest expressed
By brasses and by strings.
A little music, as they say,
To start an introspective program on its way.

Quoted in Ibid., 46.

[11] Arthur Schlesinger, Jr., *The Vital Center: The Politics of Freedom* (Boston: Little, Brown, 1949): 126.

[12] In self-abasing congressional testimony, Shaw also backed away from Popular Front political commitments during the McCarthy era, claiming naivety. It was not credible, and sadly typified a life of often feckless careerism.

[13] Max Kaminsky and V.E. Hughes, *Jazz Band: My Life in Jazz* (New York: Harpers, 1963): 157.

[14] Ibid., 172–73, 176. Society work kept Kaminsky going for another decade, when he neared retirement but enjoyed a last burst of attention in State Department-sponsored European tours.

[15] See the keen remarks of Yale Strom, *The Book of Klezmer* (Chicago: A Capella/Chicago Review Press, 2002): 180–82. A headliner in the Borscht Belt, Katz was notably based in Los Angeles rather than Manhattan, and served as a popular disk jockey there, 1951–56. That Joel Gray (most famous for a leading role in *Cabaret*, i.e., a Holocaust film of sorts) was his son and celebrity successor speaks volumes.

[16] Jonathan Kandell, "Lew Wasserman, 89, Is Dead: Last of Hollywood's Moguls," *New York Times*, 4 June 2002.

[17] Quoted in the 1986 PBS documentary, *Irving Berlin's America*, in Masha Leon, "Finding Surprises in Irving Berlin Songs," *The Forward*, 27 July 2001. The documentary was reshown at the Jewish Historical Society in 2001; musicologist Jack Gottlieb, on hand, claimed that, minus the syncopated notes, "Among My Souveniers" is actually "Dayenu," and under "A Russian Lullaby" is "Hatikvah." If so, this would be a distinct and not necessarily a pleasant surprise to most Berlin devotees.

[18] *AFI Catalog of Feature Films 1941–50* (Berkeley: University of California Press, 1999): 2874–75.

[19] Two decades later, according to Jerry Stiller, the television show *Bridget Loves Bernie* was taken off the air because of protests from Jewish and Catholic groups against the portrayal of intermarriage. Stiller Interview by David Marc, 1999, Scheuer Collection, Syracuse University.

[20] *AFI Catalog of Feature Films, 1941–1950*, M-Z: 2695–766.

[21] Hollywood censor Joseph Breen successfully demanded the removal of "offensive epithets," and a *New York Times* reviewer described it as "tasteless." See "Open Secret," *AFI Catalog of Feature Films, 1941–1950*: 1764. For Max Wilk's important role in dramatic television, see his remarks in Jeff Kisseloff, *The Box: an Oral History of Television, 1920–1961* (New York: Penguin, 1995): 113, 333–335.

[22] Sometimes it was noteworthy just to have Jewish children saved, as the two orphans (admittedly, one is only half-Jewish) in *The Pied Piper* (1942) by an English couple vacationing in the South of France in 1940.

[23] The play was cowritten by Arnaud D'Usseau, a left-winger later blacklisted. The film script was adapted by Ring Lardner, Jr., and Lee Atlas, the former a Blacklist victim, the latter a (Jewish) friendly witness with a heart condition.

[24] The personally troubled Clift had played a neurosurgeon in *Suddenly Last Summer*, promised a new hospital wing if only he would perform on a troubled young woman a procedure that was apparently a lobotomy. The troubled young woman was played by Elizabeth Taylor, a convert and a Hollywood survivor who betrayed no depth in her devotion to personal celebrity.

[25] See the excellent if brief account in Linda Martin and Kerry Seagrave, *Women in Comedy*: 234–35.

[26] "Reminiscences of Jerry Wald," 1959, Columbia Oral History Project, Columbia University Archives.

[27] See Paul Buhle and Dave Wagner, *Radical Hollywood*: 369–70.

[28] Perhaps it might be said that Jerry Lewis offered the most prominent evidence of noncommitment. His breakthrough film, *Jumping Jacks* (1951), had been written some years earlier, as a World War II script for Abbott and Costello, by blacklisted antifascist veterans Robert Lees and Fred Rinaldo, but Lewis conducted himself much as his persona in *The King of Comedy* (1983), a narcissistic celebrity. In the comedy trade, and apart from his charity grandstanding, he was best known for ridiculing women comics. As he often said, he frankly considered women best suited as baby-making machines.

[29] Kaye had already begun playing the role in *Up In Arms* (1944), as a wimpy and hypochondriac Manhattan elevator operator who is drafted and, to everyone's surprise, becomes a war hero. Full of the tongue-twisting songs that had made Kaye famous on Broadway, it was cowritten by Allen Boretz, a sometime writer for the Marx Brothers, and also a future victim of the Blacklist.

[30] David Margolick, *Strange Fruit: Billie Holiday, Cafe Society and an Early Cry for Civil Rights* (Philadelphia: Running Press, 2000): 39.

[31] I am grateful for the loan of an unpublished MS, by Jim Cullen, that treats this subject at length. See Jim Cullen, "Fool's Paradise: Frank Sinatra and the American Dream," in Jim Cullen, ed., *Popular Culture in American History* (Oxford and Malden: Blackwell Publisher, 2001): 203–32; and for conversations with Michael Meeropol, one of the Rosenberg sons who became the adopted children of the Meeropols.

[32] *AFI Catalog of Films*: 1977. *The Dolly Sisters* (1945), another lavish musical, was even more inventive with the lives of the principals, so much so that the Hungarian Jews become Hungarians only, putting aside their real-life marriages to Jewish businessmen and mobsters. George Jessel, a real-life friend of the Dolly sisters, produced the film.

[33] In later decades, the transethnic stretch was likely to prompt the Israel Lobby into action. Venessa Redgrave, a left-winger playing a courageous concentration camp resident in the telefilm *Playing for Time* (1980), stirred the wrath of the ADL; more ludicrous was the assault upon Omar Sharif, an actor whose picture with an Egyptian air force uniform brought rage until it was revealed to be a still shot from an earlier film. More important than making actual changes was the power to intimidate and prompt self-censorship, much as Catholic conservative and anti-Semite Joseph Breen had done in golden age Hollywood.

[34] William Alland, interview with Paul Buhle, Los Angeles, 1993; "The Producer from Outer Space," interview with Tom Weaver, *Starlog*, August and September 1995: 55 and 57–63, 65, respectively.

[35] The director of these and most of producer Alland's SciFi films was Jack Arnold, who had arisen as publicist in the garment industry, even making a McCarthy era semifictional documentary for and mostly about the leadership of the International Ladies Garment Workers Union, playing the evil Communist labor infiltrator himself! Arnold later improbably directed the antiwar classic *The Mouse That Roared* (1962), a remarkable near finale for an admitted hack. He closed his career working on *Gilligan's Island*.

[36] Douglas Martin, "Zeke Manners, 'Hillbilly' Who Ruled Radio, Dies at 89," *New York Times*, 22 October 2000.

[37] Kisseloff, *The Box: an Oral History of Television*: 51.

[38] See Daniel Czitrom, "Bilko: a Sitcom for All Seasons," in Paul Buhle, ed., *Popular Culture in America*: 156–62. Czitrom had interviewed Silvers at poolside, in the latter's final years.

[39] David Boroff, "Television and the Problem Play," in Patrick D. Hazard, *TV as Art* (Champaign, Ill: National Council of Teachers of English, 1966), 106–07.

[40] "New York Stories, an Oral History by Peter Biskind," special issue of *Premiere* (1994): 110.

[41] Many thanks to Al Brenner for his recollections, given in a 1999 interview in Los Angeles with Paul Buhle and Dave Wagner, and in subsequent correspondence.

[42] Jack Klugman interview by David Marc, 1999, Steven Scheuer Collection, Syracuse University: 65, 19, 31.

[43] See Steven W. Bowie, "East Side/West Side," *Television Chronicles*, no. 9 (1999): 17–32, an incisive treatment of the show including credits for all episodes. Bowie points out that another of the principal writers was Allan E.

Sloane, a Jewish friendly witness who suffered large doses of guilt for his friendly testimony.

⁴⁴ We leave aside the assorted music and variety shows, where scholarship has not yet been equal to the task of tracking anything like Jewish content. Perhaps it's enough to note that Mitch Miller, a Jewish entertainer and executive once close to the Popular Front, became in the 1950s a major producer (head of Columbia Records), responded to the threatening appearance of rock with a sing-along mode, first in albums, then on television in 1961, with the words printed on the screen. His show lasted until 1964, revived briefly in 1966.

⁴⁵ Soupy Sales with Charles Salzberg, *Soupy Sez! My Zany Life and Times* (New York: M. Evans and Co., 2001): 17.

⁴⁶ Ibid., 198.

⁴⁷ The quotation is from theater critic John Simon, see Helen Epstein, *Joe Papp, an American Life* (Boston: Little, Brown, 1994): 6.

⁴⁸ Ibid., 4–49.

⁴⁹ Ibid., 68–69.

⁵⁰ Ibid., 390–469.

FIVE

UP FROM THE AVANT-GARDE

The avant-garde story has deep roots in European history, long before *La Bohéme* lent the name "bohemians" to the restless, artistic sections of the middle class (and others, including both blue-collar bohemians and wealthy or aristocratic patrons) emerging in the middle of the nineteenth century. Social crises of the High Middle Ages had occasionally thrown distaff sections of upper-class women into alliance with a motley crew of dispossessed "beghards," crystallizing a utopianism or millenarianism articulated by intellectuals (male and female) and either crushed by force or absorbed into religious vocations. Some of the unrest and yearnings showed up in the most remarkable and innovative emerging art, like the radical works of Bosch, attacking war along with gluttony and visually creating a Woodstock-like paradise of naked innocence before the catastrophes of class society. Other signs could be found in the ostensibly religious philosophers emerging from that restless age but bearing the dialectic, destined to become the core of romantic thought and Marxist radicalism. Both art and philosophy, it could be argued, bore the indirect but definite traces of Jewish mysticism. But justly fearing surges of popular Christianity (like the Crusades), Jews had little sympathy for the millennialism of this age, or its cultural expressions.

Nineteenth-century German- and Russian-speaking Jewish intellectuals were quick to respond to romantic currents elevating the role of artist and cultural critic. Here was a perfect role, actually many roles, for the cerebral outsider. In various spots across the European map, especially the Netherlands and England, resurgent bohemianism merged with a universalist egalitarianism considerably more anarchist in spirit than Marxist. Meanwhile, in Gilded Age America, members of Jewish anarchist circles disdained marriage ceremonies (to the considerable embarrassment, in later years, of their grown children) and rushed to read the front page columns of the left-wing press boasting the ardent poetry of their champions.

In this heated atmosphere, against a background of burgeoning sweat-shops and the worst depression the nation had faced hitherto, the Yiddish poet to be known as the first bohemian of the language found and then lost himself again all too quickly. Joseph Bovshover, a young Russian immigrant who wrote verse and polemic for the anarchist *Freie Arbeter Shtimme* (Free Workers' Voice), was in the same way the earliest prominent Jewish devotee of Walt Whitman (whose style he falteringly imitated) and one of those figures whose very presence offered evidence of determined adaptation to the culture of the New World. Bovshover went mad at age twenty-six, surviving for almost two decades institutionalized.[1] Moshe Nadir depicted him imaginatively as inhabiting one of those Lower East Side tea shops where revolution was endlessly debated. Unable to speak, this fictional Bovshover tapped his knee with a pencil endlessly, lost so far inside himself that he could never come out again.[2]

The next phases of Yiddish bohemianism, determinedly reaching far into the resources of *Yiddishkayt*, inclined toward revolt against both egalitarianism and assimilationist impulses. But they involved a working-class bohemia of paperhangers and house painters who wrote furiously, driven by their mostly artistic aspirations. The truest spiritual precursors of the Beats were likely to be found in the circles of *di Yunge* as in the contemporary hobo camps influenced by the Industrial Workers of the World, rather than in the contemporary circles of the materially comfortable (if also radical) intellectuals around the *Seven Arts* and the *Dial*.

The missing connective factor, as in so much of Jewish intellectual life before mid-century, was black culture, which is to say the heart of distinctively American popular culture. Practical men (and some women) with dollars and empires on their minds were more likely to see futures for themselves in relation to this apparently exotic Americana, marketing black music for their own benefit. They were at least a generation ahead of the Jewish bohemians. In later decades, the reprogramming of the avant-garde commercial appeal to generations of youngsters was Jewish big business, in large part a cynical betrayal of whatever the avant-garde had ever meant, artistically or politically.

And yet, things could never be so simple. When I went to see Hugo Gellert, the last survivor of the old *Masses* circle, he was ninety-two, a half-century past his most creative years, an artistic Socialist realist and unflagging supporter of the by then collapsing Soviet Union. But he had quite a story to tell. Born to Jewish parents in Budapest in 1892, he moved with his family to New York in 1905, and practically grew up within a Hungarian-American workers movement rich in varied cultural activities. Winning prizes for his paintings as a teenager, Gellert drew his inspiration from contemporary Hungarian avant-garde, the mixing of folkish motifs with Secessionist styles. Emerging as an apparently apolitical illustrator for the pages of the *Masses*, he drew close to the early Communist movement after a wartime trip to Hungary, and became one of the most important artists of *The Liberator*, the heavily politicized successor to the suppressed *Masses*.[3]

Never a Communist Party member until the middle of the Depression, Gellert nevertheless became an admired illustrator of left-wing publications (his major public outlet, when refusal to make a flattering drawing of a European Fascist leader drove him from pages of the *New Yorker*). In the *New Masses* and its Yiddish counterpart *der Hammer*, by the late 1920s, black culture was very much in style, not only "proletarian" drawings of African-American workers, but Expressionist covers, jazz motifs, and assorted bows to egalitarianism with visual references abundant in crowd scenes. Illustration was a commercial sideline for him. Already known for his stage designs, he created the poster for the first production of *All God's Chillun Got Wings*, by Eugene O'Neill.[4] Gellert was, of course, a militant antiracist to the end of his life.

It is difficult to say to what degree the overwhelmingly immigrant, Jewish left-wing rank and file understood or appreciated the sympathetic move toward the Harlem Renaissance and Pan-African themes. Certainly, they supported it, in the name of transrace internationalism that encompassed the most beaten-down and exploited workers. The next heavily Jewish generation of the Left, teens at the outbreak of the Depression, adopted jazz dancing, jazz and blues music, even spirituals (within a worldview that treated religion otherwise as hopelessly backward) as part of their own Americanization and, in the Popular Front frame, vital elements of a "people's culture."

We've already seen how powerfully African-American motifs could affect theatrical lyrics, and plot, written, directed, produced, and sometimes acted in by Jews. The undercurrent would become apparent when the promised happier world of post-World War Two turned into the "age of anxiety," a refurbished American boomerism with many more Jews now included – Long Island Archie Bunkers to business executives – but others trying to find an artistic escape. These new artistic generations rediscovered black culture, as if it had been waiting for them. But then, so did the newer wave of cultural-minded businessmen who glimpsed almost limitless opportunities to cash in.

Somewhere in between was the likely to be forgotten Jew, the less than famous professional musician who took up black music as he might have taken up gypsy music a generation or two earlier, rock, rap, or even *klezmer* generations later. Consider another Max Kaminsky type, but one who actually joined the avant-garde to stay: "Red" Rodney, Jewish son of a sheet metal contractor from Kiev. Red himself, born in 1927 and raised in Boston, started playing trumpet in a local Jewish War Veterans post. He had received his own instrument as a bar mitzvah present. When the war broke out and most of the famous (even locally famous) trumpet players were drafted, he was playing in Philadelphia and Atlantic City with Benny Goodman and Jimmy Dorsey. A few years later, Rodney was invited into the official CBS radio band. Fellow sessions participants persuaded him to play bebop with Charlie Parker. Still gigging at bar mitzvahs (occasionally in *klezmer*, playing alongside the famous Dave Tarras) and weddings at the end of the 1940s, he joined Woody Herman, then returned to Parker in 1949. There he became addicted to heroin, kicking the habit only after decades of increasingly bad times, ending in a pursuit by the FBI. Near the end of his troubled life, he performed in a fluegelhorn duet for the Clinton White House. He had paid his dues in ways that the assimilationists, or for that matter Israeli musicians, rarely did.[5]

One of Rodney's most puzzled memories was the cultural turn in music during the late-middle 1940s. Suddenly, jazz became a cult among the young, magazines sprouted up and ardent devotees of specific styles could be found everywhere. Rodney certainly enjoyed the attention and the prospect of getting off the bar mitzvah circuit that Jewish musicians still consider the bottom of the not-so-magic barrel. But black nationalism not only came with bebop, it was the motivating force of bebop. Rodney felt himself spiritually excluded even while physically included, a discrepancy that no doubt had contributed to his drug problems (the music's association with blackness also contributed considerably to his FBI problems, in the continuing age of J. Edgar Hoover). Musicians borrowed and traded riffs, while fans wanted to pigeonhole styles, a source of aggravation and continuing anxiety that made Rodney an easy victim of escapism. He had begun his personal journey without any sense of identity problems, but ran into them like a brick wall. If Max Kaminsky had been satisfied with himself, Rodney was self-destructive and unsatisfied, and he was not the only one. The "White Negro" impulse of the Beat writers and their disproportionate Jewishness can be put under the same light.

But never easily or simply. Half-Jewish Lawrence Ferlinghetti, whose launching of City Lights Books (the store and the publisher) in 1953 brought the message to millions, including the similarly half-Jewish Diane DiPrima, protofeminist queen of the Beats, also introduced City Lights' all-time champion author, Allen Ginsberg, and took the heat of the would-be censors.[6] In their books, the jazzy and sexual (emphatically including homosexual) poetry reached best-seller status that their truest forerunner, Yankee-style bohemian Walt Whitman, could not have imagined. Nor could it be imagined that avant-garde and mass culture would merge, in ways further popularized, merchandized, exploited, but never totally destroyed, in music, film, and other arts in the time to come.

Howl and Other Poems (1956), in addition to being a sort of poetic declaration of Beatitude, was patently a recollection of Jewish left-wing memory held up against a crazed, postwar consumerist *goyishe* America. *Kaddish and Other Poems* (1961) intensified the dialogue through the same memory hole, vicariously recalling the Lower East Side near the turn of the century and after, Jewish generations watching Chaplin movies, hitchhiking with fellow Yipsels (Young Peoples Socialist League) long since dead, dwelling on a utopia lost but restaging it as memory never abandoned as it turns round and round within the poet's mind. The son lovingly reconstructs his mother's young Russian-flavored beauty and her hopes for a very different and kinder America, her growing mixture of Communist faith and craziness, her breakup with Ginsberg's father and her growing emotional dependence upon Allen, her heartened pause in the vibrant political moments of the Bronx, and finally her descent into madness with strange prophecies and messages. By the end, it is not at all clear that the broken woman might not be the mirror of a broken century, Jewish idealism and dreams smashed, not to be saved from despair by the usual remedies of mental adjustment, assimilation, and/or Jewish nationalism. The weight of an unredeemed vision, too much for her, is passed on to her son.

The poet, for his part, travels, sees the world, takes drugs, has a lot of sex, and moans out his loneliness and despair. But he never gets too far from mother Naomi or from his Aunt Rose, who taught him to sing Republican (*i.e.*, Popular Front, antifascist) ballads from the Spanish Civil War. Collective memory as well as humane sensibilities will save Ginsberg from the grants doled out by CIA-funded agencies boasting "cultural freedom," likewise from photo-ops at White House, or Gracie Mansion, receptions and Jerusalem Prizes. He will, at points, stumble around embarrassingly with Eastern gurus. But he unfailingly remains an antiwar crusader, a conspiracy theorist of Gentile presidents, and in his last decade, amid failing health, a determined neighborhood character. He was never less than avant-garde, but always part of a vibrant popular culture, a true inventor of the counterculture.[7]

A valuable piece of further evidence came late in life, on Ginsberg's own adopted home turf. One of his most evident enthusiasms was for artists organized around the defense of the historically sacred Lower East Side from its latest threat, gentrification and accompanying repression of unruly, i.e., property value lowering crowds in Tompkins Square Park. In 1873, a police riot there had shocked the post-Civil War republic with proof of class divisions. It was even said that Samuel Gompers, a young Jewish immigrant from Britain and a Marxist-trained cigar maker, made up his mind after that very demonstration to jettison the poor, pursuing instead the goal of a powerful labor movement restricted to a labor aristocracy sworn to convince businessmen and lawmakers that white male workers only wanted a share, not a fundamental change in society. Ginsberg, a bit over a century later, drew the opposite conclusions.

His favorite publication of these late days was said to be, not esoteric poetic texts, but a small-press comic book series: *World War 3 Illustrated*, published since 1979 by a small group that included homeboy Clevelanders Seth Tobocman and Peter Kuper, joined by a native New Yorker, Eric Drooker. Back in 1970, Kuper had been a substitute on a paper route that included Harvey Pekar, R. Crumb's oldest pal and frequent collaborator. He had come across a collection of 78s left in his parents' basement by some previous homeowner, and a friendly Pekar developed the bright notion that Crumb, about to pass through town, might be willing to trade some original art for them.

It was a brilliant connection in the spirit of earlier decades, when Jewish kids from the lower-middle classes or poorer, destined for artistic achievements, got together and discovered their talents under the most incidental, neighborly circumstances. And it was, of course, only a few neighborhoods over from the 1930s homes of *Superman*'s boy creators; some of the older Jewish Clevelanders thus might have known personally or at least seen on the streets the unlikely comics geniuses of three generations.

World War 3 was likened, by Kuper himself, to the old *Masses* in the sense of an artist's radical magazine drawing upon the art of its own time, not the Ash Can gallery work of the 1910s, but the underground comix of the 1960s and 70s. First intending to take on the big issues of the globe, the group settled for the issues of the neighborhood. Forty years after the publication of *Howl*, Drooker would make a selection of Ginsberg's verse for his own illustrations in the comic book-style *Illuminated Poems* (1996).[8] It is one of the most interesting marriages of words and images in recent literary production, equally reminiscent of William Blake and of those Yiddish poetry texts from the 1910s and '20s in the heroic age of Jewish book illustration. The great gay poet and proper descendent of Whitman, only a few years before death, wrote about the relation between writers and artists graciously, lovingly, insisting he was the one truly honored:

> I first glimpsed Eric Drooker's odd name on posters pasted on fire-alarm sides, construction walls checkered with advertisements, & lamppost junction boxes in the vortex of Lower East Side Avenues leading to Tompkins Square Park ... I began collecting Drooker's posters ... seeing in contemporary images the same dangerous class conflicts that I'd remembered from childhood ... As I'd followed his work over a decade, I was flattered that so radical an artist of late generations found the body of my poetry still relevant, even inspiring. Our paths crossed often, we took part in various political rallies and poetical-musical entertainments.[9]

Vernacular artists and organizers had their inspiration in this metaphorical vicinity, if only they knew what to do with it. The saga of the avant-garde traces the ways in which transgression against white bread America's existing expectation offered Jews opportunities to prove themselves and offer a cultural gift that could not have been accepted in outright political terms but on which a cultural avant-garde could ride in under the radar. Sometimes the most important stories got lost in the telling (or selling), and the tellers along with them, unable even to grasp what they had accomplished. But very often, their work struck home, that is, home in an American culture widened by their efforts. At any rate, the story of the American avant-garde would scarcely be recognizable without them, as unrecognizable as the tale of recorded and live folk, jazz, blues, and rock without the Jewish imprint.

MUSIC MAVENS

The revealing tale of Jerry Wexler opens, conceptually speaking, if not chronologically, just about where the Popular Front attachment to the music scene closes. Raised in Washington Heights in the days when Socialist Norman Thomas was a major hero of the mostly Jewish neighborhood, Wexler was the son of immigrant working-class types barely hanging on – in his father's case literally, he was a window washer working on skyscrapers. His mother, the driving force in his early life, was a free-thinking, dedicated reader of Marx and Freud. She couldn't keep young Jerry out of the pool halls, and later out of the Harlem flats, with live music that fascinated him more than school and set his destiny. John Hammond, the Gentile producer who spent his time with Jews and could always be seen, in Wexler's early memory, with an armload of radical magazines, was the teenage boy's model of how to live and what to do.[10]

Dropping out of college twice over, from New York to Kansas, Wexler washed windows with his dad, hung out, got married, got drafted, and after the war drifted into entertainment journalism. There he made himself an energetic promoter of rhythm and blues (actually proposing that phrase for *Billboard*'s previously titled "Race Records" listing). He championed the new, small labels that picked up artists that the majors ignored. This was the music that biracial DJ Johnny Otis furiously promoted in Los Angeles among blacks and Jews, and that, in Otis's retrospective view, was destined to be replaced by mediocre rock 'n' roll. Wexler stood somewhere tactically closer to the center.

Wexler quit *Billboard*, repelled by the assignment to do a Red-baiting "dossier" on The Weavers. That same conscience brought Wexler into the production business, first at MGM and then at a new little company called Atlantic.[11] He and his companions were eclectic but they knew what they liked: Clyde McPhatter and the Drifters, Champion Jack Duprey, Professor Longhair, Big Joe Turner, Ray Charles, and so on.[12] Eventually, Wexler discovered and promoted Aretha Franklin among many others. Wexler was no martyr to the cause of black music. But he considered himself its champion as much for its internal values as for its salability.[13]

Moses Asch meanwhile made the folk-song revival of the 1950s and '60s and beyond possible. As we've seen, the Americanization of music enriched by black and Appalachian components practically constituted a Popular Front crusade, Jewish in its main audience and in most of its producers (if not its largely Yankee folklorists). If Roosevelt had lived, or Henry Wallace had been his final vice-president and the Cold War had somehow been avoided, folk music would arguably have been taken at its face value and never been considered avant-garde at all. "This Land Is Your Land" might have become the new national anthem and Woody Guthrie the nation's troubadour. Conservatives and Cold War liberals, in demonizing the Popular Front, made it into a sort of outlaw music.

During the 1940s, folk had in fact been decisively and almost fatally attached to the Left; anticommunists (like labor songster Joe Glazer) were rare and Popular Front sympathizers like Josh White and Burl Ives copped pleas of naivety (cheerfully giving names of their erstwhile backers and fellow singers) in order to save careers. Woody was spared only by the forced retirement of deteriorating health. Not only Paul Robeson and Pete

Seeger, but dozens of the most talented, found themselves restricted to summer camps and out of the way clubs until the 1960s called them back to the spotlight.

But this was only the visible tip of the iceberg. The backbone of folk survival for decades was Folkways Records and the backbone of Folkways was Asch. No one had a more famous father in the Yiddish world: Sholem Asch, phenomenal best-selling author who was already a sensation in Warsaw before he moved on successively to Paris, the Bronx, Flatbush, and Staten Island. Born in 1905, the year of (failed) revolution, "Moe" grew up a true American boy, fascinated with radio electronics. By the late 1920s he had a thriving radio repair business of his own, loosely connected to bootleggers, but he also had a technological bug that prompted him toward improvement of microphone sensitivity, especially useful for picking up the fine notes of guitars. As a teen, he had already developed a real interest in the notion of an American folk music, and he grasped at the impetus provided by "From Spirituals to Swing," a 1938 Popular Front spectacular featuring Leadbelly among others. It created an audience, and for an ambitious youngster, major business opportunities.[14]

In a wonderful, if perhaps partly apocryphal, conjuncture of minds, Sholem Asch dialogued with Albert Einstein at the scientist's home in Princeton, in 1940, and Moe, invited to conduct the remote recording, is supposed to have exchanged some words with the notably left-leaning genius. Moe later claimed that he had regaled Einstein with the dream of recording the music of the world's people, offering this priceless treasure to one and all.[15] Whatever the exact incident and even if the two never spoke at all, it makes a great story. Moe Asch's new record company began retailing readings of his father's Bible stories for children, along with religious music by some of the famed cantors of the day. In the spring of 1941, he recorded Leadbelly, garnering special success marketing the blues giant shrewdly to Jewish New Yorkers buying records of children's songs for their kids. (Walter Winchell predictably attacked the known Pinkos, assaulting both the singer of "Bourgeois Blues" and the company willing to record a children's record by a convicted killer.) These recordings made singer Hudie Ledbetter famous and a hit on the show circuit, but he earned practically nothing from Asch, forming a melancholy pattern that would become more or less fixed for the entrepreneur and his artists across time.[16]

Wartime proved tricky due to the near absence of that crucial record ingredient, shellac, but otherwise good to Asch. The money was there for record buyers as never before, and the Jewish Left was the perfect audience for the Almanacs (with Woody Guthrie, Pete Seeger, Lee Hayes, and

Millard Lampell, a Jewish youngster from Paterson, NJ), also Josh White, Sonny Terry, and jazzmen like Art Tatum and Meade Lux Lewis.[17] Left-wing musicologist Ruth Rubin herself made one of the most famous Jewish recordings of the time, introducing "Zhankoye" among other later standards recuperated from the old country.[18] Asch's own literary contribution, i.e., the early records' liner notes, typified the effort, however primitive, to provide a documentary sensibility to the musical side of folkishness and resistance to oppression. Never a Communist and at heart always a New Dealer, Asch was perfectly in line with the Popular Front's effort to marry a homage to the Founding Fathers ideals with struggles of working people, minorities, and civil libertarians in the present day.[19]

Postwar days brought crises that would have done anyone else in, from bankruptcy to the Red Scare.[20] Launching Folkways Records in place of previous, and failed, ventures, Asch accelerated his effort at making available marvelous folk and semipop artists like the Caribbean calypsonians, only beginning to record after a half-century of vibrant Island music. By the 1950s, with librarians among the chief Folkways purchasers, Asch was recording Langston Hughes reading his own works (foreshadowing "books on tape") among other innovations. Soon enough, an enthnomusical explosion hit home (native shores, at any rate) in old-time country music and merged neatly with the recuperated strains of the New Deal era in the New Lost City Ramblers. At that, he never proved an easy partner to the musicians, especially when it came to royalties that he seemed determined to plough back into the business.

The big folk revival of the later 1950s prompted Asch to back *Sing Out!*, a crucial venue for musicians' self-interpretation, and if the world of Folkways was too small for the likes of Joan Baez (let alone Bob Dylan), the music reached hundreds of thousands of devotees consciously political or not. In the longer run, with additional folk record labels like Rounder and Arhoolie, the Folkways list bridged the gap between the 1940s and '50s and the return of the progressive coffee house music politics of the 1970s through to the '90s and beyond. Basement church hootenannies of the early twenty-first century usually offered more Celtic musicians than decades before, and included New Age components – increasingly, music from the newer immigrants groups as well – but rarely failed to have a Jewish singer, musician, or amateur producer in the lineup.

True to his own self-established limitations, Asch never got closer to the rock 'n' roll boom than the Village Fugs (later known simply as The Fugs), Jewish wild men headed by anarchistic poet Tuli Kupferberg. "Kill For Peace" was more shocking than their only hit, "Slum Goddess of the Lower

East Side," but not more Jewish.[21] In the end, the field recordings of the history of the civil rights movement would, alone, have earned Asch a permanent niche in the politics of American culture. In the end, almost at the same moment as Asch's death in 1986, Folkways archives became part of the Smithsonian Institution. All in all, it was a personal triumph but also implicitly a Jewish triumph, institutionalized.[22]

The Chess Brothers, Leonard and Phil, marked other sides of the equation in several ways, promoters of a musical avant-guard quite despite their own innate conservatism. The sons of a Jewish immigrant who made his way to Chicago, the brothers were strictly businessmen. Less like the music impresarios and more like the movie moguls who shifted their venues from hardware to films, the brothers Chess worked through a series of junk recycling and liquor stores to nightclubs, all of these natural for shrewd entrepreneurs whose Maxwell Avenue Jewish neighborhood bordered on rapidly growing black Chicago of the 1940s. Shortly after the war, uninterested in music for its own sake but keen to get out of the nightclub business, they launched Aristocrat on two thousand dollars. Shortly thereafter, Leonard found Muddy Waters, a new singing sensation on the South Side, and with the recording of "Gypsy Woman," a record legend was born. No one ever knew, or presumably ever will know, how much Chess Records made off Waters's songs, or even how much Waters himself made; but the singers and musicians remained in South Side apartments while the entrepreneurial brothers moved to suburban mansions with swimming pools.[23]

There was no doubt that the businessmen brothers put their entrepreneurial energy as well as their wallets into the work of bringing blues home to Americans of all colors. Waters, John Lee Hooker, Howling Wolf, Etta James, Bo Diddley, Koko Taylor, Otis Spann, and the early Chuck Berry, the only big artist to strategize his way successfully out of the smallish Chess world, owed immensely to the promotional efforts and improved recording studios. Chess (and an offshoot, Checkers) even made a serious go at jazz with Ahmad Jamal's Trio in 1957, along with some less soulful rock 'n' roll of similar vintage and a comedy record by Moms Mabley.

They soon added their own record manufacturing, bought a radio station with an overwhelmingly black audience, went international in distribution, and became as corporate as a one-family, one-building business was ever likely to. Occasionally investigated for payola, i.e., the well-known bribes to cooperative disk jockeys, the brothers already seemed beyond their political moment by the middle 1960s. An ardent fundraiser for Combined Jewish Appeal and Israel Bonds, Leonard Chess gave Martin Luther King,

Jr., two thousand dollars during the height of the 1963 Birmingham demonstrations – and in a few years treated King as an ingrate for opposing the war in Vietnam. Adam Clayton Powell had never received a friendly mention at the Chess radio station, WVON. Leonard described Stokely Carmichael as a "phony," refusing to play his voice for black listeners because "putting him on the air gives him dignity."[24]

Bo Diddley, Howling Wolf, Willie Dixon, and even Muddy Waters insisted that they had been robbed by various arms of the Chess empire. The suits were settled, and in the larger sense, the companies had been as good as, or better than, black artists might expect anywhere. Doubtless the Chess brothers had been shrewder businessmen than Wexler or Asch, but also never especially sincere about, or even seriously interested in, the distinctive role of black music in American culture beyond their own ability to benefit.

The irony and the complexity increased with the rapid growth of a predominantly white audience for predominantly black music. While still in their teens, Jewish prodigies Jerry Lieber and Mike Stoller had composed hits like "Hound Dog" (for Big Mama Thornton before it was covered by Elvis) for black singers. Lieber (raised in Baltimore by an impoverished single mother who ran a tiny grocery store) delivered the lyrics that ridiculed the adult world, in terms accurately described as "a white kid's take on a black kid's take on white society," for the Coasters, with his friend Mike Stoller supplying the yackety sax tunes and arrangements. By the 1960s, the Drifters carried Lieber and Stoller's current label while the two young men, now doubling as A&R men, added Brill Building lyricists and composers, nearly all Jewish, to the collection of hit makers.[25]

Lieber and Stoller's initial goal had been to break through the mostly sterile 1950s with black sounds of humor, but they later added in their work, at its best, a soulfulness sadly lacking in suburban white society. The same principle applied to the Latinization of popular music, especially in Manhattan ("seduced by the sensuality of the music," as one account had put it, "nubile Jewish chicks" known as "bagel babies" reputedly flocked in droves to the Latin dance halls). The industry-proclaimed king of salsa, likewise and perhaps inevitably, was the Bronx-born George Goldner.[26]

The explanations, or rationalizations, involving Jewishness, blackness, and American culture at large also took on new oddness with a new giant, Phil Spector, whose life remains one of the oddest stories of popular culture in the middle of the century. The tale would be merely pathetic if Spector had not made himself a multimillionaire meglomaniac, and perhaps it remains pathetic nevertheless. Bronx-born, the son of an immigrant iron worker who committed suicide (inscribed on his gravestone was the later-useful motto "To Know Him is To Love Him") by leaving the engine running in a Long Island garage, teenager Phil was moved to LA by his mother and his aunt, who were quick to spot show business possibilities for the physically slight, emotionally troubled, guitar-playing teenager.[27] They had to talk Phil out of artistic, uncommercial jazz guitar, and at that, his first rock groups were far from successful. He made a name for himself first on local LA television's *Rocket to Stardom*, broadcast live from an Oldsmobile showroom.

Like hundreds of other LA Jewish (and non-Jewish) kids in 1957, young Phil descended upon the local recording studios without the money to pay for a session. Borrowing ten dollars from kid singer Annette Kleinbard, he cut his first record and in one of the next few sessions, produced Annette singing "To Know Him." Drawing upon (or exploiting) his own pain, he had a hit with his band, the Teddy Bears, even if it took months for the record to catch fire. Then American Bandstand found him, and on a 1959 show, *Kraft Music Hall with Perry Como* taped at the Ziegfield Theater, the Teddy Bears did "To Know Him," followed by Harold Arlen's "It's Only a Paper Moon." Whole Jewish generations seemed to merge.[28] Then the Teddy Bears broke up and Phil needed another road to success.

There's another story here en route, one never likely to appear in the Rock 'n' Roll Hall of Fame annals. Trying to make a living as a court reporter, Phil found himself in the middle of the Caryl Chessman case. It was the Capital Punishment *cause célèbre* of the era with near mass demonstrations and plenty of publicity, in retrospect the California pre-cursor to the explosions in Berkeley and elsewhere to come. Spector himself was not just a low-paid legal research assistant on the case but an extreme enthusiast, downright militant in the cause, denouncing the whole system that put human beings to death. "He was very liberal, which was unusual for a teenager at the time," recalled struggling producer Lester Sill. "A lot of kids around [the studio] thought he was a Communist."[29] Spector a Jewish Communist?!? Nowhere close, but when businessman Spector took over the finances of a collapsing Lenny Bruce in 1965, pro-claiming himself and his new buddy to be twin outcasts misunderstood by society, the assertion was not entirely paranoid grandeur. Spector deter-minedly continued to see his millionaire self as the outsider in a social order run by and for insiders.

Back at the dawn of the 1960s, following Chessman's execution, Spector virtually forced himself upon Lieber and Stoller's Manhattan office, landing there suddenly without even a place to sleep. He moved in on Beverly

Ross, a Jewish songwriter with "Lollipop" behind her. She was also a producer with the right connections and together they descended happily into bubble gum music. He went on to the Brill Building, where producer Doc Pomus described him as "very smart and very politically oriented." He was, Ross later recalled, actually two-faced or perhaps lacking any real face of his own. By exploiting his own talent as well as that of others around him, Spector also made himself a music industry giant with multiple songs on the charts for years.

By that time, Spector had become the guru for the "girls' songs," and there hangs another tale. What, if anything, accounted for *their* Jewish connection? It's a good question, answered best in the early 1960s days of the Ronettes, Ronnie and Estelle Bennett and cousin Nedra Talley, homegirl Jews from the vicinity of Spanish Harlem. Eager for success and believing in themselves, they took singing lessons, got a manager and began playing bar mitzvahs. The Ronettes soon graduated to neighborhood sock hops and the Peppermint Lounge (in tight dresses and beehive hairdos), where they connected to star in a mercifully forgotten film, *Hey, Let's Twist*. Spector exploited and divided them.[30]

By the time Spector had married and dumped Annette and then Ronnie herself, his conscience had apparently vanished. Hard-working, a near-genius celebrity in his own narrow way, he ruled artists' lives tyranically and punished those near him (like no-talent Sonny and a still untapped-talent Cher), who, as he saw it, got out of line. But here was the strange and definitely Jewish thing: he never acted entirely without a degree of wounded artist's sensibility.

By the middle 1960s exalted as the "first tycoon of teen," Spector was determinedly apologizing for the predictably constrained chord changes and lyrics of his hits. ("It's very today" was his biggest claim and more defensively, "The people of America are just not born with culture.") He also hosted Allen Ginsberg in La Collina along with Lenny Bruce, who he described as "a living Socrates." He talked about making a Ginsberg poetry album. He even pretended to be a heroin addict! At least we know that he was emotionally tortured – that is, by his never-satisfied mother Bertha and by his sister, Shirley. Similarly, when he described as "nonintellectual" a group that he lost control of, the Righteous Brothers, it was probably the worst insult that he could bring to mind.[31]

It's amazing to think that the erstwhile bubble gum rocker supreme produced the Beatles' "Let It Be," but it's perhaps considerably less impressive when we learn that he was undergoing Primal Scream therapy at the time. It is even more amazing to realize that he lasted long enough in actual creative work to produce John Lennon's "Imagine," as utopian and truly radical a song as anything done in popular music for decades.

Perhaps Phil Spector, like the Chess Brothers, deserved to be forgotten as soon as he stopped making hits – if not before. Or perhaps this kind of entrepreneurial talent, so often perverse, simply cannot be appreciated as easily as that of Wexler, who had a more solid footing in a vanishing Jewish working-class life. Wexler had the saving grace of a vastly smaller ego, the dignity to be happy simply to make a living producing teenager Aretha Franklin with music right for her, and continuing to work until retirement with many other smaller names. Wexler once remarked to a critic that he should be judged by the 10 or 15 percent of the output that he believed really good, not merely the money making (that was in many cases insubstantial), to which we can say: fair enough.[32]

Of all these figures, Bill Graham may have led the most characteristically twentieth-century Jewish life of all, and, after Bob Dylan, has arguably left the deepest imprint of all Jewish movers in modern popular music. Born in 1931, Wolfgang Grajonza grew up in middle-class and Jewish Berlin as the world exploded around him. His family fled very late, in 1941–42, and one of his sisters was sent to Auschwitz, where miraculously, and unlike their parents, she survived. The boy had already been shipped off to the US and adopted in the Bronx, to a failed businessman and his wife.

He never warmed to the couple and he set his own path, starting to work early, delivering papers, groceries, and meat in the neighborhood, in part to pay his foster parents back for his upkeep and thereby owe them nothing. A born competitor and a sports fanatic, he never bar mitzvahed – thanks to a family fight with the rabbi. He found in the neighborhood movie theater his entrée into the big world of popular culture. Like so many others in every New York Jewish neighborhood, he looked to John Garfield as the model actor, the one with the "street class" that was cool in the 1940s. As he reached his midteens, he escaped to the downtown world of the live show and dancing. The Palladium introduced him to the power of music.[33]

Then came the Korean War and the draft. Wolfgang Grajonza had already become "Bill" and now he added "Graham," to stop people making fun of him. He took it from the phonebook and when he later told interviewers that he considered Bill a "nothing name," added that he had never liked Graham either. But on shipboard bound for Korea, he became the mess clerk who could magically produce snacks for the massive crap shoot every night. Never willing to see North Koreans as enemies, he nevertheless won a Bronze Star for battle wounds and got a hardship discharge. He'd learned the important lessons, on the battlefield and off.

Next stop was the Borscht Belt. A furious worker, he practiced the waiter's trade to perfection, catering personally and successfully to the most outrageous customers – which is saying something in this crowd. He also learned to despise the cheapest and meanest of the owners. A potential aristocrat of labor, or potential management trainee, he ruminated at first on which side to place himself as union drives in the resorts began. Then he made up his mind, and organized brilliantly, delivering one of the first union contracts of the circuit to the Hotel and Restaurant Workers. The respectful owner of the American palace he organized later recalled that Graham was "antiestablishment all the way but a hell of a guy to work with" because "he had a way with people" and he really knew how to please.[34]

The big opportunity lay still considerably ahead. He drove a cab and later a truck, hitchhiked coast to coast, read a part for a play, visited Europe and passed time. By the late 1950s in San Francisco, Graham hung out a bit with the bohemian crowd then in its glory years around City Lights Books, dated an actress and played some small roles in local theater, came back to New York, and tried unsuccessfully to get television work. Returning once more to San Francisco, he acquired a new girlfriend who got him into gofering for the San Francisco Mime Troupe. It was 1965.

Graham recalled that while wading through winos to get to the Mime Troupe people were talking about Artaud and Brecht, the scene seemed to him "sensational," and more than that, the ultimate compliment, "as good as the Lower East Side." It had the elements he had been looking for, the excitement of the old artistic avant-garde but also the California opening for an unconnected lad to seize the brass ring. The Mime Troupe's up-and-coming impresario, Ronnie Davis, scion of local Jewish brewery barons and student of Marcel Marceau, had worked in some of the same Borscht Belt hotels before heading for Paris. Davis was much more the political type. But they worked together well, for the moment. In the rundown office of the Troupe, Graham set up a desk with a plaque that read, "S. Hurok." Though no one else would likely have recognized it, he already had his model mixture of social commitment and personal success in erstwhile Brownsville Socialist-impresario Sol Hurok.[35]

Thanks to the times but also to abundant talent and energy, the Mime Troupe passed suddenly from obscurity to notoriety and drew large audiences, especially on college campuses. Future film star Peter Coyote (not surprisingly the adopted name of a Jewish red-diaper baby) was performing and directing, with legendary California figures like journalist Robert Scheer and counterculture icon Emmett Grogan close at hand. The benefit performances of the Troupe emerged more political events than fundraisers.

What Graham would call the "most significant evening of my life in the theater," 6 November 1965, put the Troupe and Graham on the publicity (and not merely arts) map. Thousands showed up, and the ones lucky enough to get in brought food, paid what they wanted, showed their homemade films as Graham collected the money at the door and stage managed what amounted to the first (and unintentional) Be-In. It was also the very first night of a new Haight-Ashbury. Appropriately, the evening ended in the AM with Allen Ginsberg leading the crowd in chanting mantras.

Graham had already broken with any notions of artistic purity that other members of the Mime Troupe possessed when he staged a second benefit at a venue suggested by columnist Ralph Gleason: the aged, beat-up Fillmore Auditorium of San Francisco's black neighborhood. Grace Slick, Frank Zappa, and Bob Dylan – who just happened to be in town – let it be known that they would perform. Overnight, Graham looked like the impresario of the age, at least in San Francisco. After that, it was Graham who took out the lease on the Fillmore. The Mime Troupe slipped into a lower notch in some ways, a higher one in others, acting as an artistic guerilla band whose very presence could, it was said, ignite a campus riot.[36] Graham, meanwhile, went on to one of the most spectacular careers imaginable in a category heretofore limited to nightclub and folksong impresarios, or, arguably, to the cultural mavens of mass left-wing political events: what might be called counterculture promotion.

But in odd ways, he also circled round and round his origins. One of the biggest early hits in the Fillmore, to take a case in point, was the Paul Butterfield Blues Band from Chicago. Its lead guitarist, Michael Bloomfield, a troubled Jewish youngster moved by his parents to the suburbs in his teen years, had soon begun to hang out at Southside blues spots. A fabulously talented musician who impressed the likes of Muddy Waters, he was also a longtime substance abuser who died of a drug overdose at thirty-eight. Bloomfield and the band nevertheless played what Graham described as an offshoot of "fun music," i.e., bar mitzvah and wedding tunes. In a Gentile town like San Francisco, even playing with a heavy influence by Ravi Shankar, the blues still somehow came out Jewish, and counterculture. The rabbi in the synagogue that shared an alley with the Fillmore first testified in court against Graham's continuing, then relented – after an agreement not to have shows on High Holy Days. Graham meanwhile added Lenny Bruce to his list of regular performers, a hipster by this time too far gone on amphetamines to do much more than taunt the cops, but a magic name nevertheless.

Graham had a genius for bringing together apparent opposites, like an avant-garde play by LeRoi Jones and Michael McClure with a set by the Byrds, meanwhile making hay off the Grateful Dead and the Jefferson Airplane, Ken Kesey and Neil Cassady. Outside Latin music he was pretty well lost conceptually. He could recognize the talent of Otis Redding. But he produced Janis Joplin on pure showbiz instinct. He had no trouble doing benefits for the Black Panthers at a time when the FBI identified them as the most dangerous group in the nation. He had more trouble with the Diggers, who wanted to abolish money, including the price for entry into a Fillmore show. Peter Coyote called him, if not quite accurately, "this guy who walked out of Auschwitz." Six days a week he got rich, and on the seventh, he made remarkable things possible.[37]

After that, though, it was conceptually downhill for Graham as it continued financially boffo. Promoting the Rolling Stones, actually trying for the sake of showbiz tradition to make a business deal with octogenerian Sol Hurok himself (that fell through), promoting Dylan and Crosby, Stills, Nash and Young, the genius promoter was more and more trapped inside the need for business success as he sought out the British Punks to revive the charismatic rebelliousness of a scant few years earlier. More time passed and the real Graham message, whatever remained of it, generally dissipated. Until, that is, President Ronald Reagan proposed a personal homage to Bitburg, in effect honoring deceased Nazi supporters. Graham staged a protest rally in 1985 with most of the biggest Democrats in California on hand. Holocaust survivors spoke. To his disappointment, nothing changed, except that his headquarters happened to get torched.

Graham's last promotional success was actually a political one, the kind that Phil Spector could probably not have imagined and that the Chess brothers would almost certainly have considered subversive, even anti-Israeli. He launched a global protest, through the American Peace Walk Committee, in the form of a march from Leningrad to Moscow, protesting nuclear weapons of every kind and in every national possession. It is more than possible to imagine that Graham had a different future ahead. But in 1991, coming down off Halcyon and his stint as executive producer of the movie *Come Together*, Graham boarded a helicopter heading to San Francisco. It crashed and he died instantly. The Grateful Dead, Neil Young, and others organized a free concert in memory of him, and half a million came to the by now emblematic Golden Gate Park to remember him. Joan Baez and Kris Kristofferson ended the day singing a duet of "Amazing Grace." Perhaps it was the last real Be-In event, akin to the spontaneous turnouts across the country in the hours after John Lennon's assassination hit the airwaves.

The further story of the selling of the avant-garde through rock culture could easily be told as a subscript on the Spector (and not the Graham) story. As author Fred Goodman unravels its nasty skeins, the kind of small-time promoters – most of them left-wing fundraisers – who had made Woody Guthrie's concerts possible soon morphed into music mega-capitalists running one of the most profitable entertainment industries in the world. The ones who understood the money potential best and articulated it first as the beauty of rebellious music, then second as the beauty of dollar signs, just happened to be Jewish.[38]

Out of the folky cafés of Cambridge, Massachusetts, out of the fan circles that produced 'zines like *Crawdaddy*, out of the growing need (at least, wish) for explanations of why the music was important to a new generation, came future promoters and their ultimate printed-page counterpart, *Rolling Stone*. Young men who saw in themselves, their tastes, and their intelligence the signs of the future, were quick to jump into the management of those first small radio stations willing to play off-the-beaten-track rock (and blues), and just as quick to sign musicians up with major labels when the terms proved highly beneficial all around. The scarcity of powerful women in these fast-moving circles might have sounded a warning note, but no one was listening.

At any rate, the hip corporate guys were just as eager to meet the cultural if not political revolutionaries. Warner Brothers, best remembered during golden age Hollywood for hard-hitting social dramas (many of them written or directed by future Blacklist victims), happened to be on hard times by the middle 1960s, dragged down by years of film production overruns and box office disappointments. Within a decade, music sales would outstrip film receipts, the basis for the entertainment mega-corporation of the future to take definitive shape.

Actually, Warners had been in the record business since the 1920s, taking over the old Witmark empire as its publishing division, and during the middle 1950s had already bought a label with top rock stars, including Fats Domino. Rebounding from movie losses with their own television series (and best known for the iconoclastic, youth-oriented shows like *77 Sunset Strip* and *Maverick*), Warners hit the top of the charts with the Everly Brothers, consolidating success in the early 1960s with albums by leftish folkies Peter, Paul and Mary on one hand, Jewish comic Allan Sherman on the other. Then an aging Jack Warner okayed a merger with Reprise Records, opening the door to signing the Kinks, Petula Clark, and other British stars.

Los Angeles was just the place (the second place after New York, but arguably the first place for new music by the middle 1960s) for young promoters like Barry Friedman to find performers like the Crosby, Stills, Nash and Young band that he helped put together. By 1965, the *Los Angeles Free Press* was being published by Art Kunkin (a Jewish former Trotskyist, and personal secretary to the Pan-Africanist theoretician C.L.R. James) as the voice of rebellious (and by a large disproportion, Jewish) LA-area youth eager for the new music. Back east, former club manager Albert Grossman had actually brought together Peter, Paul and Mary, and personally signed Bob Dylan. The savvy Grossman, who loved the better music of the day, negotiated contracts that allowed singers creative control of recording and packaging, arrangements virtually unknown in the middle 1960s but crucial in the phase ahead.

Grossman himself hardly had any observable politics. But he welcomed the Diggers (including Peter Coyote) to gather American support for the May–June 1968 strikes in Paris and to publicize their then famous slogan, "It's Free Because Its Yours." Grossman also brought a hip crowd to his own place near Woodstock, giving the town the cachet for its famous concert.

These were evidently the models for David Geffen, a son of Brooklyn's Boro Park, born in 1943, bad at school but heavily into chillingly accurate fantasies of himself as a future giant of the entertainment business. Going to work at the Morris Agency in 1964, he worked his way up in the music division, moving on by 1968 to manage Laura Nyro's career. He succeeded the stumbling Albert Grossman as the rock agent on the go, nabbed Joni Mitchell, and publicized Crosby, Stills, Nash and Young's heroic leap into the limelight.

The story just gets bigger from here. A Rothschild (Paul, that is) really did produce the Doors and Janis Joplin, those fabulous self-immolating acts. Jon Landau, who started out as a left-leaning critic and got MC5 back in business after the virtual repression of their incendiary *Kick Out the Jams* album, was managing and producing Bruce Springsteen by the 1980s. Jan Wenner's *Rolling Stone*, part of the countercultural press at its beginning, passed *Time* magazine in circulation. It had, like Wenner himself, long since forsaken rebellious impulses for advertising column inches. The "captains of industry," an old title for the aristocrats of nineteenth-century manufacturing and commerce, had become the rock industry entrepreneurs of the present. The passion of these Vietnam era young adults was redirected pretty exclusively at business deals. They could still be called liberals – Geffen was a major contributor to Bill Clinton's campaigns – and had a special feeling for gay rights. Nineties billionaire Geffen himself was gay, after all, and that might be the largest fact of change in Jewish-American entertainment business life.

Geffen's world of DreamWorks, with players like Michael Ovitz, Michael Eisner (son of a Hollywood blacklistee), and Steven Spielberg was also certainly Jewish as well as the first new major Hollywood studio in decades. But if nostalgia remained on the agenda, it didn't seem to be about selling rebellion any more – unless rebellion happened somehow to come back into style.[39]

But this, of course, is mainly the story told from the top including the material struggle upward, and even so, it could hardly account for the contradictions in a major musical phenomenon of the twentieth century like Bob Dylan. Jack Benny always remained "Ben" in private, while Bobby Zimmerman of Hibbing, Minnesota, had practically ceased to exist in any conscious sense by the time Dylan was playing on street corners, guitar in hand and harmonica in mouth, outside Greenwich Village nightspots. His bedside attention to the hopelessly paralyzed Woody Guthrie, his embrace of civil rights songs, spelled something different. He epitomized, although briefly, the devotion of the younger Jewish artist to the folky Left tradition whose audiences had nearly always been best in certain Manhattan venues since the middle 1930s and successful with the diaspora in places like Madison, Wisconsin, where enough removed New Yorkers were on hand to provide the hard core of an audience, not to mention promoters and reviewers.

The story of Dylan's rocketing fame, the narcissism that came with the status and idolization of him by those intimately close (like then girlfriend Joan Baez) as well as distant, has been told painfully well. Dylan's disappearance with producer-promoter Albert Grossman's bride for hours after their wedding encapsulates as well as anything the familiar story of the celebrity's moral smallness. He and the promoters, Fred Goodman rightly says, became the American aristocrats new style, not so much rebelling from the ultrarich as aping their more notorious private lives. According to some would-be decoders, Dylan met assorted mental crises with religious or at least spiritual jolts, at least once Christian, more often Jewish (reputedly touched off by the uncertain status of West Bank settlers). When young, he had arguably internalized the legacy of suffering by identifying with the oppressed; when in middle age and a megamillionaire with a secure place in entertainment history, he sometimes seemed to believe that he, as the collective Jew, himself somehow suffered. And yet he created what can only be described as an endless avant-garde, moving it solidly into the late-century mainstream.

So did another kind of artist-singer, Paul Simon. Born in Newark, growing up in Forest Hill, Queens, Simon met future collaborator Art Garfunkel in sixth grade. After college, they teamed up as a left-leaning folky duo, making a smash with "Sounds of Silence" in 1965. Following the Dylan trajectory, they became less strident and more ironic as they became more successful. The soundtrack for *The Graduate* made the best of the irony as comment on the hypocrisies wrapped up in the contemporary generation conflicts of American life, and *Bridge Over Troubled Water* (1970), pleading for social peace, remained for twenty years one of the most successful albums of music history. Another megapersonality (his role in the Woody Allen film *Annie Hall*, or perhaps it was his marriage to Carrie Fisher, confirmed this status), Simon remained nevertheless prone to multicultural efforts in music and theater that often signaled overreach – the more critical would say exploitation. But Simon was no schlockmeister like Brownsville-raised vocalist Barry Manilow (whose notable hits include "I Write the Song" – he didn't). Drawn to South African music or the motivations of New York street criminals, Simon has never ceased to be an artist struggling soulfully to remake himself as a Jew in a troubled world.[40]

Hollywood unceasingly turned up new and more seemingly bizarre examples of Jewish entrepreneurs as avant-gardist music maven-managers. In May, 2002, the *New York Times* profiled thirty-seven-year-old new kingmaker Jeffrey Evan Kwatinetz, CEO of The Firm, whose most important acts were the transgressive (or pseudo-transgressive) Korn and Limp Bizkit. He most reminded observers of Ovitz, who at a similar age in the 1970s formed the Creative Artists Agency and rose to be a giant powerbroker until he fell upon hard times and sold most of his company to Kwatinetz. Managing bands while attending Northwestern, graduating from Harvard Law, Kwatinez was a generational successor to the Chess brothers. Kwatinez was also far beyond the Chess brothers' engagement with Chicago ghetto politics and the local Urban League, in fact, he had formed a political partnership with Bush critic Richard Gephardt and noted black progressive, John Conyers. Symbol or substance? In the age of entertainment consolidation, arrangements tailored to give artists more control while giving managers more power – a synthesis of art and commerce amidst consolidation – remained at once the ideal and the deal attainable by truly hip Jewish producers.[41]

In what senses was the Jewishness of Grossman or Geffen different from the Jewishness of the profit- and power-driven Hollywood mogul a half-century before? For instance those Warner Brothers whose hard-hitting social films of the 1930s validated a message of something deeply wrong in the nation settled happily for a message of American triumphalism a bit later. And what would a degree of difference between old and new really mean? Perhaps the Jewish women rockers in the last generations had inherited the rebel seed. A largely hidden story of them might help redefine the message in a music world gone largely stale, especially in terms of social message.

Way back at the beginning of Beatlemania, Goldie Zelkowitz of Goldie and the Gingerbreads led one of the rare female groups that actually played instruments. Very briefly the rebellious rocker darlings of the New York scene toured Germany and the UK, recorded a couple of hits in London, but without making any money for themselves before dissolving. Historically speaking, they planted the idea of the serious all-female band.[42]

By vivid contrast, take the Shangri-Las, four queens of teenage angst including the Weiss sisters, Betty and Mary, from Queens. After "Leader of the Pack" (1964) and associated songs (in "I Can Never Go Home Anymore!" a thoughtless daughter screams toward her ignored and now dead mother, "Mama!"), they abandoned beehive hairdos and feminine frills for street-hip duds and attitude. Their avant-garde all image, they numbly recorded an ode to a boyfriend who proudly went to Vietnam (and another turkey, "Past, Present and Future" based on Beethoven's "Moonlight Sonata"), and promptly faded from sight.[43]

There were worse things than postfame obscurity, of course. "Mama Cass" Elliott was born Ellen Naomi Cohen in Baltimore in 1941, moving from piano lessons to guitar as she grooved to the avant-garde folk sound. She married Jimi Hendrix to keep him from being drafted, moved to LA, where Barry McGuire (of "Eve of Destruction") introduced her new group to record producer Lou Adler as the Mamas and Papas. Her size, not her Jewishness, presented the pop scene with a problem and one last reason to be daring. In 1973, she recorded the self-assertive "Don't Call Me Mama Anymore" in her briefly successful solo act (for a moment, she was a celebrity famous for weight loss). She died suddenly, at age thirty-two, of a heart attack likely brought on, notwithstanding family denials, by a contempt for body selfimage and the resulting pills popped for weight control.

More cheerful to contemplate is the microtale of Janis Ian (aka Fink), an underage folky who appeared with Bob Dylan, Pete Seeger, and the crowd at Newport in the early 1960s and had a single, stunning hit of her own composition, "Society's Child." The capture of teenage emotions at being forbidden (by liberal parents and teachers) from dating a black boy had as much protest power as any antiwar ballad. A genuine Jewish counterculture type never fond of touring, the now open lesbian Ian (her second and more daring composition of note was the self-outing "At Seventeen") had yet one more notable creation, about the abandonment of elderly Zeydas and Bobbas in rest homes. Then she retired herself – from the stage at any rate. Decades passed and she changed her mind again: Ian has been enjoying a modest comeback in the first years of the new century.

The Jewish music presence from the stage regained fresh air, sometimes a new creative life, through self-consciously regendered rock. Along with the revival of *klezmer*, before, during and after, ran developments that suggested to insiders the emergence of a new Jewish music, Jewish in spite of its apparent indifference to Jewish themes. Helen Reddy ("I Am Woman") might not count, as an Australian convert to Judaism. But newer Jewish women rockers were personified in Cyndi Lauper, whose "Girls Just Want to Have Fun" mocked traditionalist demands for personal success and/or wifehood and motherhood.

Lauper was born in Brooklyn in 1953, grew up mostly in Brooklyn and later Queens after her parents divorced. She began writing music at age twelve, and a few years later formed the popular band Blue Angels, mixing New Wave with traditionalist rock. Her older sister enlisted in the Socialist Workers Party and reputedly became a Marxist force among antiwar mobilizers. But Cyndi's rebellion took definitive shape in her first album (1983) dramatizing the female comradeship of the singer in a video, dancing with a female street gang in clothes acquired at a retro shop. A fan of women wrestling, she managed a WWF champion, considered herself a feminist, and regularly denounced the church (or synagogue), family, and government as "the three biggest oppressors of women that will ever come along." Regarded as a novelty act even while winning a 1985 Grammy, she quickly lost the spotlight, but kept working toward one modest comeback after another, most often opening for now-bigger stars.[44]

Nearer the end of the story, sporting a lesbianism validated by Holly Near, could be found singer-songwriter Phranc, describing herself at the birth of the 1980s as an "all-American Jewish lesbian folksinger." Readily discernable in person by her snappy flattop haircut, she had been born Susie Gottlieb in LA. She grew up listening to Pete Seeger records as well as show tunes and Allan Sherman, and entered the LA music scene as a "radical junior lesbian separatist." Gottlieb was ten years too young for the punks, but sang with groups like Nervous Gender and Catholic Discipline en route to her acoustic debut, "Take Off Your Swastika," an attack on Nazi fashions among some punks. Among her other typical cuts (in *I Enjoy Being a Girl*, Island Records, 1989) was "Bloodbath," about Apartheid. *Positively Phranc!* (1991) included "Gertrude Stein," a rewrite of Jonathan Richman's

Typical HELP! Fumetti, 1965

TRINA'S WOMEN. Published by Kitchen Sink Enterprises, a division of Krupp Comic Works, Inc., P.O. Box 7, Princeton, Wisconsin 54968. A free wholesale catalog will be sent to dealers upon request. Phone (414) 295-3972. Entire contents drawn, designed, and copyright © 1976 by **TRINA ROBBINS**. "Most Rosies" and "Planet Love" appeared originally in **National Lampoon**. "Panthea" appeared originally in **Comix Book**. "Lulu" appeared originally in **High Times**. "The Woman Who Couldn't" appeared originally in **Towards a Radical Art**. This issue is for Suzanne Valadon: One more time, baby!

Printing Number 5 4 3 2 1.

"The Woman Who Couldn't," by Trina Robbins, from
Trina's Women (1976). Courtesy of the artist.

Gentiles attack their own. Distaff commentary on Protestantism by Gilbert Shelton, from *Radical America Comics* (1969). Courtesy of the artist.

Portion of "Wisconsin Story," by Sharon Kahn Rudahl,
from *Snarf* (1976). Courtesy of the artist.

"Editorial," by Bill Griffith and Art Spiegelman, from *Arcade* (1975). Courtesy of the artists.

Excerpt from "Malpractice Suite," by Art Spiegelman, from *Arcade* (1976).
Courtesy of the artist.

Excerpt from Bill Griffith, "The Toad and the Madman," from *Arcade* (1976).
Courtesy of the artist.

Cover of *Cultural Correspondence* (1977) by Justin Green.
Courtesy of the artist. (The interviewer bears a likeness to the author.)

Allen Ginsberg with Eric Drooker, c.1990,
from *Street Posters & Ballads* (1998).
Photo courtesy of Eric Drooker and Arne Swanson.

"Space Creeps," by Diane Noomin, from *Arcade* (1976). Courtesy of the artist, Diane Newman.

"Real Estate," by Eric Drooker, from *Street Posters & Ballads*.
Courtesy of the artist.

"City Fights Back," by Seth Tobocman,
from *World War 3 Illustrated* (1981).

Excerpt from "Richie Bush," by Peter Kuper,
from *World War 3 Illustrated* (2003). Courtesy of the artist.

Marvin Friedman.

"Marvin Friedman," from *jews*. Courtesy *jews* and the artist.

"Summer Second Avenue," by Nicole Schulman (2000).
Courtesy of the artist.

"Pablo Picasso."[45] A handful more of Jewish women (notably Susan Silver and Lisa Fancher) worked the studios as promoters and executives, but observers predicted that there would be a female president of the US before anyone saw a female president of Sony or Warners Records.[46]

ON STAGE WITH LENNY

The Jewish avant-garde, and the American avant-garde for that matter, will not see the likes of Lenny Bruce again. The Borscht-Belt "insult comics" like Jack E. Leonard, surfacing on the *Ed Sullivan Show* in the 1950s, and then the types like Rodney Dangerfield and Don Rickles, self-stylized through insults, that are endlessly imitated but hardly emulated by stand-up Gentiles of any kind, lacked the most obvious elements of Bruce's confrontation with a shamelessly, staggeringly hypocritical society. The more cerebral and innovative comics like Stiller and Meara or Mort Sahl were permitted, in part, because of Bruce's challenge to the existing rules.[47] Readers of *Mad Comics* had, however, seen the central message and more important, the decisive technique before of holding the words up against the reality behind them. If not a textual method of analysis drawn from centuries of Yeshiva training, it was a secular Jewish response to the state of the world from the mid-nineteenth century onward.[48]

Commentators on Bruce, during his lifetime and later, have been quick to point out that he did not come from an oppressive Lower East Side background. On the contrary, Leonard Schneider was an exurban boy from Bellmore, a preserved Yankee section of distant Long Island. His father, a podiatry physiotherapist who helped patients with crippled feet, had grown up the child of English Jews (and antique shop owners in the original Soho) a few steps up from their East-European cousins. The Long Island family had the usual in-law troubles, but the real problem was the yen of Sally, Lenny's mother, for the bright lights of showbiz. Amateur shows and a broken marriage sent her onto the stage professionally, but at the same time she regarded popular entertainment as tawdry. It wasn't an unusual Jewish ambivalence. Meanwhile, Lenny grew up unhappy, a solid underachiever who couldn't even graduate from high school and enlisted in the Navy, in 1942, at the age of seventeen.[49]

Meanwhile, Sally, as Sally Mars, became a sexy stand-up comic in the entertainment-hungry war years, and one of her singer-comedienne show mates seduced the adolescent, in more ways than one, during his shore leave. Coming out of the Navy, and abandoning his father, who by this time had moved to LA, Lenny used the GI Bill to enroll in a drama workshop, with an eye cocked to Hollywood. He even claimed later to have caught the eye of Popular Front kitsch-musical producer Joe Pasternak (*Song of Russia, Anchors Aweigh*, etc), although no movie jobs followed.

Lenny spent the following years back in New York, trying to work up an act. At the close of his bit on the *Arthur Godfrey Talent Scouts* radio show, he replaced a Humphrey Bogart tag line ("All right, Louis, drop the gun!") with its Yiddishist equivalent, "All right, *Shmegegah*, drop the *Yeagah!*" He didn't write the tag line, and could not possibly have written it thanks to his own ignorance of Yiddish. But the going back and forth between Jewish in-jokes and mainstream entertainment became his key to self-exploration and to his ultimate success. It made sense of his hanging out with the real urban hipsters, deepening his knowledge and feeling for a certain mid-century, very Jewish demimonde. In the early 1950s, by the time he hooked up with bisexual stripper Honey, and found a part of himself in burlesque humor as it had descended (or grown more raw) from the golden years of the trade. He was a definite stage Jew.

Years passed and Lenny climbed out of the toilets to the better clubs. Sick Humor was suddenly so popular that a leading imitation of *Mad* was created by a competing group of Jewish writers and editors and actually called *Sick*. The term was wildly overapplied by the later 1950s. But it conveyed a sense of disillusion when the most ideologically heavy moment of the Cold War had passed.

Fantasy Records turned out best-selling albums by Bruce (I personally bought and endlessly replayed three of them) so shocking, in a variety of ways except four-letter words, that the possibility of a talent agent (who had successfully introduced Captain Kangeroo) selling a half-hour series of Lenny to the networks seems inconceivable.[50] That Bruce was on huge quantities of drugs at the time makes the notion only stranger. But as with rock 'n' roll, the youth market beckoned, along with uncounted sophisticates, and would-be bohemians in large and small towns across the nation. Lenny did get an appearance on the *Steve Allen Show* when Allen – in a rare spell of personal bravery – warned the network that if Lenny were cancelled, he'd quit. Lenny had his moment, but the medium was wrong and always would be for him; he needed the live audience response.

The story goes on from here with a fury, featuring Lenny's savage satire of everything in sight, the more vaunted (for example, the Pope) the better. No wonder he was the toast of San Francisco. More wonder that a *Time* magazine issue placed Lenny in a pantheon with Mort Sahl, Shelley Berman, and Nichols and May, ridiculing the "sickniks" and ignoring the crucial differences.[51] Before drugs killed him, and even before the struggle with authorities over drug charges had turned his act into a mixture of legal complaints and thin blue humor, he'd completed a memorable auto-biography, *How to Talk Dirty and Influence People*, thanks in no small degree to the hard work of his amanuensis, *Realist* magazine publisher Paul Krassner.

Krassner was a literary Bruce, but no druggie. Former boy violin prodigy, short-time *Mad Magazine* underling, instinctual hipster and crypto-left-winger, Krassner was eager to publish utterly outrageous satire in his irregular magazine – even if he had to write most of it himself, and limp along from issue to issue. Hugh Heffner made it financially possible for Krassner to continue, by publishing sections of the Bruce autobiography in *Playboy*.[52]

Krassner had joined the 1960s and helped to launch them. But Lenny Bruce was left behind. The film *Lenny* – thanks to a thin script, only a frail version would be captured in a vehicle for Dustin Hoffman – had suc-cessfully blasted the sexual hypocrisy of official standards. He observed, even as so many others denied or rationalized the apotheosis of violence (including the death penalty), the false claims of patriotism so brilliantly that Jewish-American political rebel and Yippie savant Abbie Hoffman could have taken the painful logic directly from a famous Bruce monologue:

> Goddamn the priests and the rabbis. Goddamn the Popes and all their hypocrisy. Goddamn Israel and its bond drives. What influence did they exert to save the lives of the Rosenbergs – guilty or not?[53]

Bruce proudly said (or perhaps he spoke through Krassner), in *How to Talk Dirty and Influence People*, that his routines were flavored with "the jargon of the hipster, the argot of the underworld, and Yiddish." "Hipster" as much as meant Jewish, and his corner of the underworld, mobbed-up club owners and prostitutes, was not so far, either.[54]

Time passes, but impulses pass from comedian to comedian. Andy Kaufman's provocations, before his early demise, carried much of the same weight, his intensity compelling audiences to get beyond expected pun-chlines and raucous laughter, a measure of his own avant-garde commit-ment.[55] Pee Wee Herman (aka Paul Reubens) reinvented the genre of the wild and unpredictable kids' show as something else very different, including a campish and unmistakably gay affect with cosmically strange characters – until an incident in a Florida film theater drove him off the air and back into the clubs.[56] In more recent days, one Sarah Silverman, dubbed by some as the new Lenny Bruce for her verbal provocations has inevitably entered something resembling the same dilemma. A former writer and cast member of *Saturday Night Live*, sometime girlfriend of Seinfeld (on the show, that is) currently either sharing the stage with puppets or providing a Julie Kavner-like voice for animation, Silverman has been described as difficult to place on the networks. Unlike Bruce she hasn't been driven out of the spotlight, so far. But like Bruce, or Andy Kaufman before his tragic death, Silverman's main complaint ("I practically have a penis") is that she doesn't get the improvisational space that she deserves.

COMICS: THE MASS AS THE AVANT-GARDE?

Comics certainly seemed, until the end of the 1940s, the least likely spot for the avant-garde. In 1940, the comic book industry was verging upon massive growth, and superpatriotism with a vague antifascist element provided the hook. Americans still leaned toward isolationism and Franklin Roosevelt reassured American mothers that he wouldn't be sending American boys into a foreign war as the Sub-Mariner leaped off the cover of his first issue tossing a U-boat out of the water. Other superheroes conducted similar operations before Pearl Harbor, but vastly more did so afterward. Jack Kirby and Joe Simon together created the *Young Allies*, a preview of the ethnic combination seen in so many wartime films and also, more glumly, of the real-life postwar consumer rush to the Right. Whites of all kinds rushed heroically (by their own lights) from tenements to suburbs, blue-collar to white-collar lives, in the process turning the collective memories of lower-class suffering into claims of racial privilege. Unlike all but a very few war films, the *Young Allies* actually had an African-American among the boys joined together to defeat the enemy. But Whitewash Jones was a watermelon-eating stereotype; elevation had its limits, and the stereotyping of the Japanese bordered constantly on racial viciousness.

Moving over to DC, the young innovators launched two more comic book kid groups: the *Newsboy Legion*, a dead ringer for the *Dead End Kids* (aka *Bowery Boys* then in the middle of a seventeen-film saga), with all the urban earmarks (like broken English) of the slums; and the *Boy Commandos*, global warriors. Other, mostly Jewish artists and scripters created *Captain America* and dozens of imitators. Will Eisner's *Military Comics* boasted the Blackhawks (*Mad Comics* ridiculed them a decade later as one of the most ridiculous of various foreign legions, as profoundly insipid in plot and dialogue as Terry and the Pirates). Smashing spy rings at home, exhibiting derring-do (but no sex) abroad, the war genre flourished as had no previous comic book series.[57]

Disclosure of anything resembling Jewishness came hard. Romance comics, which flourished in the boom of the late 1940s, might boast a degree of realism that had, in *Young Romance* of 1950, an ethnic daughter of a small-town merchant who is boycotted for being foreign until she and the family business are saved by her GI boyfriend.[58] Echoes of the anti-Semitism so evident in congressional attacks upon Hollywood for subverting America's youth could be found in the investigation of comics as well. One cannot read through the anti-comic book criticisms of the day with certainty, because the Holocaust had prompted such verbal care among those who had been so free with anti-Semitic charges and suggestions only a few years earlier. But accusing the comics of worsening the mental health of children certainly targeted the most palpably Jewish operation of the comic trade. That it would be William Gaines, who took over the deeply indebted EC Comics when his father suddenly died in 1948, taking the heat in congressional hearings of the McCarthy era could not have been entirely an accident.

Gaines's newly reorganized Educational Comics quickly made its mark by matching "New Trend" features, as adult a view of war, crime, and science fiction as the comic trade would allow, with a distinctive horror line, most inventive (and humorous), therefore also more adult and successfully creepier than competitors. Even *Two-Fisted Tales*, a match for *Frontline Combat*, had a realism that western comics almost never showed. In short, EC (first changed by Gaines to "Entertaining Comics," then dropped all but the initials) was poised to influence comics publishers in the direction of better art.

Almost as an afterthought or desire for a new title that the frenetic Kurtzman could handle personally came *Mad Comics* in 1952, followed shortly by widespread attack and threatened repression of the industry. Police and politicans' complaints against improper and unpatriotic content (*Mad*'s in-house imitation *Panic* was considered guilty of "desecrating Christmas" by publishing a satire of an old poem, "A Visit from St. Nicholas," and the Massachusetts Governors' Council resolved to ban the issue) helped to precipitate the congressional investigations in 1953–54. EC's imitators and competitors in crime and horror comics were indeed pretty dreadful, although no one could legitimately demonstrate that lurid stories had led to criminal acts. Showing only a hint of the anti-Semitism directed a few years earlier at Hollywood in the Red Scare, interrogators nevertheless sought to place the blame for juvenile delinquency upon yet another Jewish-led industry.

Altogether, EC was about to be pushed out of the mainstream. But perhaps it had been there all along, the very mirror opposite to the gung ho superhero politics, both visual and textual. A vulgarity understandable (never forgivable in its racial dimensions) during the Second World War became afterwards an increasingly repugnant reflection of the Cold War moods, a craving for revenge in a world that unsettled Americans, and the ready adaptation by some post-New Deal Jewish writers and artists to a society where the very notion of social reform had become unwanted as well as apparently unneeded.[59] EC bucked the trends and paid the price: by 1955, all their comics lines had been folded.

The process by which Gaines and his collaborators evaded the new Comics Code, a trade group promoted and enforced by the Catholic-based Legion of Decency, by launching a black and white magazine outside Code control, depended to no small degree upon the ranks of the faithful, mostly if not entirely Jewish adolescents.[60] Mad founder Harvey Kurtzman, asked by this writer about EC's "fanatical fans," pointed to the redundancy: every "fan" is properly a fanatic, and the EC Fan-Addict Club both satirized and solidified the identification. Every member got an identification card, pin, shoulder patch, and ID card, in addition to receiving the house organ EC Fan-Addict Bulletin.[61] In an era of omnipresent government snooping, it was almost like being in a secret, crypto-Jewish organization, skeptical about reality as presented, purportedly apolitical, and indeed uninterested in economics and politics as such.

Mad Comics (1952–55) was a special case, as every devotee knows. But the New York Times didn't. Mad founder Harvey Kurtzman's passing, in 1993, was noted briefly, as if he had been a medical supplies manufacturer who patented a new truss or a developer who had cleared several blocks of Manhattan's ill-used real estate. Art Spiegelman personally demanded a larger treatment, and the Times responded a few days later with a rare obituary punch-up. Apart from Spiegelman's own comic evocation of his hero, "A Fershlugginer Genius," not even the New Yorker had much to say about the real figure's historic role, however.

Kurtzman's inability to explain what he had been doing undercut his case. His last job, a twenty-year stint with Playboy scripting Little Annie Fannie was worse. When I pressed him on it, in 1970 – then a young magazine editor who wrote to him out of the blue telling him that Mad had been the inspiration of my own childhood – he sheepishly explained that he had to make a living for his family. More accurately, he had lost his niche after two further efforts to recuperate the early *Mad* madness, and needed for someone to give him both a day job and a working identity. Demanding creative control through 51 percent of stock in the *Mad Magazine* that boss William M. Gaines had launched under Kurtzman's auspices, he had gone too far. He bowed out after a year of the new venture and lost the golden chance that never returned.

For true aficionados, *Mad Magazine* has always been *Mad Comics* in a diminished formulation. And that is the enigma of the original, full-dose *Mad*: how could a mere genre satire created for adolescents possibly possess that kind of strength? Why has its impact remained undiluted by the passing of years in those who read it when they were, say, ten years old? To reiterate a main theme: R. Crumb, still considered by many our most admired comic artist, likes to say that he has spent his working life striving to reach *Mad Comics'* intensity but has no expectation of success. "Do I still feel like I'm trying to attain the kind of cohesive intensity achieved by the early Kurtzman *Mad* comics?" Crumb asked rhetorically, in 1977, in response to my questions, "Is it still an unrealized dream of mine? The answer is ... naturally ... I think that's the 'culture' works," an artist like himself reaching toward the icons of his childhood.[62] The passing decades have not altered this equation. How could they? Early *Mad* belonged to a unique time and place where readers could still comprehend tenement dwellers using a phone in a downstairs store and where jokes could be made about little old ladies talking about Bolshevism over their samovars.

Kurtzman, scripting everything for the artists to finish and embellishing almost endlessly, essentially applied elsewhere the genius for detail and the compulsion for revelation that he had built up in EC comic lines, *Two-Fisted Tales* and *Frontline Combat*. The inside notes for a magazine with an all-time perfect title made the claim forthrightly:

We were tired of the war [comics], ragged from the science fiction, weary of the horror. Then it hit us! Why not do a complete about-face? A change of pace! A comic book! Not a serious comic book ... but a COMIC comic book. Not a floppity rabbit, giggly girl, anarchist teenage type comic book ... but a comic mag based on the short story of the wild nature that you seem to like so well. THAT WAS IT! Immediately we leaped to our typewriters, our drawing boards, and our India ink ... we worked like a crew of inspired demons! In no time at all, MAD was born.[63]

The first three issues were not, actually, all that impressive. A satire on the old haunted house narrative, another on the bloblike quality of lazy humans in a totally mechanized civilization, mild runs at Frankenstein, Tarzan, and Sherlock Holmes were among other features. Artists had already advanced to a variety of visual gags that wildly exceeded the storyline, but the storylines were weak.

Then came no. 4, April-May 1952. "Superduperman," which opens with assistant copy boy of the *Daily Dirt*, Clark Bent, cleaning out spittoons (occasionally glancing into the women's bathroom with his x-ray vision), was a narrative-visual explosion. This Clark was pathetic, unable to win the attention of the very hot Lois Pain. As in the real life of the comics industry, he has to overcome Captain Marvel (here "Captain Marbles") but without the help of DC's Legal Department. Successful by getting Marbles to punch himself into oblivion, Supe presents his true identity upon Lois, who quips "Big deal! Yer still a creep!" In the following strip, the typical American girl of a romance comic story ends up selling reefers to schoolchildren. These were serious.

Thus The Shadow, protagonist of a highly popular radio show, is in the upside-down *Mad* version a deluded stage illusionist, keeping himself hypnotized so as not to remember that he lives in a dump and is frightfully homely. Or the famed film odyssey of King Kong ends back in New York City where humans have meanwhile become Kong-sized and the adventurers mere lilliputians. And so on: by 1953, Kurtzman and his artists had hit their stride.

The next time around, even the plots they had already lampooned – Sherlock Holmes, Frankenstein, the Lone Ranger – looked staggeringly different. The quantity of hilarious details multiplied, and language evolved into double-talk laced with New York references and Yiddishisms ("Mrs. Gowanus," for Brooklyn's Gowanus Canal, destroyed by misdevelopment) that Kurtzman in a later interview described as odd little memories of childhood; "I was raised on chicken fat" and even "Nit-ge-die-get" ("Don't worry" in Yiddish, not surprisingly a hyphenated version of the well-known left-wing summer camp that Kurtzman's parents sent him to in the late 1930s).[64] To take one example of riffs: Dr. Frankenstein's assistant, Bumble, is seen in successive panels as reading what may be Chinese (but has the latest Dodger-Yanks world series score), imaginary Russian, Hebrew, Italian ("Dimaggio, La Berra, Rizzuto, Cuba Libre, Toute La Horn"). In the last panel, we see that the monster has a face exactly like Hitler.

Mad Comics survived and progressed and found its audience, thanks to Gaines's willingness to lose money for the first year. Older than the normal adolescent readership of other EC comics and definitely older than the audience of most comics, it was obviously devoted to the antic in all moods, with editor Kurtzman eager to expand the range of targets. By the second volume, movies (including a memorable send-up of *High Noon*) had been added, television's right-wing classic *Dragnet* ravished (not for the last time), and *Archie Comics* (whose owners practically supervised the Comics Code) given the once-over in "Starchie." You could say that *Mad* had begun to show political muscles, while sticking to the details of the particular butt of humor.

More important, *Mad* artists and Kurtzman began playing, more and more seriously, with form. "3-Dimensions," taking off from the 3-D films current in theaters, offered a dopey-looking *Mad* scripter and artist (with two heads) working with blues and reds as they stepped through story panels, ending with something unknown in the industry – a blank page (Kurtzman quipped to an interviewer, "When you're desperate to fill space, you think of outrageous things ... ").[65]

Even more inventive in distancing the reader from the normal narrative was a two-version story, "Murder the Husband" and "Murder the Story." A simple and familiar EC-style plot (paramour takes husband on a two-man fishing trip, into a boat, shoots him after a scuffle but also shoots holes in the boat, and ends up drowning, a poetic justice) turned upside down by rendering the narrative into nonsense. First, the dialogue bubbles go wild (including a Yiddish phrase, translated as "the Danish king comes to wed in Copenhagen"), as the narrator's explanations turn to Hopalong Cassidy cap pistols and bubble gum cards, and the intended murder victims sings one popular favorite after another, "Sewanee River" to "How Much is that Doggie In the Window." "Murder the Story" not only foreshadows the deconstruction of comic form in the artwork of the 1980s and '90s, it presents a deconstructive theory of popular art as complete as any pop art work would manage in the decades ahead, albeit without the gallery setting that gave Andy Warhol's canvases their avant-garde flavor and collectors' prestige.

Mad was growing bolder politically as well. The November–December 1954 issue opened with a by now expectable takeoff from another old favorite, "Bringing Up Father," this time with the glamorous daughter at the center of the first panel reading the *Daily Worker* (with news of the Cincinnati Reds) and Jiggs sneaking off from the dreaded Maggie. Only this time, those dishes she throws actually cause the kinds of facial and head injuries that real flying dishes would cause. (Jiggs complains, "There's just so much punishment a human comic strip body can take!") The issue moved on swiftly to the meatiest contents ever: a satire of Joe McCarthy's

Senate Subcommittee Hearings, rendered as the panel show "What's My Shine?" (i.e., *What's My Line?*).

Between commercials, *Mad*'s McCarthy flashes an obviously altered photograph insisting that the witness "is in reality, a REDSKIN!" Revealing the real picture, himself with paint roller in hand and a turkey on the fence behind him, the intended victim insists, "I am not and have never been a redskin" (to which McCarthy replies, "No need to raise your voice and get angry. I realize you're not REALLY a Redskin but merely a dupe of the redskins!"). Then the two begin wrestling, throwing the scene into total chaos and dissolve. No better satire was produced, certainly not by the stunned victims and their friends.[66]

The artists continued to cut loose on form. A *Mad* satire of movie clichés (against a background of Marlon Brando in *Julius Caesar*) ends with Marilyn Monroe pulling off a mask and declaring, "I'm not really your MAD writer. In fact, this MAD comic book isn't really a MAD comic book," pulling up the page to reveal Disney characters. The whole issue, in fact, was printed upside down (or more simply, the covers were printed upside down). The end, logical and glorious, was reached in 1955, the last year of production.

If "Starchie" had been aimed at the pseudowholesomeness of Archie, "Mickey Rodent!" slashed at the larger lies in the world of children's animation. Only a few years before the opening of Disneyland (in Orange Country, in 1960), the Mickey Mouse Club was already television teen fare, the Disney strike of 1941 old news but Walt Disney's own role in the Hollywood Blacklist a familiar, continuing note in the production world of American entertainment. In the very first panel, a character is hauled away by studio guards, and another comments, "You know Walt Dizzy's orders about how we've got to wear white gloves at all times ... ". Pluto complains bitterly that only he, among the assorted animals, is denied speech; little signs like "Curb your mortal!" and "Beware of Humans!" appear on fences; and Donald finally learns that Mickey, secretly plotting against his rival for years, has set the perfect trap: Donald, without his clothes, is stuck in a zoo with other ducks.

Even better (if mainly for the recondite-minded) was the next-to-last number, the "Special ART Issue," devoted wholly to the story of artist Willie Elder ("from the time he was a tiny, miserable two-bit hack infant to the present when he is now a big, miserable, two-bit hack grown-up"). Nothing more Jewish could be imagined than the infant "shmearing" chicken fat on towels, bald heads, visitors' dresses, and convenient walls illustrated in color with thousands of blue and red lines. "Today those shmears ... are hung in various museums and signed with Elder's various pen names such as 'Braque,' 'Matisse,' 'Picasso,' etc."[67]

This much was evidently a satire of the prestigious *Partisan Review*'s New York intellectuals crowd and the early retrospectives of Abstract Expressionism, including the effusive propaganda of Clement Greenberg for his favorites within the world of what publisher Henry Luce liked to call "free enterprise art." At the same time, it was a telling comment on the fate of the cartoonists around themselves.

Could Kurtzman have read "Avant-Garde and Kitsch," Greenberg's 1939 manifesto assaulting popular culture at large and calling for true artists to retreat from it into expressions ever more devoid of social context and tradition? Not likely. But Kurtzman, even without this information, certainly knew the premier artistic trends of the time. That the MOMA had given the UPA studios a unique showing in 1955 might have been a vector in the direction of the popular arts. But comics were outside any such consideration.[68]

Kurtzman and Elder brought the story back to the hard and unartistic reality of the contemporary printed page. ("He now knew how to make beautiful drawings [sculpture and paintings] ... He was now prepared to choose which of these fine things he would devote the rest of his life to make! ... He chose to make money!") Montage takes over the narrative with ad satires, real-looking family shots, playing cards, Mt. Rushmore, George Washington, Whistler's Mother, etc. The artist completes his saga with a "normal" satire strip, *Mad* vintage, and the last page is *Senility*, a return to the scribbles of infancy when he "spends most of his time sitting around ... chewing the fat with his buddies (chicken-fat, of course)!" Interviewed decades later, Elder himself admitted to influences from Hogarth and Brueghel, and for that matter, the Marx Brothers. But, he pleaded, he needed Kurtzman's guiding genius to do his best work. Sadly, that was true, and even in years of *Little Annie Fannie*, he never had that kind of satirical guidance again.

Possibly the pace could not have been maintained in any case. But the enforcement of the Comics Code, driving nonjoiners from newsstands, would have subjected *Mad Comics* to prepublication censorship, and thereby spelled doom to the wacky collective vision. Turning the comic into a black and white magazine proved, then, an inescapable decision and, given the choices, probably a good one. Gaines was surely right in another way. Al Feldstein, editor of *Mad*'s own in-house imitation, *Panic*, before taking over *Mad Magazine* from Kurtzman, had already shown a talent for stylization (and the abandonment of color, clearly an experiment in cost-cutting). The short-lived *Panic* lacked the consistency of *Mad* but it, too, could be right on the mark, like the Mickey Spillane *Sex and Sadism Dept* satire which found the frequent murderer/detective killing women because he was a cross-dressing woman himself, tragically murdering a potential lover who was a cross-dressing man. Not bad for 1954. Elsewhere, the Dogpatch crew ended up lynched, "Trick Dacey" murdered funny-looking outlaws who cried "Liberty, equality and fraternity" as they were shot, and more of the usual nonsense. But something had leveled out.

Feldstein was neither untalented nor lacking in liberal credentials. Son of a Russian-Jewish Brooklyn dental technician who lost his lab in the Depression, the youngster won juvenile art contests, attended the High School of Music and Art, and managed a few semesters at Brooklyn College until the money ran out. He edited and sometimes wrote a half-dozen of the "New Trend" EC comics, 1950–54, that offered readers so much more than they had come to expect in the form. He even wrote a half-dozen television teledramas about psychoanalysis, some of them shown in segments of Steve Allen's late-night variety show. Politically, Feldstein had the same anti-McCarthyite sympathies as the other EC editors, but he was characteristically less openly outraged or just more cautious. Besides, he had a big production problem: Kurtzman had taken several of the best artists off to another project, *Trump*, backed (and then quickly dumped into oblivion) by Hugh Hefner.

Feldstein needed to begin in different directions with rather less than the Kurtzman-era talent. The hypertrophic advertising expansion of the age gave him a ready foil that *Mad Comics* had hit earlier with slashing satire. As in-house historian Maria Reidelbach says in her kindliest fashion, Feldstein "honed the parodies, taking advantage of the extended thematic [advertising] campaigns then in favor."[69] The new *Mad* also had the imagined anti-hero Alfred E. Neuman, created at the suggestion of Gaines after a postcard that had caught Kurtzman's attention, a wacky totem offsetting the toning down of the idiosyncratic language of *Mad Comics* (eliminating just about all the Yiddish in the process) into a smoother patter, especially stylized in satires on famous poetry, nursery rhyme, and such.

It tended quickly toward formula, although the recycling of *Mad* readers, sloughing off older ones and taking on younger ones, probably minimized the awareness of repetition. Meanwhile, *Mad* went to court repeatedly to win the right to parody music lyrics as if to carry out, in another venue, the old struggles against censorship in the comic book world. It took regular slaps over the decades at housing segregation, Republican politicians (notably Ronald Reagan with the "Greed Is Good" moralisms evoked by noticeably Jewish financiers of the 1980s and promoted among intellectuals by their favorite centrist magazine, the *New Republic*), the Vietnam War, and so on. The FBI dossier on *Mad*, running from 1957 to 1971, contains all of thirty-six files, ranging from director Hoover's own concern for certain satires, like the "Draft Dodgers Card," and satires on Hoover himself, to angry correspondence from conservative groups outraged by the magazine.[70]

In the transition from era to era, the *Mad* staffers hit a definite bump. The Beat generation literary phenomenon proved more impermeable to satire than television and movies. Student demonstrations and ghetto uprisings of the 1960s obviously made them both perplexed and increasingly nervous. Probably the younger Jewish radical intellectuals seemed intractable to the middle-aged *Mad* scripters and artists – just as they did to their parents. If Marshall McLuhan had mistakenly tabbed the early *Mad* a "TV end table," the later *Mad* tended increasingly, at least on most of its pages, to become one.[71]

And still, *Mad Magazine* went from 50,000 or so in circulation to several million, and then to many millions of readers worldwide for good reasons. If it could not have retained the original degree of manic energy, it nevertheless cast a shadow over the history of printed satire and perhaps all satire. One would be hard put to place those European classics of the earlier print age, *Puck* and *Simplicimuss*, above it. Other mass-produced and, from a personnel standpoint, Jewish-heavy satirical projects of the 1950s to 1980s, from *1000 Jokes* to the *National Lampoon*, which renewed the titillating girlie appeal of *Captain Billy's Whiz Bang* and the tenacious sailors-and-girls joke books, have come and gone. *Mad* stays, albeit under corporate ownership and with badly reduced sales. The visage of Alfred E. Neuman, never quite a cliche and the iconic staple of *Mad Magazine*, could eventually be seen on breakfast drinks packages and in Lands End catalogues. (A condom version, truer in spirit to the original *Mad*, was regrettably vetoed.) It is among other things the *most* Jewish humor magazine since the *Groysser Kundes*, with sufficient continuities that the youngest readers of the *Kundes* may have been among the eldest readers of *Mad*.

More important, in an America with an intermittently compulsive consensus and too few windows looking outward (especially before the Internet), and for the other "closed" places like Israel (where it may be more badly needed than anywhere else), *Mad* has continued its subtle role of voicing the perspective of kids by the simple means of mocking authority. Actor John Goodman, costar of *Roseanne*, once observed that as a Middle American reared in Afton, Missouri, he had received the basic education from reading *Mad* that he could have acquired nowhere else. Millions could say the same, emphatically including myself.[72]

This story ends on a collective sad note for the early geniuses. The Kurtzman-era artists almost invariably ended up in advertising, turning out undistinguished and sometimes corrupt bodies of work.[73] Within the world of comics, the end of *Mad Comics* and EC lines generally marked the sorry end of a glorious phase. Most of the lines commercially vibrant only a few years earlier were dead or dying by the mid-1950s anyway. Censorship, enforced by deeply conservative Catholic lay authorities, would probably have destroyed what was most interesting even if television had not eclipsed the industry's golden age. Comics staggered on, their highest quality lines (like *Little Lulu*, or master artist Carl Barks' *Donald Duck* series) increasingly made up of reprints. There was little new or notable to present.

THE RETURN OF FANDOM – AND THE RISE OF THE UNDERGROUNDS

The revival of comics and comic fandom by Marvel Comics during the 1960s and '70s lacked, by notable contrast to the EC Fan Addicts Club, the least element of self-satire: this time it was virtually pure promotion, an effusion of kitsch for cash. In stark contrast to the Americanization of the 1930 and '40s Jewish generation, it contained scarcely a shred of political progressiveness, quite the reverse. The America that accepted them was already democratic enough, perhaps too much so. If the "good war" against the Fascists had still seemed too warlike, its presentation too illusion-ridden for savants like Kurtzman, the Korean War was not war enough for its successors in the new mainstream. These were the veritable anti-avant-garde, and not only in political content but artistic form as well: the ironic asides delivered by the new or revived superheroes while handing out punches of banality heaped upon banality. And yet the revival of the form, unbeknownst to its chief movers, offered further possibilities for radical expression.

Along with the launching of the *Fantastic Four* in 1961, artist Stan Lee and entrepreneur Jack Kirby built upon fan interest by crediting the various contributors in a way rare to comics after the grand days of EC, and adding the "Bullpen Bulletin" of inside gossip, much of it apparently written by Lee himself. The self-conscious publication of collectable comic series followed almost as an afterthought, but also one of the most lucrative in the reduced comic book industry: rather than millions of casual buyers, Marvel and its imitators had thousands all but sworn to purchase every single item. The still disproportionately Jewish fans themselves seem to have proposed the revival of comic heroes absent since the 1940s, and even some new ones.[74]

A larger comic fandom soon kicked in as well. SciFi fandom, beginning way back in the late 1930s, had grown with the return of prosperity and the spread of low-priced, used Gestettner mimeograph machines. Presaging its role a decade later in booming SciFi films with *Star Trek*'s trekkies, fandom reached new stages, both in following and in spirit, for the baby boomers. A panel at the World Science Fiction Convention in Pittsburgh in 1960 featured Dick Lupoff and his wife with their own 'zine, *Xero*, including the first installment of his work in progress, the nostalgic and unacademic closely researched history of comics, *All In Color for a Dime*. A second fanzine surfacing at the same convention, *Comic Art*, urged the formation of an organized comics fandom. A science professor at Wayne State, Jerry Bails, really set comics fandom in motion the following year, copublishing *Alter-Ego*. Gathering addresses from the comics publishers' letters pages, Bails had his mailing list set to go. In 1963, the professor personally proposed the creation of the Academy of Comic Book Fans and Collectors, creating an academy of sorts, convoking a miniconference in which Marvel reps were on hand to help set the framework of a grown-up audience and institutionalized reputation, leading towards a comic art revival of a new kind.

By the mid-1960s, fandom gained *New York Times* notice, prompting the first published comics price guide in 1970, and thrusting a careful selection of old comics into the arena of material speculation not so different from those interested of movie posters or archaic board games. When copy shop-printed "prozine" publications appeared (or, more properly, reappeared) as vehicles for would-be professionals, the circle had been completed, albeit with a great deal more open irony than the first time around, almost two generations earlier. There was still fun, and the Jewish camaraderie (or rivalry) within the industry hadn't changed all that much – but the innocence was pretty much gone. At these fan conclaves, pimply boys and crazed collectors still abounded, but scantily clad dames with silicone breasts, and talk of film and television revenues, set the new tone. Fortunes, or at least the promise of a living wage, could be arranged with contacts made here.[75]

Exceedingly late in the day, decades after the disappearance of EC's hard-hitting series, comic book publishers did make a stab at social relevance. Leaning toward the rebellious adolescent reader, heroes now had bouts of angst, had friends who became substance abusers, and some experienced

moments of real social dissent (at least against the accredited evil, like the
KKK, fought by a new hero called Black Panther). This never went too far,
in the same way that emerging female superheroes would remain a pale
version of the feminist uprising and in some ways remain a reaction against
it. Talented DC artist Howard Chaykin, struggling to create a fresh and
stylized kind of comic book noir, later noted that his own 1970s stories
positively attacked corporate capitalism. But he was clearly the exception.[76]
Flag-waving war comics (like *GI Joe*, a big hit as the marketing of a per-
ennial toy, or *Sgt. Rock and His Screaming Commandos*) were never far away,
and never a thousandth as realistic as the EC war/violence comics published
back in the late 1940s and early 1950s.[77]

Over the following decades, fannish fascination led to a popular interest
in history, at least the history of comic book genres, styles, and publishing
companies. Jules Feiffer's *The Great Comic Book Heroes* memorably offered
an early glimpse at the origins of the form, although Feiffer's autobiographical comments were undoubtedly the most lasting contribution of
the volume. As Marvel reprinted its series from the 1960s and DC provided
readers oversized paperbacks of 1940s comics, older fans gained reasons or
rationalizations to keep up interest as well as collections. Like the baseball
fans who looked to statistics for something like a view of the world as well
as a view of the game, comics fans had by the 1980s sources for endless, if
often perhaps also contentless, contemplation.[78] Meanwhile, the scholarship
around the field continued to expand, growing beyond price lists to
directories of artists, university press (and trade) monographs or collections
of essays and minimemoirs, interviews by the dozens offered in assorted
venues. Comics respectability had almost arrived.

That future artists vastly more cerebral than Stan Lee or Jack Kirby could,
within a few years, create narratives about subjects like James Joyce, but
nevertheless based narratively on superhero origin stories, suggests how
wild postmodern impulses had become, or, less significantly, that such
efforts had no roots in comics at all, simply replicating the move of
mainstream artists through Pop and Op toward the reappropriation
("sampling") of popular culture. Less optimistically, all this might mark a
return to the 1910s origins of Dada (with Baltimore/Jewish Man Ray in the
lead) sans the seminal rebellious element.[79]

Some sections of baby boom fandom honored the field's true greats in
practice, through their own emerging art. For them, even Kurtzman's post-
Mad failures could be seen in retrospect like Moshe Nadir's imagined
skeleton after his death, bones made into walking-sticks for the next generation of artists.

After the one-shot, *Playboy*-sponsored but ill-fated *Trump* in 1955 – I can remember the day that I saw it on the drugstore magazine shelf (and like so many others, I did not buy it) – Kurtzman's next try was *Humbug* (1958–59), an impossibly small and underfunded publication using the work process of a cooperative, something like the cartoonists' union that young Kurtzman had in mind. It looked like an intense but squeezed-down *Mad Comics*. When it failed, Kurtzman went in a different direction with *HELP!* (1960–63), named after the Beatles' hit. The first US magazine to adopt the Italian mainstream's fumetti style of photos with captions, *HELP!* used them for strictly satirical purposes, some political, but most about manners and morals. The rest of the magazine was mainly filler with an occasional literary reprint (even here Kurtzman's taste was interesting, including Ambrose Bierce), gag pieces by current comedians friendly with Kurtzman (and willing to take low paychecks), and at the very back, a comics section.

Here, in these soon-to-be-forgotten pages, Kurtzman scripted for Eisner's art (in the last of their major collaborations) "Goodman Beaver," a sort of *How to Succeed in Business Without Really Trying* satire of the ad game. Here, also, some of the future stars of underground comix made their first appearance in a national venue (Gilbert Shelton of *The Fabulous Furry Freak Brothers*, and R. Crumb). This was practically the beginning of the R. Crumb story, including his *Yiddishlakh*. Despite assorted evocations of the Crumb story, including the 1995 film *Crumb*, how it all happened is one of the most intimate and misunderstood stories within American comics, or, for that matter, all-American art.

A geeky Dover, Delaware, kid, young Robert had what Art Spiegelman later described as an instinctive "cartoony" sensibility. By the time he was an early teen he, and his lost-to-the-world brother, Charles, were turning out comic fanzines with a recuperated sense of the funny animals and odd-looking humans from the 1940s vintage comic book days and earlier comic strip styles. It was, Art Spiegelman observed gloomily about his own struggles for artistic achievement, something almost impossible to learn any other way, at any later age – not that anyone could have easily ascertained its value then, for a later world from whence those particular images had almost disappeared entirely.

Crumb graduated high school in 1961 and moved to Cleveland the next year, on the invitation from a friend from the little world of comic fanzines, Marty Pahls, to become his roommate. Crumb got a day job cranking out material for American Greeting Cards, a relative giant of the field created by a former street peddler named Abe Saperstein (no relation to the savant of the Harlem Globetrotters with the same name). There the work was strictly proletarian and non-union to boot, with dozens of older skilled craftsmen working close at hand, busily doing color separations. Soon Crumb's talent was recognized and he moved to the quasi-ironic, vaguely innovative Hi-Brow line. There, at least, he was devising humorous material for money.

His free time was something else entirely, a revelation of urban life in the aging cities full of memories. Harvey Pekar, a friend of Pahl's who met the young artist about this time, remembered he and Crumb spending a lot of time in a neighborhood destined for "urban removal" destruction a few years away, but at the moment frozen in time.[80] The ethnic atmosphere of Cleveland offered a battered urban center of earlier Austrian and Czech migration, heavy also with Slavs, Jews, and most recently with a black shift into formerly white neighborhoods near downtown.[81] A look at any of the Crumb urban strips from these days, his glimpses backward for a decade, are likely to capture ethnic (mostly Jewish ethnic) types that were takeoffs from old comic strips but also reflections of living remnants.

He shared a lot with a generation that found nostalgia early, looking to pre-1950, and even more to the 1910 to 1940 designs from advertising logos to vintage automobiles, above all looking to the fading musical styles for a glimpse of a vanishing vernacular promise. In an important way, the comic book of the late 1940s and early 1950s had continued images of that world past its time. *Mad*, for example, set itself upon exploring while assaulting the details of older and transitional forms, crowded apartments and plump Jewish mamas shouting, "Villie, Villie Elder!" For Crumb and Pahls and thousands of others (including this writer), fascination with assorted fading vernacular styles meant going through stacks of old records and old magazines, looking for something unknown.

Harvey Pekar was an urban type especially valuable for Crumb's education into an avant-garde Jewishness, in recollection the "classic beatnik," a "wild intensive Jewish guy into bebop music ... this real seething character."[82] A lifelong Jewish Clevelander with left-wing parents, he had an especially politically-minded mother who, with his father, ran the ghetto grocery. Growing up in a tough mixed race neighborhood hadn't driven Pekar to the Right or into a love affair with American commercialism; to the contrary, he was a Jewish radical without a party, redefining the cause in fresh, uncharted ways.

More complex than the cartoonish figure depicted, however lovingly, in the film *American Splendor*, Pekar was the ultimate intellectual autodidact and in that sense, a definite throwback to previous generations. The high school graduate worked at the VA hospital closest to home but devoted himself to reading novels, collecting and trading "sides" (old records), trying to connect with women, and seeing pals. Too political by far to be one of the famed Jewish hipsters, uninterested in the kinds of talents and compulsions that led to pool hustling or heroin use, he was the perfect mentor and friend for Crumb's evolving tastes.

Crumb confirmed his Jewishness with his particular cravings for women. In a folknik coffeehouse near Western Reserve University, anyone hanging out would hear bad imitations of Joan Baez in addition to the heavily talked about Marx and Freud of a previous Jewish semiradical generation, and with luck meet the kind of Jewish coeds who had their own odd cravings, for male Gentiles. They accepted him; they *liked* him.[83]

An informal neighborhood salon was an extension of the coffeehouse scene, with lots of talk in 1964 of civil rights, race riots, Fair Play for Cuba, jazz, and suspiciously Dylan-sounding poet-singers. The young woman who owned the apartment introduced Crumb to Dana Morgan, a community college student, who was an instant fan of his drawings, soon Crumb's first lover and his first wife. The visions she had of a respectable Jewish family in the semisuburbs were not remotely appropriate for him. But it was hardly the Jewishness that he instinctively rejected.[84]

Crumb had already been in Manhattan for a summer, practically throwing himself into the arms of Harvey Kurtzman, who set him assisting Terry Gilliam (eventually of Monty Python) in the production work for *HELP!* To say Kurtzman was an obsession with Crumb would be an underestimation of the elder's influence. Not just the stamp of *Mad Comics* (which continued to percolate in Crumb's memory and his scarce writings) but the shaping influence of Kurtzman, getting him small jobs, introducing him around, created a bond that struck the old man as curious.[85] Here (from Kurtzman's perspective) was a talented kid who for some reason apparently did not *want* to make it big, and who regarded *Playboy*, Hugh Hefner, and *Little Annie Fannie* with outright contempt.

He was certainly looking for something. Back in Cleveland from a cheap trip to Europe (he made drawings of Bulgarian communist architecture for *HELP!*) in the spring of 1965, Crumb started smoking marijuana and occasionally dropping LSD. As Pekar and Pahls watched Crumb improve his comic styles, finding more and more uses for the Rapidograph pen that he'd adopted at work, they could see him tapping into something deep inside himself. As he observed later, he stopped drawing from life. He floated around in subconsciousness for what seemed like months at a time, inventing characters, recognizing in an intuitive way that "cartoons were just these dumb drawings of dumb guys with big shoes," a facet of "very working class, cheap amusement for the masses, like vaudeville, early movies, pulp magazines and so on."[86] The most visible part of it was the toying with vintage comic images sparked by combinations of drugs and visual memories: light bulbs, trees, bottles, and radios with faces (as on the cover of R. Crumb's *Head Comix*, commercially published in 1968). His notebooks of 1965–67 contain the essential elements of the giant leap he was about to make.

"Bop" language strips, with a remote similarity to *Mad Comics* hipster pages, were the only strips that could feature his new beastiary, from urban blue-collar types to vaudevillians, Jesus to devils, a black "natural" woman who could easily be Jewish, and Crumb's own favorite invention, the hip guru, Mr. Natural. Natural's permanent client, Flakey Foont, is surely Crumb himself (in terms of sexual frustrations, the early Crumb), neurotic, and perpetually anxious but occasionally able to enjoy drug visions. He also abandoned Cleveland and Dana (who eventually followed him, before they finally split up) for Chicago and then California. He was about to spur the birth of underground comix. And already permanently and utterly obsessed with Jewish women, intuitively and artistically rejecting the rejection of ethnic traits by so many Jewish men.[87]

In *Motor City Comics* (1969), one of his first solo books, he was already over the top. One of those comic books that Jewish women in particular (the most articulate of them Trina Robbins) would find objectionable has Crumb invent the guerilla-band leader Lenore Goldberg, whose Girl Commandos (in the name of the Women's Liberation Front) take over a meeting of leading intellectuals. Confronted by police while going out of the building, they scatter, some are brutally attacked by police – but Lenore escapes back to her apartment where, wide-hipped and lacking inhibitions, she shares glorious oral sex with her boyfriend (calling out with this small victory over middle-American repression, "Viva la Revolución!"). It was mildly satirical but also admiring, in the lustful sort of way: no victim of the usual stereotypes, he craved large, bemuscled Jewish women.

The same year, in his similarly solo *Big Ass Comix*, Crumb introduced "Dale Steinberger: The Jewish Cowgirl," adding "She's nobody's Yiddisha mama, that's for sure," and in a small box asking the readers (or himself?), "What is this strange fascination with Jewish girls??" Lenore and Dale will reappear and how could they not? In Crumb's notebooks of the next several years, she is, in the most realistic drawings of Crumb's portfolio, more or less Aline Kominsky. Long Island refugee, art school refugee, Aline became his next longtime artistic collaborator, wife, and fellow exile, with their daughter, in the South of France.

Trina Robbins later acidly observed that the violence and the sex introduced in comics by Crumb not only helped create comix but also helped kill them. The id-loosed and stylized misogyny often found in Crumb's work – only somewhat balanced with treatments of stronger women, like the semifictional Aline – gave license to the untalented artists whose work reached a limit and created a fatal bounce back effect.[88]

Robbins's version has the ring of truth, especially about the unloosed id of Crumb himself. But it oversimplifies the swift rise and collapse of underground culture in the printed page, as local antiwar newspapers came out of nowhere to gain a mass audience and were gone again by 1975, leaving behind a barely dissenting "alternative" press. Worse, it leaves aside the dozens whose métier was never sex or violence, who never found any other audience and, unlike their predecessors, shifted neither to advertising or mainstream comics but just stopped drawing for publication. Like the layout talent of the underground press, the underground comix just faded away. But for a moment, it was utterly remarkable.

We have seen, briefly so far, how *Arcade* (1975–77), edited by Art Spiegelman and Bill Griffith, sought to consolidate artistically and historically the crew of artists retreating from the collapse of underground comix. The next artistic step was taken just a bit more than a decade later. *Raw* magazine (1980–91) was the brain child of Art Spiegelman and his wife, the French artist (and future arts editor of the *New Yorker*) Françoise Mouly, dedicated to the proposition that comics could not only be no-holds-barred but also genuinely artistic. This move followed a period of self-reflection in Spiegelman that is better held until the next chapter on the self-conscious recuperation of Jewish traditions. But it is crucial that *Raw* (whose subtitle regularly changed, but was perhaps best captured in a 1989 edition, "High Culture for Lowbrows") drew heavily on non-US artists, especially, but not only, Europeans. Such a thing had never been done.

Nonconsecutive narratives, nonnarratives, sheer primitivism, lavish colored prints of sketchbooks, the early appearance of young artists like Charles Burns and Drew Friedman, emerging stars like Lynda Barry, occasional mainstream greats like Edward Sorel, joined a familiar underground crew of Kim Deitch, Bill Griffith and Justin Green with chunks of Spiegelman's own evolving *Maus*. It was, in large part, strictly unintentionally Jewish. But beneath the cosmopolitan culture and experimentation, there was more than a little familiar to older themes. Ben Katchor made his first big splash here, with evolving versions of New York and Brooklyn streets (the first published was "The Atlantic Ocean Laundry"), in what Spiegelman identified as the most Yiddish of comic artists;

Kim Deitch rehearsed the story of his parents as avant-garde, folk-singing leftists all but underground in the McCarthy era; and Spiegelman himself could be found personally in one of Drew Friedman's drawings, animatedly attacking the racism and general politics of Crumb in favor of what was evidently a Jewish, ethical (i.e., left-wing) viewpoint.

The breakthroughs that Spiegelman was to achieve in *Maus* and with the *New Yorker* covers of the late 1990s and the first years of the new century – not to mention incidental work, from illustrations of bohemian classics, to children's books – had taken shape, in nucleus in *Raw*. From the dailies and weeklies of the East Coast, the slick magazines, like *Esquire*, to hip museum staffs, Spiegelman and his assemblage of artists were an art presence in a way that comics had never been in America. But financially, *Raw* was a flop. In an exasperated moment at the 1982 First Radical Humor Festival (there was no second, or has not been one as of the present), Spiegelman described publishers as the Jews and commercial print shops as the Nazis, mainly because odd shapes and high-quality printing of color came only at outrageous prices. In the last years of *Raw*, for the nth time since the 1950s, a comic project moved from magazine to paperback format, and flopped (only *Mad* reprints had succeeded in the square-backed format, possibly because paperbacks cost only thirty-five cents in those days, but doubtless because *Mad* had a built-in market, even if the transformed layout was visually terrible).

In a curious way, less self-consciously artistic, and more openly left-wing at first, but in later years more cautious, Jules Feiffer had trod the same path.[89] Born in the Bronx in 1929 to a left-of-center family (his sister would become a Communist), he spent a year at the Pratt Institute after high school, but found his real calling when he attached himself to Eisner's operation in 1946, and drew a kid's strip, *Clifford*, on the back page of *The Spirit*. He was frankly unsuited for any other kind of comic operation outside, perhaps, EC, and had no apparent future.

Then came Korea and he got drafted. Hating the military life became his way of sketching out a political worldview and an art form. Still in uniform, he began to draw *Munro*, a militantly pacifist graphic novel (a term still far from being in use) that he finished in two years of postarmy unemployment. The protagonist kid was drafted by accident but put through the bureaucratic rigors by a system that could not admit a clerical error. In the years before he could get a commercial publisher, he drew a memorable twenty-eight-page celebrity satire for *Pageant* magazine, and *Boom*, a satire of the lies told by the Atomic Energy Commission. *The Village Voice* found him and adopted him, paying him badly for a weekly strip. He went to work briefly for Terrytoons, in the days when Gene Deitch attempted to reorganize and modernize the studio. Then Hugh Hefner offered Feiffer both the artistic freedom and the fat paycheck that he needed. *Sick, Sick, Sick* (1960), the first paperback collection of Feiffer cartoons, offered non-New Yorkers and non-*Playboy* readers, like myself, a dose of Feiffer. It was a revelation, a next step from *Mad* and *HELP!* to the Greenwich Village sophistication that had survived with its left-liberalism more or less intact.

Feiffer and his strip's ambience grew more politically moderate in the decades to follow (although no less brilliantly aimed at Ronald Reagan's entourage and Reagan himself), no doubt because of the changing character of racial politics in Manhattan, and probably because of his intimate friendships with considerably less-than-radical celebrities like Philip Roth, but almost certainly for the deeper reason that the avant-garde, rather than politics, was always the real key to his sensibility. *Carnal Knowledge* and *Little Murders*, adapted from his plays and suitably directed in film versions by Mike Nichols, captured America's postmodern heart of darkness.[90] But after the statement had been made, it was hard to go further.

Feiffer had dozens more creative projects in him, including a well-received recollective drama, *A Bad Friend*, opening in 2003, about his own slightly fictionalized Communist sister and a besieged Jewish family of the McCarthy era. In the end, Feiffer was more cartoonist and public moralist than media high roller, as were all his fellow avant-garde cartoonists of the following generation. Bill Griffith was fond of quoting gut-bucket avant-gardist Charles Bukowski calling the underground comix mavens "Baptist ministers in Popeye Suits," and this near-aphorism contained more than a little truth.[91] In music, an occasional avant-gardist might become a multimillionaire, and still be fortunate not to selfdestruct. (With a little similar experience behind him, Crumb reflected in answer to my query about himself that Dylan had been "worshipped as if he was a god … a wonder he's still alive to tell about it."[92]) Most others never had the big chance, or, like Crumb, ran from it, straight or not-so-straight back to their semi-Jewish roots (whether personal or, as in Crumb's case, borrowed). It was their strength quite as much as their weakness.

Filmmaker Edgar Ulmer, working at the bottom of the film genres almost literally until his last day on earth, had already provided the classic example of the artist going his own way, unwilling to yield. Working on ever-tinier budgets, he forged on. A trilogy of SciFi films in the dark 1950s climaxed with *Beyond the Time Barrier* (1960), warning against the poisons spread by nuclear weapons testing. He also shot a memorable noir-western made in Mexico, *Naked Dawn* (1957), with betrayal all around as a steady theme, while commencing with half-baked comedies, horror, and an ill-starred historical epic with Victor Mature as Hannibal crossing the Alps![93]

But surely Ulmer's strangest and his most avant-garde work had been *Naked Venus* (1958), often omitted from his filmography due to the calculated absence of on-screen credits. Here, a European refugee (played winningly by Patricia Conelle) falls for a GI. But after they marry, have a child and seem destined for a happy life back in the US, his mother conspires successfully to drive them apart. Here lies the betrayal of true motherhood by false moral claims: using for her wedge the well-known nudism of her daughter-in-law, she claims the child for herself as proper parent. Conelle goes to court to get back her child, defending her avocation militantly. The judge reviews the evidence, and here Ulmer's genius for cost cutting prompted him to insert lengthy clips from current European nudist camp outings (waist up only), with healthful and mostly youthful bodies male and female, engaged in volleyball or hiking but always smiling, the apotheosis of wholesomeness. Alternatively (and more likely), the availability of the footage – most definitely in the soft-core zone – actually sparked the film's creation. These, in any case, are the happiest moments of the film, when the mere love of individuals is transcended by a near-utopian innocence and collectivity.

Whatever the combination of artistic, personal, or financial urges to make *Naked Venus*, Ulmer could only be himself. He posed European society and its nonconsumerist freedoms in the starkest terms against the sexual repression of a postwar, materially bountiful America. He urgently wanted to go on making films, through whatever venues possible. But, as he told the few interviewers who bothered to pursue him, he always found himself seeking redemption. And so we can say of so many other genius Jewish popular culture innovators, most of them atheists.

NOTES

[1] One of the more remarkable texts of the intimate Yiddish literary world is the *Dud Edelshtot Gedenk Bukh* (Los Angeles and San Francisco: Dud Boshover Kommittee, 1952), a voluminous treatment of Bovshover's fellow anarchist poet, no less tragic, dead at an early age from tuberculosis. Within this text, editor B.I. Biolostoski's own essay "Fun Zeynen zey Gezen," treats Bovshover with great care: 532–47. I was kindly given this book by Arne Thorne, a few years before his own death.

[2] Moshe Nadir, *Rivington Stritt* (New York: Morgn Frayihayt, 1931), unpaged.

[3] James A. Wechsler, "From World War I to the Popular Front: The Art and Activism of Hugo Gellert," *Journal of the Decorative and Propaganda Arts*, 24 (2001): 198–205. This important essay draws upon my own interview with Gellert (housed at the Tamiment Library, New York University, Oral History of the American Left archive), among many other sources.

[4] A few years later, in 1932, he prepared an interracial mural for the Center Theater at Rockefeller Center. Unlike Diego Rivera's murals for the Center, destroyed shortly after their creation, Gellert's survived until the building was taken down in the 1940s. Wechsler, "From World War I to the Popular Front": 222–24.

[5] Gene Lees, *Cats of Any Color* (New York: DeCapo, 2001 edition): 91–121, a book burdened with the need for polemic. The author is the embittered son of Canadian left-wingers who, he insists "have no sense of real pleasure," regarding music only as a means for didactic political lessons. That narrow attitude would come as a great shock to the Jewish left-wingers portrayed in this book, and is most likely a sort of "screened memory." According to other sources, Rodney also experimented with *klezmer* in his early years, and (although not the sort of observation that Lees would likely appreciate) might have, during a different era, found in the misnamed "Jewish Jazz" an answer to his unfulfilled yearnings.

[6] It's important to note that Ferlinghetti never accepted the appellation of "Beat"; for him it was a misnomer at best, at worst a cynical marketing mechanism that repelled him.

[7] I introduced him to an audience at Brown University in 1982. His later poems were disappointing, but his early poems had lost none of their depth or piquancy. For me, it was like joining a legend, for a couple of hours – in that sense, like the short time spent with Ferlinghetti, the extended hours with C.L.R. James, and to a degree the time also with Abraham Lincoln Polonsky. They *radiated* history.

[8] See "Eric Drooker Unmasked: an Exclusive Interview" by Chris Lanier, *The Comics Journal*, no. 253 (June 2003): 82–111. He reveals here that his grandfather, a Lower East Side child of immigrants, had given him books by Frans Masereel, the great Belgian woodcut Expressionist; about the same time, Drooker was discovering Crumb. Thanks also to Drooker for a recent email. Small disclosure: Drooker, along with other artists of the *World War 3 Illustrated* circle, are contributors to a comic book format history of the Industrial Workers of the World, coedited by myself and artist-editor Nicole Schulman, to be published by Verso in 2005.

[9] Allen Ginsberg, "Afterword," to *Street Posters & Ballads* by Eric Drooker (New York: Seven Stories Press, 1998): 78–79.

[10] Jerry Wexler and David Ritz, *Rhythm and the Blues: a Life in American Music* (New York: Knopf, 1993): 3–5, 17–18.

[11] The boss, an immigrant Turk, Ahmet Ertegun, had grown up in the Turkish Embassy in DC, spending leisure time promoting jazz concerts at the local Jewish Community Center. He remains a kingmaker today, while Wexler is retired. *Rhythm and the Blues*: 76.

[12] Who were their producer-competitors? Wexler names his toughest rivals: Phil and Leonard Chess, Herman Lubinsky, Bess German, Saul and Jules Bihari, Syd Nathan, Hymie Weiss, and so on, which is to say that there was hardly a Gentile in the crowd. The same generalization holds for the managers of rhythm and blues groups except that, according to Wexler, these were "shrewd Jewish ladies." *Rhythm and the Blues*: 91, 88.

[13] Another case, less dramatic or political in the telling but equally interesting, is George Wein, an impresario who created both the Newport Folk Festival and the Newport Jazz Festival. Wein, a middle-class lad from Newton, Massachusetts, was a jazz pianist who discovered his true calling as *hondler*, married a black woman and spent much of his career promoting African-American music. See George Wein with Nate Chinen, *Myself Among Others: a Life in Music* (New York: Da Capo Press, 2003).

[14] Peter D. Goldstein, *Making People's Music: Moe Asch and Folkways Records* (Washington, DC: Smithsonian Institute Press, 1998): 1–99.

[15] Goldstein, *Making People's Music*: 92–93.

[16] Ibid., 98–100.

[17] See interview of Millard Lampell by Paul Buhle in Patrick McGilligan and Paul Buhle, *Tender Comrades: a Backstory of the Hollywood Blacklist* (New York: St Martins, 1997): 391–96.

[18] Special gratitude is owed to Ruth Rubin for granting an interview with me in 1980. Initially writing for the Left Yiddish daily, the *Morgn Frayhayt*, Rubin felt she had been given a raw deal, and strove afterward as an independent, definitely on the Left but with no "sponsors."

[19] Goldstein, *Making People's Music*: 159–61.

[20] The FBI had been watching Sholem Asch intensively for almost a decade: amid a feud with Abraham Cahan over the serialization of the elder Asch's novels in the *Forward*, Asch turned to the *Morgn Frayhayt*. Publication there was taken as an act of betrayal by the institutional Jewish community, and cause for suspicion by the investigators. He remained, nevertheless, hugely popular with Yiddish readers of all political persuasions.

[21] Goldstein, *Making People's Music*: 330–31. Gratitude on many points goes to Tuli Kupferberg for years of intermittent correspondence and occasional meetings.

[22] Not that Asch was singular in all respects. Seymour Solomon, a founder of Vanguard Records (from book publishing to politics, the word "vanguard" was almost always a subtle reference to the Left), studied at Julliard, became a music

critic and in 1950 launched the label famed for helping to break the music industry's Blacklist, signing The Weavers and Paul Robeson. "The Weavers at Carnegie Hall" (1956) is considered by some a beginning of the folksong revival, and Solomon recorded many of the participants like Joan Baez, Odette and Buffy Sainte-Marie, also blues and jazz greats like Mississippi John Hurt, Big Mama Thornton, and Charlie Musselwhite. Vanguard was also one of the first labels to market LPs, replacing the chunky "albums" of multiple 78 records. See Ari L. Goldman, "Seymour Solomon, 80, Record Label Founder," *New York Times*, 19 July 2002.

[23] Nadine Cohodas, *Spinning Blues into Gold: The Chess Brothers and the Legendary Chess Records* (New York: St. Martins-Griffin, 2000). Cohodas suggests in several places her frustration at the lack of documentation, but makes strenuous if unconvincing efforts to avoid the implication that the singers were in any way exploited by the brothers.

[24] Cohodas, *Spinning Blues*: 276–77. Even on Open Housing, the most contentious racial issue in contemporary Chicago, Chess was less than enthusiastic: he approved black purchase only if the new owner could afford a place without subdividing – a rule that could never have been applied to an earlier generation of Slavic or Jewish home owners.

[25] Among them, "Save the Last Dance for Me," written by Doc Pomus; "This Magic Moment," by Pomus and Morty Shuman; "Spanish Harlem," by Leiber and Spector; "Stand by Me," by Leiber, Stoller, and Carol King. Wexler himself discovered "There Goes My Baby" and "Under the Boardwalk" by less-remembered composers.

[26] Among Goldner's hits on mostly forgotten labels, "Why Do Fools Fall in Love?" "Tears on My Pillow," and "Shimmy Shimmy Ko-Ko-Bop." He was married to a Latina, and close to his own artists, including Tito Puenti.

[27] A suburban tale of the day: I had a Chicagoland uncle who tried suicide by the same method but didn't succeed.

[28] Actually, this particular show was a tribute to Arlen, himself on hand with Louis Jordan, Peggy King, and Eddie Foy, Jr. Thus, Spector had, so to speak, been accepted within the legacy of Jewish vaudeville.

[29] Quoted in *He's a Rebel*: 58. A monographic study of the Chessman Case, Theodore Hamm's *Rebel and a Cause: Caryl Chessman and the Politics of the Death Penalty in Postwar California, 1948–1974* (Berkeley: University of California, 2001), manages to leave out Spector entirely.

[30] Gillian A. Gar, *She's a Rebel: The History of Women in Rock and Roll* (Seattle: Seal Press, 1991): 46–47.

[31] Ibid., 214.

[32] See the lively account in David Hajdu, *Positively 4th Street: The Lives and Times of Joan Baez, Bob Dylan, Mimi Baez Farina and Richard Farina* (New York: Farrar, Straus and Giroux, 2001).

33 Bill Graham and Robert Greenfield, *Bill Graham Presents: My Life Inside Rock and Out* (New York: Doubleday, 1992): 3–64.

34 Ibid., 86–87.

35 Ibid., 116–118.

36 Speaking from personal experience, this is only a bit exaggerated. The Mime Troupe appeared on the Madison, University of Wisconsin, campus at the moment of a sit-in against recruiting by the Dow Chemical Company. In the ensuing police riot and week of protests marked by a student and teaching assistants' strike, the Troupe seemed to be everywhere, regarded by police and university officials as rabble-rousers of the worst kind, but beloved to the students, perhaps most of all to those who had never seen an art troupe at work.

37 *Bill Graham Presents*: 187.

38 Fred Goodman, *The Mansion on the Hill: Dylan, Young, Geffen, Springsteen and the Head-On Collision of Rock and Commerce* (London: Jonathan Cape, 1997), especially chapters 1–3: 3–81.

39 From the fourth to the seventeenth and final chapter, 61–379, hardly a section of Goodman's book does not consider Geffen and Geffen Records. Whatever may be said of Geffen as businessman is evidently even more true of Lyor Cohen, rap music entrepreneur turned CEO of Def Jam Music Group, whose own "risky behavior" consists of having marketed Public Enemy and Run-DMC in a notably aggressive marketing campaign, before branching out. Son of Israeli immigrants, raised by a psychiatrist and a social advocate (newspaper talk for Jewish progressive mother), Cohen took a degree in global marketing, intending to become a banker or shrimp-farmer before returning to LA and the rap music business opportunity. See Laura M. Holson, "Talking Trash, Making Cash, and Still Able to Sign Mariah," *New York Times*, 28 May 2002.

40 Darryl Lyman, *Great Jews in Music* (Middle Village, LI, NY: Jonathan David Publishers, 1990): 205–07, a classic Jewish world-style reference volume full of all manner of oddities.

41 Laura M. Holson and Bernard Weinraub, "Some See a Young Ovitz in Emerging Power Broker," *New York Times*, 11 May 2002. In a smaller but still important arena, Jewish entrepreneur Rick Rubin founded Def Jam Records and discovered LL Cool J; by the 1980s Jews emerged as rap musicians, with the Beastie Boys' *License to Kill* characteristically credited with breaking rap into suburban and frat house markets.

42 Gar, *She's a Rebel*: 61–64.

43 Ibid., 42–43.

44 Ibid., 329–31.

45 Ibid., 382–86.

46 Ibid., 438.

47 Jerry Stiller interview by David Marc, Scheuer Collection, Syracuse

University. Mort Sahl, whose father worked as a clerk for the FBI and who was in high school ROTC before being drafted, first got himself in trouble as satirical editor of the Alaska base paper. At first audiences didn't know what to make of his humor, but thanks to the management of the Hungry I he held on, growing sharper and more popular until he was purportedly ordered blacklisted by friends of Kennedy (although he had written one-liners for the 1960 election). He was certain that the CIA had been involved in Kennedy's assassination, and his efforts to educate the public resulted in his virtual disappearance as an entertainer – although he has turned up again and again, on Broadway or the radio. See his autobiography, *Heartland* (New York: Harcourt, Brace, 1976). Incidentally, Spanish Civil War veteran and Hollywood blacklistee Alvah Bessie, out of a job and harassed by the FBI, was working the stage lights at the Hungry I (thanks to the current manager of the Gateway Singers and to left-wing stand-up artist Irwin Corey) at the time, and may have prompted the young comedian's awareness of the intelligence netherworld's doings. See interview with Alvah Bessie by Patrick McGilligan and Ken Mate in McGilligan and Buhle, *Tender Comrades*: 110–111.

[48] A point made best, if with inadequate exploration of Jewish issues of self-identity, in Frank Kofsky, *Lenny Bruce: The Comedian as Social Critic* (New York: Monad Press, 1974). Here I learned that Bruce, in San Francisco, generally stayed at the North Beach fleabag where by sheer coincidence I spent part of a summer in 1963. It was next door to Finoccio's, the famed female-impersonation nightclub. I never saw Lenny in the hallway, but a junky did sneak into my room and steal my last thirty dollars.

[49] Albert Goldman, *Ladies and Gentlemen, Lenny Bruce!!* (New York: 1971): 74–91.

[50] Ibid, 223.

[51] Ibid., 256. When he watched Bob Newhart in 1960, Bruce acutely observed, "He'll make more money than me, Sahl and Berman because Parr, Sullivan and Moore need a goy comic so bad their teeth ache." Quoted in Goldman, *Ladies and Gentlemen*: 292.

[52] Ibid, 362–64. The exact role Krassner played in *How to Talk Dirty* remains in doubt.

[53] Quoted in Frank Kofsky, *Lenny Bruce*: 37.

[54] If there were any doubt that Bruce's memory lingers, it would be resolved in the successful efforts, by Robin Williams among others, to convince Governor George Pataki to issue a posthumous pardon to Bruce for his 1964 obscenity conviction following an appearance at a Greenwich Village club.

[55] The Kaufman biopic, *Man On the Moon* (1999), is most extraordinary – although treated badly by critics – because of Jim Carrey's Method acting, but this account owes most to an unpublished conference paper kindly sent to me by its

author, Prof. H. Peter Steeves of DePaul University. See also Bob Zmuda, *Andy Kaufman Revealed!* (Boston: Little, Brown, 1999).

[56] *Pee Wee's Playhouse* (1986-91) might be best seen as successor to *Rocky and His Friends* for offering stronger and more subtle doses of social satire than nighttime sitcoms; his subsequent films have been spotty, but sometimes excellent. Lawrence J. Epstein, who describes Reubens/Herman as an "odd character" that "by definition couldn't develop," is not wrong but misses the point entirely. Neither did Jerry Lewis, who seemed to do quite well with less talent than Pee Wee. See Lawrence J. Epstein, *The Haunted Smile: The Story of Jewish Comedians in America* (New York: Public Affairs, 2001): 230.

[57] Matthew Pustz, *Comic Culture: Fanboys and True Believers* (Jackson: University Press of Mississippi, 1999): 28–29.

[58] Ibid., 32. This was Simon and Kirby's most mature effort.

[59] Ibid, 36–37.

[60] *Mad About the Fifties* (Boston: Little Brown, 1997), compiled and with inside notes by Grant Geissman, offers a drastically underinterpreted sampling of the changes from the comic to the magazine, preserving, however, some avant-garde high points of the later 1950s, such as appearances from Tom Lehrer (politically controversial) and Ernie Kovacks (golden age television's brilliant madman), along with the general if never total drift into bland formula. It still had a lot of useful insights for youngsters, however. The book is dedicated "To the Memory of Harvey Kurtzman, the furshlugginer genius who started it all" – a typically generous gesture to the late Kurtzman.

[61] Pustz, *Comic Culture*: 39. Thanks also to Kurtzman for his candid if joking remarks in a 1982 interview; he resisted political labels or consciously didactic content in *Mad*, while confessing to avid union sentiments and bitter hostility toward racism and McCarthyism. His genius went to details rather than large ideas, and no doubt his bread and butter stint at *Playboy* had affected him as well.

[62] "As the Artist Sees It: Interviews with Comic Artists," in Paul Buhle, ed., *Popular Culture in America* (Minneapolis: University of Minnesota, 1987): 132. Interview reprinted from a group of interviews with underground comix artists in response to written questions, in *Cultural Correspondence*, no. 5 (1977).

[63] "Mad Mumblings," *Mad Comics*, no. 1 (Oct–Nov 1952), reprint edition (West Plains, Mo: Russ Cochran, Publisher, 1986), inside cover of original.

[64] Interview with John Benson, following no. 7 (Oct–Nov 1952), unnumbered page following last strip in reprint edition of *Mad Comics, volume two*.

[65] Interview with Benson following reprint of no. 11 (May 1953), unpaged, in *Mad Comics* reprint, ibid.

[66] Kurtzman told Benson that the *Mad* crew were desperate to bring out the satire as rapidly as possible, and managed to do so in two months from conception to production. Ibid.

[67] Will Elder himself later insisted modestly that the special issue had been a last-minute fill-in. See the extraordinary interview, "The Will Elder Interview" by Gary Groth, *The Comics Journal*, no. 254 (July 2003): 78–136.

[68] Marshall McLuhan's famed essay, "Dada in the Drugstore," was an extraordinary exception.

[69] Maria Reidelbach, *Completely Mad: a History of the Comic Book and Magazine* (Boston: Little, Brown, 1991): 52.

[70] Dave Randall, "Mad, Mad World: The FBI's Obsession with Mad Magazine," *CounterPunch*, 16 September 2002. An office visit from FBI agents in 1957 did, however, evidently did throw a scare into Gaines, prompting a letter of apology to the director and perhaps a bit of caution with sensitive topics. Feldstein recalled a second FBI visit with particular bitterness.

[71] The comic drawings of Dave Berg (1920-2001) might be taken as typical of the lighter touch in the newer *Mad*: son of a Brooklyn bookbinder who got a job inking *The Spirit* at twenty, Berg wrote scripts with young Jules Feiffer and worked for Stan Lee, first drawing for *Mad* in 1956 and becoming regular from 1961 until his retirement. Never angry at the status quo or even seemingly concerned with social issues, he traced human foibles in the daily comic strip fashion. He was president of the Marina Del Rey B'nai B'rith in his later years: a certified member of the Jewish establishment from which *Mad* had, in its earliest years, rebelled.

[72] James D. Bloom, "Funny Jews," to date unpublished.

[73] Thanks to Ben Katchor for this observation.

[74] Lee almost always managed to quash the more daring artistic efforts, while taking the credit for himself for the success of the comic series. See the critical observations by Paul Wardle, "The Two Faces of Stan Lee," in *Comics Journal*, no. 181 (October 1995): 63. Cartoonist Dan Clowes' unpleasant image of "Doctor Infinity," as meglomaniac spokesman for comic history, is dead-on Lee. Much of the rest of this *Comics Journal* issue is devoted to industry insiders' views of Lee, both positive and negative, and a memorable interview with the pulp entrepreneur, albeit dated to 1968. To put it mildly, my view of Marvel and of Stan Lee is markedly different from the fannish Tom Sinclair, "Stan Lee, the Greatest Comic Book Writer in the World!!!" *Entertainment Weekly*, 20 June 2003, although Lee readily admits that until the newer comics, he had been a total hack since entering the trade back in the 1940s.

[75] Pustz, *Comic Culture*: 46–51. To this it should be added, however, that several key former *Mad* artists specialized in public service messages, and subway riders of the 1960s–80s who recalled the receding images of their youth must have been comforted by the familiarity of health and safety warnings.

[76] Howard Chaykin interview with *Comics Journal* editor Gary Groth, in Groth and Robert Fiore, eds., *The New Comics* (New York: Berkeley Books, 1988): 34–35.

77 Pustz, *Comic Culture*: 56–59.

78 Ibid., 107–09.

79 Ibid, 144–45.

80 "The Young Crumb Story," in *American Splendor*, no. 4 (1979).

81 Captured thoughtfully by Pahls' introduction to *The Complete Crumb Comics*, no. 2 (Westlake Village, Ca.: Fantagraphics, 1988): x–xi.

82 Crumb quoted by Pahls in "Introduction," *Complete Crumb Comics,* no. 2: x.

83 Ibid., xi.

84 Marty Pahls, "Introduction," to *The Complete Crumb Comics*, no. 3 (Westlake Village, Ca.: Fantagraphic, 1988): viii–ix.

85 On Kurtzman's request, Crumb returned to New York in 1964, promised a staff job; the magazine folded the day he arrived, or the two might have spent years working together, delaying Crumb's entry into the underground comix scene.

86 "Starting Out in the Mid-Sixties I would Spin Out All Kinds of Ideas for Cartoons in Sketchbooks!" in Peter Poplalski, ed., *The R. Crumb Coffee Table Art Book* (Boston: Little, Brown, 1997), 77, a book produced by Denis Kitchen. Thanks once more to Kitchen, a friend from Wisconsin days, for supplying this book to me on publication.

87 See Dana Crumb, in Monte Beauchamp, ed., in *The Life and Times of R. Crumb* (New York: St Martins Griffin, 1998): 127–30.

88 "Trina Robbins," in ibid, 41–43.

89 Of many sources related to Feiffer, the best is "Interview" in *The Comics Journal*, no. 124 (August 1988), 37–94, covering almost all imaginable issues.

90 See Lawrence J. Epstein, *The Haunted Smile*, 181, for some observations about the nature of Nichols's comedy, one of the occasionally shrewd comments in a mostly disappointing volume of anecdotes, leaning strongly toward flattery.

91 In a 1977 interview of Paul Buhle's with Bill Griffith for *Cultural Correspondence*, reprinted in "As the Artist Sees It," in Paul Buhle, ed., *Popular Culture in America*: 135. Only in 2003 did I have an opportunity to spend some hours with Griffith, chewing over these old memories and our interview of a quarter-century earlier.

92 "As the Artist Sees It," *Popular Culture in America*: 134.

93 For an in-depth analysis of *Naked Dawn*, arguably Ulmer's best film since *The Black Cat* and *Detour*, see Buhle and Wagner, *Hide In Plain Sight* (New York: Palgrave/St. Martins, 2003): 15–16.

SIX

REFLEXIVE JEWS: THE POSTMODERN AND THE PREMODERN IN THE ERA OF SELF-CONSCIOUSNESS

Writing in the English language successor to the *Jewish Daily Forward* in 1990, literary editor Jonathan Rosen warned that the fiddler had fallen from the roof. Jewish culture could no longer live on a nostalgia that was in the process of being eclipsed, apparently for the last time, with the collapse of the East Bloc governments. Jewish culture now depended upon the "experience of contemporary Jews," i.e., whatever meaning artists could attach to it.[1] A seemingly sensible observation, except that the most dynamic sections of Jewish culture have for a century been intertwined simultaneously with both the experience of contemporary Jews and the soundings of the past.

Besides, every section of Jewish life appears to have its own agenda for appropriate memories. Frustration therefore mounts at discomforting recollections. During a 1999 CUNY Graduate Center forum, much-admired playwright Tony Kushner recalled the urgency of his yearning for Yiddish culture, and his recent adaptation of a stage classic, *The Dybbuk*, for a new production. On the dais with him, novelist-critic Cynthia Ozick responded savagely that Kushner's pursuit of *Yiddishkayt* was not only mere nostalgia but likely to be worse, yet another liberal betrayal of Israel and Zionism.[2] But like Ruth Wisse's insistence that Jewish culture is now solidly centered in Israel and is destined to grow more completely so in the future, Ozick's politically conservative and Hebraist visions cannot account for the intertwining of Yiddish heritage with American popular culture and the power of that culture to conquer global entertainment – emphatically including most popular entertainment in Israel. More to the point of this book, it cannot account for the ability and predilection of Jews to enact creatively the lives of others as well as of themselves.[3] In part an intuitive artistic expression, this last impulse is also an expression of the continuing dream, in continuing exile, from the better world that, sad to say, remains a dream still more precious in an age of virtually unrelieved cruelty and devastation.

Besides, an alternative mapping has been clear for some time. The Yiddish premodern contained a large dose of what would be taken in a later age as postmodern, a mixing of seemingly opposite forms, popular designs for comic strips and synagogues, cantorial music and *klezmer* (not to mention jazz) alike, not frequently within the work of the same artist. What is new about Jewish culture since the mid-twentieth century has been dubbed by gay Jewish television critic David Marc, in a resonant phrase summing up the most hopeful impulses of every possible medium, "reflexive at last."[4] When popular culture begins to stand outside itself in some ways, to reflect upon the medium via conversations with an audience that knows the forms well enough to process detail after detail, then something extremely interesting and rather new is taking place. For Marc, this is a case of the culture at large, specifically American culture, growing up. But I think we can see it better as the continuing saga of Jewish culture, no longer hiding its particular components within popular life (meanwhile, through continual self-satire, puncturing pretensions and refusing any special favors for being Jewish), and at last finding its destiny.[5]

Yiddish pedagogue Itche Goldberg long ago proposed that modern Jews both suffered and gained from a double alienation: rejection (in many parts of the world, persecution) by the Gentiles, but also their own rejection of the narrowness of the rabbi and merchant dominated *shtetl* life.[6] The vision of a cooperative society, once pervasive in Jewish working-class culture but also instrumental among Jewish artists of all kinds, was rooted, consciously or not, in the promise to reconcile these tensions. To come back to themselves meant for Jews to find a new sense of self, not in forms of romantic nationalism where Jews would command the weapons and territory, but as a community of Jews within some universal egalitarian prospect. Walter Benjamin, a mystic Marxist without a self-conscious drop of *Yiddishkayt*, had assayed the prospects by embracing a Jewish version of surrealism, the merging of the dream state with waking. It was up to the practitioners of popular arts in eras of vastly lowered expectations to continue the experiment in forms, seeking out universals (often cryptically, even unconsciously, Jewish values) there. Even here, with the living memories of the *shtetl* and ghettoization almost gone, and generations of secularization passed, the best way back was through the escape from normalcy and normal corruptions through the avant-garde, in an attempt to rediscover an acceptable Jewish self, if never a simple one. It was not the only way back, of course.

The commercial splash of 2001–03 film seasons, along with Harry Potter, was *Spider-Man* and its various comic-based counterparts, matching huge budgets and audience responses. Who was Spider-Man, really, anyway? There are several different stories of origin, one about as Jewish as the next. The most successful of any superhero introduced by Marvel, he appeared first in *Amazing Fantasy* no. 15 (Summer, 1962) and moved up to his own title the following year. Jack Kirby, Joe Simon, C.C. Beck (famed for creating Captain Marvel, the superhero eradicated not by ordinary villains but by industry lawsuit), and Stan Lee all had a hand in it. Lee recalled later that he came up with the hero so as to effect something different in comics, a "strip that would actually feature a teenager as a star ... a strip in which the main character would lose as often as he'd win."[7] That memory sits uneasily for Kirby, who claims that he and a small circle of others had done something similar back in the mid-1950s. Like many a fantasy film, the highflying version only happened to be the one that made it big.[8]

One has to wonder if it really matters, apart from a possible lawsuit and out of court financial settlement on a property as big as the filmic version that cleared its hefty budget within the first week of release. Perhaps not. But then again, consider the source. Peter Parker, Spider-Man's alter-ego, lives in Forest Hills, Queens, a probable next Jewish stop outward from Brooklyn (and a second stop either from the Lower East Side or latterly from the Bronx). It's not true to say, as some critics do, that only Parker, among superheroes, has a complex.[9] Actually, superheroes of all kinds have been neurotic at least since Clark Kent's crush on Lois Lane and perhaps going back all the way to Samson and his notorious haircut.[10] Besides, Spidey's teenage nerdiness has long since grown into the angst of a married man whose hours are too long for him to be a model family man (even with an unbelievably proportioned and often half-dressed wife). Nor, for that matter, is he all that clever.

Only within the extremely limited verbal repertoire of the Marvel mass-production machine would Parker/Spidey be considered a mental match for evil. Perhaps responding to criticisms of precocious readers, a current Marvel editor in chief has promised that cinematic Spider-Man will become more clever (and not just conflicted) in sequels now inevitably ahead. He was only a troubled and guilt-ridden teen of the near-burbs generation, appealing to the alienated cohorts who read comics at college. Now he's on his way to becoming sarcastic – yet another Jewish example of the verna-cular aspiring uplift to something better.[11] In another era, Spider-Man could go down as a case of successful assimilation and upward mobility. In the image of the self-reflexive, it represented something less certain, Jews more or less *as Jews* increasingly in the spotlight, in practically every imaginable venue of popular culture. It was, if more marketable, also less artistically and politically interesting than the saga of the true Jewish rebel.

The indie surprise of 2003 and counterversion of comics-to-film superheroics was of course *American Splendor*. Having been denied so much on account of his stubborn, Cleveland *menschlikheit* and by the apparently unyielding unwillingness of critics to treat his comics as literature, Harvey Pekar now seemed to be denied nothing. Reviewers in virtually every venue now enthused at the film, although more for the director, technicians, and stars than for Harvey (or for his wife and partner Joyce Brabner). Harvey stubbornly reminded the enthusiasts that the award-winning film was by no means certain to do anything much for his own continuing comics. The opposite of a superhero by his own definition, Pekar had become an icon of that very Jewish rebel unsung over generations, the neighborhood radical soaked in the *Yiddishkayt* that media stars had left behind.[12]

COMING HOME/HAYM ON THE AVANT-GARDE TRAIL

One small and especially strange incident in the continuingly strange incidents of Jewishness and identity illuminates a patch of little-explored vernacular (if also unearthly) territory. Actor Leonard Nimoy's 1975 small-press memoir, *I Am Not Spock*, is at certain points as revealing as a codex to some cryptic alphabet (like Klingon) of exile and return.[13] On landing in California at the height of the Cold War, Nimoy worked in the fading Yiddish theater of Los Angeles for several years, meanwhile taking his actors' training with blacklistee Jeff Corey (the psychoanalyst to the black soldier in *Home of the Brave*, and the leader of town rednecks in *Superman and the Mole Men*) as the guide to his appearance in Jean Genet's *Deathwatch*, acting in the notorious outré writer's first California production.[14] Here, Nimoy met future director Paul Mazursky, then an actor, and first adopted a character (as Nimoy says) who "finds himself totally alienated from both worlds, the society outside, and [from] the one within the prison walls" and who thereby comes to understand and appreciate his alien status. A few years later, Nimoy played a supporting role in Hollywood's first stab at Continental-style avant-gardism, Genet's *The Balcony* (1963) with Shelley Winters as a memorable madam, himself a schizoid general engaged in street warfare, Lee Grant as a high-class prostitute and probable lesbian (if so, she was part of an almost unknown category in American film at the time, that of the sympathetic lesbian), Jeff Corey as attaché, and Peter Falk directing an all-out civil war just beyond the walls of the bordello (or was it a sex-dispensing replacement of the Jewish ghetto?).[15]

This definitely marked a new and most unusual moment for the Jewish Hollywood avant-garde, determinedly mainstreaming itself. *The Balcony* was a recontinuation of the projects of left-wing writers, directors, and producers in the preblacklist 1940s of film noir that proposed, in effect, an agenda that Hollywood would not fulfill even in the following era of full frontal nudity and unrestrained language. Winters, daughter of a Brooklyn haberdasher convicted of arson, Miss Ozone Park, and sometime garment district fashion model, had always been fascinated by the avant-garde and its left-liberal politics.[16] Not long before *The Balcony*, she played a support role in the hitherto most daring interracial film, *Odds Against Tomorrow* (1959), secretly written by Abraham Polonsky, starring and produced by Harry Belafonte. Had *Odds* been commercially successful, HarBel Films would presumably have shocked Hollywood and the country with a series of equally tough Belafonte vehicles – just the kind to give Winters, among others, the parts that in her artistic daring, she would have most valued.[17]

Lee Grant, raised in an aristocratic Jewish family in Manhattan and an Oscar nominee for playing a teenage shoplifter in *Detective Story* (1951), had recently made her way back from the Blacklist, and was subsequently a natural for what was then some rather shocking films, from the contemptuous Jewish self-portrait *Portnoy's Complaint* (1972) and *Shampoo* (1975: she won an Oscar for a supporting role, a first for an actor returning from the Blacklist) to *The Mafu Cage* (1978, with none other than Carol Kane, a feminist mixture of incest, animal beating, and murder) before directing a film version of that Jewish radical classic, novelist Tillie Olson's *Tell Me a Riddle* (1980).[18] Starring Melvyn Douglass (in one of his last films) as a husband caring for his dying wife of forty years (played by Russian-American stage actress Lila Kedrova), with Brooke Adams as their confused bohemian Los Angeleno granddaughter, the film offered an extraordinary look backward and forward at Jewish-American life: modest upward mobility with all the built-in disappointments and no utopianism in materialist individuation.

Shot on a small budget and too realistic for Hollywood-style dynamism, it was in effect a tribute to Olson's extraordinary role, the secular, radical, and feminist Jewish fiction writer extraordinaire, erstwhile proletarian novelist, grown old uninterested in fame and, as throughout her long life, both before and after the prestige years of her attackers, the New York Intellectuals, unashamed of her Jewishness. In *Tell Me a Riddle*, her first

directorial effort, Lee Grant returned from the avant-garde to some ele-
mental American Jewishness. Then again, she had most often played beset
working-class girls and women on the stage and screen (especially dramatic
parts in golden age television drama) in her early career, until driven out by
the blacklisters. The task had been waiting for her.[19]

To backtrack further across familiar ground, Leonard Nimoy had actually
begun acting as a teenage amateur in a production of Odets's *Awake and
Sing*, and come to Hollywood, still finishing up with the Yiddish stage, as a
Brando devotee, an admiration that shifted to Paul Muni among others as
he studied old films. These angles of vision prepared him, he recalled, to be
the extraterrestrial ("a security blanket with sexual overtones," wrote Isaac
Asimov of the part) with an unexpected allure of the exotic, to fictional
Earth women, and to television audiences at large.[20] The metaphorical Jew
as obsessively logical creature, the emotionally innocent outsider whose
blood apparently can be warmed by sufficiently inventive and somehow
goyishe females traveling to strange neighborhoods, Nimoy was the perfect
outsider as insider. In short, he became or perhaps made himself the subject
of a perfect SciFi tale of something very much like Jews in (or perhaps from)
outer space.[21]

But perhaps an alternative status, the outsider as outsider narrative, has
more specifically Jewish artistic depth and durability. After the great era of
Yiddish theater, no one actor so much as Zero Mostel has been the Method-
acting Jewish engagé determined to force the world upon another ethical
path by rending his own self in public. Born Samuel Mostel to Eastern
Europeans resettled in the Lower East Side, the boy firmly resisted his
father's quest to make him a rabbi. Contacts at the Educational Alliance on
East Broadway, where Yiddishists and artists like Chaim Gross, Moses Soyer,
and Ben Shahn taught, exerted a considerable influence on the young man.
He got through a BA at City College, and aspired to be a serious painter but
drifted during the Depression. He then worked as a longshoreman and was
beaten up for supporting reformers attempting to clean up the mobbed
unions on the docks, later taking a job with the Works Progress Administration giving gallery talks to visitors to MOMA. While on that job, he
developed comic routines, moving back and forth from seriousness to
clowning, he also gained his famous gargantuan stature, and got the notion
of performing his routines for left-wing fund-raisers at Café Society.[22]

Café Society, launched in 1938 in response to discrimination against
black performers in the city's clubs, mixed comedy with serious jazz and
gave openings to the likes of Billie Holiday, Imogene Coca, Big Bill
Broonzy, Jim Backus – and Mostel. Here Sammy became Zero, doing

imitations, political satire, and monologues that were less classifiable. Concerned FBI agents described some of his more anticonservative monologues in their files as "dangerous" humor. (He also sometimes entered the set of the nostalgic play about 1910s Yiddish Broadway, *Café Crown*, while the play was in progress and ad-libbed as one of the regulars in a card game, exchanging comments with his close friend, actor Philip Loeb.) Apparently, his past attendance at Yiddish theaters then took life: the unrestrained and passionate outbursts on stage, the ad-libbing that had so often left Yiddish playwrights in a purple rage, and the engagement with theatergoers all gained new life in Mostel's moves.[23] He was, in effect, doing Yiddish in English, as veteran fans of the Yiddish Theatrical Alliance would recognize two decades later, with his stage performance for *Fiddler On the Roof.*

Mostel was, then, a comic sensation, but he was drafted in 1943, discharged after six months (perhaps for his political connections, but officially for an unspecified physical disability) and immediately shuttled overseas on USO tours to cheer up the GIs. Back at home after the war, Zero returned to Broadway with his new friend, Jerome Robbins, mixing bathos and high culture. He also resolved to become a serious actor, and managed a few interesting character roles before the Blacklist struck him down. Never a high-profile radical, he managed to appear in *Panic in the Streets* (directed by an old acquaintance, Elia Kazan) and lesser features, giving up on Hollywood about the time it became politically impossible for him to continue. Zero went back to playing the clubs, and there, too, he faced an informal Blacklist. He tried unsuccessfully to launch a little academy for the training of would-be stand-up comics and comic actors. He drank heavily, painted furiously, and made a small return to Broadway in secondary roles, before a last round of HUAC hearings in entertainment compelled him to refuse to testify against friends, driving him to the margins. For him, at any rate, the worst of the Red Scare was almost over by the mid-1950s.[24]

He had been performing for several years in road show versions of *The World of Sholom Aleichem* when it gained airtime, produced by David Susskind, in 1959 as "The Play of the Week." Not that many people had the opportunity to see it: the small educational network consisted of scattered big-city and university-based public stations.[25] But in an important way, this production marked the beginning of the collapse of the Blacklist for actors on television, although a public vindication would come only in 1962 when John Henry Faulk's suit against CBS found famed lawyer Louis Nizer crossexamining television producers and the operatives of the private blacklisting operation, AWARE. Faulk won (and himself soon appeared on a game show, appropriately named *To Tell The Truth*), ushering a small raft of mostly Jewish actors back to work. A robust series of serious drama and acting on Broadway followed. The next turning point, however, was another Mostel vehicle: *A Funny Thing Happened On the Way to the Forum*.

It was Mostel's first musical, playing a part that Phil Silvers had turned down. Famously, Mostel in an act of generosity agreed to work with Jerome Robbins, who had named (among others) Mostel's close friend Jack Gilford's second wife, actress Madelaine Gilford, an especially sensitive point because Jack was also in the production.[26] The part made Mostel a midlife star, but *Fiddler* captured him for the (Jewish) role of a lifetime. *Newsweek* pronounced, "Broadway has a new king and divinity, and there are no rivals in sight."[27] Chaim Topol was chosen for the film version, in part because of Mostel's political baggage, and the half-rehabilitated blacklistee lost out heavily.

Mostel's costarring role in *The Producers* was his only comparable success, wacko as a Broadway entrepreneur-huckster and father figure toward Gene Wilder, himself beginning a distinguished career as Jewish type. But he also had some staggeringly brilliant moments in *The Front*, written by Walter Bernstein. Actually recapturing his maddening frustrations in the Catskills of the early 1950s, swindled out of his night's pay by a club owner who took advantage of the blacklistee, he digs into the owner's pockets for his deserved payment before being tossed out the door. Elsewhere in the film, pleading to be cleared, he moans to his FBI interrogator, "It's all Brownstein's fault. I wouldn't be in trouble if it wasn't for Brownstein," i.e., his ineradicable Yiddish self that could not be escaped by a change of names or upward mobility. And at his last moment in *The Front*, in effect becoming his real-life late friend, the blacklisted actor Philip Loeb, he checks into a good hotel, has a meal, and throws himself out a window. (Loeb had taken a fatal overdose of narcotics.) Perhaps Mostel's role as a doddering elderly husband in that very Jewish film *The Angel Levine* (based on a story by Bernard Malamud, with Harry Belafonte as the black-Jewish Angel of Death, and Yiddish stage idol Ida Kaminski as the dying wife) was Zero's real finale, notwithstanding a stage revival of *Fiddler*. Zero had nevertheless done better in film than he knew. Like a Yiddish actor of lore, he had never really been comfortable on movie sets anyway, deprived of the audience's attention. He died at age sixty-two, worn out by life. And yet he had returned home, all the way back to the *shtetl* and to the exilic Brownstein, in that way a kind of model for the entertainment mainstream whose Jewishness could now be spoken.

THE MASS ENTERTAINMENT NEXUS AND THE JEWISH JEW

A half-century of evolving Jewish self-identity on narrative television, fixed by the sitcom, continues to be described historically as pre- and post-Norman Lear's sitcom legacy. But it might just as well have been described as Jewish self-consciousness come into its own. Ed Sullivan may never have been broadcast using the word Jewish – he certainly didn't use it often – and Borscht Belt veterans like Myron Cohen and Joey Bishop were still more careful never to do so, at least not on camera.[28] George Burns, as we have seen, had helped create the image of a utopian Los Angeles where half-Jewish son Ronny goes beyond mingling to merge himself with tennis-playing, blonde Gentiles. Like the very name George, it was a salesmanship that became more and more the real thing as inner identity receded to private life.

Perhaps, in retrospect, *The Phil Silvers Show, Car 54, Where Are You?* and *Barney Miller* all served as a prelude to the Jewish self-identification. But none of these remarkable shows launched the trend so observable by the 1990s of omnipresent, identified, and identifiable Jews on mainstream television. That credit belonged elsewhere.

In one of the many useful misunderstandings within popular culture, Danny Thomas the noseful Lebanese-American of the medium's golden age would be consistently identified by his viewers as Jewish. It made sense, in a way. No show in the new medium, after *The Goldbergs* moved unsuccessfully from the Bronx to the suburbs, was more completely in the radio sitcomic tradition of Jewish-style urban family confusion. Thomas's lead writer happened to be one Frank Tarloff, the blacklisted former Red. Successful radio scripts made him a lead writer on *My Date With Judy* and other typically 1940s family radio comedies featuring kindly but distracted parents, a boy-crazy girl, and an extremely annoying younger brother.

The producer of *Make Room for Daddy* (1953–64) was Sheldon Leonard. The story of Tarloff's scriptwriting and of Danny Thomas's success was thereby one of those Jewish family secrets, until Leonard flouted current network practices by awarding the writer his own credit back, effectively taking him off the Blacklist.[29] From London, where he had gone for a creative respite (and to co-write an Oscar-winning screenplay for *Father Goose*), Tarloff continued with the renamed *Danny Thomas Show* until he switched to Leonard's new premier item, *The Dick Van Dyke Show*.[30]

The creative genius of this new show was Carl Reiner, one of the major talents of television comedy writing who made a mark on Sid Caesar's various efforts. Something in Reiner's sensibilities, a progressive New Dealer delightfully keen to the pretensions and ultimate foolishness of the consumerist suburban society, fitted the antic, wacky, cosmopolitan style perfectly.[31] When the comedy-variety format died toward the end of the 1950s, Reiner turned first to the game show, unsuccessfully, and then to the sitcom. He had recently written a self-revealing play about a Jewish sitcom writer, *Enter Laughing*. It worked as a Broadway show and less successfully as a film, but Reiner recast the material around the doings of a television writer and his family, in the semisuburban setting that was the real-life average television writer's world.

Here, for the first time, a show was to treat the life of a modern American Jew as a Jew.[32] But *Head of the Family*, debuting amid the summer reruns of 1960, was no hit. *The New York Times* liked its Jewishness (or semi-Jewishness, evident but fairly soft-pedaled), and the show probably would have attracted the TV audience of the early 1950s, before Eastern urban consumers had been put into their more limited place. That wasn't enough anymore, and seeing the train wreck in the near distance, seasoned producer Leonard took charge of the issue personally. As he went over the fine points of the successful sitcom with Reiner, he suggested a decisive change of plot, with up-front Jewishness as a secondary source of gags and general interest. Leonard himself chose the new star, Midwestern Gentile Van Dyke. Borscht Belt veteran Morey Amsterdam would essentially be second (or, after wife Mary Tyler Moore, actually third) banana, gaining rather more Jewish affect in the process of the inevitable comic contrasts and the sharpened character of the supporting actor. A new production company, Calvada (made from the first names of Reiner, Leonard, Van Dyke and Thomas, in the emerging style of a leading actor sharing the proceeds) was formed, quite suitably as it turned out. *The Dick Van Dyke Show* changed television comedy, permanently.

The success of the show may possibly have been, as David Marc suggests, the weekly television version of the Neil Simon style in drama and film, the upward-mobile Jew uncertain of himself in new conditions. Seen against a background of the unsuburban, residual chaos of the City, status anxiety worked grandly. Veteran television writers and demographics experts alike quickly caught on to the potentiality of the innovations, and it soon earned multiple Emmys. *The Dick Van Dyke Show* best demonstrated its sixties-going-on-nineties mode with a small array of proto-multicultural lifestyles including not only family members of co-workers, but also a talented woman professional (a writer played by actress Rose Marie) notably not craving a marriage proposal from her boss, and of course the very Jewish

Jew, Amsterdam. Thanks perhaps to the scripts of Tarloff – called in to write a dozen or so episodes early on – African Americans were also regularly on hand and not as menials but as ordinary Americans, albeit mainly as extras. The more acute viewers quickly noticed the crafted gags unthinkable in earlier days of television, like the time our stars accept an award for interracial unity but accidentally dye their hands with black ink, thus recalling minstrelsy. Or a more famous (Jewish) episode of bar mitzvah lessons, a theme that might have baffled or annoyed millions of viewers and prompted complaints from the Anti-Defamation League just a few years earlier.

Mary Tyler Moore Enterprises (MTM) may be described as taking the already-rolling ball from there decisively forward. A key figure in the transition was writer James L. Brooks, a college dropout born in Brooklyn in 1940 and already risen to minor prominence as sitcom writer and creator of *Room 222* (1969–74), one of those classroom shows with prominent African-Americans, "out" Jews, and sex jokes all unlikely just a few years earlier.[33] Brooks proposed Moore for a new series, intended to be the first ever with a divorcée in the lead. It didn't fly, and the star became just another victim of a broken romance, before returning to hometown Minneapolis. Still, the decisive characterization had been nailed down.

The star of *The Mary Tyler Moore Show*, which debuted in 1970, could certainly not be portrayed as emotionally independent. Rather, she was ever eager to apologize to her boss, Lou (played by up-and-coming Jewish actor/activist Ed Asner) when there was the slightest cause to do so. But by contemporary television standards, she was a woman on her own, more career-connected than Marlo Thomas in *That Girl* (1966–71). In terms of Jewish characters, Mary had her often lonely but wisecracking pal Rhoda Morganstern (played by Valerie Harper) who left the Bronx and then Manhattan for a life in the Midwest. In a second spin-off from *Dick Van Dyke*, Harper returned to New York to become the signature player of *Rhoda* (1974–78), a Jew's Jew, a protofeminist, surely television's first fictive female divorcée whose terminal marriage troubles make up a principal plotline in the sitcom.[34] Unfortunately, not a successful one. Still, Rhoda's sister Brenda was played by Julie Kavner, a central figure among television's out-front Jewish women, as we will see shortly.

Brooks himself moved adroitly on to greater success and more controversy by plucking out another of the created characters, this time Mr. Grant, aka Asner. Not quite so Jewish in persona (although very much in most of his roles as actor), Asner could be rightly called a throwback to the Jewish progressive of the 1930s and '40s, or perhaps an update of the same.

Lou Grant (1977–82) marked the first transition from sitcomic to dramatic character and television melodrama into headline-chasing, sometimes creating headlines en route, much like the later and greatly admired *Law and Order*.[35] Controversy after controversy made fodder for the plots but also grist for conservative pressure groups that – not so quietly encouraged by the Reagan administration – successfully lobbied the network for Asner's head.[36] Nothing like it had been seen since the Blacklist pressures of the 1950s.

Moving from MTM to Paramount, Brooks had two more notably Jewish television contributions ahead. He cocreated *Taxi* (1978–83), a workplace drama with a taste of class conflict: comically mean-spirited boss Danny Devito versus the proles, nearly all of them aching, as in so many 1940s films of urban Jewish life, to leave the job for something better. The popular New Yorkish series also spawned one most memorable character. Lotka, diasporic representative of some imaginary but evidently Eastern European ethnic group, was deeply (even if he often didn't think so) Andy Kaufman, who we've seen as an updated Lenny Bruce, outsider as Jew and Jew as outsider. Method actor *in extremis*, inventing fresh characters on the spot and wrestling women in live exhibition matches, Kaufman recalled Sid Caeser at Caesar's wildest but in a ferocious microcosm – a Jew on the loose. He also crashed early.

Moving further with his own Gracie Productions, the restless Brooks launched *The Tracey Ullman Show* (1987–90) for the then new Fox network. It was another series for its time. Although hardly the commercial breakthrough of *Mary Tyler Moore*, it also shattered rules and established new ones by slicing the show up into comedy skits, a continuing theatrical troupe out of the *Saturday Night Live* mold but without the music and monologues. (It also won the fledgling network its first Emmys; such is gratitude that Fox dropped it after three seasons. Ullman's own Emmy was celebrated still less cheerfully, two weeks after the show had its final episode aired.) As David Marc and Robert J. Thompson observe, *Tracey Ullman* demonstrated that television comedy could assume a variety of new shapes and would need to do so in the cable era. Julie Kavner, Ullman's chief supporting star, best kept the Jewish element alive in the process. She was already a prototype for the Seinfeldian character even if none of the Seinfeld regulars could be her Jewish equal. (*Tracey Takes On . . .* , in the new century, was essentially a cable reprise with herself as short-takes auteur, heavily flavored with stinging commentary on Jewish-American excesses.)

The Tracey Ullman Show, and even Brooks himself, may ironically now be remembered best in the world of distaff comedy for introducing short cartoons by Matt Groening, whose left-of-center strip *Life In Hell* had been appearing for half a decade in the alternative press. Brooks persuaded Fox to create, with himself as coproducer, a new series based in Groening's characters: *The Simpsons*. The biggest television comedy phenomenon of the 1990s and the first animated series to offer serious social satire – indeed, more critical and more distinctly postmodern in its steady barrage of jibes than any live-action show – had Kavner herself as the brilliantly unstupid and suspiciously Jewish-sounding wifely voice. But the history of television comedy is more likely to revolve around two older Jewish creative giants: Norman Lear and Larry Gelbart.

Lear, as we've seen, was very much the veteran of the Television Writers of America and of the McCarthy era, the kind of writer who found his way through early comedy-variety television, supplying gags and sketches for Martin and Lewis, George Gobel, Martha Raye, Carol Channing, and Don Rickles. First floating a project deemed too avant-garde for the networks (according to script plans, the same star couple would play a new married or unmarried couple each week), Lear abandoned television altogether in 1959, moving over into film. His first feature, with his new partner, Bud Yorkin, was the original Neil Simon/Broadway bildungsroman (or bildungscinema) comedy-drama with a 1940s-sounding Sinatra signature tune to boot, *Come Blow Your Horn*.[37]

Then came a series of mostly unmemorable features (the most successful, *Divorce, American Style*, looked like a sitcom and starred Dick Van Dyke) and *The Night They Raided Minsky's* (1968), a nostalgic retrospective musical basically about Jewish theatrical life, starring Jason Robards, written and directed by Lear (co-star Bert Lahr died during the production), and narrated by a true period piece, Rudy Vallee. That was enough for films. Lear had apparently been biding his time until networks were ready for something different. He had it, at the very dawn of the demographics rethinking of commercial audiences. Buying the US rights to the iconoclastic British hit, *Till Death Do Us Part* (about an extraordinarily, even viciously bigoted father and his hapless family), he managed to sell it to the networks after two years of fruitless effort. Against the background of the Kent State massacre and the blossoming counterculture, CBS executives scheduled *All In The Family* as a midwinter replacement in January 1971.

It was nearly canceled because of poor initial ratings, but its daring use of assorted controversial material roused publicity of a kind unprecedented in American television. Lear writers were heard to complain later that Archie had been made almost loveable, and that the real selling point of the show to advertisers was the younger generation of consumers. In one of those typical turnarounds, controversy served the purpose: daughter Gloria and the son-in-law graduate student Meathead, played by Carl Reiner's son, Rob Reiner (described as Polish-American, but suspiciously intellectual, and, therefore, crypto-Jewish) brought viewers to products suited for them.[38]

If true, this was not Lear's intent. But network success demanded compromises that he perceived as necessary to put across a liberal Jewish message that had (although no one discussed it this way) come straight out of the Popular Front tradition. David Marc acutely described Lear as the "Zola of the small screen," the auteur who had in the mushy middle of American political (or depoliticized) culture, replaced *J'Accuse* with none too subtle jabs at racism, sexism, homophobia, and hawkish support for the war in Vietnam. Alternatively, Lear might be just as correctly seen as a New Age Clifford Odets, with the same small sets full of yelling relatives, albeit lacking the Socialist grandfather to unlock the mysteries of class struggle. True to tradition in this respect, Lear had staged his shows in front of live audiences, abandoning the laugh track to return to the original golden era television atmosphere of filmed theater, lineal descendent to the real thing.

Lear had done something genuinely different and won a top spot for years in the ratings. Rather than canceling *All In the Family*, CBS went the other way in the next few years: canceling its long-popular rural sitcoms like *Green Acres* and *The Beverly Hillbillies*.[39] Almost overnight, the new king of television comedy seemed to be able to produce big number clones at will. The most bold was doubtlessly *Maude*, a vehicle for Jewish comedienne Bea Arthur. Born Bernice Frankel, she started out in avant-garde theater playing opposite Lotte Lenya in an off-Broadway revival of *The Threepenny Opera* in 1954, originating the role of Yente in *Fiddler on the Roof* and fit perfectly for the multidivorced suburbanite who took no enemies and regularly proclaimed her devotion to the cause of women's liberation. A mere two years after CBS had ended its historic ban on shows dealing with divorcées, Arthur as Maude had three divorces behind her, and a thousand insults to deliver to sexism. She also had hot flashes, an alcoholic husband, and even an abortion.[40] Later on, as one of the Golden Girls (and an Emmy winner), Arthur's image softened but never entirely. (Spoof terrorists in the 1994 film *Airheads* demanded naked pictures of her.) Like Lily Tomlin but approaching eighty, she had her own solo stage act going into the next century in decidedly sophisticated venues of Manhattan and San Francisco.

Insiders complained that here as everywhere, the toughest emotional decisions faced by millions of ordinary viewers were avoided. Not all the spin-offs were successful or even interesting. But *Good Times*, the black clone, certainly had its moments. Inspired by the smash Broadway hit, *Raisin In the Sun*, written by Lorraine Hansberry, herself a decidedly left-wing African-American (and lesbian to boot) married to a Jewish intellectual, *Good Times* likewise focused on the difficulties of domestic life in the Chicago ghetto. It was the first time a major television series of any kind (unless *Amos 'n' Andy* is included) had made this black urban locale the source of drama or humor, and Esther Rolle delivered a performance as mama that was extraordinary by any estimation of television's mainstream. Unfortunately, as more acerbic critics observed, the show quickly reverted toward the minstrel-style antics of its teen actors.[41] Rolle herself quit. Lear had nevertheless made possible shows like *Sanford and Son* and his own, weaker version, *The Jeffersons* (a spinoff from *All In the Family*), as ambivalently or comically middle class as the Bunkers were working class.

Norman Lear had by this time gone practically as far as he could go. *All In the Family* ultimately regressed as loading dock foreman Archie took over a tavern (the typical fate of the sitcomic hero: less picaresque, more respectable, and a lot less funny), and for the auteur, a series of genuinely admirable experiments flopped. *Mary Hartman Mary Hartman* (1975–78), a late night quasi-soap opera about ordinary American dreams and seedy reality (with sex offenders and losers of all types) was surely the most innovative effort, with the even more risqué but instantly unsuccessful *Hot-l Baltimore* (1975) in second place.[42] *MHMH* broke some new odd ground with Method-style Louise Lasser and spun off *Fernwood 2-Night* (1978), a television experiment about the nature of television, with costar Martin Mull as host of a mythical talk show that moved from Fernwood to California and became, before its disappearance, *America 2-Night*.

Only by revisiting television's cautious history before cable (and before the very often Jewish-inflected *Saturday Night Live)* can it be appreciated how radical these reflexive projects really were. The erstwhile king, having proven his point and then found further experiments unappreciated, turned his attention straight to politics, creating the liberal lobby, People for the American Way. Lear thereby left the battlefield of popular culture with his status as few others would or could. In Ronald Reagan's America, and into the next century, it was the best a fighting liberal-progressive could do.

Lear had, despite his impressive results, not quite been the most daring of television producers. That honor belongs to another erstwhile TWA member and veteran of McCarthy era gag writing, Larry Gelbart. Born to a second-generation Jewish family in Chicago at the end of the 1920s, he broke into radio in the waning days of the Hollywood Left, when radio writing operated as a sort of second-tier to screenwriting, on a prestige level with writing B films, but in some cases far more lucrative. Replacing one Jewish left-winger, future friendly witness on Danny Thomas's *Folger's Coffee Hour*, Gelbart went to work under yet another future friendly witness, Woody Allen's distant cousin, Abe Burrows.[43]

Gelbart moved quickly to the new medium, writing for the usual crew of variety stars, Bob Hope to Jack Paar. Tiring of contemporary restraints and revolted by the domestic political atmosphere, he spent more than a decade in the UK, writing and producing assorted television material. He came back to work in the US with producer Gene Reynolds (a former child actor friendly to the blacklistees, and a coscripter for *Room 222* with James L. Brooks) on a series whose creation was made possible by the success of *All In the Family*, namely, *M*A*S*H*.[44] Based upon a doctor's fictionalized account of medical treatment during the Korean War, made into a then daring black comedy directed by Robert Altman and coscripted by former blacklistee Ring Lardner, Jr., its further adaptation was, in the television season of 1972, a pie thrown with hilarious accuracy straight into the face of the hawks.

Not that the Hawkeye character of the half-Jewish star Alan Alda (until then unknown, soon to become one of the most beloved figures in the history of television, especially among women viewers) and others uttered literal protests against the Korean War. Rather, it reflected the compelling, existential response to the hopelessness and unheroic character of the Asian conflict, from the weary eye of the physician and associated military staff. Antiwar protesters in America remained too controversial for sympathetic sitcom treatment, but it had suddenly become acceptable to deny military martinets the credit that they demanded for defending supposed American freedoms and for brutalizing civilian populations. In short, the old, pre-1930s Jewish (and other) pacifism, always more ironic and funny than the Christian variety, was on the march again.

No one had any doubts that Vietnam was the real subject, and the network only endured a chorus of conservative attacks because *M*A*S*H* was fabulously successful, especially, but not only, among those emerging heavy-duty consumers who loved *All In the Family*. For decades after its eleven-year run, *M*A*S*H* remained the most-watched residual in the medium's history. The medical end of the program with the expectable doctor and nurse fraternization proved a great draw, following the movies *Men in White*, *Doctor Kildare*, and so many others, likewise previewing the equally vast success *St. Elsewhere*, *Chicago Hope*, and *ER*. But the background of armed conflict with its constant stream of random deaths, the arrogance (as well as extraordinary personal privileges) of the Brass, and the inevitable craziness that could explain a sympathetic character determined to cross-dress his way out of the military, must have reminded real veterans of what they found rotten in military life, even during the antifascist conflict, let alone after 1945, when the goals of the American military bureaucracy proved steadily less noble.

Thanks to Gelbart and Reynolds, the writers (who worked in a team with input from real Korean War physicians, a true innovation within the usually insular world of sitcom writing), technicians, and actors, *M*A*S*H* was also the most artistically innovative television show to its time. A few episodes had no laugh track; some were shot in black and white; leading characters died (at the time of costar MacLean Stevenson's departure in 1975, an almost unprecedented gambit) or had nervous breakdowns. Gelbart's follow-ups were unsuccessful, and he turned to theater and to film (notably *Oh, God!* and *Tootsie*). But with this one staggering success, he had done his work.

This story has no end. But the emphatically Jewish Roseanne Barr and her *Roseanne* (1988–97) took new territory on behalf of blue-collar feminism and downright class resentment. A heroine of her own life, raised in the semirural West with scarcely another Jew in sight, she grew up overweight and inclined toward prostitution. Barr found her way into acting as therapy, finally cocreator of her own show and costar with John Goodman.[45] Perhaps only when hit by threats of cable competition did networks reassess the boundaries of the possible; in any case, *Roseanne* was practically the first to take on teenage sex, single motherhood, masturbation, drug and familial abuse, unemployment, and assorted issues as the stuff of comedy, and to lacerate corporate developers who turn small-town America into sprawl America at taxpayer expense. Arguably, huge success (by the early 1990s it beat out the *Cosby Show* for the number one spot) both made possible Barr's further creative control of the show, and paved the way for such iconoclastic hits as *The Simpsons*. (Her own efforts at comeback, like those of so many sitcomic stars of the past, were considerably less successful.)

By this time – or so it seems a few years into the new century – the self-identified Jew is a television fixture, predictably more often in sitcoms than anywhere else. Pressured by pseudoreality shows as it was earlier by other competing genres, the sitcom itself will doubtlessly survive, our comedy of manners scarcely more banal, even at its frequent worst, than the society around it.

CINEMASTERS – AND THEIR DISCONTENTS

Meanwhile Barry Levinson's *Homicide: Life On the Street* (1993–97) added something decisive to the Jewish-inflected television drama, like Sidney Lumet's *100 Centre Street* (2000–02), reminding careful viewers of both the television golden age realism and of a promise of artistic complexity and film innovation within reach of the genius touch.

Not only was it the premier police show by critical standards. *Homicide* proved to be executive producer Levinson's most widely viewed achievement after twenty years of screenwriting and directing. If he had worked more closely with the show (which he passed off to other hands in the first season, returning intermittently to direct episodes), and if it had gone on, he might possibly have climaxed one of the most interesting careers in the self-reflection of Jewish themes as mass culture. Coming from a comfortable upper-middle-class Baltimore family, Levinson admits to having missed "the immigrant experience in terms of the sweatshop and the teeming masses" of New York, and seems amazingly unaware of the lower-middle-class left-wing and liberal Jews who build the industrial unions and forced racial integration upon an unwilling, semi-southern city.[46] Rather, his work has reflected the Jewish ambience several generations removed from immigrant life but by no means removed from the Jewish craving for justice.

And that is literally what we see in his first serious film, . . . *With Justice for All* (1979), a deeply Baltimore story about a lawyer, who might more probably have been Jewish, battling the unfairness and moral corruption of the legal system single-handedly. Norman Jewison directed the picture and cast Al Pacino as the lead. Levinson's script may actually be the film's weakest point, but . . . *With Justice* was nevertheless full of wonderful Levinsonian characters, tortured and self-tortured by phantoms from the real world of pain, poverty, and duplicity.

Levinson had scraped through high school (with memories that would turn up vividly in *Diner*), indifferent to his classes and inspired mainly by movies and music, from folk to jazz. He started out a career in flunky jobs at a Washington, DC, television station, gravitating to Los Angeles where he did a leftish (by his own description) satirical club improv act that got onto a local station. Fast-rising executive Michael Ovitz, taking in the act, hired him from there to write for television's short-lived *Marty Feldman's Comedy Machine*. Moving on to the *Carol Burnett Show*, Levinson won two Emmys with the team of other writers, creating sketch material (often in collaboration with his wife, actress-writer Valerie Curtin) that would have been familiar to Sid Caesar (or *Mad Comics* artists) as updates or revisitings of satire on popular culture standards and current clichés.

Mel Brooks snapped up Levinson in 1975, and there hangs another tale. Occasionally one of the most successful filmmakers in the second half of the century, this Brooks is also one of the most blatantly Jewish. Born Melvin Kaminsky in Brooklyn, a juvenile drummer, social director, and stand-up comic in the Catskills of the late 1940s and 50s, he joined Caesar in 1949 and stayed with him, on and off, for a decade, irregularly performing on the shows himself. His script for the animated *2,000 Year Old Man* (the spritzing Jewish comic wiseman), written with Carl Reiner for a comedy record, and his creation (with Buck Henry) of the spy takeoff *Get Smart* (1965–70) put him in the very best of comic company. His maiden directorial outing in *The Producers* (which he also scripted) revealed Brooks as someone who knew no sacred cows or at least precious few. Just to stage the production number "Springtime for Hitler" made the rest of a thinly and unevenly plotted film memorable. By fall, 2001, *The Producers'* reworked musical version became the most sold-out and highest ticket-priced revival (or any play at all) in Broadway history.

Blazing Saddles (1976), for twenty years after its release still one of the heaviest grossing films ever, constituted the veritable definition of classic Brooks. Again, the plot and dialogue (coscripted by radical Jewish intellectual Andrew Bergman) were slight and full of holes,[47] but the violations of Hollywood traditions and cowboy icons would be hailed long after the farting jokes and assorted belly laughs had long since dissipated. Cleavon Little, the first black star of a white cowboy picture, was himself a constant sight gag, and Madelaine Kahn offered a perfectly fabulous takeoff of Marlene Dietrich.

Nothing Brooks did afterward had quite as many successful humorous bits. But intermittently, in most of his subsequent films, Mel Brooks managed to satirize, take apart, and reassemble some Hollywood classic poses perfectly, thanks also to the ensemble of Wilder, Kahn, and Marty Feldman. *Young Frankenstein* (1976) surely was the artistic best, because so much of the horror genre and earlier satires on it had been built around the mad scientist plot. *High Anxiety* (1977), a Hitchcock satire, began at a psychoanalyists' conference with a boasting shrink.[48] By the time Levinson caught up with the comic whirlwind, Brooks was working on *Silent Movie*, a true experiment with only music and sound effects to punctuate the action. It came fifty years too late to work either dramatically or commercially, but it was still a remarkable effort.[49] Coscripted by Levinson (who also acted briefly, in a satire on the shower scene takeoff from *Psycho* but with Brooks himself taking the shower), *High Anxiety* was better-than-average Brooks. But the comic director had already done his best work. Sharing the work and perhaps wanting some distance from the overwhelming Brooks prompted Levinson's quest to direct.[50]

... And Justice for All, notwithstanding the film's considerable limitations, earned a nomination for best original screenplay for Levinson and Curtin. The future director could now start to do what he wanted, and he next scripted *Inside Moves* (1980), a film about a crippled Vietnam vet finding a community among the riffraff of a local bar. It had heart if not much more. After cancellation of an antiwar project (later mismade as *Toys*, 1992), Levinson dug into his high school memories for a script about Baltimore adolescence during the 1950s. He found himself in more ways than one.

Diner (1982) was Jewish by way of assimilation. Trying out his wings, Levinson encouraged the budding actors to ad-lib. Their realistic gabbing is one of the most distinctive features of a film that has apparently little in common with *shtetl* memories, immigrant ghettoes, or its most logical precursor, the yearnings for the life of Westchester County tennis-court urbanity in *Fibi* (the avant-garde 1918 novella by the great Yiddish experimentalist, David Ignatov). Not by accident, *Euf Veite Vegn* (On Distant Roads), the 1931–32 trilogy by Ignatov, carrying a protagonist beyond such fantasies (however predictive of *Goodbye Columbus*), out of the real-life urban ghetto and through Marxist Socialism to a more mystical search for egalitarianism and transcendence of materialism, had been in vital ways typical of the previous generations' quest. Levinson's characters, by contrast, were already there, at the end of the assimilation road, deracinated in some sense but unable to grasp the problem that made their lives seem empty. Ignatov, the intellectual, had grown out of the Hasidism of his youth but retained its dreaminess; two generations later the dream had dwindled even as life opportunities expanded considerably.[51]

Among Levinson's later film features, it is the most intensively Jewish ones (with a single exception) that prove overwhelmingly the most interesting. *Tin Men* (1987), this time set in Baltimore in 1963 with a grown-up Richard Dreyfuss as one of the hustler-salesmen of the aluminum siding business, might be a story of competing rag gatherers from some past era, except that these guys are Jews on the shady borderline where the accepted unethical behavior of salesmen becomes illegality (better business codes cracking down for the greater good of a respectable Chamber of Commerce). Their dilemmas, their constant patter – Levinson made fine use of Danny DeVito and Barbara Hershey, competitor and lover, respectively – identify them as a type that is most likely Jewish. The combination of the theme of retro Baltimore and Levinson's work was right on the money again.

The Jewishness of *Avalon* (1990) – a film predictably attacked by Pauline Kael, avid enemy of Hollywood's blacklistees and everything Jewish perceived in a similar light – equaled anything ever done in American film about Jewishness, almost as if making up for decades of how Hollywood had been holding back the obvious equations. Randy Newman's score provided enormous help along these lines, arguably his best work in films as well. The story is straightforward, close enough to the writer-director's own family saga of reaching upward from the immigrant artisanal status of the newcomers to appliance king in a generation, with the concomitant growing puzzlement at the meaning of it all. Marvelously, at the end of the film, the Jewish grandfather lies in the nursing home trying to retell the stories from the Jewish past while the son visits and the grandson watches the ever present television: the particular past has dissolved, come to mean nothing. Levinson carefully left the moral up to the viewer.

That was the view from 1990 for much of Jewish America, rather than persistent memories of early poverty, the hopes of the New Deal, the despair of the Holocaust and mixed emotions toward Israel (to say nothing of religion). Nothing here could overcome the loss of the self-conscious identity once stamped by a very particular outsider status. Was it the absence of an ideological (idealist or otherwise) dimension in the lives of materially comfortable Jews? Was it the raw power of consumerism? Levinson and *Avalon* offered no answers to these overly large but deeply relevant questions. Perhaps too much was missing from the saga.

Homicide: Life on the Street did offer answers in small doses – not necessarily Jewish answers but not entirely non-Jewish answers either, treated in a generic old-fashioned Jewish manner of humane concern and complexity. Only Richard Belzer's character Munch was a real Jew, a life-long Baltimorean (in that sense like most of the show's characters), formerly an engagé journalist with an antiwar underground newspaper and still enraged at the Nixon-Reagan conspiracies to hide truths and to prosecute those who get in the way of the security state. And yet he was part of that apparatus himself, at this later date, as part of the law enforcement business that thrives on mollifying small minds. A survivor of multiple broken marriages, the far from charismatic Munch is one of the most existential cops of an existential television cop era. (Banished with the end of *Homicide*, he returned in *Law and Order: Special Victims Unit*, regrettably now a mere New Yorker, and a less counterculture memory than in Baltimore.)

The Baltimore of *Homicide* was also at the opposite end of the scale from the neighborhood of the lamenting, but definitively neoliberal, *Hill Street Blues*, placed in the hopeless slums of some unidentified city. From the grimy waterside to the blue-collar hillbilly "Pigtown," the ghetto streets to Levinson's own suburbs, this is one very particular place that perhaps LA and Manhattan cannot be and indeed few television glimpses of urban life have ever been. It's home, a ragged and frequently despairing home as *haym* must always be until the birth of a more enlightened and humane age.

The appearance of the legal drama *100 Centre Street*, in January 2001, lent a similar savant role for Sidney Lumet, the senior version of Levinson with his feet firmly planted in vintage 1930s drama. The Cable series gave viewers the extraordinarily interesting and deeply Jewish figure of a troubled liberal judge, played by Alan Arkin, at the very center of the drama. Unintentionally letting a future killer off the hook, he is already the Jewish bleeding heart liberal under siege in the first episode and thereafter. Right out of the old school of progressives, updated to the point where he describes himself as a former hippie (surely a little old for the part, a late beatnik, more likely, not so far from real-life Arkin, the 1950s folksinger in the left-wing group, The Tarryers), he's a supremely Lumetish Jewish character who talks about Paul Robeson records and even mentions the Popular Front.[52]

Like so many in Jewish popular life, the inspiration goes back to a family story. Baruch Lumet, a Polish émigré, reached American shores in 1919, worked in Yiddish theater during the 1920s, but without notable success. His breakthrough was a fifteen-minute radio serial, *Der Zayde* (the grandfather), launched in 1929 with various members of the family, including young Sidney, playing parts. It ran eight years and the elder Lumet never took a credit on the air, convinced that it would lower his status as an artist. Young Sidney found the road that his father never did, making supreme popular art in his own name.

He had made his theatrical debut at five in the Yiddish Art Theater and appeared frequently in both the Yiddish theater and on Broadway during the next decade as a child and prepubescent actor. After working radar in the Far East during the war, he returned to theater for a time, broke off from Group to found (with friends) an experimental troupe, and taught high school drama. He joined CBS in the new medium at the ripe age of twenty-six, where he directed some of the best live drama, including the live-action *Danger* (1950–54) and *You Are There* episodes written by three blacklistees including Walter Bernstein and Abraham Polonsky. In the era of Paddy Chayevsky, *Playhouse 90*, and more than two dozen anthology competitors, mordant cop dramas like *Naked City* with sympathetic criminals and (just a little later) a liberal conscience presentation like *The Defenders*, Lumet was an uncrowned king.

Lumet's film directorial debut, *Twelve Angry Men* (1957), made on a budget of less than $350,000, was classic liberal Jewish material. The cast of Henry Fonda, Lee J. Cobb, Ed Begley, E.G. Marshall, and Jack Klugman was virtually the best of the best lineup of liberals showing the moral edge of contemporary television drama. One juror, played by Henry Fonda, must convince the other eleven that a guilty-seeming boy may very well be innocent. It wowed critics, got the director, along with the film, nominated for Oscars, and was performed in public schools for a decade.[53] It also set Lumet in a lifelong cinematic career.

Lumet's subsequent films included the atomic war political shocker *Fail-Safe* (1960, written by Walter Bernstein), the police department muck-raking *Serpico* (written by another blacklistee, Waldo Salt, and based on a real-life massive corruption case in the New York City Police Department), the documentary *King: a Film Record . . . Memphis to Montgomery*, and several other of the most extraordinarily Jewish films ever made in Hollywood. A continuing giant decades later, his breakthrough Jewish film, *The Pawnbroker* (1965), would still seem to many moviegoers as the most significant. The memories of the Holocaust were then close enough and the agonies of black/Jewish confrontation immediate as to spark monumental episodes of emotional conflict around Method actor Rod Steiger in his best-ever role as survivor and proprietor of a Harlem pawn shop. The plot was so small, a hold-up by a Puerto Rican employee who craves to know the Jewish secret to success, and the imaginative vistas so large (like his being offered sex by the employee's black girlfriend, whose sexual offer reminds Steiger suddenly of seeing his wife being prostituted to German officers before being murdered in the camps) that the film was brutally hard to take. Watching it was a sobering experience, that rarest of Hollywood affects.[54]

Bye Bye Braverman (1968), destined to be the kind of commercial failure that nevertheless looped endlessly in many Jewish minds, was the only novel by black humorist, in-joking Wallace Markfield ever to reach the screen, and a very difficult one for director, actors, and viewers alike. Most of *Bye Bye* basically consists of four middle-aged Jewish men from Manhattan driving around lost in Brooklyn, looking for the funeral parlor where an old companion is laid out. Being fussy and competitive intellectuals, they weren't actually fond of their late friend, or of each other for that matter. But the task itself compels them to examine details of the world in front of them, a world so Jewish that Godfrey Cambridge plays a street character who speaks Yiddish – and even the fact that they end up at the funeral of the wrong Braverman doesn't matter in the end. *Bye Bye Braverman*, with its smart aleck intellectual types, was an effective homage to memories still vivid in the 1960s that were quickly growing dim as the era passed and renewed political passions along with better career opportunities loomed for younger Jewish intellectuals.[55] Like *Seize the Day* (1986), in which a most improbable Robin Williams (the Gentile as perfect outsider and on that account, perfect Jew) is Saul Bellow's utterly unlovable hero at loose ends as he enters middle age, *Bye Bye Braverman* offered up the intellectual of the 1950s getting older, without losing any of the generational passions and prejudices.

Probably no major director but Lumet would have taken on *Daniel* (1983), the still untouched and likely untouchable subject of the executed "atom spies," Julius and Ethel Rosenberg. Based on best-selling history fictionalizer E.L. Doctorow's *The Book of Daniel*, it avoided the innocent-or-guilty question that had obsessed public discussion of the case from the beginning, and instead focused on the status of the two surviving children trying to live in a world that had made their parents the enemies of the State. Never, perhaps, has a Bronx left-wing, lower-middle ambience been rendered more beautifully, in a glimpse of the family just before catastrophe befalls them. The delicacy of treatment throughout guaranteed (if the subject had not rendered it so already) that exhibitors would ignore the film. Sympathy for the Rosenbergs, parents or children, must have hastened its departure from the theaters into oblivion.

Lumet had garnered his revenge in advance with the amazingly powerful *Dog Day Afternoon*, in which Brooklyn crowds chant "Attica! Attica!" at police about to trick and assassinate would-be bankrobber Al Pacino. He must have taken solace in multi-Oscared *Network* (1976), not a great film but notable for being very nearly the last word of Paddy Chayevsky, once the prince of Jewish-style live drama on 1950s television, and for being an unremitting attack upon the subsequent (further) corruption of the medium. Lumet had many other memorable credits, but *Running On Empty* (1988) was a small gem of a Jewish family drama, this family on the run from bombing a university lab during the Vietnam war, and suffering mainly because the growing boy needs to settle down in a stable family to prepare for college.[56]

No other director could equal Lumet's Jewish moral themes, but Sydney Pollack occasionally came close. Child of Russian Jewish parents, trained by Group veteran Sanford Meisner, he broke into directing through television in markedly liberal crime shows like *The Defenders, The Fugitive*, and *Naked City*.[57] His breakthrough film, *They Shoot Horses, Don't They?* (1969) got him a deserved Oscar nomination for an evocation of 1930s hopelessness. *The Way We Were* (1973) was not the film that the gay Jewish writer of the original, Arthur Laurents, intended, but it was arguably the one that could be successful as the ultimate Barbra Streisand vehicle for Jewish left-liberal politics from the 1930s to the 1960s.[58] It was also, as some critics observed, crucial to Jewish filmic feminism: for nearly the first time, a young and marriageable Jewish woman had escaped the spoiled princess role, and refused the temptations of personal assimilation by standing up for her own identity, including her political identity.[59] Director Joan Micklin Silver's *Hester Street* (1974), projecting an immigrant wife's story into the definitely non-feminist novella by Abraham Cahan, did something similar on a tiny budget, thanks in no small measure to the bravura role of Carol Kane, who earned her Academy Award in the starring role.[60]

Was it possible to separate reflexive from *shtick*, whether comic or strictly serious? One candidate would be another Jewish Brooks (1947-), this one Albert, son of an Eddy Cantor comic foil (playing a stage Greek) and like his father, a stand-up comic. Performing on television from 1969, reaching the status of in-group (but what an in-group!) script auteur with his little films for *Saturday Night Live*, 1975–76, Albert soon moved into full-scale directing, including an oddly Jewish early hit, *Private Benjamin* (1980), but most memorably his own deeply personal films, like *Lost in America*. From then on, Brooks offered audiences regular doses of someone very much like himself, the lonely bachelor self-consciously Jewish in every postpoverty sense, shy, foolish, troubled by relations with mom and every other woman, but sincere, and, despite everything, hopeful. The films meandered by any usual standard of plotting, but for aficionados, they were deeply meaningful in being about someone who could easily be themselves, at least their male selves or their relatives.

The one writer who best epitomized the conscience from midcentury continued to the latest new era was surely Herb Gardner. A close friend of Paddy Chayevsky, but a considerably less successful writer in 1950s television, Gardner brought to the stage and then films his own intense take on media life and on contemporary Manhattan: *A Thousand Clowns* (1965). Perhaps filmable only because of other contemporary dropout films, it featured Jason Robards as a former kid's show writer who is utterly dis-illusioned but feels compelled to drop back in, so as to raise a nephew who lives with him. Although television culture is a sham at all levels, New York is amazingly real, an adventure possible any day for the bold and humane.

Decades and not many successes later, Gardner brought *I'm Not Rap-paport* to the stage (where it won him another Tony on Broadway) and then to film. Here, Walter Matthau in his last great role is the former left-wing activist who comes to share a park bench with a fellow ancient, a nearly blind janitor, played by Ossie Davis, more cynical about life's prospects and just as ravaged by age and bitter experiences (or good experiences now vanished). Very much like Robards in *A Thousand Clowns*, Matthau considers himself bedeviled by younger relatives (in this case a daughter, played by Amy Irving) who feel both obligated and annoyed almost beyond endurance. But by then, Manhattan was not so inviting.

The most moving scene in the play and even more so in the film (starring Judd Hirsch in the Matthau role) shows the aged Jew as a boy, at the famous meeting of needle trades workers in 1909, roused to the prospect of extreme suffering in order to vote for a general strike of the trades. One of the most extraordinary Jewish moments of the century that had been put away in distant memory by those who perceived different and contrary morals in the modern Jewish experience was never captured so well in mass entertainment; it alone would have verified Gardner's purpose. The pain in the passage of generations and causes that are so important to Jewish self-consciousness and the loss of it, but also the New Yorkishness of it, had come home here. As he says to his impatient companion,

> **OK, OK, the Soviet Union, throw it up to me; everybody does. They screwed up, I'm the first to admit it ... I gave up on them ... but I never gave up on the ideas. ... the ideas are still fine and beautiful, the ideas go on, they are better than the people who had them.**[61]

The film version was to begin (or end) with Rappaport in his unwanted rest home, organizing the attendants into a union. Prompted by an urgent phone call from the playwright looking for an angle, I recalled the life of Clara Lemlich, the proletarian adolescent whose speech had actually launched the 1909 strike. Her heroic moment of youth is indeed recalled in *I'm Not Rappaport* and the old age home organizing really happened, naturally with her in the lead. The scene, which might have worked perfectly but also might have taken the edge off the tragic/comic affect, didn't make the final cut.[62] *I'm Not Rappaport* was, in any case, an Odets for the end of an era, when those who could remember Odets plays being performed in the 1930s had grown fewer and fewer. But perhaps it was also Odets for the new generations of Jews.[63]

Meanwhile, the newer generations of Jewish Hollywood took on fresh projects (some of them Jewish, some of them worthy, most of them neither) without reservation of comparable ethnic competition. Does all this mean that Jewish movies had really come of age?

The question remains. A 1988 survey by two scholars of Jewish film directors found most of them unwilling to designate *any* Jewish influence or Jewish element to their work, and that likely continues to be the case. By and large, they think of themselves as artists who happen to be Jewish. Perhaps things have changed decisively in the subsequent fifteen years. But, more likely, not.[64]

Then again, perhaps Woody Allen personally marked, in his best years and despite his foibles, a kind of turning point that would remain forever in the sight of at least some history-minded filmmakers. Early in his career an act at Camp Tamiment, the old Socialist spot in the Catskills, he emerged beyond stand-up as the literate satirizer of Jewish liberalism's Cold War champions and their obsessions aimed simultaneously at erudition and public success. In *New Yorker* literary pieces, as he prepared himself to burst onto the screen, he delivered send-ups of literature and lit crit not far from the best of college humor columns. His cinematic satires of the liberals' predilections and their continual pursuit of self-interest (in 1977's *Annie Hall* he famously announced that *Commentary* and *Dissent* were merging – as *Dysentery*) had already climaxed, in a small way, when in *Sleeper* (1973) he described the nuclear holocaust as triggered by Vietnam hawk Albert Shanker, who in his darker moments had ordered thousands of teacher's curriculum guides withdrawn from use and destroyed – all for the sin of treating Malcolm X, Shanker's literal bête noir, sympathetically. *Zelig* was a pastiche about the "little Jew," the one who didn't fit into great historical events and had to infiltrate them.[65]

Riding the success of the antiwar generation, Allen became the champion of the blacklistees and their Jewishness in *The Front* (1976), and then went further deep inside himself, to the world of Jewish lower-middle-class life past in *Broadway Danny Rose* (1984), *The Purple Rose of Cairo* (1985), and above all *Radio Days* (1987). He lovingly rehearsed his own memories of neighborhood personalities, the longings and fantasies of childhood in the 1930s and '40s, and the odd fragments that remained behind. In *Crimes and Misdemeanors* (1989), his most serious drama, he came sharply to the present (and earned multiple Oscars for it) of the Jewish generation that became wealthy fiddling the books while applauding themselves for their philanthropy. Never political, he could not have been Rappaport – but he sensed the necessity of a Rappaport for Jewish life, and he more than sensed the overpowering of Jewishness by the blacklisting no goodniks of the Jewish establishment.

Allen's loving audience, often learning about the existence of the very subjects while watching his films, could only agree with him. He had made a particular historical, semi-Yiddishist corner of the American experience closer as well as artistically possible in cinema. Then he lost the subject, trapped inside the celebrity that he analyzed so brilliantly in *Star Dust Memories* (1980) and as actor-writer-director further perusing the old film genres, evidently running out of things to say. It remained to be seen how well others would carry the narrative possibilities further.

COMICS, ONE LAST TIME

The underground comix failed to overcome its status as a second-class culture not only because its artists were unrelenting avant-gardists or traffickers of visualized sex and drugs, but because they could not become what they were not already. Throwbacks in some ways to an earlier era of Jewish life, they undercut their own potential ascendance into artistic acceptance unconsciously, when not determinedly. Even when accepted and celebrated in the art and illustration world – Spiegelman and Katchor offer the best cases, with Harvey Pekar an unpredicted third – they actively sabotage the expectations for them as respectable artists and respectable Jews. Avant-garde they remain, but they are also reflexive Jews in more crucial, telling ways.

Kim Deitch offers a sodden early example. Best known for his time travels through the dreams and hitherto suppressed memories of marvelous characters, Deitch is, like Crumb, fascinated (or obsessed) with the vernacular creations of the 1910s-30s, especially in the demimonde of B entertainment like the circus and carnival. He's also the only descendent, among the underground circles, of a famous and decidedly left-wing animationist. His father was Gene Deitch, a UPA and Terrytoons artist who created *Tom Terrific*, one of the first projects to move fresh animation into television.

By the time Kim Deitch was a teenager, he'd met the likes of Jules Feiffer and John Hubley (the Disney animator who helped lead the studio strike of 1941), and been exposed to jazz and folk music and lots of radical talk. Later on, after his parents split, his father, Gene Deitch, left for Czechoslovakia where he became a major animator. Before he left home, he'd taught the boy a great deal about visual storytelling techniques and the broader world of American popular culture. And yet, by the son's account, *Mad Comics* remained decisive, destined to be studied obsessively not just for the satirical value but also for the complex subtle connections between the original and the lampoon.[66]

More confused than assisted by a model of success in the family, Deitch dropped out of the Pratt Institute, unable to fit into art school. Shipping out to sea Melville-style, working odd jobs (including a stint as psychiatric aide in a White Plains hospital with an intact 1930s ambience), he painted with oils and came across the work of Windsor McCay, the dream-like turn-of-the-century comic strip artist. Between psychedelic drugs and the appearance of his strips in the *East Village Other*, Deitch found his way to the flower child (circus freak on acid) *Sunshine Girl* strip in 1966. In a life often troubled by substance abuse, he and fellow artist Trina Robbins moved in together.[67]

Robbins, the daughter of a left-wing Yiddish journalist, was genetically meant to be a radical and instinctively a feminist who would become the foremost figure among the circle of artists, herself editing *It Ain't Me Babe* (1970, the first of a series of such comics of the Bay Area crowd collectively producing later ones variously titled, mostly *Wimmen's Comics*, not to be confused with another feminist creation out of Laguna Beach, *Tits 'n' Clits*). Trina had been, before her comics days, a highly talented and modestly successful clothes designer and boutique owner on the old Lower East Side. Turning to comics, she hooked up with Deitch and they left New York together for San Francisco in 1969, moving in (at first) with Crumb and his first wife, Dana, into the Haight-Ashbury neighborhood, for several generations known for its lower-middle-class Jewish ambience. Soon, Robbins had set herself up among new friends and associates, separate from, and in contrast to, the emerging crowd of underground comix guys.[68]

If Trina Robbins grew up very much in the cerebral districts of the Jewish Left, she also delved *Wonder Woman* and *Sheena, Queen of the Jungle*. Her work in the decades before she became the major historian of women's comics and cartoon art was in large part an artistic exploration out of those fantasies, but with a twist. From her earliest published drawings to the erotic *Wet Satin* (a 1977 comic of sex fantasies by women artists), her heroines got laid almost as often as they wanted – sometimes even in (completely nonviolent) rape fantasies that other feminists found considerably less than acceptable. Some of her most charming material, however, could be traced to her childhood memories of *Rosie the Riveter*, a typically left-wing productivist vision of women, and to her historical vignettes of forgotten women artists who slept with the artists while learning to paint, and had to deal with their male childishness as she – Trina, that is – struggled to raise a daughter, make her own art, and eventually become one of the serious scholars of women artists.[69]

Most notable about the Jewish artists among other self-consciously lib-
erated women was not the constant sexual references either serious or
humorous, not the lesbianism, nor the mostly leftist politics directed
(especially) against 1980s Reaganite America. Rather, it was their hyper-
consciousness about their Jewishness, the vapid materialism of their parents'
lives, and their own strivings for an escape that was still somehow (and
perhaps more) Jewish.

Nothing could exceed Aline Kominsky's *Bunch Comix* (1980) as high or
low in generational sex exploration. Blabette and Arnie, mother and father,
come out of teenage years of the big war into marriage in 1947, and Arnie
sells Studebakers while Blabette has two children (Aline is the oldest) and
craves bigger and better suburban houses. Family fortunes collapse with the
Studebaker, and before Arnie dies of cancer, Blabette discovers herself in
success at sales. The kids grow up totally neurotic but adolescent Aline
escapes into hippiedom, promiscuity, art school (where, as she admits, she
couldn't learn much in technical terms) and finally underground comix,
creating an autobiographical fiction. Arguably, especially set off against
Crumb's goyishness in their joint comic *Dirty Laundry* and their anthology
series, *Weirdo*, she becomes more Jewish than ever.

Aline's pained as well as hilarious descriptions of escape from suburban
Jewry into her own choreographed destiny seem, at any rate, a world away
from the Jewishness of Harvey Pekar's Cleveland. But looks could be
deceiving. Pekar managed his own artistic escape from suburbanizing Jews
by staying behind in the city.

His *American Splendor* ("From Off the Streets of Cleveland Comes … "),
written entirely by himself and drawn by various other hands, by now
possibly the least element of Pekar's emerging renown, is one of the
longest-running of all comics (1976-present). One of the back covers of an
early number has an ethnic-looking local crank on the street yelling at a bus
of the outward-bound heading westward to tonier climes: "You fuckers can
leave if you wanna, but I'm stayin' in Cleveland an' fightin'!" This was the
familiar spirit of d.a. levy, who had sworn to make himself a "discrepancy in
Cleveland" (an anthology of his work, published shortly after his 1971
suicide, was titled obligingly *Ukanhavyrfukincitibak*) rather than just one
more artist among the beautiful people in New York or Los Angeles.

It was Crumb's fascination with old comics, as we've seen, that introduced Pekar, the weekend writer of criticism for *Downbeat* and assorted
music venues, to the idea of comics, and it was a decade of rumination,
along with a visit from Crumb, that brought forth *American Splendor*, a title
not quite entirely ironic. Pekar has kept alive an avis rara in popular (or any

other) art, certainly in the US: a combination of the oral history of others, and a personal commentary about the quality and anxieties of his daily life, including that rarely seen life on the job, in his case, the VA hospital where he worked until 2001 as a filing clerk and trouble-shooting advocate of the patients.

The appearance of *American Splendor* had more than metaphorically marked the eclipse of alternative culture. Its finest Cleveland moment had arguably been poet levy's *Third Class Buddhist Junk Mail Oracle* (1968–70), mixing Jewish themes compellingly with Eastern religion, psychedelics, and other totems of the 1960s. A little guy with great charisma, d.a., as he preferred to be called, had staged a public campaign for more public poetry in his home town, and faced with arrest for printing impermissible language, with Allen Ginsberg and others to fly in for his public defense. Then things got too much for him. He left Cleveland for Madison, for a month or so, and I got him to agree to let a dozen or so poems go into a quasi-political poetry book that I published through my magazine, *Radical America*.[70] Things hadn't improved by the time he got back. His paper's final issue featured a front-page poem asking for financial help to get him to Israel to "dig holes in history." Shortly after he shot himself (his Gentile mother having ruined his prospects for making *aliyah*), dispatching, it seems, a final, amazingly undepressed postcard to me and perhaps to others as well.[71]

The crisis of comix had almost simultaneously arrived, only a few years after its counterpart in the underground press. The head shops that provided comix their over-the-counter outlets and represented unrespectable commerce generally, from bongs to black lights and radical posters, were closing down thanks to new ordinances and rising storefront costs. The familiar combination of sex, dope, and antiestablishment humor had lost its aura of rebellion as coke parties, middle-class promiscuity, and the cynics of the *National Lampoon* took (over) the stage. To launch an unfamiliar art form then, in comic book format, was strictly a loner's project as well attempted in Cleveland as San Francisco or Manhattan. Pekar did practically everything but the printing himself.[72]

American Splendor was also, from its earliest issues, profoundly about memories of popular urban life, in these years mostly the hidden life of ethnic neighborhoods, flea markets, and resale shops, with ample references to Kielbasa and Yiddishisms. Strikes years before where company thugs and police attacked strikers with heavy violence, aging memories of girlfriends (or near girlfriends) mixed with the tales of their second-generation families, nostalgia tales told about Eleanor Roosevelt, all these memories that led one way or another back to the teller, Pekar himself. It was, after all, *his* Cleveland, in some sense all an extension of his own family turf.[73]

Crumb's all-too familiar limitations became Pekar's strength. For Crumb, women in particular and black people in general tended to be used as a foil, larger than life even if the women were modern, if the African-Americans looked like they'd been taken from cartoon strips of the 1920s, and if he often treated both with an extraordinary tenderness (his drawings of Aline and of black musicians and their lives, the latter from storylines not his own). For Pekar, black fellow workers in the hospital were neither smaller nor larger than life; they were human beings of the first degree.

Mostly his fellow workers, they could be ignorant or ill-educated, speak in dialects that he faithfully reproduced, or not, and like the same music as him or hate it, and come up with the most peculiar theories for behavior. But they were shrewd as well as kindly, and instructed him in their own lives and in his, too. Likewise with women: Pekar's early troubles with women characters reflected his doomed marriages, sexual frustrations, and troubles in relationships where his own neurotic responses evidently hold most of the blame. Later on, in a strong marriage, his personal life revolved around a sometime artistic collaborator who is also more emotionally solid.

There's nothing new about the comic scripter who does not draw, although the importance of this difference remains unknown or vague to most of the juvenile audience. But Pekar had something new to add. In terms of comic content, with but few exceptions, comix had remained at the narrative level of fantasy. Even the most serious comic books (like *Classics Illustrated*) had extracted its narratives from imaginative literature. We've seen what Harvey Kurtzman tried to do in war and action comics, before this genre returned to bloodthirsty nationalism. Pekar had a more ground-level view of reality, the reality in front of him.[74]

It was a vital point for comics that had somehow not been made convincingly along the line, no doubt because the very limitations of the form imposed by the audience and publishers disuaded talented artists from attempting extended experimentation. Comics were capable of visualizing anything, if not in a magic encompassing venue like film or television, then in their own ways. In his first appearance on *The Late Show with David Letterman*, Pekar had tried to make this point clearly.[75]

But realism alone would never satisfy Pekar. Despite any disclaimers of didacticism, Pekar's work has the unmistakable stamp of *Menschlikheit*, a way of seeing that amends Spiegelman's judgment of Ben Katchor as the "most Yiddish" of the comic artists. Katchor has the form, the ambience, down cold; Pekar has sentiment that could be taken from the pages of Sholem Aleichem. In that sense, it may not be postmodern at all, at least in narrative terms but human and humane, egalitarian in a low-key sense of human decency, and deeply reflective, about the writer's own life and the life of his city. We see memories of his parents' seven-day week in the (literally) mom-and-pop grocery store, his father's occasional moments of near violence, the son's disappointments in school and rage at a less than lower-middle-class life for himself, the lost relationships along the way, old pals who come back from out of town for a visit and leech off him for weeks, Pekar's endless fascination with old jazz and blues, his hopes for an egalitarian revival of the inner city – all his dreams met with the cold reality of Cleveland but warmed by folks that warm to him, including hometown admirers of his comics.

The enhanced realism of a personal relationship (to Joyce Brabner, a Jewish reader who moved to Cleveland to marry Pekar), the experience of living through a cancer operation (rendered as *Our Cancer Year*, a full-length book), and the humility of the writer-as-artist have all added depth to Pekar's work. Indeed, in his reflexiveness, Pekar suggests the artist who has come to terms fully with his fate. Celebrity called on *Letterman* – and he threw it back at the celebrities. If he enjoys an occasional fantasy (a recent *Entertainment Weekly* strip of him at Cannes, as drawn by his old colla-borator Tom Dumm), it's not too serious. He is most likely to come back, as he did in a *New York Times* strip drawn by Bill Griffith, to complain that Cleveland had been trashed. He made his moral choices a long time ago.

By the late 1990s, Pekar was drawn to a very special corner of Jewish history, the *klezmer* revival by the neo-Jewish composer, producer, and saxophonist John Zorn. This brought Pekar back toward the early begin-ning of his critic's life, the music criticism that had dominated his creative output from the dawn of the 1960s until *American Splendor* took him over. And it helped bring him to a more comfortable Jewishness that recovered Jewish traditions as bearing a non-exploitative connection with black cul-ture. True child of an all but vanished Jewish urban neighborhood and factory life, the greatest loss in his forced retirement was the everydayness of the hospital and his black coworkers.[76] Harvey had not so much dwelt on Jewish self-consciousness as lived it.

The apex of comic artists' collective self-reflection, as observed briefly in this book's introduction, had decades before been reached within the seven issues of the commercial flop, *Arcade: The Comics Revue* (1975–77). *Arcade* succeeded aesthetically, if briefly, as the premier effort of self-conscious vernacular artists, but not only to explore the kinds of connections higher and lower forms of art and popular culture so vividly display in *Mad Comics'* treatments of superheroes and abstract expressionism alike during the early

1950s. *Arcade* was also intended to move the project one step further, adopting an explanatory purpose about the inner history of popular culture, framed with a necessary (and necessarily Jewish) irony about the whole effort.

This saga may be conveniently relaunched, one last time, with a fuller version of the Art Spiegelman story. Almost accidentally on the margins of the underground, he was younger than most of the others, and un-Californian in the extreme. But as a New Yorker with serious artistic intentions, he was the chosen one, destined to bring the comics aboveground, if never to a collective respectability.[77]

His family – it's no secret – was all but destroyed by Hitler and the Holocaust; his mother, scarcely a survivor, later committed suicide. As *Maus* shows, the middle-class Czechs barely survived, in no small part because his father as a wheeler-dealer could land on his feet (and if necessary on someone else's neck, a point rarely made by admiring reviewers, to the dismay of Spiegelman himself). Spiegelman's mother only survived in the technical sense, because she committed suicide in 1970. As a teen on the verge of adulthood, still in New York, young Spiegelman worked with former *Mad* artist Wallace Wood, collaborating on Topps cards. (A decade later, Spiegelman returned to cards, producing "Garbage Pail Kids," a takeoff on the heavily merchandized Cabbage Patch Kids: a small revolution in this humble line of work.) He had already gone without graduation from SUNY-Harpur College, a domain of the artistic-minded but low-income New Yorker, where he encountered Ken Jacobs, underground filmmaker and mentor to a large handful of talented youngsters working in popular formats.[78]

To imagine Spiegelman making a living off bubble gum cards of illustrations for poverty row *Playboy* imitations like *Gent* and *Nugget* is to come to grips with the low levels of artistic estimation that he inherited with the comics trade.[79] He returned to San Francisco in 1971. The underground comic was then only two years old and barely Jewish at all, by personality or in its contents. The *goyishe* character was especially evident in a scarcely cerebral, Texas storytelling style of books coming out steadily from Rip Off Press. There hangs a final tale that I can claim, to some slight degree, as my own corner of the comics trade, i.e., the bottom and mostly Jewish shelf of popular culture.

A curious coincidence brought me to the edge of this lively world through my own journal, *Radical America*. Willy-nilly, I helped bring Rip Off into existence in 1969, through turning over a grant given to the promising New Left bimonthly by the Louis M. Rabinowitz Foundation. A high-minded Old Left institution with a diminishing fund (drawn, at least apocryphally, from bra-snap patents lately expiring), the Rabinowitz was in its last years as a little slice of the needle trades that had brought so many American Jews either wealth or revolutionary expectations and sometimes both, at different times of their lives.

Radical America itself was ostensibly and mostly serious, treating its historical subjects, like the Wobblies (i.e., Industrial Workers of the World), with especially loving care. The Wobs' early ideologue Daniel DeLeon, a Sephardic Jew from Curacao who had reshaped American Socialism, had been my favorite intellectual during several years spent between the civil rights and antiwar movements, and *Radical America* carried over a kind of syndicalism from the memory of the First World War into the vibrant new movement around the Students for a Democratic Society. The magazine's stated purpose was to educate the young activists by relocating radical legacies among the masses, and if its editors were mainly Gentiles (thanks largely, I think, to its home base in Madison, Wisconsin and to the fact that most of the Jewish graduate students in history were more interested in a European or global focus) its readers were largely Jewish – a neat if entirely accidental reversal of some important and rarely discussed radical traditions.[80] But I'd recently fallen in love with *Heads 'n' Feds*, a self-published Texas comic book entirely drawn by Gilbert Shelton, an Austin party-going friend of Janis Joplin, also a history graduate student dropout who had moved on from his *Mad*-style *Superman* satire *Wonder Wart-Hog* to the updated hippie *Fabulous Furry Freak Brothers*. Shelton's evangelical theme was definitely peacenik and acid-oriented – if ordinary Americans could "turn on," perhaps they wouldn't need to be so repressed or war-oriented – but more than anything story-based. His narratives offered imaginative, satirical tales of counterculture life, roughly a million miles from *Terry and the Pirates* or for that matter, *Spider-Man*.

Radical America Comics, created by Shelton with the check that I signed over, appeared shortly after Crumb-dominated *ZAP Comics* no. 1 and no. 2. Rip Off proved one of the outstanding outlets of talent during the next decade. If the full-length San Francisco-based comics arguably constituted a whole new artistic genre, then *Radical America Comics* was the third number. (It was also, counting the normally cerebral *Radical America* itself as one more typical left-wing American magazine, my second entry into the Jewish trades.) Lamentably, Crumb was busy with other matters, Shelton drew upon his own crowd for contributions, and for that matter, the Spiegelman of that day would have been invisible to me, just another artist caught up in psychedelic themes. The result was noticeably (as I look back) *goyishe* humor, with LSD in the foreground, indubitably true to comics tradition, but not to Jewish comics traditions.

Landing in San Francisco just a bit later, but after the first great burst of comix energy, Spiegelman fell in with Bill Griffith, Justin Green, and others who would join together in *Arcade*, in time for serious rumination but too tardy for the short-lived underground comix commercial boom. By the mid-1970s, growth in the number of artists coincided with the decline of underground culture at large. The future looked grim. But within this microworld of popular art, things were changing in another important way.

Spiegelman introduced dimensions that other artists could hardly have imagined. In the midst of psychedelia, "real dreams" recalled and rendered by the artist were relatively rare. So were apparent genre strips about detectives or romance characters in which Picasso's visage suddenly appeared along with his misplaced-eye women, the comic artist was seen dead, and Potato Head was the heavy. *Ace Defective, Midget Hole* ends with a Jewish (or is she German-American?) housewife full in accent, and the protagonist-detective lost in his own fantasies. It was Spiegelman's version of postmodernism run amok, and it was only 1973.[81]

The acknowledged king of the undergrounds, R. Crumb, had meanwhile unconsciously absorbed a Jewishness with his attraction to past commercial and comic art. The obsessions and artistic expressions of his second wife and collaborator Aline Kominsky, were to play a central role in the direction of the rest of his career. Crumb was already on the path. Love, hate, fascination, resentment, and sheer confusion about women – Crumb was not one to straighten out his emotions, only draw them – had everything to do with Jewish women and some deeper artistic connection that he could not elucidate.

Spiegelman had met R. Crumb years earlier through a mainstream comics editor Woody Gelman, who had the future king of underground comix working on a project of his intended to be called *Nostalgia Illustrated*, a sort of updated anthology of old-time comic strip drawings. Spiegelman and Griffith intended, during the early 1970s, to publish a comics tabloid called *Banana Oil* (the once-famous cynical retort thrown at fabulators by Milt Gross characters three generations earlier).

Griffith was another interesting character, like Crumb a Gentile (and like him with a talented, excessively self-conscious Jewish wife and fellow artist, Diane Newman, aka Noomin) but coming at Jewish culture from a somewhat different angle. He grew up in Levittown, Long Island, the original suburban sprawl where lower-middle-class escapees from Manhattan and Brooklyn could become home owners, unless of course they didn't happen to be white. By one of those marvelous coincidences, the Griffiths' next-door neighbor was a famous SciFi and detective pulp illustrator, Ed Emshwiller, who was a bit of a bohemian and doubtless an encouragement to Griffith's mother, a minor SciFi writer herself. Griffith's father was (like Crumb's) a career military man, an especially strong reason for generational rebellion at the moment. Griffy went to art school, sought to become an abstractionist painter and more or less fell into comics. He began coediting a well-selling satire series, *Young Lust*, by the early 1970s.[82] But from his first appearance in the underground, his beat was more general: the odd perversities of mass culture at large.[83]

His early protagonist was Mister Toad, at some level a combination of Phil Silvers and Sgt. Bilko and more than a hint of Froggie the Gremlin, that troublesome magic character of 1950s Saturday afternoon television (he haunted host Andy Devine's storytelling sessions, forcing the porcine straight man to say foolish things in front of children wildly laughing at adult pretensions).[84] A few years later, Griffith switched to *Zippy the Pinhead*, zen-like moron-hero of his long-syndicated strip whose fondest readers still think of themselves as outsiders and (at least in their own minds) potential avant-gardists eager to roll back the suburbs and smite a suburban, hopelessly McDonald's-eating, Republican Middle America.[85]

Arcade took shape in the spring of 1975, as no comics anthology ever had or would again. With a Crumb cover, a more than full-bodied young Jewish woman oblivious to the funny animal creatures around her, and a collaboration of Spiegelman and Griffith in a comic "editorial" alongside the old-fashioned column of insider chatter, it opened up to Spiegelman's "Cracking Jokes: a Brief Inquiry into Various Aspects of Humor." This was serious stuff (with Freud caricatured) on the origins of humor as aggression and hatred, the self-inflicted pain of the humorist over the ages, marked finally by Mark Twain's epitaph that "everything human is pathetic." Inside we find a nuthouse Long Island story from the 1930s drawn by Kim Deitch. In the last pages, Aline recalls some of her tortured Long Island childhood. An anthology of pals, the issue climaxed with Justin Green's version of *The Winter's Tale*, with Leontes played by a familiar Uncle Sol Jewish character from Green's narratives about the entertainment business.

Green was yet another Jewish adaptee. Raised in suburban Chicago in a mixed marriage with a Gentile mother, he first discovered the weirdo in himself when the family moved to Skokie, home of the Jewish upward-bound. (Like myself in Yiddish class, he was the *goyishe-kopf*, whose literal translation, "Gentile head," actually means dumb-head: same thing.) His private obsessions turned Catholic and remained so (although also occasionally Zen) in a dialectic of the searcher after mystic symbols destined to be disappointed. But the jokes were Jewish.[86] Only in the pages of *Arcade* would Green bring back Sgt. Bilko in a sixteenth-century *Comedia dell Art*, with his troupe intact. Green even redid *Dante's Inferno* at the gates of purgatory, complete with Chicago accents ("So you had a heart attack at Devon and Kedzie, huh? I usta live on th' nort' side, too").[87]

Coeditor Griffith himself used the pages of *Arcade* to do something that the underground comix had heretofore avoided. He explored his favorite cutting-edge predecessors, like Henri Rousseau (and Rousseau's friend, dada-precursive Alfred Jarry) as precursors of the underground crowd in the turn-of-the-century French avant-garde circles. Recounting strange characters and their often sad lives, devising art unappreciated by contemporary critics (and patrons), it must have been consolation as well as experimentation.

With a mixture of Green's reflections on classic literature (Uncle Sol makes another appearance in *Crime and Punishment*, a satirical version of the *Classics Illustrated* version, as the police inspector who hunts down Raskolnikov, a lunatic intellectual considerably funnier than the original), a revisitation to the birth of avant-garde art, vaudeville, and the Russian Revolution, fiction by William Burroughs and Charles Bukowski among others, *Arcade* was probably too introspective to last.[88] It should have succeeded, and might have succeeded in lifting up comic art to the level of serious acceptance still barely achieved by the end of the century. Spiegelman laconically remarked to an interviewer for the *Comics Journal*, some years later, that *Arcade* was intended to be a "life raft on the sinking shop of the underground comix scene."[89] Then the life raft went under.

But at the very least, it had provided a transition for Spiegelman himself. The failure of *Arcade* after six issues, punctuated by Spiegelman's own return to Manhattan, pointed in another direction. In only a few years, he (joined by his new wife, Françoise Mouly) proceeded with *Raw Magazine*, both a bold venture and a *very* New York thing to do, with enough newsstand presence and enough international readership to keep it going, if never prosperous, for a decade. *Raw* and the success of *Maus* led straight to the pages of the *New Yorker* for Spiegelman and Mouly, as is well known. Spiegelman remained intrigued with the vernacular, but also did what a good Jewish liberal-radical in rotten times would be expected to do. Making his cover drawings for America's most dignified weekly both poignant and controversial (an African-American and a Chasidic man kiss each other; or police frolic with shootings of unarmed black suspects, "forty-one shots, ten cents," a reference to the Amadou Diallo killing;

the *New York Post* editorialists called him a "creep"), he horrified and
enraged Jewish conservatives, but not only them. Rudolph Giuliani
denounced one cover, as did Governor Pataki, and 250 police officers
picketed the offices of the magazine. Spiegelman took it with aplomb,
noting that he was drawing upon the pudgy policeman comic strip in the
old *Daily News*, altering details with the real change in police behavior. Had
Spiegelman's nineteenth-century precursor, master-caricaturist Thomas
Nast, famed for his revelations about the notorious Tweed Ring in City
Hall, been beloved for attacking corruption? Not by all.

By the mid-1990s and perhaps before, Spiegelman and Griffith had all
but eclipsed Crumb, the artistic exile living in the South of France whose
enduring fame, especially among younger generations, might by now be
attributed to the 1994 documentary film directed by Crumb's old friend
Terry Zwigoff.[90] A remarkable work of art in itself, *Crumb* offered a
memorable tour through the hell of a dysfunctional and sometimes violent
family, broken survivors (all but Robert himself), and the garishness
imposed upon his artistic imagination. Gene Siskell urged a special Oscar.
But only indirectly, mainly via the observations of Aline, did his early
attachment to the city life of the streets, the ethnic characters, and most
especially the Jewishness of the artist's imagination manage to re-emerge.
Zwigoff had not seen the whole dimension or had regarded it as less dramatically effective than sex and psychic horror.

It was as if the filmmaker had entirely missed an inner logic of *Introducing
Kafka* (1994), whose preparation by Crumb and literary collaborator David
Zane Mairowitz had preoccupied the same years. For the artist, it capped
off an artistic lifetime of Jewish seductresses at once caricatured, reduced
repeatedly, and all the while, urgently desired. The introduction books
appearing since the later 1970s had been heavily illustrated or narrated
mostly through pictures, and some had been quite funny. But none had the
psychological depth of Kafka, thanks only in part to collaborator Mairowitz,
fellow exile and author of *Wilhelm Reich for Beginners*. The depths of the
weirdness came in the drawings, among the strangest that Crumb ever
delivered.

Indeed, this Kafka is more than a little like Crumb, who himself makes an
appearance in the early pages listening to the very kinds of modern
sophisticates that the artist despises, maddened by their throwing around the
neologism "Kafkaesque." At the end of the book we have contemporary,
post-Communist Prague with McKafka Burgers, Ghetto Pizza, and horrible
American tourists (a few years later, Crumb might have detailed the five
megamalls that now surround Prague and threaten to turn the old city

district into a theme park of suburbanites). The boy Franz grows up in a scary society of anti-Semites, but his worst fear is his violent and psychologically abusive father (not unlike Crumb's own experience). The psychological source of Kafka's literature was the writer's seeing himself through his father's eyes: not the manly son that he wanted, but instead a wimp – by no accident, also Crumb's own traumatizing experience.

And yet it was no less Kafka, including an incisive visual retelling of *The Metamorphosis* and parts of *The Trial*. An even more incisive retelling of the doomed writer's ill-starred careers and his romances, each of them an intended escape from himself, pauses here and there in Crumb-like fashion to sketch social history and the bohemian artist-intellectuals' circles of the time. In the penultimate visual tale, in a second excerpt from *The Trial*, the condemned protagonist, drawn erotically to a woman who brandishes a webbed hand, looks unmistakably like Crumb himself (perhaps because this is the only one of Kafka's characters to achieve sex, even if a tortured variety of it). The next pages show the author as the hopelessly wandering Jew craving that which repelled him. The rest of the book is about Kafka's final years fighting tuberculosis, marrying the most obviously Jewish of his lovers, his death, and the speculation set loose by his writings. In Mairowitz's words, the tragedy of Kafka's Czechoslovakia under the Austrians, Germans, and Russians has been succeeded by the "fake American dream." It's not a happy ending.[91]

Nor had Crumb especially sought one. *Weirdo* magazine, with a bit under thirty numbers from the early 1980s to the early 1990s, was the definitive last of the underground comix-style anthologies. Sometimes very funny (Crumb revived the fumetti-style photos with captions that Kurtzman had overseen in *HELP!*), often autobiographical (above all about Crumb and Aline, their past and present), it introduced new artists, but was preoccupied with being politically incorrect. Here, too, Aline came into her own. If her drawing remained (by her own characterization) a studied version of childish perceptions, it hinged upon constantly shifting self-consciousness. So much had to do with the Jewish materialism and neurosis of the 1950s and '60s, the look backward at strivings that brought mostly unhappiness (not to mention bad taste), that her work constituted a coherent generational/gender statement. Then again, it was also a deeply personal statement of living with an artistic genius who also happened to be a crank. Too bad she didn't particularly want to continue.

The continuing energy of the undergrounds, transmuted by time and politics, could best be seen in *World War 3 Illustrated*, a more or less annual series in its twenty-first year by 2003, steadily becoming the quality anthology that both *Arcade* and *Raw* had promised earlier. Spiegelman, alienated from the *New Yorker*'s political drift, could be found here, also Sue Coe, the Cleveland protégés of Pekar, Peter Kuper and Seth Tobocman, along with a whole new generation of radical artists, most (but not nearly all) of them Jewish. Nicole Schulman, born in 1975, a youthful reader of *World War* 3 and an eager visitor to the MOMA exhibit of Spiegelman's *Maus* drawings in 1995, was the youngest of the crew taking hold by the early years of the new century. A realist along the lines of the old Ash Can artists, Schulman, like *World War* 3 (whose issues she sometimes edited) guaranteed a kind of continuity of political and artistic intent at once forcefully Jewish, of internationalist and secular variety. The radical artists of the 1910s–40s would easily have recognized her as one of their own.[92]

In a curious way, the work of artists Katchor and Spiegelman, who didn't start out with comic strips in mind, have meanwhile circled back to Jewish hipster/artists who might as well have been called cartoonists but escaped the labeling. Larry Rivers offers a last, major case in point. Born Yitzroch Loiza Grossberg in 1923 into a Bronx Jewish and Communist milieu, a young jazz musician in the 1940s who came across modern art by chance, he took art classes on the GI Bill, but immediately rebelled against abstract Expressionism – and refused to drop his left-wing sentiments (which, doubtless, at least as much as his art, caused the ever-influential Clement Greenberg to launch an assault on his work). Most notably, his parodic *Washington Crosses the Delaware* (1953) broke abstractionist rules, threw the Henry Luce vision of free enterprise art into the face of the art world's rulers, and opened the way to pop art. Incorporating everyday objects into his work, Rivers constructed his grandest object, *History of the Russian Revolution*, a thirty-three-foot construct of boxes, paintings, drawings, wooden rifles and so on, based mostly on his reading of Trotsky's famed volumes. Mocking US foreign policy and domestic racism, he never stopped being the left-wing troublemaker and jokester that, for him, would remain an essence of Jewishness.[93]

REDUX, OR AN AGE OF SEINFELDS?

That Adam Sandler (who must have been joking when he titled his production company Revolution) ran a close second to Jerry Seinfeld among American Jewish grad students as favorite Jewish celebrity at the start of the new century was probably just a blip on the ever-shifting radar screen. But the compulsive commentary on the symbolism that Sandler's characters explored was nevertheless revealing. The former *Saturday Night Live* celebrity and (by less admiring accounts) "termite comedian" of youth-oriented fart-joke films, including an increasing number that he has directed, certainly hit a nerve with his platinum hit, "The Chanukah Song." Whenever he gets depressed, Sandler confesses about the downsides in his rise to fame, he thinks about Jewish film and television stars and the Jewish influence on popular culture.[94]

It's a strikingly different self-identification from the Holocaust Jewishness that has swept the barely identified in the wake of *Schindler's List* and lives on in gut response to Israeli crises, but in terms of lived experience among younger generations, the kind of experience likely to be more intimate and more lasting. Sandler, according to ever-shrewd film critic J. Hoberman, is a Jew without Jewish ideology or conscious affect – just a Jew.[95]

Jerry Seinfeld, just below Sandler in the poll of favorite Jewish person-alities, had made a point of never actually identifying Jewishness, although late in the series the telltale signs were made more and more freely. In veteran actor Jerry Stiller's observation, the free association mode of comedy allowed characters (but also actors) to change the existing rules that render the Jewish underpinnings visible. According to Stiller, who played George Costanza's father, the television persona reveals his Jewishness best either when with his parents (where the humor of embarrassment is inevitable) or when cavorting with *shiksas*, for whom his Jewish oppo-siteness to them is his main attraction and biggest laugh. But like *Saturday Night Live*'s Gilda Radner character, Roseanne Rosannadana, stumbling into a deconstruction of the superficiality of news reporting, Seinfeld has moved beyond the sitcom mode. Arguably, he hit his peak with his reflexive commentary on television, during a famous episode brainstorming a sitcom "about nothing."[96] This is more understandable because originally, according to Seinfeld scripter Gregg Kavet, a top NBC executive dismissed the original pilot as "too Jewish," and the star had seized a second chance by avoiding specifically Jewish plots. He innovated because he needed to. From the standpoint of Jewish officialdom, on the other hand, the show often seemed all too Jewish, too satirical of Jewish looks and behavior. And it was a smash.[97]

But not the only model for success. Beloved sitcom star and ultimate modern Manhattanite Paul Reiser embodied another postmodern type, the fictive documentary filmmaker, in *Mad About You*. This popular 1990s show, based on memories of New York situations but shot almost entirely in Los Angeles, has something unmistakably, if also indefinably, Jewish in ways that might actually have seemed more natural to the television audience of the 1950s.

Jewishness was fast being naturalized, shedding off the often transparent disguises of most television history.[98] Indeed, as Jeffrey Shandler observes, the increasingly frequent appearance of discernibly Jewish characters in comedy and action dramas during the late 1970s and 1980s (including *LA Law, Thirtysomething, Murphy Brown,* and *Hill Street Blues*) became, by the 1990s, a reverse if virtual return to Greater New York, where no less than twenty shows were fictionally set (shot, course, in LA) with Jews more or less omnipresent. *Brooklyn Bridge* (1991–93) was easily the most elegiac, a memory of a boy growing up with a proletarian dad in the fictive shadow of Ebbets Field, the city scene (albeit Flatbush rather than the Bronx) that the Goldbergs had blithely left behind.[99] Was *this* the eclipse of alienation? Or, as Larry Gelbart among others complained, was it merely a sidebar to the replacement of sitcom writers with a background in radio, film, and literature by younger men and women self-trained as couch potatoes and given mostly to inside jokes?[100]

Not likely. In a Jewish world where surviving or reviving Yiddish at once takes on a gay affect (the marginal re-embracing the marginal) and a musical zest (*klezmer*), a world still largely ignored by the powerful Jewish institutions (or cursed as somehow non-Zionist and by that measure, self-hating), anything is clearly possible. A *Forward* arts editor celebrating the moment of Art Spiegelman's Pulitzer Prize described the artist's *Maus* as "a dark passageway from Auschwitz" but "with all the charm, the disquieting appeal, of popular entertainment," in short, "something new in American Jewish art."[101] This judgment was wrong on one crucial point: only the official recognition was new. Spiegelman's metaphorical calls for transcending the racial and ethnic lines separating Jews from other stricken peoples were nothing if not familiar. His famous etching made immediately after the attack on the World Trade Center (his daughter was going to school nearby), will surely remain among the most interesting of *New Yorker* covers, unremitting serious art for the masses (at least the masses reading the *New Yorker*).[102] Artie had always been there: the son of survivors and himself a survivor in a related sense, he had never been driven into conservatism or conformity.

Jewish music savant and promoter Henry Sapoznik recalls, in a similar spirit, going on the air in 1990 with the first new *klezmer* radio show aired in nearly a half-century. When he and his colleagues abandoned the show due to the studied indifference of the station management, four years later, it was also one of the last of the Yiddish hours on station WEVD. The failed effort to produce a successful cross-fertilization of the old *Forverts* hour and the *Prairie Home Companion* had thereby marked a larger eclipse, as the station itself was sold just a few years later.[103] But Sapoznik, musician and *hondler*, persisted. By the time another decade had passed, his collecting of records made for Yiddish radio broadcast had germinated into a major traveling show, visuals (with translations of the Yiddish), live music, and Sapoznik's own dramatic presentation on the road for memories of *Yiddishkayt*. KlezKamp, his brainchild, became the hottest of the new summer camp ideas to stir young Jews to an egalitarian Jewish self-identity.[104] Those thousands who attended the *Yiddish Radio Show* tour in a dozen cities during 2002 would not easily forget the wash of memories, real and borrowed, that Sapoznik and his friends (including a few now aged radio originals) managed to choreograph into a mental world of the vanished but not forgotten.[105]

It's fascinating that Sapoznik can readily locate his own roots in the wandering Jewish musicians of nineteenth-century Europe – often passing themselves off as gypsies – and in band members of the good times music of the weddings and bar mitzvahs of the 1910s-50s Jewish America. All the way along, "Jewishness" was deepened, one might say achieved for the first time in modern conditions, precisely through borrowings, adaptations, and downright swipes from surrounding cultures. Not that religious music and the sound of the cantor were absent (Sapoznik's own father, a famed cantor, dragged him to endless recitals in his childhood, thrusting him toward "Old Time" Gentile music until he rediscovered his Jewish muse). They were never really set off from the rest of the diasporic musical tradition. Unenthusiastically received in Israel, modern *klezmorem* found themselves most amazingly welcomed by Jews and Gentiles alike in parts of Europe where the revival of Jewishness would have been considered utopian only a decade or two earlier.[106]

Tony Kushner has described the pained humor of the much-awarded *Angels in America* as extremely Yiddish, its contents as the imaginative rearrangement of old parts, its architecture as the mixture of new and old, novelty and truth, and perhaps most of all, its striving to overcome the great American myth of individualism. To that artistic observation of *Yiddishkayt* and the lasting impression an older diasporic Jewishness upon Jewish and popular culture, nothing need be added.[107]

NOTES

[1] Jonathan Rosen, "Beyond Nostalgia," *The Forward*, 25 May 1990.

[2] Beth Pinsker, "Yiddish Debaters Draw Tough Questions," *The Forward*, 30 April 1999.

[3] Ruth Wisse, ed., *The Modern Jewish Canon* (New York: Free Press, 2000): 29. Wisse makes the claim only for literature, but it is clear that she means it for every writer, screen to book, and probably for every other artist as well. No one else can be truly canonical. In a lucid commentary on the book, "Mapping the Contours of a 'New Tanakh,'" *The Forward*, 13 September 2000, a reviewer observes what Wisse overlooks, that Israeli writers, like Israelis at large, remain (with important exceptions) extraordinarily and even willfully ignorant about the Yiddish cultural past; and further, that Israelis will perforce find their own way, likely creating an artistry owing increasingly less to Zionism, more to the blend of peoples including Palestinians, and to the varieties of "world pop" connecting Israeli popular art to that of postmodern Europe, Africa, and Latin America as well as the US and Asia.

[4] David Marc, *Demographic Vistas*: 129–66. Even if Marc had contributed nothing else, this observation would earn him the status of a chief observer of Jewish life, and not only in the US.

[5] So the same *Forward* pronounced editorially about the success of *The Producers* as a musical: "Half of us can't take a joke anymore, and the other half can't remember what 'Jewish' is. Mr. Brooks has restored that treasure, big time. Thanks, you crazy nut." In "Springtime for Jewish Humor," *The Forward*, 8 June 2001.

[6] Most of Goldberg's precious insights have been delivered in Yiddish; an exception is in his "Introduction," to Chaver Paver [Gershon Einbinder], *Clinton Street and Other Stories*, trans. Henry Goodman (New York: YKUF, 1974): vi.

[7] Quoted in Ron Goulert, "Spider-Man," *The Comic Book Readers' Companion*: 153.

[8] And in making it big, engendered further struggles over the booty. Chairman Emeritus Stan Lee broke with Marvel after sixty years and sued them for a share of the profits from the film. The legal wrangles will take years (and millions of dollars) to iron out. See Michael Dean, "News Watch: Spider-Man or Spider-Clone? Marvel and Sony Battle over a Bigger Piece of the Spidey Pie," *The Comics Journal*, no. 253 (June 2003): 19–21. See also Tom Sinclair, "Stan Lee: The Greatest Comic-Book Writer in the World!!!" *Entertainment Weekly*, 20 June 2003, for a cheerleading interview with Lee on the legal battles and other Lee sagas.

[9] Carla Mann, "Tobey Maguire's 'Spidey' Has the Chops But Lacks the Chutzpah," *The Forward*, 17 May 2002.

[10] It has been suggested recently that some of them might have good social-psychological reasons for the neurosis: they were gays and lesbians. At least, that is the inference that could be drawn, figuratively and literally, from the belated introduction of such characters in 2002. The Jewish artists and industry editors involved are in some cases gay themselves. Judd Winick, who draws the *Green Lantern*, is the best known, and his lesbian character Sunfire, in the series *Exiles*, is so far the most important. See "A Comic Book Gets Serious About Gay Issues," *New York Times*, 13 August 2002. Further live-action films based on comic book figures have regressed into childish action features without the psychological edge that might have instilled Spider-Man, and definitely touched Superman and Batman film adaptations at points.

[11] For Jack Kirby's side of the controversy, see, e.g., Paul Wardle, "The Two Faces of Stan Lee," in *The Comics Journal*, no. 181 (October 1995): 63.

[12] I wish to express my gratitude to Harvey, but most especially to Joyce during the event-filled months, for talking at length to me over the phone about matters large and small. Viewers of *American Splendor* who wonder about the dynamics of the real Harvey and Joyce do not need to go on wondering: the depiction is highly accurate, even if the details are altered and the personalities somewhat adjusted to movie fare.

[13] Leonard Nimoy, *I Am Not Spock* (Milbrae, Ca.: Celestial Arts, 1975): 5–7, 24–25. The title should not be taken too seriously, save perhaps as self-consciously ironic commentary. Star Trek's Klingon has occasionally been likened, in sitcoms, to Hebrew; language of a warrior people. If so, it ill-befits Yiddish.

[14] Gay as well as Jewish, drawn to the Black Panthers and reviled by Jewish institutional leaders, Genet would end an artist's life dedicated to the most unacceptable identities in the official Jewish world, the collective survival and self-realization of the Palestinian community.

[15] A sometimes wonderful, sometimes incoherent film, *The Balcony* was the only American-made avant-garde film of the European type available on the usual circuit. It stunned me with its boldness. Later, I learned that it had been adapted (from Genet, of course) and produced by blacklistee (and reluctant friendly witness) Ben Maddow; Lee Grant told me that despite its limitations, it was exciting, and one of her early returns from the Blacklist. This was the first time she met Nimoy, whom she remembered as an especially intense young man.

[16] J. Hoberman has a nice thumbnail sketch, "Shelley Winters," in J. Hoberman and Jeffrey Shandler, *Entertaining America: Jews, Movies, and Broadcasting*: 176. Her big break was reprising Judy Holliday's role in summer stock, and playing opposite John Garfield in *He Ran All The Way*, the final appearance of the actor almost literally on the run from HUAC, between subpoenas.

[17] According to insiders, Paul Newman walked away from the deal – and shortly later formed a production company with Martin Ritt to create social films

more commercial in nature. The production company did not last, but it gave Ritt a boost toward several of the most daring and important interracial films of the 1960s–70s, including *The Great White Hope* and *Sounder*. See Buhle and Wagner, *Hide in Plain Sight*: 149, 188.

[18] Again, gratitude to Lee Grant for several conversations; her later role in television is noted below.

[19] See Paul Buhle and Dave Wagner, *Hide in Plain Sight*: 31. I was lucky enough to exchange letters and phone calls with Tillie Olson; unlucky never to have spent time with her.

[20] It also defined and has certainly confined his career. Nimoy returned to film, outside the *Star Trek* series, with the remarkable anti-western *Catlow*, directed by blacklistee Sam Wanamaker, and to the stage with productions of *Fiddler On the Roof*. In later years, he turned out volumes of photography and poetry from the same small press that produced his memoir. The world took little notice of his artistic seriousness.

[21] One of the oddest of the crank theories among the assorted Cold War era theories of aliens inseminating the foundling generations of homo sapiens was French in origin, that Jews were the extraterrestrials, not quite hidden among the Gentile normals but not quite apart. It was never entirely clear whether this was a philo-Semitic or anti-Semitic projection.

[22] Jared Brown, *Zero Mostel, a Biography* (New York: Athaneum, 1989): 1–22.

[23] Ibid., 29–31, the conclusion is my own, although inferred in Brown's text.

[24] A revival of "Once over Lightly" in 1955 had blacklistees Zero, Jack Gilford, and Sono Osato in the cast with blacklistee Stanley Prager directing. Yip Harburg proposed whimsically that it be renamed "The Banned Wagon." Brown, *Zero Mostel*: 123.

[25] Ibid., 147–49.

[26] An otherwise fascinating picture book by Christine Conrad, *Jerome Robbins: That Broadway Man* (London: Booth-Clibborn Editions, 2000), skips over the Blacklist testimony and its effects entirely, finding the trauma only in the post-1965 change of musical styles. *Fiddler* comes off as a spiritual return to his parents' European origins – although as Conrad notes (193), his father frankly wanted to go to Hollywood, i.e., become a real American entertainer.

[27] Quoted in Brown, *Zero Mostel*: 242.

[28] The most famous or notorious Jewish story of the *Ed Sullivan Show* was the firing of Jackie Mason for acting "too kikey" on camera. A few years earlier, at the height of the Cold War, Sullivan the columnist had demanded the blacklisting of Jewish artists considered "Reds," pinpointing the cerebral noir artist of the Hollywood Left, Abraham Lincoln Polonsky.

[29] And a bit more secret than Leonard's long-standing connection with the left-leaning Jewish Hollywood milieu of his own days playing gangster. One of Tarloff's

best friends, and the director of many *Make Room* episodes, happened to be Artie Stander, younger brother of Lionel Stander, the original Hollywood Red (by this time exiled to Rome, until he returned to Hollywood for television parts, probably best remembered as chauffer on *Hart to Hart*). Thanks for recent conversations with Bella Stander about her father.

[30] Due to the severe limitations of writers' credits on radio shows – producers customarily grabbed them all – we will probably never know what effects the presence of many left-leaning writers had, if any, upon the most popular radio shows of the 1940s. But it is a most interesting subject for further study in the growing field of radio scholarship, and probes questions that my generation and older ones must have for memories of shows like *Our Miss Brooks*, *Suspense*, and anything with Fred Allen.

[31] He had other reasons. Reiner had been a great admirer of Paul Robeson during the war. Before being drafted, he worked as a comic with Abel Meeropol in an upstate New York bungalow colony during 1942; and he had many other mutual friends in the Left. See David Margolick, *Strange Fruit*: 58.

[32] David Marc, *ComicVisions: Television Comedy and American Culture*: 98.

[33] Brooks also coproduced *Welcome Back, Kotter* (1975–79) with the very Jewish Gabe Kaplan returning to his old high school where he must seek to instruct the "sweathogs" at the bottom of the academic charts, including John Travolta. It might be described as the sitcomic, ABC version of Jewish social work, so notable in *East Side/West Side* a decade earlier.

[34] Jeffrey Shandler acutely describes Rhoda's return from Minneapolis as reversing the Goldbergs' outward journey to the suburbs, from comic outsider among the Gentiles to a homegirl again, even if a career washout. Shandler, "At Home On the Small Screen: Television's New York Jews," in *Entertaining America*: 247.

[35] In one respect at least, Asner had the last laugh: seven Emmy awards amid fifteen nominations, five Golden Globe and two Critics Circle awards. He had no more hit series, however. Reaganism, with the neoconservatives running the ideological department, had taken its toll. In later decades, Democratic Senator Joseph Lieberman became the most ferocious attacker of Hollywood in Congress. Not surprisingly, Lieberman attracted only hostility from Hollywoodites in his own run for the White House; Lear, Rob Reiner, and others were early supporters of Howard Dean, the antiwar candidate equally cursed by neocons and neolibs.

[36] By that time, Asner was president of the Screen Actors' Guild, a rocky regime best remembered for its effort to include the low-prestige heavily Jewish screen and television extras, and for Asner's personal opposition to the role of the Reagan-sponsored Contras in Nicaragua. SAG conservatives, led by NRA spokesman Charleton Heston, managed to dethrone Asner after two terms, but

not to deflect a reconciliation of the SAG with its preblacklist sympathy for the rest of organized labor. Heston, the Gentile, had reaffirmed his position by calling for state right-to-work laws, outlawing the Union Shop and inevitably further reducing union membership. Going too far, the Right did not regain SAG leadership, but managed to prevent the organization from merging with its cousins, AFTRA and a poor relative, the union of screen extras (considered mere amateurs by Heston and his younger allies, like Tom Selleck).

[37] It may not be quite accidental – after all, his career practically began in the old socialistic Camp Tamiment of the Pocanoes – that Simon's career-making theatrical hit, *Come Blow Your Horn*, was directed by Hollywood blacklistee Stanley Praeger. Simon's future efforts, notably the telefilm *Bound for Broadway* (1995). carried the Odets-like themes of the old radical grandfather as far as this playwright was likely to go, although later work, especially *Lost In Yonkers*, occasionally referred to the Blacklist. See Simon's autobiography, laced with discussions about the prefilm original, its semiautobiographical content, its bumpy ride to success and so on: Paul Simon, *Rewrites: a Memoir* (New York: Touchstone, 1996), especially 12, 16, 32–36, 50–52, 58–83, 124–25, 175–77, and on "Stosh" Praeger, 59–61, 66–68. Praeger's status is not mentioned.

[38] This account owes much to David Marc, *Comic Visions: Television Comedy and American Culture* (Boston: Unwin, Hyman, 1989): 174–87.

[39] Another irony: the rural sitcom was spawned by the Jewish Paul Henning (1911–). Raised in Kansas City, a radio sketch-writer who turned to television, wrote for *Burns and Allen*, and formulated the *Bob Cummings Show* before creating *The Beverly Hillbillies*. *Green Acres* and *Petty Coat Junction* followed. He was finished by 1972. See David Marc and Robert J. Thompson, "Paul Henning," in *Prime Time Prime Movers* (Syracuse: Syracuse University Press, 1995), 30–37.

[40] There was still a more dangerous but unsuccessful version of *Maude*: the one-season *Fay* (1975–76) starring avant-gardist Lee Grant as a plainly Jewish woman who divorces her philandering husband and becomes a swinging single in her forties. It received much critical praise but could not survive the competition of family-hour offerings. Thanks to Lee Grant for yet another conversation, about this series.

[41] Thanks to Carlton Moss, a blacklisted African-American Hollywood writer, for making this point to me in a 1992 interview in Los Angeles.

[42] Some of the first successful women comedy writers on television – almost uniformly Jewish – wrote for Lear vehicles. See interviews in Denise Collier and Kathleen Beckett, eds., *Spare Ribs: Women in the Humor Biz* (New York: St. Martins, 1980), including Gail Parent and Lynn Roth (who moved on to "comedy development" at the film studios). Only *Saturday Night Live* had as many (also Jewish) women writers in the era before *Sex In the City* and other series enshrined what seems a secure place. One of *SNL*'s early writers was Rosie Shuster,

daughter of Frank Shuster (of the Canadian comedy team Wayne and Shuster) and more amazingly, niece of Joe Shuster, cocreator of *Superman*.

⁴³ Burrows played an important role in the early days of Woody's rise. A personality in the early years of network television, he hosted *Abe Burrows' Almanac* (1950), but made his big name later with musicals, writing the book for *Guys and Dolls* and *How to Succeed in Business Without Really Trying*, and the script for the Judy Holliday vehicle, *The Solid Gold Cadillac*.

⁴⁴ Reynolds, as producer of *The Ghost and Mrs. Muir*, had brought blacklistees Alfred and Helen Levitt out of the cold (although not yet with their own credits); for their part, they were quietly holding seminars to encourage black writers and actors to move ahead in television and films.

⁴⁵ *Roseanne: My Life as a Woman* (New York: Harpers, 1989) is in some ways the most remarkable of celebrity autobiographies. She recalls learning, in childhood, that comedy was "a place where a Jew can speak as a Jew": 163.

⁴⁶ David Thompson, ed., *Levinson on Levinson* (London and Boston: Faber & Faber, 1992): 108. Notwithstanding his film scholar reputation, auteurist Thomson evidently lacked the Jewish knowledge, or the inclination, to push Levinson harder on these kinds of points.

⁴⁷ Bergman, a former student of gay radical historian Harvey Goldberg on the University of Wisconsin campus was a bit of a local legend. He also scripted and directed the garment-district comedy, *So Fine* (1981). His script collaborators on *Blazing Saddles* included Richard Pryor, Norman Steinberg, and Alan Ungar.

⁴⁸ In the mid-1990s, the Comedy Channel boasted its own animated series, *Dr. Katz, Professional Therapist*, with versions of famous Jewish comics as his patients.

⁴⁹ Remarkable in its sincerity but no more successful was Brooks's direction of *Jacob The Liar* (1997), a Second World War drama about a ghetto character played by Robin Williams, here far from top form. More dramatically successful if not financially so, *Willie and Phil* (1980) has two Jewish men both in love with a *shiksa*, played notably by progressive Margot Kidder, an actress under bitter political attack from neoconservatives for her avowed opposition to the First Gulf War.

⁵⁰ The richness of discussion about Jewish directors forbids further detail here on assorted hands, but of the highly productive, Paul Mazursky is the most interesting by a large degree, at least in his Jewishness. *Alex in Wonderland* and *Next Stop, Greenwich Village* are fascinating as thinly disguised autobiography of a younger generation, *Moon Over Parador* essentially a remake of a beloved Danny Kaye-type liberal film with Richard Dreyfuss in the Kaye role, and *Enemies, a Love Story* perhaps the most successful creation of a Yiddish-American 1940s or '50s atmosphere anywhere, as well as the single film rendition made from Isaac Bashevis Singer's fiction. See Mazursky's memoir, *Show Me the Magic: My Adventures in Life and Hollywood* (New York: Simon & Schuster, 1999).

[51] Lamentably, Ignatov's works have never been translated. The abbreviated comments by Charles Madison, *Yiddish Literature: Its Scope and Major Writers* (New York: Ungar, 1968): 296–97, give a general sense of the novelist's accomplishments. Of those creative writers for film with little output, Marshall Brickman and his decisive contribution to *Annie Hall* must top the list.

[52] Lamentably, *100 Centre Street* did not survive its second season. Like the Richard Dreyfuss vehicle, *The Education of Max Bickford* (2001–02), its demise was a terrible blow to soulful Jewish television, as much for the character actors as for the stars and plot.

[53] It also called back from the Blacklist film editor Carl Lerner, who would go on to a series of distinguished projects, finally *Klute*, before dying prematurely. His widow, famed women's historian Gerda Lerner, has left a priceless retelling of the lives of herself and Carl, in *Fireweed* (Philadelphia: Temple University Press, 2002). Thanks are given to Gerda Lerner for conversations about Carl's film work, and her many kindnesses over the years.

[54] This and several others of Lumet's projects were wounded by especially vicious reviews from the influential Pauline Kael, apparently enraged at the director for his Old Left ties. See Paul Buhle and Dave Wagner, *Hide In Plain Sight*: 178–79. Rod Steiger, married at the time to actress Claire Bloom, had a few years earlier costarred in the Odets drama about Hollywood disillusion, *The Big Knife*.

[55] See the description of the film in J. Hoberman, "Flaunting It: The Rise and Fall of Hollywood's 'Nice' Jewish (Bad) Boys," in *Entertaining America*: 225–27. Lester D. Friedman, *Hollywood's Image of the Jew* (New York: Fredrick Ungar, 1982): 208–210. Friedman was outraged at the treatment of the modern rabbi, in a cameo played by Alan King, as standup performer; no doubt it was too close to real life.

[56] Among notable if minor efforts by assorted hands less able than Lumet's: *Just Tell Me What You Want* (1980), starring a brilliantly repugnant Yiddish-cursing Alan King as a Jewish businessman, and his screwball affair with *shiksa* Ali McGraw; and the sadly neglected *Made for Each Other* (1971), a hilarious comedy about an Italian and his Jewish girlfriend who fall in love and then suffer all the dissonance of ethnic contrasts.

[57] *The Defenders* as noted above, because of its liberal writers and cast, some of them returnees from the Blacklist; *The Fugitive* because it was created and produced by television's most notable friendly witness, Roy Huggins (another gentile among Jews); and *Naked City* because it reprised blacklistee Jules Dassin's noir film of the later 1940s.

[58] Pollack also directed the documentary *Sanford Meisner – the Theater's Best Kept Secret* (1984), one of the most effective documentaries about a dramatic coach ever made.

[59] Friedman, *Hollywood's Image of the Jew*: 261.

⁶⁰ A Midwestern daughter of Russian immigrants, Silver had directed educational shorts before her developer husband raised the $370,000 needed for full production. Everyone worked scale and Silver shot on the Mott Street of the early 1970s. She made Kane the real protagonist of the narrative, a decisive change from the original. The film made back its budget in six weeks. See the perceptive comments (including excerpts of an interview with Kane) in David Zinman, *Fifty Grand Movies of the 1960s and 1970s* (New York: Crown, 1986): 99–104.

⁶¹ Gardner, *I'm Not Rappaport*: 20.

⁶² My grateful memories extend to Gardner for asking my advice – even if he didn't take it. His 2003 death marked the end of an era in which the young intellectuals of 1950s television could recall their social tilt in far-removed decades. Walter Bernstein is among the last remaining, along with Lumet.

⁶³ Of Jewish pathos without Odets's message of potential deliverance, an encyclopedia of recent Hollywood could be written. But one of the more fascinating cases, surely, is actor Harvey Keitel, child of orthodoxy raised in Brighton Beach, a high school dropout for the Marines, a Method actor who, despite his highly successful career, describes himself as "always in turmoil." See Marshall Fine, *Harvey Keitel: The Art of Darkness* (New York: Fromm International, 1998).

⁶⁴ David Desser and Lester D. Friedman, *American Jewish Filmmakers, Trends and Tradition* (Urbana: University of Illinois, 1993): 33–35.

⁶⁵ See Eric Lax, *Woody Allen: A Biography* (New York: Random House, 1992): especially 102–03, 223–27. It should be added, though, that Allen considered Saul Bellow a great literary comic, formal politics and pomposity notwithstanding.

⁶⁶ "Kim Deitch Interviewed by Monte Beauchamp," *The Comics Journal*, no. 123 (July 1988): 56–62. Thanks also go to noted antiglobalist writer and filmmaker Naomi Klein for several communications. Her uncle was another of the Disney strikers later blacklisted: an important life's lesson passed on to a family successor.

⁶⁷ Ibid., 64–69.

⁶⁸ Prominent among them: Sharon Kahn Rudahl, who projected her distinctively raven-haired Jewish look back into assorted characters of history, and forward into the story of her own life as bohemian, sometime free lover, mother, and middle-aged political militant.

⁶⁹ Gratitude is extended to Robbins for occasional personal meetings, letters, and calls over the years. See also my short interview with her in "Interviews with Women Comic Artists," *Cultural Correspondence*, no. 9 (Spring, 1979), 10–12.

⁷⁰ d.a. levy, *Stone Sarcophagus* (Madison: Radical America, 1971). The selection was mostly made by Dave Wagner, cultural editor of *Radical America*, then the editor of the town's underground newspaper.

⁷¹ His enigmatic message about thought traveling like a little bird may have referred to me as a writer/editor with pet birds flying around the room; or to

Jewish lore, or to Buddhism. I never found out. The card is in the Radical America Collection, State Historical Society of Wisconsin.

[72] "Harvey Pekar & Joyce Brabner: By the People, for the People," interview by Stanley Wiater and Stephen R. Bissette, in Wiater and Bisette, eds., *Comic Book Rebels: Conversations with the Creators of the New Comics* (New York: Donald J. Fine, 1993): 131. Printing and mailing costs were not, of course, nearly what they would become a decade and more later. I had launched my journal *Radical America* on the same frayed shoestring in 1967, likewise doing just about everything but the printing myself. It was possible.

[73] One could rightly complain about *American Splendor* that if the human element remained in Cleveland, the physical remains seemed massively depressing in ways that ever buoyant city fathers must find less than the desired depiction. The urban Cleveland in which Pekar grew up and spent his younger years was largely wiped out by destructive redevelopment, its remnant the modern monstrosity of a Veterans' Administration hospital that we see in *American Splendor*.

[74] The sensitive reading given by Joseph Witek, in *Comic Books As History: The Narrative Art of Jack Jackson, Art Spiegelman and Harvey Pekar* (Jackson: University Press of Mississippi, 1989): 153, owes in part to a visit that Witek made to Cleveland to interview Pekar, something that I should have done as well; I've been paying penance, over the years, with phone calls.

[75] Witek, *Comic Books As History*: 154.

[76] Deepest thanks to the candid comments and emails from Joyce Brabner in the fall of 2002, when the latest of his *American Splendor* appeared, this time a two-part book taken from an oral history of a black Clevelander's years in and after the Vietnam War, and on the near eve of the Drama award for the film *American Splendor* at the Sundance Festival. Had the screenwriter received the festival's Waldo Salt Award, the cross-generational correlation would have been perfect.

[77] Much of the following is drawn from "Interviews: Art Spiegelman," in *Comics Journal*, no. 180 (September 1995), and an interview that I happened to do with Spiegelman and Francois Mouly in 1982, in preparation for the first (and apparently last) Radical Humor Festival at New York University that year. Spiegelman and Mouly were prominent participants in the festival, along with Jules Feiffer and a handful of other artists. The spirit of the well-attended event is perhaps captured by my keynote address, "Humor's Magic History," in Paul Buhle, ed., *Popular Culture in America*: 245–50.

[78] Another was David Marc, himself briefly a network sitcom writer; still another is media scholar Daniel Czitrom, author of *Media and the American Mind*. Both these writers were fellow editors of the magazine *Cultural Correspondence*.

[79] In fact, Garbage Pail Kids was such a hit that Topps executives offered to make Spiegelman a company vice-president, with salary and perks worth over $100,000 at the moment when, happily, he had the self-confidence to quit.

[80] Among immigrant radical Germans and Hungarians, at least, the frequency of Jews in editorial positions, turning out copy for a mostly Gentile ethnic working class, was not exactly a secret but treated as unimportant, as I learned interviewing then ancient Hungarian-Americans. It had probably been so in a number of other groups, presumably also for English-language publications (like Chicago-based Socialist and later, Communist dailies) where the Left had a large ethnic following, with Jews an overrepresented minority.

[81] *Short Order Comics*, no. 2 (1973), also featured a one-pager by "Griffy" with seven panels about the hated Walter Winchell, Red-baiter and the butt of Clifford Odets's *Sweet Smell of Success*, ending in a quotation about him in the *New Yorker* and showing him shooting the head off his only companion, a dummy. It begins (after an inside cover collage by Spiegelman) with Griffith's "Schlockpeople," a Jewish garment baron creating yet more ridiculous styles.

[82] *Young Lust* actually outlasted *Young Love*, on which it was satirically modeled. Griffith's long-time coeditor of the series was Jay Kinney, a Chicagoan and an anarchist who contacted me in the early 1970s, re-establishing my connection to the underground artists. Many thanks go to Kinney, who went on to publish the mystic *Gnosis* magazine and become, adopted Californian as he is, a figure in the Gnostic Church, and is still an occasional cartoonist. See his strip on the underground cartoonists' effort to become a Wobbly local, in *The Wobblies*.

[83] See the full-length interview of Griffith by Gary Groth in *The Comics Journal*, no. 157 (March 1993): 52–98, with many biographical details.

[84] Mr. Toad was, in part at least, actually a manifestation of Griffith's father, as he told me, a realization made during a nightmare after many years of drawing Toad.

[85] A useful, subsequent interview with Bill Griffith by Joe Sacco appears in Gary Groth and Robert Fiore, *The New Comics*: 170–79, shorter and more technique-oriented than the interview in the note above. In any case, Griffy's predilections continue, best expressed in collections of his daily strips (reprinted as *Annual Zippy*, continuing volumes published by Fantographics) that confirm has fascination, grim and otherwise, with roadside fantasia, and his strictly grim fascination with the steady spread of suburbia. Thanks for a conversation in Griffith's studio and a nearby diner in July 2003 that Zip would surely have approved.

[86] See the interview with Justin Green, by Mark Burbey, in *The New Comics*: 158–66.

[87] Thunderstruck at the end of *Arcade*, I interviewed several of the artists, including Crumb and Griffith, also feminist artists Robbins and Terre Richards, in a 1977 issue of my next journal, *Cultural Correspondence*. Justin Green designed the issue cover, depicting an artist suspiciously like himself coming up out of a manhole: no. 5 (1977).

[88] The more usual reasons given for its demise were the inability as well as unwillingness of distributors to find a place for it; *Arcade* didn't look like other

comics and it didn't look like existing magazines, and it didn't last long enough to find its audience.

[89] *Comics Journal* interview: 97.

[90] Zwigoff's next film was *Ghost World* (2001), a rendition of a comic strip narrative by Dan Clowes, about a Jewish teenager's alienation as she graduates from high school with one main interest (apart from not being bored): cartooning. It was, in parts, very touching.

[91] Peter Kuper added his own Kafka note with a memorable adaptation, *The Metamorphosis* (New York: Crown, 2003).

[92] Thanks go to Schulman for these autobiographical details. She has been artistically active in a wide variety of social movements, rent control to antiwar activism, meanwhile drawing for publication. She is coeditor of the forthcoming *Wobblies: A Graphic Story History of the Industrial Workers of the World*, to be published by Verso in time for the IWW's 2005 centenary.

[93] Sharing a panel on culture and politics with Rivers in 1996 was an unforgettable experience. He liked to play the naïf in details of history, deferring to the "experts," and clearly enjoying the ruse. See "Larry Rivers, Artist, Shake and Cultural Provocateur to the End, Is Dead at 78," *New York Times*, 16 August 2002. See also Helen A. Harrison, *Larry Rivers* (New York: Harper & Row, 1984), for a useful overview that, however, has little grasp of his grounding in the Old Left and its successors.

[94] Andrew Silow-Carroll, "The Featherman File," *The Forward*, 24 November 2000.

[95] Actually, Hoberman is rewriting Philip Roth's vision in *The Counterlife* of a Jew who has no Zionism, no Judaism, no apparent Jewishness at all but who is still an unassimilated Jew. Hoberman, "Adam Sandler," in J. Hoberman and Jeffrey Shandler, *Entertaining America*: 203.

[96] Thanks to Professor James D. Bloom, in a still unpublished manuscript on "funny Jews," for driving home this point to him.

[97] Interview of Jerry Stiller 2001, by David Marc, Scheuer Television History Collection, Syracuse University.

[98] But sometimes also helpfully maintaining an aura of mystery. *Monk*, USA Network's comedy-edged detective drama, has Tony Shalhoub playing a protagonist so cerebral and hypochondriac that he can only "feel" Jewish; his tarty single mom assistant Sharona, played by Bitty Schram, could as easily be Los Angeles Jewish as anything else. In a typical irony, *Monk*'s boss, Captain Stottlemeyer, is in real life Ted Levine, i.e., the Jewish actor playing the *goyishe kopf* (dumb head) Gentile to the hilt.

[99] Others included *Will and Grace*, with a lesbian Jewish character, *The Nanny*, *Friends*, and *Foley Square*, the last of them an ironic title because of the trials of mostly Jewish Communists in Foley Square during the 1950s. Jeffrey Shandler, "At Home on the Small Screen," *Entertaining America*: 248.

[100] Michiko Kakutani, "Culture Zone: Master of His Domain," *New York Times Magazine*, 1 February 1998.

[101] Jonathan Rosen, "Beyond Nostalgia."

[102] "9/11/01," *New Yorker*, 24 September 2001.

[103] See Henry Sapoznik, *Klezmer! Jewish Music from Old World to Our World* (New York: Schirmer Books, 1999).

[104] Small memory: I was the token Gentile on the program at the 1997 centenary celebration of the Jewish Bund, in Manhattan; the high point of the afternoon was a Yiddish chorus from KlezKamp, proof positive that *Yiddishkayt* retained a voice among the young, at least some of the young.

[105] *The Yiddish Radio Show* toured in 2000–01, with excerpts played on National Public Radio. I attended an unforgettable performance in the Palace of Fine Arts theater in San Francisco.

[106] See Yale Strom, *The Book of Klezmer* (Chicago: A Capella; Chicago Review Press, 2002): 183–84. Strom, like a number of other *klezmer* musicians, turned a negative (lack of reception in Israel) into a positive, the warmth of the European audience, increasingly Jewish in Germany among other places, by relocating himself and his musical career there for considerable stretches.

[107] Tony Kushner, email to Paul Buhle, 21 October 2003.

POSTSCRIPT:
ONE LAST LOOK BACK

Ending this book demands turning a final page that I am most reluctant to turn. How can it be over already? It will seem as if I have said a final goodbye to a history that is a large part of my own inner life as well. One bittersweet look backward remains, then, with a last glance at a few representative personalities, mostly those who can still be close only through memory and its capacity for revivifying certain unforgettable images.

The first and oldest of the personalities drew me further into the world of Yiddish, at a critical point for me and for *Yiddishkayt*, a culture retained for generations within insular New York neighborhoods. The slightly younger one, who had lived in vastly more modern worlds, restored memories of what film and golden age television meant to my own childhood, and helped bring me to a degree of artistic understanding or appreciation otherwise unimaginable. In my mind's eye, the two have presented historical stages, as real as the ever-changing, but ever-related, possibilities of working with the mundane materials at hand, making something marvelous out of them.

The painter-poet had been utterly forgotten with the disappearance of his generation. I still can't quite accept the finality of never returning to a badly aged apartment building in Brighton Beach, Brooklyn, where Moishe – Maurice in the Americanized English that I could not accept – Kish lived. More details than I can assemble coherently overtake me when I gaze casually at the two lesser canvases that the artist gave me, one of them at home, the other over my office desk, and likewise when I work my way, now and then, through the Yiddish of his poems. I wish that I had taken photographs, to bring back to memory now the walls of his modest three rooms lined with fantastic paintings of Coney Island and city subjects, his palette and canvas in a corner, two windows overlooking the boardwalk with rich ocean smells wafting up from below.

Moishe was short and sturdy, the twinkling-eye sort of old-fashioned character by the time I found him in the later 1970s. He was a little mentally drifty already; a few years later, as my regular visits eased, his mind proceeded to slip away into nothing. I'd been looking a long time for radical-tinged books and art that did not make a fetish of realism but granted it a proper place along the products of less-restrained imagination. In one of the forgotten Yiddish journals, I came across a print of a painting of a Coney Island carousel with its horses untethered. It was a faded, grayish version of a splendid midnight dream of liberation. But the breaking of the bars that held them in place, the steeds prancing into the waves, the roller coaster set behind the carousel and the moon and clouds above, fairly stunned me. As with some of the best Yiddish poetry, it was what I had been looking for, without my ever knowing it. On a tip, I simply looked up the artist's name in the Brooklyn phone book. Sure enough, an answering voice with a heavy accent revealed age but also enthusiasm, no suspicion. I should definitely take the long ride out. For my first time in New York, I stayed on as a train emerged from its tunnel onto an elevated track, looking down on approaching neighborhoods that signaled 1920s and '30s and a veritable boyhood Woody Allenland.

Kish was lonely, but worse than that, neglected. Born in Russia in 1906 where his family recognized his talent early, he was a real proletarian in the new land, for decades a highly skilled craft worker in a Manhattan factory that made glass vases. Just as he had begun to place his paintings in mainstream museums and public shows, the 1940s came and the vogue of Abstract Expressionism conquered. He was left behind, much like Coney Island itself. The festive atmosphere that had persisted since the 1890s when the trolleys brought the toiling masses and rising accompanying real estate values quickly deteriorated after the war, and then collapsed. Luna Park, jewel of the Island lit by a quarter-million incandescent lights in its time, inevitably Kish's all-time favorite spot for painting, writing poetry, and people watching, closed permanently in 1948.

Growing aware of his impending isolation, Kish painted more furiously, spending weekends around Luna and the remnants of the larger scene, finally retiring early and, after his mother died, relocating from Brooklyn's Brownsville neighborhood (where he had lived since coming from Russia) to Brighton Beach. A former amateur boxer, also a former dance instructor in the Catskills, and published Yiddish poet, he was still occasionally playing handball during the 1970s in the famous Brighton courts. He knew that he was running out of time and anyway he was melancholy, deeply nostalgic for the way Brighton Beach had been fifty years earlier. So was I, although of course the memories weren't mine.

He served nominally as the final chair of the arts division of a badly faded organization, the Left-linked Yiddishe Kultur Farband (Yiddish Culture Association, YKUF). I'm not sure that he actually did anything in his official status. He had never been much drawn to organized activity as such, mainly going along with the crowd through the Yiddish sectors of the Left, thence with his aging pals into a generalized, post-Communist but very immigrant-Jewish egalitarianism. Like the all-time best-selling Yiddish novelist Moses Asch in the novel *Uncle Moses*, pronouncing the holiday life in Coney Island more truly socialistic than the Socialists themselves, Kish intuitively treated the Ferris Wheel, the Tunnel of Love, the bathing beach, and the whole scene as containing the unrealized promise of a disappointing twentieth century. In his choice of composition and color of one canvas after another, he sought to illuminate and thereby to save, in some way, the possibilities of the artist's subject in the mass.

Kish's one poetry volume, *Di Velt Iz Mayn Lied* (The World Is My Song), contains almost all the poems that he ever intended to publish. The title is his credo, and reading it gave me a sense of discovery, also a profound sadness.[1] Reading the verses and looking at his paintings is a great deal like looking at a vanished New York, before Robert Moses and the superhighways, back in the days when the world of skyscrapers rose by the handful rather than the hundreds, still as marvelous as in Alfred Steiglitz's photos. Days, that is, when working-class Jews gave the daily scene a particular character, masses living the New York life but with memories of another world in their heads, and only minutes from Broadway lay the real countryside. It's a dream that, as I say, is mine only by second remove, at best. But I cling to the remnants of it. In fact, Moishe and I had one contemporary bit of popular culture in common: we both loved the television show *Barney Miller* and occasionally watched reruns together.

I like to imagine Moishe as the Chagall of Brooklyn, because my memories of him offer up metaphors of an existence in the Pale, then a New York experience, a particular way of looking at the world now gone forever except in artistic recreation. Also because, like every left-wing Yiddishist interested in art, Moishe had been at receptions during the 1940s years when Chagall was the biggest personality in the crowd, and almost certainly shook the great man's hand. Unlike the master Chagall, who was lucky enough to be able to work almost to the end, Moishe lost his eyesight and physical capacity some years before he died. Rather than giving up, he returned to a kind of caricature in oils, visualized memories of his own childhood *shtetl* life with comic strip-like figures, each representing a type that he had known from close observation and now remembered with the increasing vividness of old age. The effort was more impressive than the result, but it gave him something to do as his friends and relatives steadily disappeared.

I was able to guide him on subways and buses to a few places, to Yiddish-language political meetings in Manhattan and a public lecture or two, state Humanities Committee-sponsored arts meetings in Brooklyn where I showed slides of his work that he had given me, describing its value to me, the only Gentile in the crowd and the only one under sixty-five as well. I published several of his paintings in a cultural magazine that I was then editing, alongside poems of his that I managed to translate with the assistance of another old-timer, a long-retired master embroiderer from Montreal. The first issue of an intended City Lights annual (it failed after one number), adventurously called *Free Spirits*, carried his most surrealistic painting on the cover, of trapeze artists painting pictures of themselves, his satire of Abstract Expressionism but also something quite beyond that. In connecting him with the Chicago-based disciples of the André Breton surrealist movement, I probably found his truest English-language audience. But it wasn't a big one. Around this time, I also managed to write a piece about him for the *Village Voice* with a near full-page reproduction of one of his strangest paintings, the mocking *Funeral of an Undertaker*, with everyone in a crowd frowning except the smiling corpse.

As I was going to see him intermittently, several of the paintings were exhibited at the venerable ACA Gallery and he was suddenly asked to loan his paintings for a one-man show in Brooklyn. (He was too nervous to turn them over, even temporarily.) Kish seemed on the verge of late life rediscovery, but time had run out on him. One day I called up to get him ready for my visit, and he was gone. I learned that he was already in a Long Island rest home *non compos mentis*. He died a few months later. His epitaph is properly a poem of his that I translated (with help), and published, called simply "My Address Book":

I strike out the names and addresses
Of people – they exist no longer.
Names I cannot forget.
Relatives, comrades, friends.

Bitter it is to strike the names out, erase them

As it is hard to go to funerals
My little book is full of black stains
Names hardened into stone.

I heard those names so often
The people – I still see them clearly.
Soon not one will remain.
So disappears a generation.

I had names and addresses collected
But my book will now be empty
No one will remain
Tell me: who will strike out my name?

My cotranslator, the Canadian Yiddish poet who visited me occasionally in those days, exclaimed, in answer to the poem's final question: "You will!" And it was true. I literally struck out Moishe's name from an address book, in those days before we erased mere electronic impulses with a touch on the computer.

Maurice Kish's death went unnoticed, except in the pages of the Yiddish newspaper *Morgn Frayhayt*, which folded in 1987. The *Frayhayt*'s editor, Pesach Novick, then in his early nineties and quite a literary figure himself, was at once an assiduous critic, time-tested essayist, and lecturer. He delivered a beautiful literary column every week (that is to say, every issue, as the paper receded from daily to semiweekly, and then in its last decade, weekly appearance) full of both Russian literary and Torah references, with snippets of American slang. Novick had been with the paper since its inception in 1922. It was Novick who advised me to call Kish when I went to the newspaper office off Union Square, in one of the last times that I visited the office. Soon, as my old Yiddish-language friends fell away, I wondered what would ever cause me to begin interviewing again.

One of my more extended field trips had already supplied the answer, although I didn't recognize it for years. Interviewing aged poets and Yiddish cultural activists in the tenaciously Jewish but changing (steadily less secular, more Chasidic) Fairfax neighborhood of West Los Angeles, I'd asked casually if the old-timers had had any contact with the Hollywood blacklistees. They were, after all, also secular left-wing Jews, only a half-generation or so apart. "Not much!" was the standard answer, not even back in the 1940s, before repression had decimated the Left film milieu. Yiddish-speakers had always kept mostly to themselves. But "linkies" or left-wingers had been physically proximate to the Yiddish "right-vingers" (actually social democrats) in former Jewish neighborhoods like Boyle Heights; both sides were now even sharing park space on weekends. As members of historically opposed groups they never became real friends, but nevertheless bizarrely waved their greetings at each other across distances of a few hundred feet in regular weekend outings. In truth, all the surviving groups had for decades supported and criticized the Democrats and the Israelis to about the same degree; the rest of the differences were over memories, past hurts, and hopes that could not be forgiven or forgotten.

But fading Yiddishists of all kinds knew about the Hollywood Left, naturally, and all factions flocked to the city-run theater in the same La Brea Park on Sundays when one of the old-time films like *Woman of the Year*, *Action in the North Atlantic*, *Gentleman's Agreement*, or anything with John Garfield or (from more recent decades) Barbra Streisand was played. Even if they preferred a world of Yiddish, they were all big-time movie fans, no different in that sense from other Americans of their generation.

It was Gerda Lerner, a teenage Viennese refugee from Nazism, by middle age a legendary women's historian and widow of blacklisted film editor Carl Lerner, who choreographed my next move. (Her husband's most important work after banishment from Hollywood proper was the moral classic, *Twelve Angry Men*, and his last, suitably enough, was the arch-feminist *Klute;* together, the couple wrote and produced the 1964 antiracist shocker, *Black Like Me*.) Everyone knew about the victimized Hollywood Ten, she insisted. Those eight writers, one director, and one producer who had gone to prison for refusal to testify had certainly left behind vivid memories that garnered more open sympathy, now that so much time had passed and the Cold War was over. But what about all the others blacklisted? They were dying off fast. And few enough had put their lives on tape.[2]

She had me there: once more, it was case of now or never for a slice of almost uniformly Jewish culture, very different from the Yiddishist old-timers but alike in more sensibilities than either group probably imagined. With a retired optician as chauffeur and foot-in-the-door assistant, I soon covered the territory from Malibu to Pecoima, from hole-in-the-wall offices maintained for no apparent reason, to a Beverly Hills mansion with a real Chagall painting, but mostly quiet little homes and apartments. Only a couple of the interviewees, actors naturally, were memorable from my own childhood; I recalled them from kids' films and television. But of the movies others wrote, I had seen dozens.

There was one glowing exception to the assorted private meeting places: a cinematic artist regarded by many as the last living master of left-wing noir insisted on gathering in the café of Niemann-Marcus, where models struck poses as we talked about films, Jewishness, and *his* New York. We discussed the erstwhile writer-director's Manhattan childhood of Yiddish grand-parents, his radio broadcasting with partisans behind German lines, the movies made from his scripts and others written but never made, the assorted careers that he had begun and discarded – all answered with more quips than straightforward replies. Abraham Lincoln Polonsky's wife, I learned later, was back in the penthouse a few blocks away, dying of cancer. He managed to be chipper, probably because the conversation gave him a small break from caregiving. In the next six or seven years, after Sylvia Polonsky died, I made repeated visits to him at home.[3]

The main reason I went, at first anyway, was that other survivors of the Blacklist would say, with particular emphasis, things like, "If you want to talk about *ideas*, Abe is the one." What and who else was Polonsky? In that Niemann-Marcus opener, I knew so little about his work that I fumbled through my usual framework of life story narrative, misidentifying a film or two as his, then wincing with embarrassment as he corrected me. Later, as I put it together, his was one of the oddest of the many odd Hollywood stories that I collected. Son of a Bronx druggist (and soda jerk in his father's Lower East Side store), Columbia Law School graduate who quickly lost interest in the law and turned to radio writing (for Gertrude Berg's comic *The Goldbergs*), he became a CCNY lecturer on modernist literature and a campus unionist. Following a stint as a union educator, he enrolled in the Office of Strategic Services and after overseas duty, quit when the bureaucratic temperament shifted from left- to right-of-center. Thanks to the success of his potboiler action novelettes in the slick magazines, he was quickly discovered by Hollywood after the war. Studio informers for the FBI at once noted his talent and damned him by labeling him a Marxist and a troublemaker. A figure of great interest to the bureau – no doubt it was because of the intelligence agency background as well as the growing reputation – he only lasted a few years before being forced out.

A fighter behind enemy lines in more ways than one, Polonsky was now submerged again. Writing television shows under pseudonyms or behind fronts (his most memorable reinterpreted the lives of Galileo, Freud, Michelangelo, Beethoven and Milton), he would be discovered once more. This time interviewers of all kinds accepted him both as the final author-itative voice of the blacklistees, and so a noir-minded Martin Scorsese put the best of Polonsky's films, *Force of Evil*, back into video re-release with an on-camera imprimateur/introduction.

You Are There rang the bell to my childhood, and I could remember from age ten several of the episodes that he had written. Polonsky's movies now quickly came to mean a lot to me, too. I scrutinized them as carefully and repeatedly as I had Moishe Kish's poetry and paintings. *Force of Evil*, ironically or apocryphally observed (by a British critic) to be written "in blank verse" because of its uniquely stylized dialogue, encompassed brotherly betrayal and Wall Street revelations into a total moral collapse. From one angle, it was written as if for a 1949 Manhattan, Jewish version of Poe's "House of Usher." It was also a particularly vivid piece of political interpretation.

The writer-director himself was more likely to describe it as a visualized poetry, an experiment in film art with John Garfield, in his best role ever, at the center. *Body and Soul* is not so subtle, but way up among the best boxing films of all time. It cast Garfield brilliantly as the slum boy corrupted by power (while the women around him know the score and resist the lure). *I Can Get It For You Wholesale*, a second wave feminist feature a quarter-century before its time, was released in 1951, just weeks before the screenwriter's showdown with HUAC questioners.

Then came the next underground phase, climaxing in *Odds Against Tomorrow*, about which we've seen some sideways glimpses. *Odds* wasn't even close to a box office success, and a planned series of uncompromisingly tough interracial films to be written by Polonsky and produced (as well as starred in) by Harry Belafonte ignominiously collapsed. It was one of those great moments of Jewish/black collaboration that never happened.

To be overly generous, the country probably needed a few more decades to get itself ready. To be less generous, it still isn't ready, at least not for the untamed and somewhat threatening films the two planned on issues like antebellum sex and race in the South and nuclear catastrophe (a farce, as meant to be played by Belafonte and Zero Mostel). After some drift and unmemorable film work (at least unmemorable work under his own name – he stoutly refused to give details about the fronts he used for all or parts of scripts that he wrote sans credit), he wrote and directed *Tell Them Willie Boy Is Here* (1969). Denounced for its purported "New Left existentialism," *Willie Boy* turned the western epic on its head in ways artistically opposite from, but quite spiritually close to, *Blazing Saddles*. Polonsky effectively closed out his career with *Romance of a Horsethief* (1970), a film that he took over in a collapsing mid-production, and that was destined to be his last directorial effort because his own near-collapse, his weakening heart, would not allow the further exertion.

Horsethief may, for all its weaknesses, be the most Yiddish film ever made in English, or at the very least second to *Enemies, a Love Story* but with few benefits of quality production. The nearly allegorical saga of a distant *shtetl* in 1905 was based upon the transgressive Yiddish stories by Joseph Opotoshu, considered shocking back in the 1910s for portraying the lives of Jewish thieves. Under Polonsky's hand, it can best be seen as a revolutionary, semisurrealist version of the considerably less Yiddishist, more Broadwayesque *Fiddler On the Roof*.

Two rascally but loveable characters, played by Eli Wallach and Oliver Tobias, live by their wits, thanks also to the help of the local madam (played by Lanie Kazan) who is romantically attached to Wallach. Back from a Paris education comes a local Gentile (Jane Birkin), entranced with revolutionary ideas – just as the Russo-Japanese war worsens conditions drastically and will prompt the famed uprising led by (among others) the Jewish Bund, the dress rehearsal for 1917. Here, in the provinces, things take a less spectacular and more plainly hilarious course. The local Czarist proconsul, played with the silly dignity of the King of Siam, is none other than Yul Brynner, an old friend of the Left and perfectly suited for the character's pomp. He has to tell the Jews that their men will be drafted for a pointless distant war, and he knows that he has a problem. The problem grows suddenly larger as Tobias, so as to impress a fair lady, showers the crowd listening to Brynner's war speech with antiwar, virtually insurrectionary leaflets. Repression threatens.

Since the horses are to be conscripted along with the men, the jolly thieves also face an economic crisis. They solve their dilemma by posing as the Czar's special envoys who are to halt the spread of a virulent equine epidemic by removing sick horses to be slaughtered. The garrisoned soldiers, they explain, will need to have their uniforms burned as well. By the time the plot is discovered, the thieves are racing for the border, followed by hundreds of men on foot, chasing them in underwear! Stuck with the prospect of ultimate humiliation (and reprisals against local Jews), proconsul Brynner chooses to explain to superiors that the horse disease has been banished along with the most restless of the local population. Along with some idyllic footage shot in Yugoslavia, Polonsky had also shot one of the most surrealist of modern films. In a postproduction interview, he insisted that he could hear the voice of his grandmother, the one who had read him Huck Finn stories from the *Forverts* in the Yiddish, only altering the protagonists to be a Jewish boy on the Volga, escaping civilization with a fugitive serf. Bad editing and worse music after Polonsky left the project did great damage to *Romance of a Horsethief*. But what remained was the extraordinary work of the Jewish imagination, reaching back into the European past for treasured legacies that survive even the Holocaust.[4]

Polonsky had viewed culture all his life, if not as a weapon (in the old

Communist phraseology that he had never accepted), then potentially as a tool of collaborative selfexpression. This was for him the real value of movies, which he repeatedly described as the *only* new art form (unlike theater, dance, painting, and even sport) invented since antiquity. Movies, commonly regarded as trash culture, could aid humanity in reinventing itself. And where would the dreams for a better world come from? Critics across the political spectrum sharing a hostility toward mass society and mass culture could not have felt as he did about film. "For me," Polonsky told an interviewer,

> movies are irrevocably and richly rooted in kitsch, in childhood, in story-telling, in the rubbish of paperbacks and sitting under the streetlights while off in the zoo across the lots flowering with burdock, lions roared out their fantasy of freedom ... It was a great pleasure to make a movie again. Nothing is better; perhaps revolution, but there you have to succeed and be right, dangers which never attach themselves to making movies, and dreaming.[5]

These are, of course, memories of his own Bronx childhood of the 1910s superimposed upon an artist's lifetime endeavor. The Jewish radicals involved in every avenue of art – but for my purposes, the main avenues of popular culture as well – did not make the social transformation of their dreams. But from humble Moishe Kish to noir genius Abraham Lincoln Polonsky, not to mention all the others up to the present day and into the foreseeable and unforeseeable future, they did capture something of our common dreams, they do leave and will leave behind an imperishable heritage. If I have engaged the reader to look more carefully at that heritage, to draw some fresh lessons of both form and content, then I will be more than satisfied.

NOTES

[1] Maurice Kish, *Di Velt iz Mayn Lied* (New York YKUF, 1967). I tell part of Kish's story in "Maurice Kish," *Cultural Correspondence*, no. 9 (Spring, 1979): 45–50, with several of his poems translated.

[2] See Lerner's own searing memoir, *Fireweed*.

[3] Some of this story is recorded in Paul Buhle and Dave Wagner, *A Very Dangerous Citizen*.

[4] Buhle and Wagner, *A Very Dangerous Citizen*: 210–13.

[5] Abraham Polonsky, "Making Movies," *Sight and Sound*, 49 (Spring, 1971): 101.

INDEX